"As any one of Marvin Wilson's countless students could tell you, the treasury of learning, insight, and wisdom found in this book emerges from a lifetime of integrity and faithfulness. This long-awaited sequel immediately takes its place alongside his best-selling *Our Father Abraham* as mandatory reading for all who participate in our educational programs."

— JAMES C. WHITMAN
president of Center for
Judaic-Christian Studies

"Wilson's *Exploring Our Hebraic Heritage* shows how Judaism and Christianity can mutually enrich our faith communities despite the great tragedies of the past. . . . Offers a wonderful resource for any rabbi or minister wishing to better understand how Jesus' ethical teachings fit within the context of early rabbinical tradition and theology."

— RABBI MICHAEL LEO SAMUEL
author of *A Shepherd's Song:
Psalm 23 and the Shepherd
Metaphor in Jewish Thought*

"Cut off from its Jewish roots, Western Christianity has lost its way — and its credibility. . . . Faith in Jesus need not, and indeed must not, obliterate the (Jewish) faith of Jesus. Wilson's book points the way toward authentic Christian renewal."

— DAVID N. BIVIN
editor of JerusalemPerspective.com

Exploring Our Hebraic Heritage

A Christian Theology of Roots and Renewal

Marvin R. Wilson

WILLIAM B. EERDMANS PUBLISHING COMPANY
GRAND RAPIDS, MICHIGAN / CAMBRIDGE, U.K.

Published 2014 by
Wm. B. Eerdmans Publishing Co.
2140 Oak Industrial Drive N.E., Grand Rapids, Michigan 49505 /
P.O. Box 163, Cambridge CB3 9PU U.K.

Printed in the United States of America

20 19 18 17 16 15 14   7 6 5 4 3 2 1

Library of Congress Cataloging-in-Publication Data

Wilson, Marvin R., 1935-
Exploring our Hebraic heritage: a Christian theology of roots and renewal /
Marvin R. Wilson.
pages   cm
Includes bibliographical references and index.
ISBN 978-0-8028-7145-9 (pbk.: alk. paper)
1. Christianity — Origin.
2. Church history — Primitive and early church, ca. 30-600.
3. Judaism (Christian theology) — History.
I. Title.

BR129.W55   2014
261.2′6 — dc23

2014005078

www.eerdmans.com

Dedicated in remembrance of the life of

Dwight A. Pryor

Cherished friend and humble servant,
Beloved scholar-teacher of our Hebraic heritage,
Man of deep faith who first implanted the vision of this book.

May his memory ever remain a blessing.

Contents

Contents

Contents

Pronunciation Key for Transliterated Hebrew Words

Vowels

a	as in *father*	(*dabar, shalom, lappidim*)
e	as in *red*	(*ha-zeh, mishteh*)
i	as in *machine*	(*li, dodi*)
o	as in *cold*	(*torah, kenegdo, zimrot*)
u	as in *tune*	(*ketubah, nissu'in, galut*)

Consonants

ḥ   represents the harsh guttural sound of Hebrew *ḥet* (*yiḥus, mish-phaḥah, orḥim, ḥokhmah*)

kh   represents the spirantized sound of Hebrew *kaph* as in the German word *Bach* (*shadkhan, hakhnasat*)

tz   represents the Hebrew *tsadhe* (*mitzvah, matzot*)

b   after a vowel is pronounced *v* (*dabar, ketubah*)

ʾ   represents the separation of sounds of Hebrew *aleph* (*nebi'im, nissu'in*)

ʿ   represents the separation of sounds of Hebrew *ayin* (*da'at, me'at*)

Hyphen

-    the hyphen in Hebrew words is a grammatical indicator to separate an article from the word that follows (*ha-zeh, ha-ba*), or an indicator that connects the conjunction "and" to the word that follows (*ve-nithazeq, u-she'on, ve-hagita*)

Preface

Roots and Rot

Christianity's Hebraic heritage is multifaceted and rich. For years, I have reminded my students that Christianity was not invented out of whole cloth, nor did it originate *de novo;* instead, it was a development from Judaism. To understand anything of the depth of biblical Christianity and its teachings one must understand Judaism. This is sometimes particularly difficult for Christians living in the Western world to grasp. Throughout our history, we have tended to be influenced more by Greek and Latin expressions of Christianity than by those of the Semitic world of the East.

The history of Christian-Jewish relations mainly chronicles a troubled past. Although originally the first-century church had sturdy Jewish roots, by the middle of the second century and the "parting of the way" many of those vibrant roots were beginning to rot, wither, or die. Instead of thriving with its (Jewish) "olive tree" connection (Rom. 11:18), within a century — especially outside the land of Israel throughout the Mediterranean world — the church was less and less Jewish in its composition, influence, and expression and more and more had developed religious patterns and practices reflective of the wider culture of the day. The de-Judaization of the church would have lasting effects on the history, teachings, and practices of Christianity.

Let us briefly highlight some of the important developments that brought change to the church. The church began as a movement totally within Judaism, "enjoying the favor of all the people" (Acts 2:47). For the first twenty years of the early church — up until the middle of the first century — unless someone was born a Jew or had chosen to convert to Judaism (a proselyte), that individual was excluded from the church. Like a number of first-century Jewish sects or parties, such as the Pharisees, Sadducees, and Essenes, the early Jewish followers of Jesus, the sect of the Nazarenes, were another expression among the various "Judaisms" of the day (see Acts 24:5).

In A.D. 49, the Council of Jerusalem was called (see Acts 15). The Jewish apostles and church leaders wanted to find a way for those outside the commonwealth of Israel to share in the heritage of the ancient people of God. Belief in Jesus and in the apostolic witness about him became the criterion for membership within the fledgling Jewish church. As the gospel message began to spread rapidly outside the land of Israel, many Gentiles responded to the gospel message and joined Jews as those newly grafted into the "olive tree" (see Rom. 11:17-24). But unlike Jews, the physical descendants of Abraham who bore the "sign of the covenant" in their flesh (see Gen. 17:13), Gentile believers did not have to undergo the painful rite of circumcision. Further, Gentiles were not obligated to perform the hundreds of commandments of Judaism, many of which were intended to set the Jewish people apart from the nations.

By the second century, with the rapid advancement of Christianity into the non-Jewish world, an adversarial relationship had begun to develop between church and synagogue. As the number of Gentiles quickly grew within the church, Gentile leadership of the church grew correspondingly. This gradually led to the emergence of an anti-Jewish polemic accompanied by a spirit of triumphalism, arrogance, and outward hostility. Jews were increasingly viewed as those of a dead and legalistic religion, cursed by God for their rejection of Jesus.

Christianity became more and more de-Judaized in expression. The Septuagint or Greek version of the Hebrew Bible was a factor in hastening this process. The de-Judaization of early Christianity was likewise aided and abetted by a number of influential early church fathers who brought certain neo-Platonic teachings and philosophical constructs into early Christian thought. The rise of various branches of Gnosticism, with their spiritual and esoteric teachings, also brought a corrupting influence upon the "flesh and blood" emphasis that early Jewish Christianity had inherited from Judaism.

Conflict also arose over various theological issues. Differing points of view arose concerning Jesus and claims about his messiahship, divinity, and resurrection. Further, many traditional Jews, upon realization that Gentiles were not required to keep all the Law of Moses — including circumcision, Sabbath worship, and dietary regulations — considered such religious negation the very evisceration of Judaism. The interpretation of such actions was that *these people have left Judaism.* Indeed, in the beginning, the modification of the practice of Jewish Law through the exempting of Gentiles from various Jewish commandments probably created as much discord between communities as theological disagreement did, if not more. Adding further to the controversy, Gentile believers saw the church as the "new" Israel, replacing Jews — the "old" Israel. This teaching of supersessionism was picked up by the middle of the second century in the writings of Justin Martyr.[1]

Two competing interpretations of a common Scripture (the Hebrew Bible) also began to polarize the communities. The Christian Scriptures proclaimed Jesus as the messianic fulfillment of the prophetic teaching of Israel. The New Testament writers saw in Jesus the coming of a new era. Its hallmarks included a new revelation, a new redemption, and a new kingdom. Traditional Jews had a different interpretation of the person of Jesus and the meaning of his life and death. A sibling rivalry between church and synagogue was now well under way. Accordingly, each group sought ways to define themselves over against the other, to distance themselves, and eventually to come to a mutual rejection.

In addition to the above conflicts, Jewish followers of Jesus who continued to attend the synagogue had to deal with an exclusionary curse or malediction that considered them sectarians or deviants. Further, two Jewish wars against Rome (A.D. 66-73 and A.D. 132-135) and various persecutions of the other also significantly contributed to the split. The parting of the way, however, was not sudden. It was gradual (over many decades), complex (multiple factors involved), and oppositional (included both Jewish rejection of Christians and Christian rejection of Jews).

Today, in light of the long conflict that has existed between church and synagogue for most of its history, it is often easiest to take the low road and settle for a recital of our seeming differences rather than to assess realistically our commonalities. I would argue, however, that despite our long and painful adversarial relationship from the close of the biblical era through most of the twentieth century, we must remember that the areas we share in common are far greater than those teachings, beliefs, and practices that divide us. It is all too easy to define or dismiss the other by a hastily spoken negative. For example, to hear a Christian define a Jew as simply "one who rejects Jesus and/or the New Testament," and to hear a Jew define a Christian as basically "someone who rejects the Torah and upholds creeds rather than

---

1. See Peter Richardson, *Israel in the Apostolic Church* (Cambridge: Cambridge University Press, 1969), p. 1.

deeds," is to hear this brash division. Such facile statements or partial truths do not advance Christian-Jewish understanding or interfaith relations.

Jesus, Jews, and Common Ground

Do Christians and Jews have considerable common ground? I believe they do. Both groups, however, are often uninformed about it or are unwilling to explore the breadth and depth of this territory. For Jews, Jesus has long remained a controversial figure, sometimes summarily dismissed with the superficial declaration, "Whoever Jesus was and whatever he had to say is not what Jews believe." Such a response usually lacks an understanding of the life and background of Jesus, what he taught, the overall Jewishness of the Gospels, and the rich diversity of Second Temple Judaism. In recent decades, however, works of Jewish scholars such as David Flusser, Jacob Neusner, Amy-Jill Levine, and others have "reintroduced" Jesus as a Jewish sage whose vibrant Jewish teachings resonate with many strands of traditional Jewish thought and practice.[2]

To be sure, over the centuries Jews and Christians have interpreted Jesus differently. The apostolic church and early church fathers had their interpretations of Jesus; the rabbinic sages and medieval commentators had theirs. To the discredit of the church, however, much of the modern Jewish misunderstanding about Jesus and his teachings has been influenced by the long history of anti-Judaism and anti-Semitism. Christians have always made Jesus the focal point of their faith. But many Christians today are uninformed about the centuries of suffering and persecution inflicted upon the Jewish people in the name of Jesus by those in the church or those identified with the church. Thus, given the history of crusades, disputations, expulsions, forced conversions, and pogroms, one should not be shocked to learn that the person of Jesus has, until recently, largely remained unexplored or unknown in the Jewish community. The name Jesus was not always associated with a person good for the Jews.

These historical tensions greatly contributed to Jews wanting to avoid

2. See, for example, David Flusser and Steven Notley, *The Sage from Galilee: Rediscovering Jesus' Genius,* 4th ed. (Grand Rapids: Eerdmans, 2007); Jacob Neusner, *A Rabbi Talks with Jesus* (Montreal: McGill-Queen's University Press, 2000); Amy-Jill Levine, *The Misunderstood Jew: The Church and the Scandal of the Jewish Jesus* (New York: HarperCollins, 2006); and Amy-Jill Levine and Marc Zvi Brettler, eds., *The Jewish Annotated New Testament* (New York: Oxford University Press, 2011).

Christians and any understanding of the teachings of Christianity. Until the last half of the twentieth century, Jews and Christians understood very little about the other; each community lived largely separate lives. With little personal knowledge of the other, Christians continued to build their faith around Jesus; Jews, on the other hand, largely continued to make the study of Torah the centerpiece of their lives.

Today, owing to an increasing openness in Christian-Jewish relations, a remarkable change is underway. Increasingly, a sincere desire to understand the other has resulted in mutual respect and self-correction. Jews are acquiring a greater knowledge of the first-century Jewish world and the Jewish origin of Jesus' teachings. In the process, Christians are profiting immensely from Jewish scholarship, books, and articles and a variety of interfaith educational events. This current rediscovery of Jesus the Jew could come about only through an honest assessment of the past, social change, and a new interreligious encounter that is willing to take risks, readjust attitudes, and right wrongs. At the same time, through this new engagement of the other, Christians are becoming more sensitized to the Jewish Scriptures — especially the foundational value of Torah — the commentaries, and the essential teachings of Judaism. In this contemporary conversation, Christians are coming to discover and understand their indebtedness to Jews and Judaism and something of the vastness of the church's Hebraic heritage.

Judaism: A Living Tradition Guided by Texts

Christians tend, on average, to be much more familiar with the pages of the New Testament and the subsequent theological writings of the church fathers and the Reformers than they are with the church's Hebraic heritage. In this book I have chosen to define *Hebraic heritage* as more than the Jewish Scriptures, or what is contained in the Tanakh, namely, the Law, Prophets, and Writings. Christians must recognize that the heritage of the Jewish people is not static but dynamic and organic. The Jewish theological and ethical legacy involves more than the Written Torah; it also embraces the Oral Torah and the rabbinic commentaries within a living tradition.

Why are these extra-biblical Jewish texts important for Christians? What is the value of Jewish sources such as apocalyptic literature, the Apocrypha, writings of Josephus, the sectarian documents and commentaries of Qumran, the Targums, the Talmud (Mishnah and Gemara), and *Midrashim?* These works serve as valuable tools to help clarify the understanding and application of the expressions and concepts of the Hebrew Bible, of Judaism of the Second Temple or pre–A.D. 70 period, and of the teachings of the New Testament.

These texts also help frame the political, historical, social, and religious world from which the canonical Scriptures come. In historic Christianity, the biblical writings alone are divinely inspired and authoritative Scripture. But grasping the precise meaning of various biblical texts — without being able to locate them in their wider religious and cultural context — would be exceedingly difficult if we could not draw upon extra-biblical Jewish literature (for example, John 10:22; Jude 14-15; and see 2 Pet. 3:16).

Further, these non-biblical texts display something of the spirit and rich complexity of Judaism as a living tradition in light of its need to adapt to changing circumstances. The religion of the Hebrew Bible was far more dynamic than static; the understanding of the faith of Israel (as in Christianity) and its traditions continued to be shaped and reshaped by social expansion, cultural interaction, political developments, and significant events such as the exile, the destruction of the Temple, and the codification of the Oral Law.

To illustrate the above, one may observe how the meaning of *tahat ayin tahat*, "an eye for an eye," evolved throughout the history of Israel. By the time of Jesus the expression had come to mean something different from what it had earlier meant in the second millennium B.C. in the ancient Near East world of Moses — the cost of an eye (Exod. 21:23-25; cf. Matt. 5:38). A further example one may cite concerns the number of children that satisfied the first commandment of Scripture, *peru u-rebu*, "be fruitful and increase in number" (Gen. 1:28). Judaism came to define this requirement as two children (either two sons or a son and a daughter) as set forth by the major schools of Jewish thought that had emerged during the Second Temple period (cf. Mishnah Yebamoth 6:6). Another example of the importance of extra-canonical Jewish literature relates to our understanding of the *kohen gadol* or "high priest" and of the "Azazel-goat" or "scapegoat" on *Yom Kippur*, "the Day of Atonement," in the Temple at the time of Jesus. These matters are carefully described in tractate Yoma of the Mishnah and must be compared and contrasted to the description of the Day of Atonement and the function of the high priest in Leviticus 16. Thus, Leviticus may contain the first word about the "scapegoat" but not the last word on how this ritual on the Day of Atonement was carried out.

Christian Need of Jewish Texts

Christians must not whimsically or reductively take the position that the extra-biblical tradition may be ignored because it is not "Christian" literature. If early non-biblical Jewish sources do not shed light on the New Testament itself or the cultural background of the times, they likely will illumine modern Judaism and how Jews learned to adapt to changing circumstances in order to make their faith relevant to the times. In short, these writings, traditions, and theological reflections often reveal the parameters, elasticity, and spirit of Jewish thought. They are necessary to fill out the context, background, and developing teachings of the Jewish people. Christians need to be reminded that Jews have a history of nearly four millennia and that the understanding and application of biblical texts are seldom frozen. Rather, these texts are very much alive, adapting to new, real-life situations.

To illustrate the above, do the biblical instructions about masters and slaves hold the same relevance for Jews and Christians today as they did in the biblical world (Exod. 21:1-11; Eph. 6:5-9; Col. 3:22; 4:1; Titus 2:9)? Obviously, No! Thus, we must ask: In what way does the history of our tradition and modernity affect how we read and apply the biblical text? As a further example, consider how the invention of modern medicine and its painkillers effected a change in the thinking of Christian women concerning their understanding of the "curse" long associated with childbearing: "I will greatly increase your pains in childbearing; with pain you will give birth to children" (Gen. 3:16). In addition, consider how a woman today might do "just obedience" to the text in the second half of that verse: "[your husband] will rule over you." To be sure, it would be exceedingly unwise for a Christian to suggest that a strict and literal meaning of the above texts should be frozen and enforced for all time and that these texts should never be rethought in light of modern scientific advances — not to speak of deeper theological and social reflection about women. Few Christian women today would say that they are in conflict with Scripture by taking medicine to reduce the sometimes very uncomfortable and tearful pangs of childbirth. So, in the community of faith, Scripture lives, breathes, and sometimes must be rethought and reapplied in the face of new discoveries and gifts that God graciously (and sometimes unexpectedly) provides for his people. Extra-biblical literature may prove to be one of those gifts for those willing to consult it.

Some Christians may question the advisability of exploring literature written by non-Christians. These people may express concern that Jewish writings, in particular, have the potential of uprooting the truth of Jesus by posing alternative perspectives of thought. To the contrary! That is to misunderstand the correct place of early, non-biblical sources. The purpose of studying such texts is not to undermine the words of Jesus or the Hebrew Scriptures that he taught; rather, it is to make the Christian student more knowledgeable and obedient as a *talmid* or "disciple" of Jesus.

Extra-canonical Jewish sources are not the Word of God. Accordingly, these sources must be carefully studied and weighed the same way all commentaries on Scripture must be evaluated by any thoughtful Christian student of the Bible. A statement is not helpful, valuable, or true simply because it is old or because one recognizes the name of the author. All words must be tested against the overall tenor of Scripture and its established teachings. In regard to commentaries, the presuppositions and even biases of an individual writer must be considered. To be sure, even the Bible itself must also be carefully read. We must distinguish between what the Bible reports and what it teaches. Why? The Bible records both the evil words and actions of individuals as well as the good. Job's "philosopher" or "comforter" friends give inaccurate or irrelevant advice. Further, even Satan is able to quote Scripture (Matt. 4:1-11). Thus, one must primarily establish the meaning of Scripture by Scripture, but also make use of relevant principles of exegesis, the history of biblical interpretation, commentaries, early extra-biblical sources, and listening to the voice of the Spirit within (1 Cor. 2:13-14).

Today's church needs early Jewish sources, hermeneutical studies, historical studies, linguistic studies, anthropological studies, archeological studies, geological studies, and knowledge of comparative religions to help in understanding the biblical text and cultural world of the Bible. We are several thousand years removed from the original context of Scripture. Thus, we need all the help we can get. The meaning of words and knowledge of historical background are rarely — if ever — given as a direct grant from the Holy Spirit. Rather, this useful knowledge to assist us in exegetical studies is acquired by careful research and study of the above. That God occasionally seems to bless and even use a poorly exegeted passage or distorted or incorrectly understood biblical teaching does not condone or justify the idea that textual and background study may not be important. Rather, it only reminds us how gracious God is. He sometimes works in spite of us, not because of us.

Much useful knowledge and wisdom is found outside the Bible; much of this comes from non-Christian thinkers. Such truth may be partial, incomplete, limited in perspective, or reflective of a certain degree of truth; however, we should not ignore it or dismiss it without first testing it. God, because he is kind and gracious, enables others to grasp truth even if limited or lacking in one or more aspects. All truth comes from God wherever it is found. Despite the cloud of sin that hovers around humanity, providence, nature, moral law, human conscience, and common grace all witness to the divine, and in some measure may be grasped by all. Christians acknowledge Jesus as the living Word of God and the ultimate divine revelation and expression of truth. However, the mere confession of a Christian that one claims to "know Jesus" or "has the Holy Spirit" does not guarantee infallibility in interpretation or full, accurate understanding of truth.

Accuracy in handling Scripture comes primarily through study, utilizing the best research available, and practice. It may be helpful, here, to illustrate this point from a different field. A Christian brain surgeon must do more than pray; the skills of this specialist must also be honed *before* operating through years of education, internship, residency, continual research, and much hands-on practice in the operating room. While prayer is important for a Christian physician prior to operating, successful surgery cannot be accomplished if credentials are limited to prayer alone. A brain surgeon is not a praying but untrained, incompetent, and unqualified novice. "Holy shoddy is still shoddy." So, Christian scholars of the Word are expected to do their part in acquiring knowledge through personal study. Jewish sources can provide some of the valuable resources in a serious student's toolkit to enable that person to be a more capable, competent, and skilled "surgeon" of the Word (see Heb. 4:12).

We must emphasize that it is this post-biblical Jewish reflection on the teachings of the Hebrew Bible which is often missed, unknown, and left unappreciated by the Christian community. Thus, the chapters of this book seek to give particular attention to how Jewish scholarship has reflected upon the Hebrew Bible. In the pages that follow, our aim will be to expound some of the more important themes from the Bible of Jesus (the Hebrew Scriptures) that are compatible historically with the thought and practice of Christianity and are, at the same time, also significant to Judaism in the thinking of the sages and rabbis.

Why This Volume?

My aim in writing this volume is primarily to explore some of the theological, spiritual, and ethical themes that more directly affect Christian understanding and experience rather than to explore specific, narrowly focused, highly theoretical, or abstract legal issues that may lack relevance and applicability to most Christian readers. I believe Christians have unity of the Spirit, not full unity in doctrinal matters or in practice of the faith. Through love, compassion, and grace, God desires believers to shun atavistic legalism and compulsory practices that have sometimes polarized or destroyed the body of Christ. Our Hebraic heritage is not an exploration of Jewish "legalisms" or a call for people to practice ancient or modern Judaism. Ours is a call to explore and to learn more of the richness and depth of the roots of the Christian faith. Through the Spirit of love, God permits personal freedom and group diversity in biblically grounded practices. In that sense, "pluraformity" is ordained in the plan of God. However, we *may* — not *must* — choose to engage in the exercise of different teachings and practices as long as our liberty is exercised unto him. In addition, this must always be carried out with sensitivity to the conscience of others and with the goal of edifying all believers within the body.

More importantly, restoring Hebraic heritage is a call to know and follow Jesus and his teachings more closely and thoughtfully. Likewise, a personal rediscovery of Hebraic heritage is a summons to the study of Scripture, to greater obedience to it, to faithful discipleship, and to teach the Word, with humility, to others. Such will make us wiser, deeper, and richer in contending for the faith entrusted to the people of God (see Jude 3).

In my earlier volume, *Our Father Abraham: Jewish Roots of the Christian Faith* (1989), I sought to lay a broad introductory foundation to the world of Hebraic thought, a discussion upon which much of this present work is built. This prior publication primarily explored the history of Christian-Jewish relations, the contour of Hebraic thought, and its application to a number of themes relevant to the church. The work also dealt with the relation of church and synagogue and how we may build and allow the flourishing of Christian-Jewish relations in the modern world. In this present volume, I have sought to avoid any extensive duplication of themes already introduced in *Our Father Abraham*. If this present work omits a number of themes or concepts central to an understanding of the Hebraic heritage of the church, there is a strong likelihood that I may have intentionally left these out because of their inclusion in earlier published works.

One of the main reasons I have written this book is to seek to bring to Christians of every stripe and background a renewal of perspective on various biblical themes. With great predictability, most Christians depend only on other Christian commentaries of the past or present to understand, explain, and apply the main themes and concepts of the Bible. It is certainly understandable why most individuals tend automatically to seek out the thoughtful works, useful sources, and favorite authors within their own respective religious traditions. Many are taught to do this; in addition, we are creatures of habit. This practice of not reading much outside our own religious tradition may also be influenced by our past educational training, theological bent, works available, and language proficiencies.

Obviously, many benefits can be derived from such an approach; but more often than not, this may result in a rather in-grown experience, ending up with little more than a recycling of many all-too-familiar perspectives. One often ends up working materials over and over again within the same frame of reference. Such an approach can become so mechanical, stilted, familiar, and uncreative that it yields, in the end, very diminished returns. Indeed, such study can quickly become stale, predictable, and even counterproductive. While theology and theological presuppositions matter every time we open the Bible, readers and interpreters can easily become prisoners of their own routine, pre-digested, in-house theories and miss the stimulus of an often richer, deeper, more edifying open textual conversation by engaging those from outside their own theological frame of reference.

Christians and Jews are set apart in an unusual relationship, for, as the great Jewish scholar Martin Buber observed, "We share a Book, and that is no small thing."[3] Reading from this shared Hebraic heritage can provide an antidote for the above practice, providing a set of fresh eyes and enabling the reader to suggest new insights and ask new questions.

There is no quick-fix "Jewish remedy," however, for understanding the message of Scripture. Nevertheless, to limit oneself to only Christian sources when seeking to understand Jews, Judaism, and the Jewish origins of Christianity is both unwise and myopic. Why the encouragement for this broader engagement? It is not for the sake of being "untraditional," avant-garde, or novel. Rather, it comes from the necessity to reflect on, comment on, and ask useful questions of the text. This engagement can often stimulate one to rethink the text from a new perspective, frequently challenging the passive default position potentially characterized by a pernicious or incestuous interpretive point of view.

Another benefit of engaging Jewish commentary on Scripture is the value it places on dialogue and conversation. Many Christians spend too

3. Rabbi David S. Rosen calls attention to Buber's point about this special relationship made possible through a "shared Book" in Rosen's dynamic final words of the public television documentary based on *Our Father Abraham,* here quoted in the *Study Guide* to the documentary, *Jews and Christians: A Journey of Faith,* ed. Marvin R. Wilson (Potomac, MD: Auteur Productions, 2000), p. 40.

much time talking only to themselves, a perceived place of security and safe answers. Christians and Jews, however, have a shared Hebraic tradition. That tradition requires a living conversation regarding its meaning. Interfaith conversation has great potential to provide insight into the text from one tradition that a person coming from another tradition may not have. Steeped in the history, teachings, and traditions of Judaism, Jewish sages and rabbis — though often neglected or undiscovered by Christians — are an indispensable source of knowledge concerning the heritage of their faith and its practice.

Acknowledgments

At the outset of this book, I wish to acknowledge the profound influence the writings of the late Rabbi Abraham Joshua Heschel have had on my thinking and life. For more than forty years I have taught a senior seminar on Heschel and continue to rejoice in seeing how positively my students too respond to his works. Next to the Bible itself, the writings of Heschel have done more than any other texts to challenge and shape my thinking about God, Israel, the prophets, spirituality, awe, the meaning of being human, the Jewish roots of Christianity, and the importance of Christian-Jewish relations. Various footnotes scattered throughout this book indicate something of the sense of debt I have to this scholar whose works remain so instrumental in understanding the God of Israel and the Scriptures and people of Israel and making them come alive to me.

By way of additional acknowledgments, I am very grateful for the encouragement and contributions of various individuals, organizations, and resources that have had a role in my writing this work on Hebraic heritage. In the first place, I am very appreciative of the helpful feedback from numerous readers and various reviewers of *Our Father Abraham* — both Christians and Jews. This overwhelmingly positive response to my attempt to lay out the foundational groundwork of Christianity's Jewish roots is one of the main reasons I am motivated to write this present companion volume. Further, I have been encouraged by the number of individuals and institutions who have successfully used my first volume as a study text or for discussion. This has further led to a variety of requests for foreign translations, which underscores that the subject matter is of international interest.

I also owe a debt of gratitude to my students at Gordon College. Their response remains very positive to my teaching emphasis on the Jewish roots of the Christian faith and on the usefulness of the Hebrew language, Judaism, and Jewish studies for informing a biblical foundation to the Christian faith and for guiding them in respectful conversation with the Jewish community in this modern world.

Another driving force behind *Exploring Our Hebraic Heritage* grows out of my personal involvement in the development of the television documentary *Jews and Christians: A Journey of Faith*. This national two-hour public television program is based upon various themes presented in *Our Father Abraham* and provides a visual educational venue for communicating the importance of the Jewish roots of the Christian faith to an interfaith audience. Co-produced by Auteur Productions and Connecticut Public Television, the documentary received several awards. As primary scholar of this film, I was assigned the responsibility of writing several thousand questions to be used in the various interviews with the experts and — upon the completion of the film — also assigned to create a detailed educational study guide for use with the segments and themes within the documentary. As much as possible, these discussion questions were honed to the individual strengths of each of the ninety scholars, rabbis, and religious leaders interviewed on camera. While only some of the experts interviewed made the final cut, this unusual opportunity to interact with such a large variety of Jewish and Christian institutional leaders and academics proved very informative and personally enriching. It was much like participating in a graduate school seminar on Judaism and the history of Christian-Jewish relations. In this regard, I must express deep thanks to Auteur's producer Gerald Krell and cinematographer Meyer Odze for allowing me to work closely with them in arranging interviews with various scholars and educators here in America and also in Israel. Having the extraordinary opportunity to be on site and actively present at dozens of these on-camera interviews prompted me to pursue additional research on a number of topics found in the present book.

My appreciation also goes to Professor Steven A. Hunt, one of my faculty colleagues at Gordon College who provided additional stimulus for writing this book. In celebration of my seventy-fifth birthday, Steve worked tirelessly to collect and edit a volume of twenty scholarly essays under the title *Perspectives on Our Father Abraham* (Eerdmans, 2010). The collection includes essays by both Christians and Jews. Many were penned by my faculty colleagues in the department of biblical studies at Gordon College, some by former students, and others by personal friends — professors or rabbis — serving at other schools or institutions. This engaging Festschrift of Professor Hunt provides considerable creative reflection on Judaism and various aspects of the life and theological significance of father Abraham, a foundational theme I have continued to reflect upon in the present volume. Further, in regard to the subject of Abraham, I wish to acknowledge that portions of two chapters I have written in the second main division of the present volume are based on my previously published essay "Abraham: A Point of Convergence and Divergence for Christians and Jews," in *Jews and Christians: People of God,* edited by Carl E. Braaten and Robert W. Jenson (Eerdmans, 2003), pp. 41-64.

A personal debt of gratitude also goes to Gordon College for providing me with a sabbatical leave in the spring of 2012. This time of release from my regular teaching duties enabled me to complete a significant amount of the research and writing involved with this book.

Further, I am very appreciative of the valuable support of various students I have had as teaching assistants. Three I must single out, each a promising young scholar. First, Kirsten Heacock Sanders contributed significantly to much of the initial research done on this book. In addition to Kirsten, I am very grateful to Kevin Capel for his organizational input and editing skills. Kevin's sharp theological mind, sage advice, and faithful support have done much to help bring this work along. Last, but not least, my deep appreciation also goes to Chelsea Revell. In addition to her insightful assistance in editing, Chelsea played a major creative role in the development of the study and discussion questions found at the end of each chapter.

A word of thanks also goes to my wife, Polly, who has encouraged the writing of this book in innumerable ways. She has provided input on some of the topics in this work about which I have publicly lectured. In addition, like the present writer, Polly values our Hebraic heritage, the land of Israel, and the importance of strong Christian-Jewish relations. I am grateful for her talented piano playing and love for the music of Israel that she continues to bring to my Modern Jewish Culture course, a class I have annually taught and in which she has assisted for more than fifty years.

My final words of appreciation go to the experienced and supportive editorial staff at William B. Eerdmans. I am grateful for the enthusiastic support of Jon Pott, editor-in-chief. In addition, my deep thanks go to Jennifer Hoffman, whose superb editing skills were most valuable in bringing this work to publication.

The Hebrew heritage of today's church is both deep in its exploration potential and forward-looking in how it may edify. The Jewish roots of the Christian faith that have largely been rotting in the ground since the "parting of the way" are available and vital for bringing renewal and restoration to us in the church. This book goes forth with the hope that its contents will be helpful in the renewal process by providing some theological, spiritual, and ethical insights and commentary essential for today's church in building a fuller, richer, and more biblically authentic lifestyle. The "history of contempt" combined with overt and latent anti-Judaism has prevented many in the church from tapping into the root system of their faith. It is imperative that all Christians look back at their foundational roots in the Jewish people and in Jewish thought so that they may move forward into a more thoughtful, informed, and hopeful tomorrow.

Judaism and Christianity confidently believe that biblical faith is founded upon a rock, father Abraham (Isa. 51:1-2). Accordingly, here is a firm and faithful reminder that Christians alone do not hold the patent on a brighter tomorrow. The promise of Abraham was centered on hope in the God of Abraham; he was "looking forward to the city with foundations, whose architect and builder is God" (Heb. 11:10). Like father Abraham, the man who "believed the LORD" (Gen. 15:6; see Rom. 4:3), the Hebrew Scriptures admonish all humanity to hope and trust in the Lord (Ps. 42:5; Prov. 16:20). May this text for study be a means of encouraging and deepening that end.

MARVIN R. WILSON
Wenham, Massachusetts

PART I

Theological Sources and Methods

CHAPTER 1

Stepping-Stones and Pitfalls in Theology

Some practical guidelines are necessary for doing theology. Why? In every believer there is the potential for articulating strong theology, weak theology, or something in between. There are beginners in theology; there are also mature theologians. Naturally, one might anticipate that a theological neophyte has the greatest potential for making mistakes and missteps. This is often the case, but there is also much potential; the novice's situation is similar to a beginning musician or athlete, seeking daily to improve by applying the dictum "practice makes perfect."

Success in the development of one's personal theological position has as much to do with how one holds one's positions as with the actual positions one holds. As a pastor friend of mine sometimes reminds me, "Some theologians are like porcupines: they have a lot of good points, but you can't get near them!" Indeed, in the art of theological discourse, positions of intolerant and intractable dogmatism or of extremely inclusive and syncretistic broadmindedness are both potentially self-destructive.

It could be simplistic or deceiving, however, to think that a life dedicated to the study of Scripture and theological writings always produces a mature and thoughtful lay or professional theologian. It is possible to be in a category similar to those described in the New Testament as "always learning and never able to arrive at a knowledge of the truth" (2 Tim. 3:7, ESV). How so? Is not theology a black-and-white discipline? Isn't theology a matter of laying out a list of the authoritative truths sincere Christians agree on?

Good theology is, at the same time, both complex and nuanced, yet also based on beliefs and convictions. However, at the end of the day, the most venerable and mature theology is probably not like listening to a simple creed piously recited. Rather, it is more like a glorious tapestry patiently interwoven with a rich variety of colored strands by an Author who has left us to figure out how each part relates to the whole. As each human life is built as a complex work of art, with certain threads of life more important than others in defining who a person is, so theology combines major motifs with minor motifs in the revelation of God's big picture of himself and his relation to the world.

The aim of this chapter is to lay out some of the more important stepping-stones in the journey that leads toward greater maturity in theological reflection. At the same time, I will also discuss some of the common pitfalls that can limit or hinder the development of strong and mature theological thought. Many of the observations below grow out of many decades of teaching theology and out of personal theological reflection. Their purpose is to help minimize theological missteps and help bring a greater biblical balance, richness, and integrity to this vital discipline.

Theological Eclecticism

One of the questions biblical and theological professors often debate is, What is the central theme or the theological heart of the Old Testament? Is there a dominant theological concept that holds the Bible of Jesus together? A great variety of answers are typically offered and positions taken. Is it covenant? Is it the kingdom of God? Is it redemption? Is it promise-fulfillment? Is it holiness? Is it law? Is it love? And the list could go on. What seems to be the key concept or uniting motif of the Jewish Scriptures, the Tanakh?

I believe the best answer is not one theme but many themes. It is all of the above theological concepts and more. While the dynamic presence of the living God is the centerpiece who fills the pages of Scripture, there are many theological themes that relate to his character and nature, his work in history with Israel, and his purpose and will for the world. It is impossible to attempt to systematize or to reduce to one motif the varieties and richness of theological themes found in the Old Testament. Taken together, however, as powerful strands of truth, they are as critical to bringing theological connectivity to the testaments as the numerous cables of a suspension bridge, strung together, are in providing strength, support, and ultimately a form of life-and-death dependence for those moving between two shores.

Hebraic theology cannot be simplistically reduced to one key strand of thought. While there is a complex congruity and continuity between the testaments, they have very different approaches. Order, logic, organization, system, and symmetry are often more characteristic of a Greek mindset than of a Hebrew one. The ancient Greeks had tidy minds. Everything was reasoned out and had its place. Their approach was that of philosophy. In the early post-biblical history of Christian doctrine, chiefly through the influence of the Greek fathers, many of the above features of Greek thought sought to bring coherence and structure to doctrinal expression. The Hebrew Bible and Jewish mindset, however, tended to take a different approach. Martin Stohr comments on what he describes as "the Jewish way of doing theology" by noting "its constant questioning and counter-questioning, its emphasis on the whole, its inclusion of contradictory traditions, its rejection of schematization, and its willingness to forgo seeing Holy Scriptures as a unity or finding in them some 'material principle.'"[1]

Here is a fitting reminder that Hebraic biblical expression (and the rabbinic discussions thereof in the post-biblical centuries) seldom involved a singular approach to theological truth. Historically, Judaism is not famous for its "creeds" the way Christianity is. Rather, several perspectives are often set forth, each usually debated in the process. Post-biblical theological thinking is approached dialogically, through commentary, rather than systematically. One position is usually held in dynamic tension with the other(s). Theologically speaking, matters are seldom reduced to an either/or alternative. Instead, there is a repetitious cycle: a question and answer simply leads to another question.

In regard to Christian theological reflection on Scripture, when doctrine is limited to one "correct" position on a subject — for example, that of one particular theologian, a certain theological school of thought, or a particular denomination — such a conclusion may be flawed. But we do not necessarily mean flawed in the sense of being wrong, errant, or heretical; rather, the conclusion may be flawed in the sense of being a partial, imperfect, unbalanced, or one-sided statement. Selected biblical passages, particularly those that are very pregnant theologically, often give us windows on truth, but seldom the whole truth. Thus, for Christian theological understanding in general, it is usually preferable to think of *points* of view (plural).

Accordingly, in my view, it is usually very risky and problematic to believe and teach that one particular theological tradition has it all "right," and the rest of the traditions have got it "wrong." Why? Varying views of biblical interpretation, the history of Christian thought, church authority,

---

1. Quoted in Pinchas Lapide and Ulrich Luz, *Jesus in Two Perspectives* (Minneapolis: Augsburg, 1985), p. 19.

and other matters — even one's gender or ethnicity — often significantly influence theological perspectives. These are issues of great consequence. Who speaks for the church, or do all individual Christians speak for themselves? What role should church councils, church history, and church tradition play? Thoughtful Christians have had considerable disagreement on these and other questions. At the end of the day, Christians must learn to think theologically as individuals, but never in total isolation from the church, the corporate body of which they are a part, not apart from.

In seeking to harness Hebraic theological expression, it is usually wise to take an eclectic approach. Eclecticism deals with choosing or selecting from a variety of streams or sources. Instead of following one system of thought or one interpretive scheme, the individual chooses from and reflects upon various theological streams. It is always tempting to play one's favorite theological hobby. However, given the complex relation between the testaments and an honest acknowledgment of the dissimilarities as well as similarities present, it is normally preferable to select from a number of theological themes and emphases. In addition, some texts may have multiple theological meanings, as opposed to one "correct" meaning. Theological eclecticism eliminates a major problem of trying to force varied currents of thought into one comprehensive — yet potentially limiting — single-theme approach. Just as an evangelist cannot legitimately find the salvation message of John 3:16 hidden in every other passage of the Bible, so no single theological theme can be forced to serve as the indisputable theological center of the Old Testament.

Theology as a Product of Human Reflection

Scripture is divine revelation, uniquely inspired by God's Spirit. As the Word of God, it is fully trustworthy and dependable in matters of faith and practice. Theology, however, is different. It is the product of human reflection upon Scripture, not Scripture itself. This is an important distinction. Theology is exceedingly valuable, but not a perfect science. Sometimes imprecise and incomplete, theology is the formulation of fallible human beings. On occasion, theologians are driven by personal agendas. Therefore what theologians discuss and write is always susceptible to error and revision. Such is rarely intentional; rather, it is part of being human, lacking experience, or sometimes lacking appropriate checks and balances. Indeed, there may be a difference, from time to time, between what the Bible says (Scripture itself) and what the reader/interpreter thinks it means (theology). What God says is infallible. Human understanding of that Word may lack precision, show bias, or be something quite different from what the original author may have had in mind. Accordingly, Ben Witherington calls for an emphasis on what the Reformers termed *semper reformanda*, "always reforming," for there is "the temptation to form our theology almost independently of doing our exegesis."[2]

Archeological, historical, and linguistic discoveries also occasionally make it necessary to tweak slightly some theological concepts. If no two English versions of the Bible are exactly the same, how much more is there likely to be theological diversity? Much of the diversity in theological expression is in nuance or emphasis, not in substance by an attempt to rewrite major concepts of doctrine. But theology always needs vetting and some rewording and even excising from time to time, for it comes from godly, yet sinful, human beings. In 1543, Martin Luther wrote some terrible things about the Jewish people. His words were so offensive that the Lutheran community, more than four centuries later, issued an apology and formally disassociated itself from these remarks. Post-Auschwitz theological reflection has led other major denominations to make significant self-corrections to denominational liturgy and teaching concerning the Jewish people. In addition, passion plays have undergone theological revision.

We must not forget that human beings have different degrees of sophistication and experience in this task of theological reflection. In addition, most people have unconscious biases. They may also possess predispositional allegiances or wounds that make theological objectivity difficult. To illustrate, the prophets teach that God is a "father" (Jer. 31:9; Mal. 1:6). If God is like a father in the relation he has with his people, what are the possibilities of a person creating a theological distortion of this father image if the person's own father is remembered as an uncaring, unfaithful, and cruel man? No one has a *tabula rasa* or clean slate when opening the Bible. We all have potential baggage that can affect how we read the text and how we formulate theology from it. We all have different presuppositions, life experiences, and church backgrounds that can potentially influence our theological understanding.

For the reasons cited above and others not mentioned, one needs to envision the writing of theology with a pencil and eraser, not with indelible ink or by chiseling it in marble. Sometimes — but certainly not always — theology may seem more like a train schedule: "Subject to change without

2. Ben Witherington III, "The Problem with Evangelical Theologies," *Christianity Today*, November 2005, p. 68.

notice." Why? One major reason is that theology students, pastors, and even professional theologians do not have all the answers. Their understanding of God, like that of every Christian, is a work in progress. Another reason is the fact that no theologian — and the church has had some great ones — has ever said it all. Theology is often hammered out through the pressures of the times, in response to particular situations, or as a result of the need to correct or clarify some new teaching.

Theological expression, therefore, must be open to review, revision, updating, and even correction. This does not mean that nothing in theology can be nailed down. Neither does it mean that everything theological is really unglued and of no permanence, mere opinion that can, at any moment, be cast aside. To the contrary! Theological convictions are a necessity, not an option. Most major theological teachings have developed corporately over centuries of time. However, to be adept and successful in theological conversation, one needs a spirit of humility in order to listen, learn, and grow wiser, deeper, and more biblically focused in theological expression.

Scripture Not a Slave to Any System

One of the great difficulties and honest challenges in theological study is answering the sometimes all-too-real but uneasy question, Where does the theological buck stop and one's highest allegiance lie? In short, does a Christian's highest loyalty come in defending the theological slant of a particular religious denomination or tradition, or does it lie in support of what one believes the text of Scripture is teaching? A candid grappling with this question is no easy matter, for it sometimes ruffles feathers. With a view to being a "biblical Christian" who seeks to hold to a "biblical theology," it simply asks the simple question, How close does one's local church or fellowship group come to this norm?

Looking at global Christianity today, the perspective of many Christians on Scripture is often largely defined and circumscribed by a particular denomination. Indeed, some Christians take great pride in their denominational distinctiveness. Occasionally, one finds almost an elitist attitude associated with the particular church denomination to which certain Christians belong. In fact, these Christians sometimes judge other Christian groups by how close they come to, or how far they are removed from, the allegedly "pure and true" system of theology typically practiced in these Christians' highly regarded "official" and "historic" denomination.

Now there is an upside and a downside to denominationalism. Among the positives one usually finds some degree of historical development and awareness. There is also the expectation of quality control. In short, denominations have standards and expectations. And these standards are usually adhered to or enforced. Thus, church visitors usually know in advance pretty much what to expect about the ambiance and emphases of the worship experience. They know the style of worship, the liturgy employed, the traditional hymns used, and the order of service. Usually, there is a predictability about the worship service, expectations as to the educational level of the pastor, and the overall theological slant and parameters held by denominational executives and denominational seminaries. Such positives add a sense of stability, familiarity, and expectation, as well as usually a sense of theological predictability and distinctiveness.

There are often potential negatives, however. Within certain denominations, the theological standards being upheld and theological emphases being experienced are often institutionally tied to a particular theologian, Reformer, church father, lauded saint, or group historically linked to the preservation — in some degree — of a specific culture or ethnicity. While the theological giants and doctors of the church have had a very important and vital role in shaping the development of Christianity, these great theological minds of the church are not God. Neither are their writings — as profound, erudite, and formative as they are — the inspired, canonical Scriptures, Holy Writ. Names such as Karl Barth, Søren Kierkegaard, John Calvin, John Wesley, Martin Luther, Francis of Assisi, Thomas Aquinas, Augustine, Origen, Tertullian, and others are among the most brilliant and influential theological minds the church has ever known.

However wise, valued, groundbreaking, or game-changing their lives and works, none of the above theologians said it all. None is without need of eventual updating, modification, or addition. None, for example, was able to make use of the Dead Sea Scrolls, the modern Jewish-Christian theological encounter, modern theological commentaries and dictionaries, modern theological libraries, and computer-generated research. These and other formidable, trailblazing greats of church history served their generations well. We must continue to hear, study, and ponder their weighty theological voices in the modern church; we must continue to engage respectfully and seriously their works and ideas. However, we may not always be comfortable moving beyond these denominational heroes, who still, for all their wisdom, did not see the entirety of things.

In my view, one should be a Christian who happens to be a Baptist, or happens to be a Methodist, or happens to be a Presbyterian, or happens to be a Catholic, or happens to be a Lutheran, and so on. One should be cautious and aware of the potential theological restrictiveness that may come when one chooses to define oneself as an *Episcopalian* Christian, a *Presbyterian* Christian, an *Assembly of God* Christian, a *Congregational* Christian, and so on. Such a self-definition may contribute to an unwise theological exclusivity. How so? When one's denominational label precedes the word *Christian,* it may be exceedingly difficult to free oneself — if or when one's theological conscience may deem this necessary — from a particular, distinctive theological or ecclesiastical practice that one is not convinced is soundly biblical. While the Bible, tradition, reason, and expediency all play a role in the thought and practice of most Christians, there are times when the stance of a denomination or its executives may conflict with the biblical and theological understanding of an individual believer. Many Christians will tend to ignore or slough off these matters as differences of opinion, assuming that others know more than they do. On the other hand, we may point to some examples from church history — those with deep theological convictions such as Martin Luther and John Wesley — who courageously championed theological reform and renewal. God calls the church to unity. So any decisions related to theological interpretation must always be weighed thoughtfully, carefully, and with much prayer and personal counsel.

Theological systems or denominational interpretive schemes do affect how Scripture is read, understood, and applied. For example, Covenant theologians and Dispensational theologians traditionally have had significant interpretive differences on such matters as the relation of Israel and the church, law and grace, the kingdom of God, covenant, end-time events, the earthly and heavenly Jerusalem, and literal versus symbolic interpretation of Scripture.

Theological disagreement also sometimes happens when a particular *deductive* system of biblical interpretation comes in potential conflict with an individual's *inductive* study of Scripture. The one who makes an open inductive theological investigation of Scripture is not usually out to defend a certain predetermined schematic or systematic position. Such an individual is willing to let the theological chips fall where they may. Personally, I do not believe the Bible should ever be held hostage to any interpreter's pre-established theological grid or system (e.g., Reformed, Wesleyan, Pentecostal, or others) that the interpreter may wish to impose on the Bible. A commitment to the largely inductive nature of biblical theology, however, and also a commitment to eclectic theological thinking, will usually provide a healthy check-and-balance system should the Bible be in peril of being a slave to any deductive theological system.

Theological systems are a double-edged sword. They can be valuable; but they can be dangerous too. Jewish theologian Leo Baeck sharply warns against rigid systems of truth:

> Every system of thought is intolerant and breeds intolerance because it fosters self-righteousness and self-satisfaction — it is significant that the most ruthless of inquisitors have come from the ranks of the systematizers. . . . A system cuts itself off from all outside . . . and thus prevents the living development of truth. On the other hand, the prophetic word is a living and personal confession of faith which cannot be circumscribed by rigid boundaries; it possesses a breadth and a freedom carrying within itself the possibilities of revival and development.[3]

In offering a Christian response to Baeck, I can say that I believe the discipline of systematic theology can be a very useful organizational tool for the various categories of theological thought. Indeed, the Bible is more than a storage place for spare parts, just as our bodies are not a bank for spare organs. Each part is made to function organically in relation to the others. So the Bible is not a dump for detached or isolated verses. The Bible has structure and holds together with continuity. Accordingly, systematic theology has often proven beneficial in helping to identify and concretize many of the basic theological and confessional truths by which the church lives. In addition, an understanding of systematic theology and many of its venerable teachings has often prevented the church from wandering into aberrant teachings and unproductive, passing religious fads.

We should acknowledge the organization and doctrinal clarity that theological systems have often provided the church. But I would argue that it is usually preferable to find structure and system internally, within Scripture, rather than importing or inventing theological pigeonholes and then trying to fit theological proof-texts into them. Furthermore, systematic theology may have little regard for the specific context out of which the theological teaching derives. Unlike a more inductive approach, attempting to systematize theology carries the danger of placing all verses on the same level of importance, for the simple reason that they are all in the Bible.

In this discussion about varieties of theological emphases and systems,

---

3. Leo Baeck, *The Essence of Judaism* (New York: Schocken, 1948), p. 43.

we must not forget that God is greater than our theologies. We may attempt to box God in with our theological formulae. But he is alive and active, not to be taken captive and made prisoner to any theologian's sometimes far-too-limiting theological propositions. Jeremiah 18:5-10 reveals that God's decisions are not always final but may be conditional. How God carries out his word is often tied to human response. If humans change their perverse ways of behaving, God may relent from acting in judgment and show mercy (cf. Jonah 3). God is greater than the systematic theological statements to which we sometimes blithely confine him. Tennyson's poem "In Memoriam A. H. H." beautifully grasps the nub of this point:

> Our little systems have their day;
> They have their day and cease to be;
> They are but broken lights of thee,
> And thou, O Lord, art more than they.

Whatever theological system, if any, one may be inclined to adopt, it is critical to seek to mold that system by Scripture, not Scripture by that system. In the very nature of the case, systems tend to be too rigid and inflexible, not pliable and able to expand as the evidence may dictate. They need to be expandable, accommodating all the phenomena of Scripture. So any theological grid or system through which one may feel comfortable reading Scripture should be an open system.

Opting for a more inductive approach to theology may be too messy for some because it has the potential for theological loose ends and dangling threads. As difficult as this may be for some to accept, I believe this approach best fits the often open-ended and dynamically flowing Hebraic pattern of theological discourse, far better than the more closed and tightly reasoned approach characteristic of the ancient Greeks. Among Jewish interpreters of the Hebraic tradition, there has never been a rule that the theological understanding of a text is exhausted once one interpreter discovers the "one correct meaning." In the rabbinic tradition, Hillel and Shammai were prominent sages with very different opinions and interpretations, but the wisdom of both was highly valued in theological discourse. Furthermore, for Jewish interpreters, no hermeneutical rule exists that forbids one to have a category of theological thought titled "mystery" or "paradox."

Heresy: Pressing a Truth Too Far

One might think that most theological heresy comes from modern "liberal" theologians who sit down together to decide in cavalier fashion what ancient, established teaching(s) of the church they feel it would be "hip" to deny. Seldom, if ever, does heresy originate this way. Rather, heresy often arises when a recognized belief or truth is taken and then pressed too far.

Take, for example, the Christological controversies of the early church, especially in the fourth and fifth centuries. Was Jesus only a human being, a mortal man? Was he God, a divine spirit? Or was Jesus fully human and fully divine, two natures (human and divine) in one person? The New Testament presents Jesus as the God-man. However, in the early Christian centuries, the heresy of Gnosticism arose. The Gnostic belief about Jesus provides a concrete example of taking a mainline New Testament teaching (the divinity of Jesus) and pressing it too far by seeking to obliterate the humanity of Jesus. Most Gnostics held that Jesus did not have a real body but was a spirit. This "spiritual" thinking of the Gnostics was apparently influenced by neo-Platonic thought. As a result, Gnosticism considered the physical body and the material world as inferior to the spiritual. The humanity of Jesus the Jew, however, is fully affirmed in the pages of the New Testament.

There are many other theologically related concepts in Scripture that must be held in tension and balanced with some other truth. To deny one concept in favor of the validity of the other not only creates potential heresy but, in the end, destroys both truths. For example, one may inquire whether knowing God through the objective stability of doctrine is more important and dependable than knowing God subjectively through experience. Reading theology is an exercise of the mind. Theological reasoning is usually content-based and tends to be more precise and objective, for it deals with written texts that provide an intellectual, cognitive, and conceptual understanding of faith.

Knowledge of God by personal experience, in contrast, is far more subjective; God is no less real, but attempting to define his presence experientially, including his often mysterious and unpredictable ways, can be difficult. In a life situation, to intuit the realness of God through an encounter in the depth of the human heart is not the same as reading about God with one's theology book in hand. Some of the earliest theology recorded in biblical narrative is that of divine-human encounter of the angel of the LORD (Gen. 16:7; Exod. 3:2).

To deny the intellectual aspect of knowing God is to leave one floundering without the concrete theological definition of a God who, according to Holy Writ, has again and again revealed himself by intervening in history. To deny that God is also personal and can in some way be existentially experienced is to brand the witness of countless believers over the centuries a lie and eviscerate the biblical record of both Judaism and Christianity. Theologians of the first order are both theoreticians *and* practitioners. They cognitively know God through study of sacred texts; they also experientially know God as they encounter him in their respective spiritual journeys. Theology requires one to *think* and to *do*.

The Bible is the Word of God, but it is also the thoughts and words of human beings. There is a mystery in how the divine and human are meshed in the process of biblical inspiration. To give balance to both sides of this polarity we may describe the Bible as God's voice in human words. On the human level, we must study the Bible as any other book, using normal principles of literary criticism. Within their cultural boundaries, the biblical authors personally used vocabulary; grammar and syntax; figures of speech; rhetorical, rhythmic, and onomatopoetic devices; and the like, all influenced by the writers' level of education, research, and life experience. Thus, we must comparatively approach and analyze their writings as we would any other human literary document, within its respective genre, its stylistic expression, and the period of time during which it was written.

To be sure, the Bible is a monumental masterpiece, an anthology of gifted human authors; but it is likewise a magnificent mouthpiece of the living God. In short, the Bible is of divine origin, not simply the script of sages. In the words of Abraham Heschel, "It is as if God took these Hebrew words and breathed into them of His power, and the words became a live wire charged with His spirit. To this very day they are hyphens between heaven and earth."[4] This does not mean that God "dictated" his will through passive human instruments, who copied words verbatim as God infused them into their minds. Rather, there is present a mysterious work of God's Spirit guiding and superintending the authors, literally "breathing into them" and carrying them along in this process (see 2 Tim. 3:16; 2 Pet. 1:20-21). Thus they were empowered to choose words from their own background and memory, words familiar to them and appropriate to the theological concepts and teachings God intended for them to get across to their readers.

Some have incorrectly understood the divine dimension of Scripture.

---

4. Abraham J. Heschel, *God in Search of Man* (New York: Farrar, Straus & Giroux, 1955), p. 244.

They have taken the term "God's Word" to mean that the Bible is a kind of magical book, a talisman or oracle out of which God speaks via Holy Spirit–sent lightning bolts to address virtually any human situation or need. These and other types of biblicists have misunderstood revelation and tried to turn the Bible into a kind of supernatural "wand" that it was never intended by God to be. In and of itself, the written Word of God does not have the power of a magic wand to compel belief or to make people repent, quiver in reverence, and start worshiping. It is often forgotten that it is the presence of the living God behind the written text, through the power of the Holy Spirit, which is necessary to energize and ignite those words and to make them real to the reader or hearer.

The example of Holy Scripture illustrates how heresy may unintentionally arise when two theological truths are not held in tension, when one theological truth is pressed too far. We have also seen the damage this may do and how it may be corrected. Within the community of faith, when either the human or the divine dimension of Holy Scripture is emphasized to an extreme — even when this is done unwittingly — the divine-human balance of this unique book may be seriously distorted or destroyed.

Holding the Truth in Love

Theology is more than a cerebral exercise. At the heart of Hebraic heritage is the command to love God totally and to love one's neighbor as oneself (Deut. 6:5; Lev. 19:18). Christians are urged "to contend for the faith" (Jude 3). But this is not to be done in a contentious spirit. Rather, one is to speak "the truth in love" (Eph. 4:15). This means that theological convictions must be articulated not with arrogance but in a humble manner. Let it be acknowledged that there are degrees of theological certitude. All biblical theology is not on the same level of clarity or importance.

Further, the precise application of theological thought in light of modernity may be far from clear. In their historic commitment to the authority of the Hebrew Bible, the Jewish people have tended to stress certain teachings more than others. Some of these include the seeking of peace, the reverence of life, the pursuit of justice, the holiness of deeds, the folly of idolatry, the integrity of the family, the cherishing of freedom, the love of learning, and the demonstration of compassion toward the weak and powerless. All are central themes of Judaism. Other teachings are more on the periphery, not at the heart of Judaism, things that are difficult, debatable, problematic, or sketchy in detail, such as the specifics of the afterlife. While Christians will differ from Jews on what theological, ethical, and spiritual themes stand at the heart of the Old Testament, from the list of biblical teachings above it is clear that both communities share considerable common ground.

Jewish theology is like an "incessantly gushing fountain,"[5] a living source, rooted in God himself and his teachings, that habitually slakes the thirst of all who would come and drink (Prov. 14:27; Isa. 55:1-4; Jer. 2:13). The theology of the Hebrew Bible is the very life-sustaining source of the theology of Jesus, Paul, and the early apostles. They knew no other theology. As Stuart Blanch observes, "The New Testament does not alter that [Hebraic] theology, it simply points it up and announces that God's purpose . . . was now to be seen as supremely effective . . . in Jesus of Nazareth."[6]

Theology must be applied with great compassion, sensitivity, and love. We do not have all the theological answers; and those we do have are often partial answers. Theology has lacunae. The Torah points out, "The secret things belong to the LORD" (Deut. 29:29). Commenting on this verse, Jewish scholar J. H. Hertz notes that here is "a great law of life. There are limits to what mortal beings can know. Certain things are in the hands of God alone, and must be left with Him."[7] God has revealed many things to us in Scripture. But we cannot approach theology honestly without acknowledging up front that God has mysterious ways beyond our comprehension. God declares, "As the heavens are higher than the earth, so are my ways higher than your ways and my thoughts than your thoughts" (Isa. 55:9). Given our own finitude and sinfulness, we must therefore be charitable toward those whose theology may differ, in points, from our own.

In this life, perfect understanding of theology, on the personal level, is not possible. Neither is total agreement within the community possible. It is always becoming, never having fully become. Sometimes Scripture is obscure. But most theology runs the risk of being incomplete, biased, or defective because human beings are flawed, limited in information and in perspicuity. So we humans are often tempted to speak for God where he has not spoken for himself. But we must be charitable, patient, and compassion-

5. Byron Sherwin, "An Incessantly Gushing Fountain: The Nature of Jewish Theology," in *Contemporary Jewish Theology*, ed. Elliot N. Dorff and Louis E. Newman (New York: Oxford University Press, 1999), pp. 7-22.

6. Stuart Blanch, *For All Mankind: A New Approach to the Old Testament* (New York: Oxford University Press, 1978), p. 89.

7. J. H. Hertz, ed., *The Pentateuch and Haftorahs*, 2nd ed. (London: Soncino, 1975), p. 880.

ate toward one another as we seek individually and collectively to understand more perfectly the theological foundation of our faith. Presently, we know only in part, for "we see but a poor reflection" as in a mirror; "then we shall see face to face," as Jacob and Moses once saw (1 Cor. 13:12; see Gen. 32:30; Deut. 34:10).

UNDERSTANDING CHAPTER ONE

1. What does it mean that success in developing one's theological position "has as much to do with how one holds one's positions as with the actual positions one holds"?

2. What artistic metaphor is employed to describe venerable and mature theology? Explain the metaphor in your own words.

3. How does the author respond to the questions *What is the central theme of the Old Testament* or *Is there a dominant theological concept that holds the Bible of Jesus together?* How is the metaphor of suspension bridge cables used to illustrate his response?

4. In what way did the Greeks have "tidy minds"? From a Western Christian perspective, do you recognize an influence from their methods of thought on your own thought patterns? In contrast, how did the Jewish mindset handle theology (refer to Martin Stohr's comments)?

5. Why is Judaism typically not famous for its "creeds" in the same way Christianity is? Alternatively, how was theological thinking in the Jewish tradition generally approached?

6. In what sense can singular theological positions be flawed? Why is it usually preferable to think in terms of *points* of view (plural)?

7. The author states that Christians must learn to think theologically as individuals but never in total isolation from the church. In relation to this assertion, in your opinion, what is the importance of being familiar with not only the church of the present but also the church of the past?

8. Which particular theological approach does the author view as wise, and why?

9. What important distinction does the author make between Scripture and theology?

10. What does the term *semper reformanda* mean? Why does Ben Witherington call for an emphasis on it?

11. How do selected writings of Martin Luther function as a powerful

example of the fact that theology must always be open to reformation? From a Western Christian perspective, what effects does the tension of Luther as a revered theologian and as a man who produced very ethnically offensive remarks have on your sense of both human potential and fallibility? Do you feel a need to test the theology that has been handed down to you?

12. In what way does no one have "a *tabula rasa* or clean slate when opening the Bible"? Are you able to identify some of your own presuppositions that stem from your background, identity, or preferred theological positions?

13. Why does the author hold that theology should be written "with a pencil and eraser"? How, at the same time, does this not mean that nothing in theology can be "nailed down"? In what sense can the two convictions coexist?

14. What are some of the upsides and downsides of denominationalism? From a Christian perspective, what do you see as some of the strengths and weaknesses of your own denominational background or present denominational context? Are there other expressions of Christianity that you find more admirable in these areas?

15. Briefly summarize the author's reflections on both the value and limitations of formative Christian theologians of the past. In general, do you agree? Why or why not?

16. What are some potential negative effects of one's denominational label preceding the word "Christian" when self-identifying? What do you see as the healthiest way for loyalty to a denomination to be expressed?

17. What example does the author provide as support for the statement that theological systems affect how Scripture is read, understood, and applied? For additional discussion: explore and evaluate the positions of Covenant and Dispensational theologians in the areas of thought listed.

18. In what ways can particular "deductive" systems of biblical interpretation come into conflict with an individual's "inductive" study of Scripture? The author personally encourages commitment to which line of thought when seeking to interpret the Bible?

19. Review Leo Baeck's comments on systems of truth. How do you respond to his position?

20. In what ways is systematic theology worthy of credit? At the same time, what dangers accompany it?

21. Review Jeremiah 18:5-10. How do these verses remind us of the poten-

tial conditionality of God's decisions, and why is it important to keep this in mind?

22. How does the excerpt of Tennyson's poetry illustrate God's transcendence of human theology? How do you understand his powerful choice of words in describing theological systems as "broken lights"?

23. What is an "open system" of scriptural interpretation? Are you more eager or more hesitant to adopt such a system of thought? Why?

24. Consider the fact that in the Hebraic tradition, there has never been a rule that the theological understanding of a text is exhausted upon discovering "one correct meaning." From a Christian perspective, is this mindset typically present or absent in your denominational background or present context? Which should it be?

25. What five-word definition of heresy is given in the heading on p. 13? How does heresy usually arise? What was Gnosticism, and how does it serve as a powerful example of this point?

26. Consider the author's comment that "one may inquire whether knowing God through the objective stability of doctrine is more important and dependable than knowing God subjectively through experience." How would you respond?

27. Discuss the following statement of the author, "Theologians of the first order are both theoreticians *and* practitioners."

28. How is the description of the Bible as "God's voice in human words" a useful phrase in grasping biblical inspiration? Review Abraham Heschel's statement about the origin of Scripture. How does he develop the visual analogy of the words of Scripture as "hyphens between heaven and earth"?

29. Note the author's understanding that the writers of Scripture were empowered to choose words from their own background, memory, and vocabulary. To what extent do you think this should prompt Christians to regularly seek to familiarize themselves with the historical and social contexts from which Scripture emerged?

30. How is theology "more than a cerebral exercise"? How should this truth influence the ways in which we uphold and contend for our faith?

31. What are some of the teachings of the Hebrew Bible that Jewish people have tended to stress more than others? While it is true that Jewish and Christian communities differ in some emphases (note the example of a theme that is more peripheral in Jewish thought, for example), what is clear from the list?

32. Review Stuart Blanch's observation that the New Testament does not

alter Hebraic thought. Rather, it does what? From a Christian perspective, how does Jesus take on the role of an "incessantly gushing fountain," in Byron Sherwin's words? For additional discussion: explore John 7:37-39 and identify other passages of Scripture that connect Jesus with this role.

33. How do you interpret the author's statement, "Theology has lacunae"? In what verse of the Torah does J. H. Hertz find a "great law of life"? Why?

CHAPTER 2

Theological Quest for Hebraic Heritage

If today's church is to uncover more of the depth and breadth of the Christian faith, concern about accessing the very foundational teachings of Christianity, our Hebraic heritage, is not an option, but a necessity. Here is an enriching task that may require a reorientation to include new areas of study and theological learning. But I believe this oft-omitted emphasis in religious education is crucial if we are to overcome some of the shallowness and superficiality found in this current culture. Today's Christian often lacks a deep and intellectually informed faith; he or she too easily settles for an emotional Christianity, lacking seriousness about discipleship within the body of Christ.

Why do seemingly few in the church sense a malaise regarding this lack of teaching concerning the Hebraic roots of the faith? Why are many in the church unaware of the importance of the common theological and ethical tradition that undergirds Judaism and Christianity? Its lack of emphasis in Christian seminary education is one reason. But there is another historical reason that is prior to the failure of the curricula of present-day theological seminaries. Indeed, for centuries many in the church taught that Judaism was simply a propaedeutic for Christianity. That is, Judaism was only necessary until Christianity was born. This view held that God canceled the "old" covenant with Israel and replaced it with a new covenant established with the church. Sadly, in the process, the very Hebraic theological foundation of the church was negated.

The discipline of theology is primarily concerned with the study of God and his relation to the world. Succinctly put, theology is human thought and reflection on God. Biblical theology begins with two presuppositions: God exists and has revealed himself in Scripture, the Word of God. These starting points for the study of theology are not rationally proven, but are matters of faith. As Augustine wisely said, "I believe in order to understand." Unlike much of modern theology that often starts rationalistically with an inward subjective human experience, Scripture emphasizes that theology begins with the supernatural and outward. The revelation of God is mainly perpendicular; it comes through divine initiative. The Bible is not primarily the story of man's search for and discovery of God; rather it is God, in his grace, disclosing himself to man.

In the discipline of theology, it is important to point out that when one declares acceptance of theological teachings such as the existence of God and the divine inspiration of Scripture, one is making a faith statement requiring an attitude of belief and trust. But the Christian faith is an informed or reasonable faith; the divine inspiration of the written Word is often corroborated through history, archeology, fulfilled prophecy, and the experience of the believer. Revelation begins with God, not with humanity. Scripture assumes God's existence and declares that God's Word is trustworthy. Thus, to do theology effectively, our port of entry into this discipline requires an act of faith in God and his Word; we believe in order to understand.

Hallmarks of Hebraic Theology

Often Embedded in Historical Context

There are several important hallmarks or features of Hebraic theology. First, throughout Scripture, theology is often deeply embedded in historical context. This is especially true of the Hebrew Bible. The God of Israel is a God of history; he reveals himself in visible ways through events and concrete, this-worldly circumstances. As I often like to remind my students, "The Bible didn't come out of heaven on a parachute." Rather, the theology of the Bible is inextricably interwoven into the chronology, places, and circumstances of Israel's history. God is known by his ways. Hence, the Ten Commandments are not abstractly listed. Rather, they are introduced with these words, which recall a pivotal historic event fifty days earlier: "I am the LORD your God, who brought you out of Egypt, out of the land of slavery" (Exod. 20:2).

As we formulate our theological terminology, the Bible emphasizes the God of Israel is not an unknown deity mysteriously concealed in heaven; rather he is known by the revelation of himself and his will on earth. Biblical events typically involve acts/deeds and also the (prophetic) theological understanding of them. The Bible is a record of divine revelation to humanity.

A "First Word," Not the Last

A second feature of Hebraic theology is that it is often in the process of maturing. In other words, it may be God's first word, but probably will not be his final word. Throughout the Hebrew Bible, God gradually keeps building on earlier revelation by clarifying it, expanding it, nuancing it, or illustrating its significance to a later generation in a new context.

The understanding God gave to Israel concerning himself and his teachings was progressive in nature. This is one of the most important reasons why we must not atomize the Bible or use it for proof-texting. To dip arbitrarily into one part of the Bible and yank out a verse or phrase in an attempt to support a predetermined meaning one is looking for is the questionable practice of *eisegesis,* reading meaning "into" the text instead of *exegesis,* "out of" the text. This practice is as risky as trying to prove something true from a phrase within a sentence without reading the complete sentence from beginning to end. It is only the whole sentence that gives appropriate context and correct meaning to any of its parts.[1] Note, for example, Psalm 14:1, a classic text some have tried to use (either tongue-in-cheek, or otherwise) to support the idea that there is no God (agnosticism or atheism), "The fool says in his heart, 'There is no God.'" Accordingly, there is an appropriateness to the dictum, "A text without a context is a pretext."

The revelation of God and his Word often comes in different stages, each stage advancing the depth and breadth of the truth found in the previous stage. Therefore, Hebraic theology is not confined to the Torah alone. Torah must be read within a larger canonical context (Old and New Testaments) and also in light of the teachings of the sages and rabbis.

---

1. In the seventh of his classic principles of interpretation, Hillel (first century B.C.) emphasizes *dabar halamed me'inyano,* "deduction from context." See Yaakov Elman, "Classical Rabbinic Interpretation," in *The Jewish Study Bible,* ed. Adele Berlin and Marc Brettler (New York: Oxford University Press, 2004), p. 1848.

Focused on a Personal God, Not Abstract

A third hallmark of Hebraic theology is its God-centeredness. God is not simply an impersonal concept for investigation, or an object of theological inquiry. Rather, God is subject, a living Being, One who has an intimate relation to the world. To be sure, "God is not a blurry power living somewhere in the sky, not an abstraction like the Greeks proposed, not a sensual super human like the Romans worshiped, and definitely not the absentee Watchmaker of the Deists. God is 'personal.'"[2]

The dynamic, active presence of the living God is one of the most central unifying themes of the Hebrew Bible. The temple of Solomon was completed so "all the peoples of the earth may know that the LORD is God and that there is no other" (1 Kgs. 8:60). Accordingly, God commanded his people, "Be still, and know that I am God" (Ps. 46:10).

Dynamic Revelation, Not Static

Fourth, throughout the Bible, revelation is not simply static but dynamic and active. Stephen, a Hellenistic Jew, emphasizes this point in his speech to the Sanhedrin. Linking himself and his own generation to their great spiritual ancestor Moses, Stephen states that Moses received "living words *(logia zonta)* to pass on to us" (Acts 7:38). Revelation, to many Christians, is defined only as a theological proposition. Indeed, truth about God may be found in words, but not dead words. The Bible is the Word of God written. But God's self-revelation is not abstractly confined to intellectual or theoretical knowledge acquired only through the mind by means of the printed text. As Abraham Heschel asserts, the central thought of Judaism is *"the living God."*[3] Indeed, the minimum meaning associated with the word *God* is that "he is alive."[4]

To the Semitic mind, knowledge of something was not (like the Greeks) primarily reserved to the intellect in a theoretical way, but the reality of something was often interwoven in the experience of life. To know was to understand personally, existentially, or practically. To the Hebrews, God is a person to be experienced, not simply an idea to be thought. Truth may be known through God's actions and ways.

---

2. Philip Yancey, "The Bible Jesus Read," *Christianity Today,* January 11, 1999, p. 68.
3. Abraham Heschel, *God in Search of Man* (New York: Farrar, Straus & Giroux, 1955), p. 25.
4. Heschel, *God in Search of Man,* p. 126.

Redemptive in Its "Big Picture"

A fifth major characteristic of Hebraic theology is that it is redemptive in nature. The story of the Bible is that of a loving God calling the world to himself. God, a holy, wise, and powerful Creator, brings humanity into being. But human beings become disobedient and flee from God's presence. God calls Israel into a covenantal relation with him. They are to be a holy people and to bring the message of God's will to the world. The revelation of the one true God and his teachings were given through a particular people, Israel, to be a blessing for the entire world (Gen. 12:2-3).

As God redeemed Israel through a mighty deliverance from four hundred years of slavery in Egypt, so the theme of freedom and salvation echoes throughout Scripture. According to the prophets, this message of the redemption of God's people Israel would one day be realized universally through a redeemed world (see Isa. 11:1-10). Thus comes to consummation the redemptive program of God in search of man.

Concerned with Ethics or "How to Live"

A final characteristic of the Bible of Israel is its strong emphasis on theological and social ethics. God is the Author of right and wrong. The ethical teachings of the Bible are divinely revealed truths on how to live in harmony or *shalom* within one's family and in relation to one's neighbor. The ethical principles of the Tanakh concern how people are to conduct themselves in public and private.

Good conduct was directly connected to the Almighty, the Supreme Moral Being whose nature and attributes the children of Abraham were expected to model. As the God of Israel was merciful and just, so his people were to emulate him. Accordingly, the Bible has a decisive preference for the poor, marginalized, and disenfranchised. The widow, the orphan, and stranger are among those particularly singled out for preferential treatment. But social ethics concerns how all human beings are to live successfully and cooperatively with each other. The Hebrew Bible holds a high reverence for life; it lays out the broad moral guidelines on how respect and honor is due all human beings, for each is precious, created in the image of God. In many ways, the entire Bible is a commentary on the command, "Love your neighbor as yourself" (Lev. 19:18; Mark 12:31).

Christians and the Old Testament

The reason I have chosen to title this chapter "Theological Quest for Hebraic Heritage" is because this heritage is not an heirloom that can be acquired instantaneously; it involves an active search, pursuit, or quest for the roots of one's faith. For Christians, at least, there is no agreed-upon consensus of what constitutes Hebraic heritage. At the outset, the term "Jewish Scriptures" has long been considered a pejorative by many Christians. Due to the church's longtime use of the term "Old Testament," Christians are often semantically preconditioned to regard the Hebrew Bible as inferior or antiquated in relation to the New. There is a whole vocabulary that often leads one initially to believe the word "New" implies that which is superior or better, and the word "Old" conveys what is inferior, less important, or sub-Christian in comparison. Christians have been historically influenced to think pejoratively about the Old Testament because of negative terms such as "superseded," "abrogated," "annulled," "done away with," or "replaced" simplistically attached to it. The church may never get beyond its conventional terminology of referring to the Tanakh as the Old Testament. However, as one antidote to the above, in addition to Tanakh, Christians would do well to frequently employ other terms such as First Testament, Original Testament, or Older Testament.

Further, large sections — as well as individual verses — of the Old Testament have posed problems for the church since the post-apostolic period. Some taught that the ethical and moral standards of the God of the Old Testament were different. This Old Testament deity was said to be a God of war and bloody sacrifices, harsh and cruel in punishment. It was claimed this God seemed to condone slavery, polygamy, and gross acts of violence. Things appear sanctioned in the Old Testament that most Christians cannot relate to and would never think of doing today. There is also a strangeness about various laws concerning sacrifices, purification rites, dietary matters, and other issues.

Christians have had a variety of responses to the above "problem" of the Old Testament. The first major response came from Marcion, a second-century church father. Marcion argued to remove the Old Testament from the Christian canon. He claimed the God of the Jewish Scriptures was different, a Demiurge, one of cruel battles, a "dirty bully." This Old Testament Jewish God stood in stark contrast to the "God of love" he found in the New Testament. Fortunately, Marcion was condemned in Rome as a heretic. But vestiges of virulent neo-Marcionistic thinking continue to plague

26

the church, especially in various expressions of Judeophobia, anti-Semitism, and anti-Zionism.

The church fathers were another early segment of Christian leaders who had difficulty with the Old Testament. While Marcion wanted to remove it, the church fathers chose to rescue it, mostly because the Old Testament contained hidden prophetic truth and had Christian meaning for the church. The solution of the church fathers, therefore, was to look for Christological, allegorical, or symbolic meaning in the Old Testament. Typical of this approach are the words of Augustine, "The Old Testament is the New Testament concealed; the New is the Old revealed." While the church fathers argued that the Old Testament contained messianic promises applicable to Christ and the church, the nation of Israel, God's covenant people, tended to evaporate spiritually and to be replaced by the church. In addition, the extensive and excessive application and considerable misuse of the allegorical and Christological method tended to render the Old Testament and Israel as little more than the launching pad for Christianity. This approach within the church severely undercut the ongoing historical and theological validity of the Jewish people. In Augustine's view, for example, Jews need not thrive; they need only survive.

Christians have also tended to neglect much of the Old Testament, not knowing what to do with it. The option of flat-out rejecting it or excessively spiritualizing it left many Christians uncomfortable. Over the centuries, while most Christian interpreters understood the Old Testament as witnessing to the coming of Christ, considerable disagreement existed on what else from the Old Testament can be legitimately salvaged. This troubling feeling concerning the largest portion of the Word of God has often been resolved with a sort of cherry-picking approach. John Bright has explained this rather commonly employed Christian solution.[5] Christians make a value judgment on the contents of the Old Testament based on New Testament teaching in order to separate the relevant elements of timeless validity from those that are ancient, useless, and sub-Christian.

The above approach can lead to highly subjective or arbitrary judgments on what parts of the Old Testament are timeworn rather than timeless. Furthermore, it leads to the ignoring of large portions of the Old Testament either because the New Testament writers do not quote from the particular Old Testament passage in question or because a Christian reader feels it is in

---

5. John Bright, *The Authority of the Old Testament* (repr. Grand Rapids: Baker, 1975), pp. 95-100.

some way incompatible with New Testament teaching. If this criterion were fully valid, how should interpreters of the New Testament deal with certain issues like slavery, foot washing, and use of head coverings for women at worship?

In our quest for Hebraic heritage, today's church must recognize that the above approaches to the Old Testament are at best too limiting and, in the end, unsatisfactory. Any approach that does not hear all the Old Testament text as the inspired Word of God is unacceptable. The New Testament authors had only one text, the Hebrew Bible (or its Greek equivalent, the Septuagint). They did not see problems with the Old Testament the same way that present-day Christians see problems. Granted, not every part of the Hebrew Bible is of equal value, relevance, and application for Christians or Jews today. However, Christians in particular must not antecedently make negative judgments on the Old Testament as a whole; it is all the holy Scriptures *(hiera grammata),* and these Scriptures thus must all be weighed carefully as the Word of God (see 2 Tim. 3:15).

The New Testament writers appealed to and lived by the teachings of the Old Testament Scriptures. Their starting point was not the New Testament (as it was for Marcion, the church fathers, and others). Thus, they had to take all the Old Testament seriously, as the written Word of God. Hermeneutically, if we, like they, approach all the Old Testament as a Word from God without initially making an interpretive judgment on it, we will respect the integrity of far more of the Old Testament than if we prejudge its value, meaning, or authority from our New Testament perspective. It is the theology of the Bible that is authoritative. Thus, after beginning with the Old Testament text and hearing it in its historical and canonical context, we may then go to other sources such as the New Testament, Oral Law, and rabbinic commentary to come to a fuller understanding of the meaning and application of that text.

Theological Methodology and Hebraic Roots

Engaging in the task of theology is far more an art than it is a science. There is not a set of hard-and-fast rules to follow in order to guarantee perfection. But the quest of theological reflection does require some guidelines. There are many factors one must keep in mind when reading and interpreting texts with a view to uncovering the theology therein. In this section of the chapter, I will set forth a number of foundational observations on some of the more important aspects of theological method. Because this work mainly concerns how Christians may better understand their Hebraic theological heritage, most of my observations, principles, and reflections found in the remainder of this chapter will focus on the Old Testament Scriptures.

Developmental and Progressive Thought

In Bible times, as well as today, individual authors often stood on the shoulders of earlier pioneers. Many of these spiritual giants of Israel deposited legacies of cherished wisdom — both oral and written — within their own community of faith. As a living tradition, this was often drawn on and reworked by later generations. Sometimes, however, the Israelites went outside and borrowed from other cultures various teachings, laws, or sayings appropriate to their God-inspired purposes. For example, some of the laws found in the Law of Moses are found recorded centuries earlier in the Law Code of Hammurabi; some of the sayings in the Book of Proverbs likely came from an Egyptian source, *The Wisdom of Amenemope,* and were recast into the Hebrew wisdom tradition. Israel could also draw on a vast pool of wisdom and knowledge found within the common East Mediterranean cultural continuum.

The development of theological thought through various time periods of Israel's history is critical to understand, for not all theology is on the same level, neither is every theological theme clearly present in each time period. Revelation is progressive. Theology, like a flower, moves from bud to fuller flowering. For example, the emphasis on corporate responsibility found in the Book of Joshua associated with the sin of Achan is different from the individual responsibility for sin emphasized in the Book of Ezekiel (see Josh. 7:1-26; Ezek. 18:1-32). Teaching on the resurrection and the afterlife is not a primary concern of the Law of Moses; but it mainly develops as an emphasis in the latter prophets and in Daniel.

Like a snowball, theological truth is often cumulatively acquired and tested through the various periods of Israel's history. Theology, in a profound sense, never ends; redemption of this world and the kingdom of God is not yet consummated. Even though the ink of a Hebrew prophet's pen may have dried on the scroll, we must ponder anew the depth of Abraham J. Heschel's sage observation: "No word is God's last word."[6]

6. Abraham Heschel, *The Prophets* (New York: Harper & Row, 1962), p. 193.

Grasping the Setting of Scripture

Biblical theology is rooted in history. The goal is to get back there so that one can hear and understand the words and meaning of the author in the context of his world and his day. This requires a grammatical-historical method of interpreting the text. Such study may well involve the original languages of Scripture. It emphasizes the meaning of the words in their historical, literary, and archeological context. There is considerable truth in the saying, "The best commentary on the Bible is the Bible." The analogy of Scripture or comparing Scripture to Scripture is a most essential tool in this process.

Sound theological method is concerned with the *Sitz im Leben,* the life setting or cultural context out of which the text was composed. Rarely is theology the result of a *Bat Kol,* a voice direct from heaven; inspired theology derives from the mysterious collaborative interaction of the Divine and the human. God may speak, but he does so in human language, employing godly-minded human vehicles. The concern of the theologian, then, is to listen to the author through the text. What truth does God intend to communicate through the words of this author? How would the first readers have understood this message? How were their circumstances similar to, yet different from ours?

Questioning and Answering

The big picture of theology is simply this: God speaks, and the hearer answers. God speaks forth his will for humanity through revelation. The theology of the Bible is authoritative in human lives. In the Hebrew Bible, the history, culture, customs, and daily lives of its characters often provide the setting through which the theology emerges. Exegetical study of Old Testament texts reveals real theological issues and concerns that motivated their inclusion. The goal of sound theological method is to uncover in a given text of Scripture what God is teaching about himself and his relation to humanity. Biblical exegesis (what the text says) must lead to theological exegesis (what the text means and teaches). This theological exegesis is concerned with laying bare the timeless message of that passage. For Christians, later theological reflections from the pages of the New Testament and also other extra-biblical sources may be useful in determining the theology of the passage. Theology is written to give normative truth for our generation as well as to produce life. The final step is to ask how this theology applies to us today in our actual life situation.

The Scriptures are a dialogue between God and his people. As Abraham J. Heschel states in his classic work, *God in Search of Man,* God himself takes the initiative in searching for man and revealing himself; he has done so from the beginning of sacred history. God's question to Adam, "Where are you?" (Gen. 3:9) is an inquiry that "goes out again and again" and accordingly, Heschel emphasizes, "Faith in God is a response to God's question."[7] To Abraham in Ur, to the nation of Israel at Sinai, to the prophets and beyond, God uniquely and dynamically revealed himself and his will. The Hebrew Bible, the New Testament, and the rabbis are all in agreement that, in addition to faith, sacred deeds or *mitzvot* are an appropriate response to God's revelation (see James 2:20-26). Divine revelation requires that we, God's people, also formulate a reply. Our answer to the question of revelation is mainly through applied theology. Our response is highly ethical; it is concerned with how we live, not simply what we believe.

Personal Participation in the Text

Texts must do more than record past events. They must also, in some existential way, engage the reader. In some personal way the reader must "get back there" and seek personally to relive those sacred moments. When the Israelites stood with Moses at Sinai agreeing to the terms of the covenant in the presence of the Lord, all Israelites of future generations were likewise standing there receiving the law (see Deut. 29:15). In the celebration of the festival of Passover each year, the Mishnah instructs all Jewish participants at the Seder that each has to "regard himself as if he (personally) came forth out of Egypt" (Pesahim 10:5). This vicarious reliving of deliverance from Egypt through liturgy, music, and the eating of symbolic Passover foods long ago led Jews to remind others, "At Passover, Jews eat history."

Theology can be cold, dry, and detached. Theology is intended to revitalize, not anesthetize. Thus, those who would study Hebraic theology must bring themselves into a living sympathy with the subject matter of the text. In short, theology must become incarnational, something that is prayed. An Orthodox rabbi I have known many years once told me, "I do not daily sing Psalms, I *am* a Psalm."

---

7. Heschel, *God in Search of Man,* pp. 136-37.

Personal participation and identification with the text is necessary in some re-creative or imaginative way so that the relevancy of the past can break forth in the present. If the Scriptures are impersonal, this is unlikely to happen. After Moses personally had come through the Reed Sea he confidently proclaimed in song, "He is my God, and I will praise him" (Exod. 15:2). Like Moses, when the God of our ancestors becomes personally alive in our own spiritual experience, we realize theology is more than a dead, abstract discipline or creed. Theology lives.

Faith and Theology

Faith is necessary to know God. Abraham, the acclaimed patriarch, believed in God (Gen. 15:6; see Rom. 4:3). One can neither access God nor please God without faith (Heb. 11:6). Faith is not a New Testament theological concept. Many of Israel's heroes of faith are celebrated in Hebrews 11 for their confidence and trust in God. It is especially the gift of faith that enables Scripture to come alive and makes it personal to the reader.

It is difficult to read Scripture with insight and personal identification if one does not sympathetically share the faith of the men and women of the biblical text. Stepping inside the circle of faith gives one the ability for inner understanding and appreciation of the narrative. In terms of knowing, is it not normally more authentic to write about something one has personally experienced from the inside out rather than theoretically from the outside in? It is one thing for a little boy to go inside a candy store, buy candy, and taste its sweetness; it is another matter for a little boy to stand outside a candy store and simply look at the candy — face pressed to the glass window — and yet never get inside to experience its sweetness.

Scripturally speaking, the apostle Paul makes the same point: unless one is a person of the Spirit and thus alive and aware spiritually to the subject matter of Scripture so as to have insight into it, the text will be enigmatic, baffling to one's understanding. In Paul's words, "The man without the Spirit *(psychikos anthropos)* does not accept the things that come from the Spirit of God, for they are foolishness *(moria)* to him, and he cannot understand them, because they are spiritually discerned. The spiritual man *(pneumatikos)* makes judgments about all things" (1 Cor. 2:14-15a). For Paul, faith is the key to spiritual insight acquired by the "spiritual man." In that the Bible is a book about faith, theology is done best when faith is present. Apart from an appreciation of the literary beauty of the Bible, the ability of an individual to submit voluntarily to all its teachings and to accept its claim to supernatural origin as the Word of God is virtually impossible without faith.

Dialogue with the Living God

Theological method must be characterized in anticipation of the reader coming to the biblical text and carrying on a dialogue with the living God. God speaks to the reader through the text. Helmut Thielicke insists that theology must be carried on in the second person of the verb.[8] The second person of the verb employs the word "you," a personal subject pronoun as in the phrase, "you are speaking." On the other hand, the third person of the verb is often used for the impersonal pronoun, "it," referring to what is inanimate. For example, "It (the book) is heavy."

Thielicke's point is that in theological discourse one must beware of beginning to think increasingly with the "it" of the third person instead of the personal "you" of the second person. Such an impersonal reference can be a form of theological reductionism; theology must center on a personal relation with God ("you") rather than God becoming reduced to a merely impersonal, nondescript, technical reference ("it says"). The Bible must be more than an object of academic inquiry, a bound mass of paper and ink used for exegetical investigation. Rather, Thielicke insists, God is personal, and theological thought can only breathe in an environment of dialogue with God who speaks through his living Word.

Hebraic Theological Reflexes

The goal of any theological methodology rooted in Hebraic thought is to acquire reflexes for thinking and acting biblically. If one is to respond to the varied phenomena of life instinctively as one who is a believer, namely, a person led by the Spirit of truth, such a response will require a disciplined knowledge of that truth. Further, it will require an understanding that this goal, like so many other spiritual realities, can never fully be achieved, but is always a work in progress. Thus, we engage in biblical

---

8. See Helmut Thielicke, *A Little Exercise for Young Theologians* (Grand Rapids: Eerdmans, 1962), pp. 33-34.

studies in order to acquire a biblical mentality or a biblical mindset, one increasingly capable of displaying biblical reflexes. As Robert Martin-Achard points out, Christians committed to this task of pursuing their Hebraic heritage personally realize they have "become spiritual Semites in the midst of a generation which feels and even thinks outwith [sic] the biblical categories."[9]

Those committed to building Hebraic theological reflexes are able to respond to the issues of the modern world as the men and women of faith did in Bible times. Every Christian must especially realize, as Norman Snaith has emphasized, "The message of the New Testament is in the Hebrew tradition as against the Greek tradition. Our tutors to Christ are Moses and the Prophets, and not Plato and the Academies."[10]

UNDERSTANDING CHAPTER TWO

1. What are some of the major reasons that many Christians today are unaware of the importance of the common theological and ethical tradition undergirding both Judaism and Christianity?

2. With what is the discipline of theology primarily concerned? Provide a brief definition of theology.

3. How does Augustine's statement, "I believe in order to understand," demonstrate the nature of faith as the beginning of theology? How must this statement also be part of our own port of entry into theology?

4. What six major hallmarks of Hebraic theology does the author discuss? From a Christian perspective or from your own experience, which of these do you think are most strongly retained in Christianity today, and which are less pronounced?

5. How does the introduction of the Ten Commandments reinforce the fact that Hebraic heritage is often deeply embedded in historical context? The Bible emphasizes that the God of Israel is known how? In what way is your own theology embedded in your personal history?

6. Explain how Hebraic theology in the Bible is often in the process of

9. Robert Martin-Achard, *An Approach to the Old Testament*, trans. J. C. G. Greig (Edinburgh: Oliver & Boyd, 1965), p. 79.

10. Norman H. Snaith, *The Distinctive Ideas of the Old Testament* (New York: Schocken, 1964), p. 159.

maturing. How does this characteristic in and of itself serve as a warning against atomizing the Bible or using it for proof-texting? What did Hillel emphasize in his writings on the classic principles of interpretation (see note 1)?

7. What is meant by the dictum, "A text without a context is a pretext"? Why is an active awareness of this principle critical when interacting with Scripture?

8. In what way is Hebraic theology focused on a God who is personal? How is he different from the deities perceived by the ancient Greeks, the ancient Romans, and the Deists?

9. What is meant by the description of Hebraic theology as dynamic and active? How might this differ from many Christians' perceptions of revelation? What does Abraham Heschel state is the "minimum meaning" associated with the word "God"? To the Greek and Hebrew minds respectively, what did it mean to *know*?

10. How does the Hebrew Bible illustrate redemptive theology? In the big picture of redemption, what is the role of a particular people, Israel, in relation to humanity universally?

11. Concerning Hebraic theology's emphasis on ethics, in what ways can the Bible be said to be a commentary on the command, "Love your neighbor as yourself"?

12. Why has the author chosen to title the chapter "Theological *Quest* for Hebraic Heritage"?

13. What have been some consequences of the church's designation of the Hebrew Bible as the "Old Testament"? In your opinion, what is the best way (or ways) for Christians to refer to this body of Scripture? Why?

14. Since the post-apostolic period, in what ways have some taught that the ethical and moral standards of the God of the Old Testament were different? How do you respond to this suggestion?

15. Who was Marcion, and what did he claim and propose concerning the Old Testament? What was the short-term result, and what long-term results continue to affect the church?

16. In general, how did the church fathers treat the Old Testament? Why? What effect did excessive application and considerable misuse of the allegorical and Christological method have on the rendering of the Old Testament?

17. Regarding the treatment of the Old Testament, what is the cherry-picking approach? What are some of the effects of it?

18. In considering how Christians today should view the Old Testament,

why is it significant that the New Testament authors had only one scriptural text (the Hebrew Bible)?

19. Which major aspects of theological method does the author discuss in this chapter? Comment briefly on the significance of each.

20. What does the author mean by his statement that to engage in the task of theology is far "more an art than it is a science"?

21. Provide examples of cases in which the Israelites likely borrowed from various teachings of other cultures. How does this mode of acquiring religious tradition reinforce the reality that theology is developmental in nature?

22. Briefly discuss (1) corporate and individual responsibility and (2) teachings about the resurrection and the afterlife in relation to the assertion that revelation is progressive.

23. Since biblical theology is rooted in history, what is required to interpret the text?

24. What is the *Sitz im Leben* of a text? Why must sound theological method be concerned with it? What does the rabbinic expression *Bat Kol* mean? How do each of the following texts illustrate this apparently rare phenomenon: Daniel 4:31; Matthew 3:16, 17; Acts 9:3-9?

25. Biblical exegesis must lead to what? Why?

26. In his work *God in Search of Man,* what does Abraham Heschel state about humanity's relationship with the divine? Why must humanity formulate a response to God? What do the Hebrew Bible, the New Testament, and the rabbis all agree is an appropriate response to God's revelation? Why is applied theology critical?

27. What does the author mean by stating that those who would study Hebraic theology must "bring themselves into a living sympathy with the subject matter of the text," and that "theology must become incarnational"? Why is it important to relive sacred moments in Scripture? Discuss Deuteronomy 29:15 and Pesahim 10:5 of the Mishnah in relation to the significance of "reliving" history.

28. In what way is faith the key to spiritual insight? What do Paul's words to the Corinthian church in 1 Corinthians 2:14-15a reveal about the necessity and power of faith?

29. What is Helmut Thielicke's point in saying that theology must be carried on in the second person of the verb?

30. What is meant by the phrase "biblical reflexes"? Why and how must one work to acquire them?

CHAPTER 3

Foundational Sources of Hebraic Thought

Biblical faith is first and foremost a way of life. Conduct strongly matters to God. He is concerned with what people do, not only with what they think. If an individual desires to love God, both Moses and Jesus teach that it is necessary to show that love to one's neighbor. While theologically conservative expressions of Christianity have often put greater emphasis on what a person *believes* rather than how an individual *lives,* they are both important to any biblically balanced expression of Christianity. Belief must affect behavior, creed has to express itself in conduct, and doctrine determines more than destiny; it demands deeds.

The Tanakh: Bedrock of Hebraic Teaching

In Judaism and Christianity, the Tanakh or Hebrew Bible is the foundational document on how a righteous person should daily proceed upon the path of life. Hebraic thought, mainly conveyed to the church through the Old Testament, serves as a needed corrective; it anchors Christianity to this earthly world. A Christianity severed from the Bible of Jesus may be precariously perched to go doctrinally airborne and take a spiritual flight from this world to the heavenly world above. An understanding of Hebraic heritage and of Judaism, the religion that developed directly from the religion of biblical Israel, is particularly crucial in helping Christianity maintain balance and avoid the temptation to escape the struggles and painful realities below for contemplated pleasures above. Among the many reasons why Christianity stands in need of Judaism is this point: Judaism serves to keep Christianity grounded in this world by addressing the most challenging of human needs and real-life problems. From Bible times to the present, Judaism has never been a religion indifferent to the here and now.

In the Judeo-Christian tradition, the guiding foundational principles for such a caring, community-centered way of life go back to God's great revelation of himself and his will at Sinai as recorded in Scripture, in Torah. But these biblical teachings are further developed, commented on, and explicated for daily living in the Hebrew prophets and in other later sources such as the Mishnah, Talmud, and Codes. As the New Testament documents are primarily a commentary on ideas, stories, and teachings within the Hebrew Bible by Jewish followers of Jesus, so the sages and rabbis began to reflect on, comment on, and even reformulate their understanding and meaning of the Hebrew Bible. These sources were especially necessary in the religious life of the Jewish community due to the destruction of the Temple in A.D. 70 and the scattering of the Jewish community from the land.

If the withered or rotted roots of today's church are to become revived through a new understanding of the church's Hebraic beginnings, the church must nourish itself from the sources, those central documents vital to Hebraic thought and life that have shaped Judaism over the centuries. The foundational bedrock on which biblical thinking rests is the Tanakh, or Jewish Scriptures, the Christian Old Testament. The Tanakh has three main divisions: the Law or Torah, the Prophets, and the Writings. The Torah, or Written Law, contains the very root of Hebraic heritage.

In traditional Jewish thought, all of the main teachings of Judaism go back to the revelation at Sinai. In the words of Jewish scholar Michael Wyschogrod, "All Jewish values are ultimately rooted in revelation and to pretend otherwise is to play a charade which will convince no one."[1] But revelation is more a process than a once-and-for-all event. Study of Judaism and Jewish civilization begins with the Written Law itself; it extends from there into the Prophets and Writings. But Judaism also teaches that the revelation at Sinai also extends to the Oral Law (Mishnah) and in the rabbinic commentaries and codes. However, this teaching is particularly brought together in the rabbinic development of *Halakhah* or "religious law" set forth to provide specific guidance on how the Jewish community was to think, to act, and to live. Thus, these early rabbinic sources that reflect on the Tanakh, mostly unknown or unexplored by Christians, are

---

1. Michael Wyschogrod, *Abraham's Promise: Judaism and Jewish-Christian Relations* (Grand Rapids: Eerdmans, 2004), p. 2.

vital in helping Christians to deepen their appreciation of the depth and breadth of Hebraic heritage.

Accordingly, in addition to the Bible itself, this book draws from many of these extra-biblical Jewish sources. The reflection of Jewish scholars on their own Scriptures, the original Testament, gives a valuable and unique "in-house" perspective from the very community who directly received, copied, preserved, and commented on those first Scriptures. Such reflection is quite different, for example, from the early teachers of Islam, a religion that was not established until the seventh century in Saudi Arabia and that claimed a totally new revelation of God (Allah) and his will, thus revising both Judaism and Christianity.

Who Owns the "Book of Books"?

The Bible is the priceless religious treasure God gave to the world through the Jewish people. Indeed, as Bruce Chilton has wisely observed, "Neither Judaism nor Christianity owns the Bible . . . any ownership is God's. Scripture is divine property. We (Christians and Jews) have really been arguing over the lease we hold on the property."[2] Historically and theologically, the question of "lease" boils down to whether the Jewish Scriptures are prophetic of Jesus or not. The church says Yes, the synagogue, No.

While neither Jews nor Christians may lay claim to personal possession of the Bible, each faith community reads the Bible differently. Accordingly, Judaism emphasizes the importance of observing all God's teachings, "Do not add to it or take away from it" (Deut. 12:32; see 4:2; 5:32). A similar note is struck in the final chapter of the Book of Revelation in the New Testament. The author warns about "adding words" or "taking words away" from "this book" (22:18, 19).[3] Christianity needs the Tanakh to explain its origin. But for Judaism, the reverse is not so in regard to the New Testament Scriptures.[4] Despite this difference, the Tanakh contains considerable common ground shared by both faith communities — and it should, parenthetically, be noted that we are intentionally excluding some "highly Jewish" sections

2. Bruce D. Chilton and Jacob Neusner, *Classical Christianity and Rabbinic Judaism* (Grand Rapids: Baker Academic, 2004), p. 265.

3. Also see David J. Zucker, *The Torah: An Introduction for Christians and Jews* (Mahwah, NJ: Paulist Press, 2005), pp. 193-94.

4. See Willem Zuidema, *God's Partner: An Encounter with Judaism* (London: SCM Press, 1987), pp. 30-31.

of New Testament Scripture such as many verses in Jesus' Sermon on the Mount (Matthew 5–7).

In Jewish tradition, the Tanakh is referred to as *Miqra,* namely, "that which is read."[5] Among Jews, the word *Miqra* is interchangeable with Holy Scriptures or Hebrew Bible. In referring to the inspired Scriptures of Israel, the Christian "Old Testament," Paul uses the term *hiera grammata,* "holy Scriptures" or "sacred writings" (2 Tim. 3:15). The term underscores the written nature of the text, historically an important concept for Christianity, through its direct connection to Judaism.

Christians, true to their Hebraic heritage, take the Bible and textual study seriously. Indeed, the word "Bible" has reference to sacred writings, a term derived from the Phoenician port city of Byblos, famous for exporting paper (papyrus) or writing material. Long before Christianity was born, the Jewish people impressed the world with their strong emphasis upon sacred text. Hence, Jews were the first to be called "People of the Book." But God owns the Book. It is his holy Word. Jews were simply the chosen human channel for bringing the divine revelation to all peoples and nations (Isa. 42:6).

On one occasion in the 1980s, I was invited to join a group of Christian leaders at the Israeli Embassy in Washington, D.C., to hear an address by the Honorable Chaim Herzog, president of the State of Israel. I remember distinctly what he had to say about the Bible in his remarks. His words were humorous, yet illustrative of my above point. Herzog said, "It is painful for me to admit, but with Israel's currently high inflation and other economic woes, we really blew it!" He then wryly explained, "The Jewish people gave away the Bible to the world but never charged for this Book; we didn't receive one shekel in royalties!"

The above anecdote underscores the irony of it all: the greatest and richest spiritual treasure of Judeo-Christian religion, the Book of Books, was written by the Jewish people not for themselves alone, but to be given as a free gift to the world. In the plan of God, this was pivotal in the fulfillment of God's promise to Abraham: "All people on earth will be blessed through you" (Gen. 12:3b).

---

5. Joseph Lowin makes the observation: "Originally, a *qara* was a 'biblical scholar.' In later rabbinical literature the word *qara'im* was applied to the sect that accepted only *miqra* and rejected rabbinic teachings, the 'Karaites.' An offshoot of Judaism that believed in reading was Islam; its primary text is the *qur'an,* 'that which is read.'" See *Hebrew Speak* (Northvale, NJ: Jason Aronson, 1995), p. 155.

"A Letter Written This Morning"

The Jewish biblical scholar Samuel Sandmel has called attention to how the Bible contributed to the survival of the Jews: "The Bible was the adhesive that held the Jews together, that fed and nurtured their loyalty to the notion of being Jewish. . . . Without the Bible they would have surely disappeared, and quickly. With it, they preserved both their ethnic sense and their developed ways of living."[6] Through its teachings and precepts, the Bible was the lifeblood that defined Jewish identity. The Jewish people "clung tenaciously to its teachings in spite of all obstacles."[7] The ability of Jews to persist defiantly and with audacity, despite their detractors, and in the face of the catastrophes and the absurdities of life that confronted them, is one of the most remarkable stories of history.

The immediacy and freshness of the Tanakh enabled Jews to overcome obstacles by asking questions of Scripture in the face of difficult daily circumstances. Jacob Neusner points out, "The rabbinic sages read Scripture as a letter written that morning to them in particular about the world they encountered. That is because for them the past was forever integral to the present."[8] To read Scripture as today's mail, speaking a relevant word from the past into the situation of the present, is an extraordinary insight on how Jews related to Bible reading. This aspect of Hebraic heritage was passed on from Jews to Christians. As the great German Jewish leader Leo Baeck observed, "When Christianity spread among the nations, it already possessed in Israel's Psalms and prophetic books the rich treasure of consolation and assurance to meet all the trials to which it was subjected by the powers of the world."[9]

While the Hebrew Bible is the foundational, authoritative document of our Hebraic heritage, it is necessary to remember that the religion of Moses, David, and the prophets was far more dynamic than static. Israel's faith continued to be shaped and reshaped by social expansion, cultural adaptation, and pivotal events such as the destruction of Solomon's Temple, the Exile, and the Restoration.[10] From antiquity, it was believed ancient

6. Samuel Sandmel, *Judaism and Christian Beginnings* (New York: Oxford University Press, 1978), p. 17.

7. Francine Klagsbrun, ed., *Voices of Wisdom: Jewish Ideals and Ethics* (New York: Pantheon, 1980), p. xxiii.

8. Jacob Neusner, *Questions and Answers: Intellectual Foundations of Judaism* (Peabody, MA: Hendrickson, 2005), p. 234.

9. Leo Baeck, *The Essence of Judaism* (New York: Schocken, 1948), p. 75.

10. See Marvin R. Wilson, "The Bible and Contemporary Judaism," *ESV Study Bible* (Wheaton, IL: Crossway, 2008), p. 2623.

Hebrew religious life flowed rather seamlessly into the religion of Judaism established by Ezra, a scribe and priest. In the centuries to follow, sages and eventually rabbis continued to hold firmly to the commandments of the Bible, but dynamically reinterpreting some, as the changing political and social environment demanded for the preservation of life and community. In the evolving circumstances of Israel's history, however, the people never separated themselves from the Bible. As Michael Fishbane observes, "It has been a tenet of rabbinic Judaism since antiquity that all the features of Judaism, no matter how innovative, have their ultimate source in the Bible. . . . Hence the adage of Judaism, 'Israel and the Torah are one.'"[11]

Christians are different from Jews in the way they read the Bible. Of necessity, Christians read the Bible backwards. That is, Christians come into the relation of divine sonship, adoption into God's family whereby they cry "Abba," then go back as children of Abraham and spiritual Israelites to "discover the story of God's ways with his people."[12] Christianity is not a total annulling of Judaism but an expansion and reinterpretation of it. Bruce Chilton summarizes how Christians read the Old Testament differently from Jews:

> So the Old Testament is every Christian's story, whether "Jew" or "Greek" because it is the record of how faith came to fruition, how it grew and developed like a plant, bobbed and weaved like a boxer, and broke through to the promise of a new heaven and a new earth in the poetry of vision that scholars call apocalyptic. That faith is the promise Christ fulfills, and for us the patriarchs and prophets and psalmists equally sing our song — and sing it in our words. But the melody, Christianity insists against Judaism, is that of prophecy rather than Torah.[13]

Without minimizing the importance of the Psalms and prophets to the typical Christian reader of the Old Testament, it would perhaps be surprising to many Christians to discover the first five books of the Bible, the Law of Moses, is the place Christians and Jews often find considerable common ground. Themes such as creation, covenant, redemption, revelation, worship, holiness, love, compassion, moral law, ethics, and social justice are central to the teaching of the Torah and are, correspondingly, foundational to Christian

11. Michael A. Fishbane, *Judaism: Revelation and Traditions* (San Francisco: Harper & Row, 1987), pp. 27, 30.

12. Bruce D. Chilton and Jacob Neusner, *Classical Christianity and Rabbinic Judaism* (Grand Rapids: Baker Academic, 2004), p. 264.

13. Chilton and Neusner, *Classical Christianity and Rabbinic Judaism* p. 263.

biblical thought. Writing out of his Hebraic tradition, Paul insisted, "the law is holy, and the commandment is holy, righteous and good" (Rom. 7:12). Hence, Paul said, "I delight in God's law" (Rom. 7:22).

The Meaning of Sinai

The Law of Moses and Sinai go together. One of the greatest theophanies of Scripture occurred at Sinai. Some fifty days before Israel arrived at Sinai, God had miraculously split the waters of the Red Sea and delivered Israel from the tyranny of the Egyptians (Exodus 14; Ps. 136:13-15). While Israel was encamped at the base of Sinai, God again made a dramatic appearance in behalf of his people. The Torah says that God came down to the top of the mountain, and Moses went up to meet him (Exod. 19:20). At the base of the mountain, Israel trembled in fear, observing a scene of thunder, lightning, earthquake, smoke, fire, and loud trumpet blasts (Exod. 19:16-19). This encounter between God and Moses was to have far-reaching implications for the history of civilization. On Sinai, God revealed his covenantal teachings to Israel, including the moral and ethical imperatives that were to govern humanity.

For centuries scholars have debated the significance of the revelation at Sinai. What exactly happened when the invisible God of heaven met the man Moses on the mountain? Scripture tells us that God spoke to Moses on Sinai and gave him two tablets of stone, "inscribed by the finger of God" (Exod. 31:18; see 34:1). Revelation is not the culmination of man's search for and discovery of God. Rather, revelation is the story of God coming to man, in history, to impart a message and/or revelation of his will. But this is not without human instrumentality. There is a pattern in Scripture. God initiates; man responds.

The pattern begins long before Sinai. God reveals himself to Adam in the Garden of Eden, to Noah regarding the flood, to Abram in Ur, to Jacob at Bethel, and to Moses at the burning bush. Without making his presence known in coming to man, God's will could not have been perceived. The metanarrative of Scripture presupposes the act of revelation and the presence of the supernatural. To say "the Bible is the Word of God" is to make a faith statement. The one making such a statement acknowledges that God exists and that he has in Scripture, in some *bona fide* yet mysterious way, communicated his will to humanity.

The apostolic writings comment on the supernatural authorship of the

Jewish Scriptures: "For prophecy never had its origin in the will of man, but men spoke from God as they were carried along by the Holy Spirit" (2 Pet. 1:21). However, as Abraham J. Heschel observes, "More decisive than the origin of the Bible in God is the presence of God in the Bible."[14] It is God's intention that individuals respond to this scriptural revelation because the Bible is a means of discovering the presence of the living God. In Heschel's view, God is subject or living Presence; he is not an inanimate object to be exegeted or interpreted. The Bible is a path to that presence. Thus, the reader must intuitively open up and respond to the divine Word. In response to this point of Heschel, many Christians would argue that their ability to open up and respond to Scripture comes externally through the illuminating power of God's Spirit rather than inwardly through the intuitive capability of the human reader.

Rabbis have understood revelation in a variety of ways.[15] How the divine and human factors meshed in the giving of the Law at Sinai is at the heart of the debate. If God spoke to Moses and gave him the Law, what did he hear and record? Did God give him only principles or ideas, or did Moses record literally each word God gave? How much of the Law did Moses receive on the mountain of God? Was it a portion of the Written Law or all of it? Is revelation uniquely limited to Sinai or does revelation extend beyond Sinai? What role should biblical criticism play in this debate?

In a pivotal passage, the Mishnah states, "Moses received the Law from Sinai and committed it to Joshua, and Joshua to the elders, and the elders to the Prophets; and the Prophets committed it to the men of the Great Synagogue" (Abot 1:1). The rabbis have normally understood this to mean both the Written Law and Oral Law were handed down from Sinai. In the second century, Rabbi Akiba and his followers held that all revelation (Torah of Moses, words of the prophets, Oral Law, debates of the rabbis, and future questions of scholars) could be traced to Sinai. Some scholars describe Akiba's position as a "maximalist view" and compare it with a "minimalist view" of Rabbi Ishmael, another influential scholar of the second century.[16] Ishmael insisted that Moses could not have learned the whole Torah (written and oral) in the forty days and forty nights he was on the mountain. Rather,

---

14. Quoted in Maurice Friedman, *Abraham Joshua Heschel and Elie Wiesel: You Are My Witnesses* (New York: Farrar, Straus & Giroux, 1987), p. 59.

15. See the thoughtful discussion of this theme in Gilbert S. Rosenthal, *What Can a Modern Jew Believe?* (Eugene, OR: Wipf & Stock, 2007), pp. 41-50.

16. Rosenthal, *What Can a Modern Jew Believe?* pp. 44-45.

he likely received the general rules or principles that Moses himself, and later the prophets and sages, worked out in detail in the generations following.

The evidence of Scripture itself seems to support the idea that revelation was not confined to one event at Sinai but was repeated again and again as God imparted his truths and teachings to other spokespeople within the community of faith. After Sinai there were ongoing encounters with God. When considering the big picture, in Judaism, revelation seems to be far more a process that happened over time, a continual dialogue between God and his people, rather than a single event. Sinai, however, with its dramatic setting of fire, earthquake, and trumpet blasts, points to the supernatural dimension of the Torah and all of Scripture to follow. The Bible finds its origin in God, not Moses. It is the Word of God, something Israel was to never forget.

Abraham J. Heschel suggests Sinai implies a "minimum of revelation and a maximum of interpretation." By this, Heschel apparently means the essence comes as a revelation from God but understanding and explanation is from humans.[17] Heschel sees a mystery in prophecy and its inspiration. The work is one of synergism. The language "Torah from Heaven," argues Heschel, is formulated for the human ear, but seriously dissipates when taken literally. Literal-mindedness limits words to one meaning when often they are meant as indicative words to be understood responsively with more than one meaning.[18] In a somewhat similar vein, Rabbi Michael Samuel argues that revelation is really "a timeless theological conversation," a dynamic dialogue, as truth is evolving through a text that is living. Thus the Torah embraces a dialogic pattern with many facets of meaning, the text fabric never finished.[19]

While Christian views on revelation and inspiration vary, many Christians uphold the position that God uniquely spoke through many centuries, on numerous occasions and in many ways, to the authors of the Jewish Scriptures (Heb. 1:1). As long as the sacred canon of the Tanakh was open, God was still working through his Spirit in the composition and shaping of these writings. Once the canon was closed, however, the church began to make a careful distinction between authoritative, inspired Scripture and other,

---

17. See Rosenthal, *What Can a Modern Jew Believe?* p. 46.

18. Abraham Joshua Heschel, *Heavenly Torah: As Refracted through the Generations*, trans. and ed. Gordon Tucker (New York: Continuum, 2006), pp. 666-67, and Abraham Joshua Heschel, *God in Search of Man* (New York: Harper & Row, 1955), pp. 178-83.

19. Michael Samuel, *Birth and Rebirth through Genesis: A Timeless Theological Conversation* (Coral Springs, FL: Aeon, 2010), pp. 25-34.

extra-canonical literature. Jesus seems to allude to the threefold division of the canon of Jewish Scripture (Luke 24:27, 44). In reading and responding to Scripture, therefore, many Christians prefer to use the word "illumination" rather than "revelation." They understand the work of the Holy Spirit in "speaking to them" is illumination, the bringing of spiritual understanding or deep inner meaning of the text (John 16:13). Such a distinction may appear to be semantic to some. While the Spirit may illumine the human heart in revealing God's truth, such personal revelation is never synonymous with the inspired Written Word of the Revealer.

In this process of personal understanding or application of a truth, this may come directly through the biblical text itself or indirectly through another source commenting on it. There is considerable insight and understanding that we may derive from extra-biblical sources. As the adage states, "All truth is God's truth." Accordingly, we must acknowledge that Jesus and Paul drew teaching material from the oral traditions of the sages of Israel as well as the Jewish Scriptures, all under the guidance of the Holy Spirit.[20] While for Christians, the Bible alone is inspired, the written Word of God, it is important that Christians understand that in Jesus' day, both oral and written laws were viewed as Torah. The oral and the written flowed together. This inclusive nature of Torah constitutes more than the revelation at Sinai. It also includes the midrashic process of textual interpretation. In sum, "Torah encompasses a whole, unique, pious approach to life that centers around faith in God, study of his Word, and obedience to his will."[21] Just as the teachings of the apostolic fathers are important for understanding early Christian thought and practice, so the sayings and commentaries of the sages and rabbis are inseparable from understanding Jewish thought in antiquity.

The Delight of the Law

The longest chapter in the Tanakh, the 176 verses of Psalm 119, centers on the joy of the Written Law, the five books of Moses. Indeed, God's law is the Psalmist's "delight" (119:77, 174). The word *torah*, often translated "law," means guidance, direction, instruction, or teaching. That is why Israel rejoiced in the Torah. They rejoiced that God had not left them to figure out

---

20. Dwight A. Pryor, *Unveiling the Kingdom of Heaven* (Dayton, OH: Center for Judaic-Christian Studies, 2008), p. 21.

21. Brad H. Young, *Meet the Rabbis* (Peabody, MA: Hendrickson, 2007), p. 82.

life by trial and error; he had given them guidance and direction for the path of life. To the Jew, that was worth celebrating. The highly negative and pejorative definition of Law, namely, some prohibitory system that kills joy and serves as a legalistic straightjacket, sometimes found in Antinomian versions of Christianity, is not what Jews mean by Law.

In modern Jewish religious life, after the weeklong observance of the Festival of Sukkot (Tabernacles) each fall, Jews celebrate another holiday, Simchat Torah, literally, "rejoicing in the Law." Great celebration takes place in the synagogue as Torah scrolls are removed from the ark and paraded around the congregation, amidst singing, hand clapping, and small children waving flags. The Torah is lovingly cradled and carried in exuberant congregational dancing. A Torah is fully unrolled from *Bere'shit* (Genesis) to *Debarim* (Deuteronomy). Simchat Torah marks the conclusion of the annual Torah reading cycle and also initiates the start of a new cycle. God's teaching, embodied in the Torah scroll, allows the Jew to celebrate Sinai anew, to take joy in the trans-generational and eternal importance of Torah.

Solomon Schechter, architect of the American Conservative Jewish movement, sheds light on all-out joyful praise by Jews, making use of their entire body. Schechter points to King David, the main contributor to the Book of Psalms. Schechter observes, "David praised God with every limb in his body, . . . with his head, with his eyes, with his mouth, with his ears, with his throat, with his tongue, with his lips, with his heart, with his reins, with his hands, with his feet, as it is said, 'All my bones shall say, Lord, who is like unto thee?' (Ps. 35:10)."[22]

As the Law consisted of five distinct works, so the Book of Psalms, the "Hymnbook" of Israel, had five separate anthologies or "books" (chapters 1–41, 42–72, 73–89, 90–106, and 107–150). The entire collection of Psalms opens on the theme of how the righteous man delights in the law of the LORD (Ps. 1:2). According to Psalm 119, God's laws are "righteous" (v. 7), "good" (v. 39), "precious" (v. 72), "unforgettable" (v. 93), "loved" (v. 97), "sweet" (v. 103), and "true" (v. 151). Indeed, "Blessed is the man who fears the LORD, who finds great delight in his commands" (Ps. 112:1). The righteous man's "delight is in the law of the LORD, and on his law he meditates day and night" (Ps. 1:2). After Ezra the priest had spent hours reading the Torah to a large group assembled in a Jerusalem square, all greatly moved by the experience, Nehemiah the governor sent the people on their way with these encouraging words: "the joy of the LORD is your strength" (Neh. 8:10b).

22. Solomon Schechter, *Aspects of Rabbinic Theology* (New York: Schocken, 1961), p. 156.

The "Text within the Text"

The origin of the Oral Law may be traced back to the biblical period. Ezra, a fifth-century B.C. priest and scribe, was especially influential in this process. Ezra instituted various reforms, including the public reading of the Torah (see Neh. 8:1-9). Ezra apparently worked closely with the "men of the Great Synagogue," a group of 120 elders who accompanied Ezra back from exile, enacting new rules and teachings to guide the post-exilic community (see Mishnah, Abot 1:1).

During the Intertestamental period, the literacy of the Sopherim, or "scribes," and the Pharisees had an important role in helping to preserve various traditions. From the first to the third centuries, the Tannaitic era, the two basic techniques of *Halakhah* were established: Midrash and Mishnah.[23] Midrash involved a careful search of the biblical text, drawing out or deducing implications, often in aphoristic style, for the life of the community. Emil Fackenheim has emphasized that no midrash wants to be taken literally, but every midrash wants to be taken seriously, for its stories and parables seek to convey universal religious truths to the reader.[24] According to Norman Cohen, "The Rabbis believed not only that the Torah given at Mount Sinai anticipated all that would happen in the course of history but that all new interpretations are an implicit part of the original text. . . . Therefore, the written text (of the Bible) and its interpretation (by the rabbis) . . . were thought to be part of the same revelation." Cohen concludes, "What is deduced from the biblical text is not separate from it, but rather a latent part of it. It is the text within the text."[25]

Brad Young, a Christian scholar of Judaism, makes a similar, yet slightly different, distinction of the "text within the text":

> The revelation of Torah to Moses on Mount Sinai is the foundation of Jewish faith and practice. The pious Jew chooses a course of life and pursues the fulfillment of God's will by obedience to the commandments. But the words of the Torah can be interpreted in different ways, and the oral commentary that accompanied the revelation to Moses on Mount

23. Elliot N. Dorff and Louis E. Newman, eds., *Contemporary Jewish Theology* (New York: Oxford University Press, 1999), p. 304.

24. Emil L. Fackenheim, "The Human Condition after Auschwitz," in *An Introduction to Judaism*, ed. Jacob Neusner (Louisville: Westminster/John Knox, 1991), p. 363.

25. Norman J. Cohen, *The Way into Torah* (Woodstock, VT: Jewish Lights, 2000), pp. 54-55.

Sinai is the unwritten guidebook that must be preserved in memorized form by committed disciples who pass it on. . . . The Oral Torah is of almost equal importance in Jewish thought to what is written, largely because it reveals the meaning of the recorded text and is upheld by its authority. Still it is not considered to possess the same authority as the Written Torah.[26]

The Mishnah, or Oral Law, was codified around A.D. 200. It had its beginnings, however, in the teachings of the sages, or even before the time of Jesus. When a problem or difficulty arose, scholars would arrive at a decision based on their ethical perceptions, often informed (but not always overtly expressed) by Scripture. "The Oral Torah was a living tradition used for continuous interpretation of the written code as changing circumstances demanded."[27] *Aggadot* (narrative sources of the Oral Law) were especially inspiring and edifying; they expounded theologically on human activity and the work of God in the world.[28] *Midrashim*, homiletical rabbinic commentaries on the Hebrew Scripture, are an extension of the biblical text by using the criteria of Aggadot.

The Gemara is the commentary on the Mishnah. The Gemara developed in the academies from the third to the sixth century. The rabbis used dialectical argument, employing questions and answers with movement of thought back and forth from point to point.[29] The Mishnah and Gemara together comprise the Talmud. The Babylonian Talmud was finalized around A.D. 500.

An exploration of commentaries, teachings, reflections, illustrations, and applications of the sages and early rabbis will be of interest and value for Christians intent on understanding the meaning of texts related to Hebraic heritage. The continual, dynamic shaping and reshaping of traditions rooted in the Bible of Jesus is important for serious Christian study of the roots and early development of Christianity. This "text within the text" will help illuminate, expand, enrich, and nuance some of the foundational — yet largely undiscovered — themes of Hebraic thought — especially those that

26. Young, *Meet the Rabbis*, pp. 198-99.

27. David Bivin, "Jesus the Rabbi," in *Roots and Branches: Explorations into the Jewish Context of the Christian Faith*, ed. John Fieldsend, Clifford Hill, Walter Riggans, John C. P. Smith, and Fred Wright (Bedford, UK: PWM Trust, 1998), p. 38.

28. Dan Cohn-Sherbok, *The Jewish Heritage* (Oxford: Blackwell, 1988), p. 70.

29. Jacob Neusner and Bruce Chilton, *Jewish-Christian Debates* (Minneapolis: Fortress Press, 1998), p. 22.

emerged following the separation of church and synagogue. In addition, such study will provide needed insight for more effective interfaith dialogue on methodologies employed by Jewish teachers and on the similarities and differences between Judaism and Christianity. Finally, such study will lead to a greater appreciation of Jesus the Jew and his *Aggadic* storytelling style so central to his parables and other teachings.

Some Observations on the New Testament and the Law

The Torah, both Written and Oral, contrary to what some Christians have often taught, is viewed in Judaism as a means of blessing and living a productive and fulfilled life, as God intended it to be (Deut. 30:19, 20). Jesus taught in the Sermon on the Mount, "Do not think that I have come to abolish the Law or the Prophets; I have not come to abolish them but to fulfill them" (Matt. 5:17). Among the thousands of pages of the Talmud, only one New Testament verse is cited (Shabbat 116a-b); it is the above verse indicating that Jesus did not come to diminish the Law of Moses, a verse obviously very "congenial with Judaism."[30] As a teacher within the household of Israel, Jesus came to uphold and establish the Torah, not to cancel it out. A faithful Jew, Jesus was "born under the law," and for thirty-three years lived a Jewish life that embodied its principles (see Gal. 4:4).

Mishpatim *and* Huqqim

Biblical law distinguishes between *mishpatim* and *huqqim*. The *mishpatim* are "laws" or "judgments." Originally, some of these laws may have included legal decisions of judges. But one of the main features of *mishpatim* is that this "justice" is often expressed in commandments or prohibitions that are self-evident, rational, or obvious to all civilizations as, for example, the forbidding of murder, adultery, and theft. These laws are vital for the preservation of individual, family, and societal life.

The *huqqim*, divine "statutes" or "decrees," are commandments, laws, and rituals given specifically to the Jewish people without any apparent reason or explanation. The dietary laws (Leviticus 11) and laws concerning

---

30. See Marc Saperstein, *Moments of Crisis in Jewish-Christian Relations* (Philadelphia: Trinity Press International, 1989), p. 12.

purification after childbirth (Leviticus 12) are examples of *huqqim*. Such laws were followed by Jews because God commanded them, not because they necessarily made sense.[31] Many *huqqim* were apparently intended as "boundary markers" to set Israel apart from the nations and to thwart total social integration. Today, certain Reform and secular Jews have either re-interpreted or dropped *huqqim* in light of rationalistic, scientific, or other modernistic explanations. In addition, many of these *huqqim* only had direct relevance to ancient society and in the land of Israel around a sanctuary. The church also came to reinterpret many of the *huqqim*, especially those pertaining to religious ritual and ceremony. Noteworthy, for example, are the laws of sacrifice surrounding the priesthood in Israel. These laws become spiritually or Christologically gathered up in the sacrificial death of Jesus, his high priesthood, and the presentation of himself as a new teacher of Israel, in certain ways like Moses.

Jesus: A New Moses?

The structure of the Gospel of Matthew closely ties Jesus to Moses. This highly Jewish Gospel presents Jesus as a new Moses, a new Israel. Mary and Joseph take the child Jesus to Egypt and then return, a reminder of Israel's enslavement and escape from Egypt. In Matthew, Jesus goes up a mountain to deliver his Sermon on the Mount, the first of five major discourses of Jesus in Matthew. This great Teacher, on a mountain, echoes Israel's coming out of Egypt and Moses then going up a mountain to receive the Five Books of the Law.

Jesus undergoes baptism in the River Jordan and spends forty days in the wilderness, there experiencing temptation. This reminds Matthew's audience of Israel's coming through the waters of the Red Sea and enduring forty years in the wilderness, with various temptations. Matthew also de-scribes Jesus and Moses carrying on a conversation together on the Mount of Transfiguration, the place where the face of Jesus "shone like the sun" recalling the radiant face of Moses on the top of Mount Sinai (Matt. 17:2; Exod. 34:29). Thus, Jesus links himself to the prophet Moses as a new Teacher in Israel. Through his own life, Jesus recapitulates stories from the history of Israel that would resonate with any Jewish audience.

---

31. David S. Ariel, *What Do Jews Believe? The Spiritual Foundations of Judaism* (New York: Schocken, 1995), pp. 88-89.

Old Wine Is Better

Contrary to popular belief, Jesus did not come to establish a new religion but to renew and revitalize his ancestral religion. His approach focused far more on the inner condition of the heart rather than on external appearances. In his approach to renewal, Jesus succinctly and rather cryptically affirms, "The old wine is better" (Luke 5:39). What did Jesus mean? This text has given rise to a number of different interpretations.

In his book *Jesus the Jewish Theologian,* Brad Young astutely points out that the old wine refers to "the ancient faith and practices of the Jewish people." Adds Young, "The purpose of Jesus was to revitalize the people spiritually by a revival through the old wine. . . . He did not desire to put away the noble traditions of the ancient faith . . . but was seeking wholehearted reform from within."[32] As the prophet Jeremiah called Israel back to walk in the "ancient paths," the "good way" of their godly ancestors, so Jesus called his countrymen back to the stable foundation of sincere prophetic faith (Jer. 6:16). Jesus did not come to abolish the Law or the Prophets (see Matt. 5:17).

Jesus and the Oral Law

Jesus apparently attached considerable importance to the Oral Torah and in some way regarded it as authoritative. The Pharisees upheld the Written Law and the Oral Law. While Jesus, in the usual dialectical style of Jewish sages, often clashed with the Pharisees on various issues, Jesus did admonish his disciples, "You must obey them (the teachers of the law and the Pharisees) and do everything they tell you" (Matt. 23:3). Jesus was referring to the oral traditions of the Pharisees and their interpretations of the Written Torah.[33] Such, however, need not be a *carte blanche* endorsement by Jesus of all Pharisaic teachings. Nevertheless, it must be recognized that the Written and Oral laws were usually so interwoven and flowed together within the religious practices and culture of Judaism, it was not always easy to separate the two. Jesus, however, was not prescriptively enslaved or chained to one interpretation of the law, but allowed its spirit, fluidity, and dynamic life-changing principles to break forth in each new situation (see Mark 2:27).

32. Brad H. Young, *Jesus the Jewish Theologian* (Peabody, MA: Hendrickson, 1995), pp. 156-57.

33. See Bivin, "Jesus the Rabbi," p. 39.

Law and Grace in Judaism

In his groundbreaking work, *Paul and Palestinian Judaism,* E. P. Sanders did much to clarify the relation of law and grace in Judaism. The old perspective on Paul, commonly held by Christians, was influenced by certain strands of Reformation theology and reflected a rather cursory reading of the Pauline corpus, significantly lacking in Jewish contextual background. The old perspective largely characterized Judaism as a "works righteousness" religion whereby Jews claimed they could earn merit and God's salvation by keeping the law. Sanders and other scholars, however, in presenting a new perspective on Paul, have largely countered the earlier legalistic framework. This has come about through a more careful and thorough study of early Jewish texts. The main sources of these texts include rabbinic literature, the Dead Sea Scrolls, the Apocrypha, and Pseudepigrapha.

As Sanders puts it, "The pattern [of Judaism] is based on election and atonement for transgressions, it being understood that God gave commandments in connection with the election and that obedience to them or atonement and repentance for transgressions, was expected as the condition for remaining in the covenant community. The best title for this sort of religion is 'covenantal nomism' . . . the covenant by God's grace and Torah obedience as man's proper response within the covenant . . . obedience maintains one's position in the covenant, but it does not earn God's grace as such."[34]

It is not in the purview of this chapter — or even this book — to try to solve all the questions surrounding Christians and the law. But some concluding observations are in order. The exact place of the law in Christianity has long been debated and doubtless will continue to be debated. There is no one single answer that will satisfy everyone. How then may a balance be struck that takes God's revelation of the law seriously as well as the New Testament Scriptures?

The main message of the New Testament seems to be one not of bondage but of total liberty in Christ. This freedom is intended to enable one to live a life of love that honors God and respects one's neighbor. Living a life of love requires all the help that a serious believer can get; led by the Spirit, one will be informed by the fullness of God's teachings, including the law.

---

34. E. P. Sanders, *Paul and Palestinian Judaism* (Philadelphia: Fortress Press, 1977), pp. 236, 420. For a valuable, additional perspective on grace in Judaism, see David R. Blumenthal, "The Place of Faith and Grace in Judaism," in *A Time to Speak: The Evangelical-Jewish Encounter,* ed. A. James Rudin and Marvin R. Wilson (Grand Rapids: Eerdmans, 1987), pp. 104-14.

The moral law is a paradigm of what the law of love demands in a variety of concrete situations. It is expressive of an attitude and lifestyle toward God, family, and society. Thus the law must be taken seriously, for it is a concrete expression of the will of God. When adhered to out of love, God's law will contribute significantly to one's personal welfare and the stability and structure of an all-too-chaotic world. In the above sense, when correctly understood and applied, the law is a gracious gift of God. It was given to guide a people already secure in the covenant in their walk of faith.

End of the Law?

The New Testament states that "Christ is the end *(telos)* of the law" (Rom. 10:4). This would not seem to mean the termination or cessation of the law, for the law is quoted from extensively in the New Testament to establish its arguments. Also, Jesus said he did not come to do away with the law but to fulfill it by establishing its intended meaning. Jesus embodied the Torah; in his life he fleshed out its meaning. Thus, "end" of the law would appear to refer to the purpose of the law. The New Testament sees the law "put in charge" as a tutor to guide people to Christ (Gal. 3:24). According to the New Testament, many of the types, shadows, and promises found in the law are fulfilled in the life and ministry of Christ. The New Testament writers see its fullest meaning — especially in the holy days and the rituals performed in the sanctuary — in him. The Christocentricity of the New Testament documents thus underscores a different overall purpose of the law than that found in traditional Judaism.

Christ freed believers from the condemnation associated with law. Accordingly, with a new heart through faith, believers are empowered by the Spirit within, rather than tightly controlled by requirements of the law without. Many of the specific ceremonial and civil laws that applied directly to ancient Israel, a "holy people" among the nations, are no longer directly applicable to either Jews or Christians today. Didactically, however, or by principle, when these laws are understood in context, many carry significant meaning about God or the timeless priorities he wishes to establish for his people.

The moral law, however, primarily encapsulated in the Ten Commandments, is to be kept as part of God's international moral code in respect of him and in honor of one's neighbor. We must emphasize that perfect keeping of the law was impossible in Israel, although often strived for. This is something every Christian should understand, in that the failure to meet every expectation of the law in Israel is just like the impossibility of today's Christian living a fully flawless and perfect life that corresponds at every point with the teachings of Jesus. (One should try living by the Sermon on the Mount, if there is any question about this standard being fully attainable.) While keeping the law in Israel was not optional, God made provision for forgiveness of sin, through repentance, offered freely to those with a sincere, humble, and broken heart.

Thus, in biblical Israel, it was God's intention for his people to observe the law as a response of love and obedience to God's gracious offer of the covenant. The expectation to keep commandments was not to secure favor from God but was to guide the people, who were already secure within the covenant. So too, in New Testament Christianity, one of the proofs of love is in obeying commandments (Matt. 28:20; John 14:15, 21; 15:10; 1 John 3:24; 5:2, 3). "We love because he first loved us" (1 John 4:19). Thus, for Jew or Christian, one was not to be indifferent regarding the keeping of commandments, but the law itself was never intended to save. To the sensitive believer seeking to know and do the will of God, however, the law illumined and distinguished the pathway of a righteous and holy life that God desired his people walk.

UNDERSTANDING CHAPTER THREE

1. What have theologically conservative expressions of Christianity often emphasized? Yet what is necessary for a biblically balanced expression of Christianity?

2. For which reason in particular does the author point out that Christianity stands in need of Judaism?

3. The foundational principles in the Judeo-Christian tradition go back to what event in history? How did the Mishnah, Talmud, and Codes develop?

4. What must be done in order for the church to revive her understanding of her Hebraic beginnings? What is the foundational bedrock of biblical thinking, and what are its main divisions?

5. In Jewish thought, all the main teachings of Judaism may be traced to what? In what way, however, is revelation more than a once-and-for-all event? What does revelation extend to beyond the encounter at Sinai?

6. What does Bruce Chilton observe about the ownership of Scripture? How does he figuratively describe the actual role of Jews and Christians?

7. How is the Tanakh referred to in Jewish tradition? How does Paul refer to the inspired Scriptures of Israel, and what does the term underscore?

8. From where does the English word "Bible" derive? What does this reflect about Christian tradition, and in what way is Christianity in debt to Judaism for this characteristic?

9. What distinction does the author note concerning the roles of God and the Jews in the title "People of the Book"?

10. Through a humorous anecdote, what does the author point out was and is the intent of the "Book of Books"?

11. In what way does Samuel Sandmel suggest that the Bible contributed to the survival of the Jews?

12. What does it mean to read Scripture as "today's mail"? Review Jacob Neusner's comments on the rabbinic sages' readings of Scripture. Why is their mindset so extraordinarily insightful? Review also Leo Baeck's observations. From the outset, how did Christianity already possess an assurance to meet all trials to which it was to be subjected?

13. Since the time of Moses, David, and the prophets, how was Israel's faith continually shaped and reshaped? What kind of elasticity developed in the Jewish sages' and rabbis' interactions with the Bible? How do Michael Fishbane's thoughts illustrate that, amid evolving circumstances of history, the Jews never separated themselves from the Bible?

14. In what way do Christians read the Bible "backwards"? Rather than an annulling of Judaism, what is Christianity's relationship with it?

15. Review Bruce Chilton's quote. In what way is the Old Testament every Christian's story? How do you understand his statement that "the melody, Christianity insists against Judaism, is that of prophecy rather than Torah"?

16. In which division of the Bible does the author emphasize that Christians and Jews often find considerable common ground? Is this the division that would have come to your mind first in thinking about common ground? Why or why not? List at least six of the themes mentioned by the author that are central to the teaching of Torah and, correspondingly, to Christian thought.

17. Using Romans 7:12, 14, and 22, sum up Paul's attitude toward the law and commandments.

18. How did the encounter between God and Moses have implications for the history of civilization?

19. What pattern of revelation is found in Scripture? How is Sinai emblematic of this pattern, and how was the pattern also in place prior to this crucial event?

20. What striking anthropomorphic figure of speech is used for the means God used to record the law on tablets of stone (see Exod. 31:18; also 34:1)?

21. What does Abraham Heschel emphasize by stating that "[m]ore decisive than the origin of the Bible in God is the presence of God in the Bible"? In what way does Heschel envision one's response to the divine Word taking place? How might many Christians' perspectives be distinct from this?

22. What questions might be considered when exploring how the divine and human factors meshed at the revelation at Sinai? What does Abot 1:1 of the Mishnah state, and what, consequently, have the rabbis normally understood this to mean? What did Rabbi Akiba and Rabbi Ishmael have to say about revelation, and how was one's view "maximalist" while the other's was "minimalist"? Which view do you tend to gravitate toward?

23. How does Scripture itself seem to testify to revelation as a process rather than exclusively one event? If revelation is carried out in stages throughout time, what do you think is the purpose of more dramatic, single-event cases of revelation (e.g., Sinai)?

24. What does Abraham Heschel mean by suggesting that Sinai implies a "minimum of revelation and a maximum of interpretation"? What phenomenon does he put forth as a threat to the language of "Torah from Heaven"?

25. How do many Christians view revelation concerning the Jewish Scriptures? At what point did Christians begin to carefully distinguish between inspired Scripture and extra-canonical literature?

26. Why might many Christians prefer to use the word "illumination" rather than "revelation" when speaking of reading and responding to Scripture?

27. Why is it important for Christians to take seriously the adage, "All truth is God's truth," when considering extra-biblical sources? In Jesus' day, what, in addition to the written law, was also viewed as Torah? From what did both Jesus and Paul draw teaching material?

28. What is the subject of Psalm 119? What does the word *torah* mean? Because of this, why did Israel rejoice in the Torah? In what sense has the "Law" sometimes been understood in American Christianity? Why is it so critical that this misunderstanding be addressed?

29. What is Simchat Torah? What happens on this occasion, why, and what does it represent for those celebrating? The Gospels inform us that Jesus celebrated Passover (Mark 14), Sukkot (John 7), and Hanukkah (John 10), so would you conclude that Judaism is a more "celebratory" religion than Christianity? What events rooted in the Bible do you celebrate?

30. Structurally, how does the Book of Psalms mirror the Law? On what theme does the entire collection of Psalms open? How is the Law described in the Psalms? From a Christian perspective, do you think these expressions in the Psalms are typically taken seriously? Does anything need to change in the church's mindset or focus? Why or why not?

31. To when can the origin of the Oral Law be traced? Who was particularly influential in this process, how so, and with whom did he work?

32. What contributed to the preservation of Jewish tradition during the Intertestamental period? What two basic techniques of *Halakhah* were established during this era? Define *Midrash*. How is Emil Fackenheim's statement that "no midrash wants to be taken literally, but every midrash wants to be taken seriously" particularly helpful in understanding the purpose and value of midrash? Does such an enhanced understanding open doors for Christians to more comfortably explore midrash? In your opinion, should Christians do so?

33. Recall the section titled "The 'Text within the Text,'" and locate the phrase within Norman Cohen's observations. What is the "text within the text"? How does Cohen's use of the word "latent" provide a helpful framework of thought for those seeking to better understand the rabbinic mindset concerning new interpretations of revelation? How does Brad Young offer a slightly different understanding of the "text within the text"?

34. What is the Mishnah? What prompted its development, and when was it codified? What are *aggadot,* and in what way were they especially edifying?

35. What is the Gemara, and when and how did it develop? How do the Mishnah and the Gemara together relate to the Talmud? Around when was the Babylonian Talmud finalized?

36. Briefly summarize the author's comments on the value of Christians' exploring rabbinic material. From a Christian perspective, how could such a pursuit open new doors for theological growth and spiritual maturation in your own Christian community and context?

37. What did Jesus teach about his role in relation to the Law and the Prophets? From a Christian perspective, do you think Christians generally honor this part of Jesus' teachings appropriately? What is the only verse of the New Testament that is cited in the Talmud?

38. What are *mishpatim* and *huqqim*? What was apparently the role of many *huqqim*? How have various religious communities today either reinterpreted or dropped *huqqim*? As an example, how did the church reinterpret the laws of sacrifice surrounding the priesthood?

39. What are some of the ways in which the Gospel of Matthew ties Jesus to Moses? From a Christian perspective, does this reinforce for you the esteem with which Moses was and is held in Judaism? From a Jewish perspective, do you find Jesus' ties to Moses as a leader of God's people encouraging in any way?

40. The author states that, contrary to popular belief, Jesus did not come to establish a new religion but to do what? How does Brad Young interpret Jesus' affirmation that "the old wine is better"? In what way were the calls of Jeremiah (see Jer. 6:16) and Jesus similar?

41. Cite an instance in Scripture that indicates Jesus attached considerable importance and, in some measure, authority to the Oral Torah of his day. What does the author mean to point out, however, by stating that this "need not be a *carte blanche* endorsement by Jesus of all Pharisaic teachings"? What is a preferable way to understand how Jesus perceived and interacted with the Oral Law?

42. How did the old perspective on Paul, commonly held by Christians, characterize Judaism? In contrast, what perspective did E. P. Sanders present, and which sources played a particularly prominent role in his study?

43. Review E. P. Sanders's comments on the pattern of Judaism. What does he mean by "covenantal nomism"? How does this alternative understanding contrast with the more strictly legalistic framework of the old perspective? From a Christian perspective, did your Christian background present the old perspective or the new perspective more fully?

44. With the purpose and role of the law in mind, what does the main message of the New Testament appear to be? What is the moral law a paradigm of, and what kind of attitude is it expressive of? For Christians today, how does the law remain pertinent and a gracious gift of God?

45. What interpretation does the author see as preferable regarding the statement that "Christ is the end *(telos)* of the law"? How does the New

Testament ultimately underscore a different overall purpose of the law than found in traditional Judaism?

46. How are many specific ceremonial or civil laws no longer directly applicable to Jews or Christians, yet can potentially carry very significant meaning?

47. In the closing paragraph of the chapter, the author emphasizes what reason for God expecting biblical Israel to observe the law? How is New Testament Christianity similar in its view of obedience?

PART II

People of God: An Abrahamic Family

CHAPTER 4

The People We Join

More than two billion Christians are alive on this planet today. And the numbers are growing.[1] Many within the church claim to embrace "biblical" Christianity and its scripturally rooted teachings. This, they would say, is a hallmark or distinctive of their faith. In truth, however, many have never made a serious personal exploration of the biblical texts that undergird their faith.

Also troubling is the fact that "biblical" Christians may be in the church for a lifetime and yet remain largely uninformed about the biblical origins of their belief system. They may have some general understanding of certain Christian teachings and practices. But they often lack knowledge of Judaism, the religion that gave birth to Christianity. Many Christians are surprised to hear the Christian religion was not "invented from scratch" or "from the word 'go.'" Hence the main focus of this book is to explore the Hebraic foundations of the Christian faith. Today's church is in need of renewing. If it is to reflect its biblical origins, the church must have an understanding and appreciation of its Hebraic heritage and the Jewish people to whom Christians are indebted for bequeathing so much of their spiritual heritage.

Would a marriage counselor urge a client to become seriously involved with one of the opposite sex without first exploring the value system, family background, and traditions of one's potential life partner? Would a realtor advise a potential buyer to purchase a house "sight unseen," or would the realtor insist first that the client carefully check out the property, the history

---

1. See David B. Barrett, George T. Kurian, and Todd M. Johnson, *World Christian Encyclopedia*, 2nd ed. (New York: Oxford University Press, 2001), pp. 12-15.

of its ownership, and the neighborhood where it is found? Would a high school guidance counselor advise a college-bound senior to choose a four-year school without first learning about the school, its reputation, and the specific programs of study it has to offer? In virtually every area of life we are encouraged to make informed decisions. Before one buys in to something it is needful and wise to do one's homework. If such reflective study is crucial in the everyday areas of life, how much more should this be the case when it comes to our faith commitment? We should desire to know what we believe and also the origin or source of those beliefs and teachings that inform our faith. Though not always understood or acknowledged, biblical Christianity is Hebraic to the core.

Living in the Tents of Shem

Genesis 10 contains the Table of Nations of the world. Seventy names are listed. They comprise the lines of Noah's three sons, Shem, Ham, and Japheth. Twenty-six nations are listed from Shem, thirty from Ham, and fourteen from Japheth. The total of seventy suggests completeness. God told Noah and his sons, "Be fruitful and increase in number and fill the earth" (Gen. 9:1). Accordingly, these seventy descendants of Noah "spread out over the earth after the flood" (10:32).

Abraham was a Semite, a descendant of Noah's son Shem (Gen. 11:10-32). In the Noahic narratives, the Lord, the God of Shem, is blessed (9:26). He is the object of praise because it is through this God of Shem and his descendants — the most immediate and noteworthy of whom is the patriarch Abraham — that his covenantal promises would be realized. One of the most intriguing blessings of Scripture is in regard to Japheth and his relation to Shem. The book of Genesis says, "May God enlarge Japheth and may he [i.e., Japheth] live in the tents of Shem" (9:27). In the Hebrew text of the first part of this verse, one may hear the artistic play on words between the terms *yapht*, "enlarge," and *leyephet* "[to] Japheth." While some interpreters understand this passage to mean God will dwell with Shem, the overall context suggests otherwise, for its focus is a blessing on Japheth. Many of Japheth's immediate descendants settled in the general area of Eurasia. While it is attractive to try to find a precise fulfillment in some historical situation of the Old Testament when Gentiles came under Israelite domination, as at the time of the conquest, judges, the united monarchy, or later, such is impossible to say for sure.

The above passage appears to have a deeper meaning suggested by the New Testament. As G. Charles Aalders correctly observes, "to live in anyone's tent involves sharing in that person's lot. In other words, what we have here is an announcement that Japheth would share in the blessing of Shem."[2] The descendants of Japheth will worship the God of Shem. In light of the heritage of Shem via Abraham and the people of Israel, Japheth, i.e., the Gentiles "now share in the nourishing sap from the olive root" (Rom. 11:17). In the words of Gordon Wenham, "It is certainly attractive to see the incorporation of Gentiles into the Shemite fold as a *sensus plenior* of this saying [regarding Japheth]."[3] Wenham, however, comes short of specifically linking this text to the New Testament, where believing Gentiles are incorporated into the Semitic family of Abraham (see Gal. 3:29). Thus, we believe Wenham misses the deepest meaning of this passage, in that spiritually Christians are all "Shemites" (Semites). In contrast to Wenham, Derek Kidner cites Ephesians 3:6 (". . . Gentiles are heirs together with Israel, members together of one body") to support the conclusion, "the fulfillment of the words [about dwelling in the tents of Shem] leaps to the eye in the New Testament in the ingathering of the Gentiles."[4] Indeed, all Christians are spiritual Semites, for they share in the inheritance of Abraham's family. A Christian cannot make sense of the Bible unless he or she knows what it means to be a spiritual Semite. Shem's tent of blessing through Abraham is large enough to include every Christian. The question is whether every Christian is large-minded and wise enough to enter that tent to explore and appropriate the richness and depth of that blessing.

Who Joins Whom?

Much confusion exists regarding the relation of Jews to non-Jews, the relation of Israel to the church. When Christians are asked to articulate their spiritual identity, often the first thought many use in defining themselves is in relation to theological concepts rather than in relation to people. While theology is very important in giving definition and shape to Christian thought and practice, New Testament theology does not originate with a

2. G. Charles Aalders, *Genesis*, vol. 1 (Grand Rapids: Zondervan, 1981), p. 211.

3. Gordon J. Wenham, *Genesis 1–15*, Word Biblical Commentary (Waco, TX: Word, 1987), p. 20.

4. Derek Kidner, *Genesis*, Tyndale Old Testament Commentary (Downers Grove, IL: InterVarsity, 1967), p. 104.

creed but with a person. That person, however, is not the one most Christians initially think about.

Paul defines the issue in his letter to the church at Galatia: "If you belong to Christ, then you are Abraham's seed" (3:29). According to this text, Christianity does not begin with some impersonal or abstract theological idea or statement; it begins with a person, father Abraham.[5] It is significant to note that Christians find their earliest spiritual identity not with Paul or Jesus but with Abraham and his people.

The question of who joins whom ought to be of vital interest to every Christian.[6] Some Christians teach that Israel and the church are two separate entities but that God's will is to eliminate that distinction by having Israel convert to Christianity and join the church. The ultimate conclusion of such teaching would of course be the disappearance of Israel. The apostle Paul, however, has a different answer to this question of who joins whom.

For Paul, the destiny of Jew and Gentile is mysteriously and inextricably bound together throughout the church age (see especially Romans 9–11). As self-proclaimed "apostle to the Gentiles" (see Rom. 11:13; Gal. 2:8), Paul argues that non-Jewish believers are grafted into the olive tree, Israel (Rom. 11:11-24). Through the use of this metaphor of the olive tree, Paul depicts non-Jewish believers as wild olive branches. Gentiles are not "natural" branches but "wild." Thus God, by his mercy, graciously grafts them into Israel. Accordingly, non-Jews are allowed to partake of the rich sap derived from the root of the olive tree, that faith-filled channel of spiritual nourishment found in Abraham and his descendants. In this way non-Jews join the faithful remnant of the Jewish people. But Halvor Ronning is correct in pointing out that "even the secular Jews must be accepted as somehow a part of the family. However problematic it may seem, we gain some kind of special relationship even to them."[7] Thus the biblical answer of who joins whom is clear: we non-Jewish believers, formerly excluded from partnership with Israel (see Eph. 2:12), are joined to Israel in this divinely ordained olive tree connection (Rom. 11:24). In short, Israel is the people we join.

Through faith, as exemplified in the life of father Abraham, non-Jews

5. For a biblical exposition of this theme, see my earlier work, *Our Father Abraham: Jewish Roots of the Christian Faith* (Grand Rapids: Eerdmans, 1989); in addition, see in this present volume chapters 5 and 6 below: "Abraham: The World's 'First Jew'" and "Thinking Theologically about Abraham."

6. See the helpful exposition of this point by Halvor Ronning, "The Land of Israel: A Christian Zionist View," *Immanuel* 22/23 (1989): 125-26.

7. Ronning, "The Land of Israel," p. 125.

come into the family of Abraham (Romans 4). When an individual becomes a follower of Jesus and exercises genuine faith like Abraham, that new believer is grafted into the Abrahamic people. This olive tree connection allows those on the outside — Gentiles who have no claim on the promises of God or the spiritual heritage of Israel — to be joined to Israel through the mysterious process of ingrafting. From our Christian perspective, at the moment of belief, Israel's God becomes our God; her Scriptures become our Scriptures. Israel's prophets, psalmists, and sages become our spiritual mentors. Israel's family history becomes our history. A new realization grips us: it was *our* ancestors under Moses who passed through the waters of the Red Sea (1 Cor. 10:1, 2). Israel's heroes of the faith become our heroes (see Hebrews 11). The ethical, spiritual, and worship principles that governed Israel's relationships now become a vital part of our walk with God. Israel's anticipation of a fully redeemed society becomes our hope too.

This priceless heritage is not genetically acquired; it must be personally owned. It is not a gift to be *passively* received but a legacy that must be *actively* seized. Our biblical, Hebraic heritage is not the dead faith of the living but the living faith of the dead. It is not a relic to put in a museum but a life-giving source to embrace. There is no way the church may define itself without being connected to the people of Israel.

Christianity 101

The idea that Christianity 101 begins with Abraham is a stark and difficult notion for many Christians to grasp. But this is how the New Testament explains it. The earliest church saw itself as an extension of Israel, not the replacement of Israel. This is one reason why Abraham is appealed to again and again in the pages of the New Testament. His life was an inspiring example for the apostolic church. He was *their* man. The New Testament was not written to provide information about a new plan God had devised on how humankind can build a proper relation with God. To the contrary! Paul's argument is that an individual must come into a relationship with God Abraham's way or that one has chosen the wrong way. Abraham was a man of faith. He believed God and it was credited to him for righteousness (Rom. 4:3). He therefore sets a course of spiritual action, a righteous standard for all who would follow him and be his true children (see Gen. 18:19). Abraham's life is characterized by trusting or believing God. But Abraham's faith was more than an attitude of the heart; his faith was also an action. This man of faith voted with his feet. Amidst a polytheistic environment, God called and Abraham responded in faith. He "obeyed and went, even though he did not know where he was going" (Heb. 11:8).

In a profound sense, Abraham's name is crucial to the beginning and the end of the New Testament story. (See the next two chapters for a fuller discussion of this point.) The New Testament opens prominently with Abraham: "A record of the genealogy of Jesus Christ the son of David, the son of Abraham. Abraham was the father of Isaac . . ." (Matt. 1:1-2). The story of the New Testament ends with the triumph of Abraham. How so? In Genesis, God promised this man, "all peoples on earth will be blessed through you" (Gen. 12:3). Abraham's seed is the vehicle through which many spiritual gifts would come to the entire world. As God's chosen, Abraham's descendants were to be "a light for the Gentiles" (Isa. 42:6) and a source of "riches for the Gentiles" (Rom. 11:12). Through a particular man, Abraham, God's faithful servant, God purposes to bring universal blessing to the world.

Jesus builds on this point in his teaching regarding the outworking of the kingdom of God in the age to come. In Jesus' day, the righteous dead were gathered to the bosom of Abraham (Luke 16:22). In this connection, Manfred Gorg observes, "Abraham is truly the root and home of all the righteous. This idea is connected also to the meaning of the word *heq* in Hebrew, which can mean both 'lap' and 'breast' or 'bosom.' The meaning is very simple: one can lean on this Abraham because in the consciousness of Israel and Judaism he *is* the righteous person as such. All the dead can rest in him and take to themselves the bliss of the presence of the righteous father of faith."[8]

Further, Jesus says Abraham will appear at a heavenly banquet and will sit at table with the righteous from all parts of the earth. At this eschatological banquet, "People will come from east and west and north and south and will take their places at the feast" (Luke 13:29). This marks the triumph of Abraham. Here is the connecting of the two dots: Abraham of the past (promise) and Abraham of the future (fulfillment). God accomplishes what he said he would do through Abraham. Thus Abraham fittingly has an important place in the final chapter of Christianity 101. (For additional reflection on Abraham, see chapters 5 and 6 below.)

---

8. Manfred Gorg, *In Abraham's Bosom: Christianity without the New Testament,* trans. Linda M. Maloney (Collegeville, MN: Liturgical Press, 1999), p. 130.

Saving Face

Throughout the centuries, Christianity has to some degree become covered over by various masks. Not every mask fully obliterated or significantly distorted the original Jewish face of Christianity. All movements grow and change with time, but from the perspective of our spiritual forebears of Bible times, some aspects of modern Christianity may appear unrecognizable or even faceless. It would seem that a primary task of one who seeks to be a "biblical" Christian would involve a commitment to try to recover and restore as much as is possible of the original face of Christianity. For a faith to declare itself "biblical," it must make every effort to understand itself in biblical categories. This may require peeling off some of the masks or layers, which hide, paint over, or make obscure the rich first-century Jewish context of the early church.

When we scan today's church scene, what do we often see? We observe cosmetic or surface-type expressions of Christianity that lack any real depth or rootedness, any sense of historical connectedness. Shallowness, superficiality, and emotional mush have unfortunately become apt descriptors for many current expressions of Christianity. If the Hebraic features of the church's original face are to be uncovered and warmly embraced, it may require considerable time to scrape away at some of the layers built up over time. This is the road to acquire the legacy. But is it worth it? I believe so, for it has the potential to lead the discoverer to a more biblically authentic expression of Christian thought and practice. Should that not be one of the great essentials of the Christian life?

Today's church attracts men and women for a variety of reasons. Some become involved with the church primarily for social-psychological considerations. They may be hurting, but they sense the need to connect with people and enjoy the fellowship of the body. Others may be drawn to a church because they like a particular pastor's personality or preaching. In other situations, people may fellowship with a congregation because they like the music, the liturgy, or aesthetic touch of the sanctuary. Some individuals attend church services because they want to adhere to a longtime family tradition or because they sense attendance is an expectation of the culture around them. Then there are those on the extreme periphery of the church who are minimalists, those whose connection with the church could be dubbed as representative of the hatch, match, and dispatch syndrome. In this last case, the church is primarily a local religious vehicle for necessary life-cycle events such as baptism, marriage, and burial.

Many of the above reasons motivate people to connect with the church; they have an important role in helping Christians fulfill their various family, social, and personal needs. All of them, however, are lacking in another very basic Christian need. All Christians need solid scriptural grounding through regular study of the Word of God. Scripture is the bread of life and all believers need to be fed by that Word. Here the teaching function of the church comes into play. Because believers need to be edified in the Word of God, the need for communal study must also be a critical priority in motivating Christians to be part of the church family.

Why should Christians study? The church has a venerable theological and ethical history behind it that must not be neglected. The church seems perpetually to go through an identity crisis. Its historic identity, however, derives primarily from the biblical world. That foundational identity is established in the biblical text, but it is also further clarified through other ancient sources that shed light on the biblical text. Though the identity of the church may be marred or seemingly eroded, the church indeed has a face. We discover the contour of that face when we go back to the foundations of the church. The foundations of our Christian faith reveal a face we in the West may not readily recognize — for the face has Hebraic features. In the Western world, when one observes a congregation at worship at a typical Sunday morning service, the face of the church often does not reflect its eastern Hebraic origin. The church's Jewish roots have often become truncated or obscured due to hundreds of years of adversarial history between the synagogue — the ancient context where the church began — and the modern church.

A further reason why the Hebraic face of the church has largely disappeared is a result of faulty theological thinking within the church. Especially during the early Christian centuries when the church and synagogue were in the process of parting company, each community sought to define itself over against the other. There was a tendency to emphasize dissimilarities, those areas where one differed from one's opponent. Over the centuries this "oppositional" language of the church — a people unfortunately too eager to put distance between itself and those in the synagogue — left the church largely disinterested in and disconnected from its Hebraic past.

The division was further exacerbated in the church through an emerging theology that understood the term "new covenant" to mean "brand new," "first edition," or "newly invented." Since there was a "new covenant," many Christians — without giving "new" much thought — became semantically preconditioned to understand "old covenant" as that which was passé, fully antiquated, and superseded. Rather, the theological expression "new covenant" builds on the earlier "old covenant." Thus "new" suggests a "refreshing," "renewing," or "recent updating" of the original (older) covenant of grace that became enlarged anew and to its fullest expression of grace in the coming of Jesus (see Luke 1:32, 33, 67-73). The earlier Abrahamic covenant was one of grace; it was later enlarged and expanded in expression and features through the establishment of the Sinaitic covenant and the Davidic covenant. In short, Christians believed their "new" covenant had replaced the older covenant God had made with the Jewish people. As the saying goes, "Who wants to keep an old car if you can have a new one?"

The above misunderstanding by Christians of "old" and "new" covenant further led to faulty thinking about God, the plan for his people, and the overall importance of the Jewish Scriptures. This was largely born out of a misreading of Scripture that essentially taught that God's Plan A, found in the Old Testament, was a failure because it was based on law. For Old Testament people, God had set up a system of keeping commandments, bringing animal sacrifices, and performing good deeds. Israel, however, failed to perform what God required. So God scrapped the old covenant and instituted a "new covenant," Plan B. This new covenant would be characterized by and built upon faith, grace, and love, not one of law and good works.

Thus the Jewish Scriptures (the Old Testament) largely became deprecated by many Christians. The Old Testament Scriptures were viewed as being of little value because they represented a dead and legalistic faith, one superseded by a better way, the Christian way. In the process, tragically few within the church considered the fact that the Bible, which the church had declared "old" and hence inferior and so replaced by a "new" testament, was in reality the Bible of Jesus and the early church. The message of the Hebrew Scriptures (the Old Testament) and the ongoing significance of God's eternal purposes for the Jewish people must be affirmed by today's church if biblical Christianity is spiritually to save face.

Family Resemblance

If the above argument is valid, that Gentiles are grafted into Israel and that Abraham is the father of every Christian, then there ought to be a family resemblance between Christians and Jews. When we carefully look at this question historically, we can begin to understand why Christians and Jews today share far more in common — even after two thousand years — than they differ. First, in terms of spiritual genealogy, Christians and Jews have the same grandparents, those God-inspired people who developed the religion of ancient Israel. The Hebrew people, through the Holy Spirit, produced the Scriptures of the First Testament, beginning with the Writings of Moses. These Scriptures were the foundational source influencing New Testament thought and practice. Accordingly, every Christian today is theologically dependent upon them and is shaped by them.

Some examples of the above are worthy to note. Genesis provides the Hebraic roots for our understanding of creation, the fall, covenant, faith, and the messianic promise. The Book of Exodus reveals the power of the God of Israel in the plagues and release from Egypt. Exodus also instructs us on the Passover (the background to the Last Supper), redemption, and the ethical foundations encapsulated in the Ten Commandments. In Exodus we have the Hebraic origin of the seven-branched *menorah* or candelabrum used in many churches, and we are also introduced to the concept of a sanctuary for worship. Leviticus gives us an understanding of the priesthood, sin, atonement, and the holiness of God. Leviticus also commands us to love our neighbor as ourselves (Lev. 19:18). Numbers provides principles of organization, leadership, and accountability for God's people in transition from the wilderness to the Promised Land. Deuteronomy affirms the oneness of God and his desire that his people intently love him in all their ways (Deut. 6:4-9). The book of Deuteronomy also gives us foundational teaching on the family and human sexuality, and on issues of social justice such as caring for the poor, widows, orphans, and strangers.

It is in the Torah of Moses that we also learn about the Hebraic origin of the altar, use of vestments by religious leaders, and the practice of self-denial, commonly expressed in fasting (Lev. 16:29). Furthermore, here we have the earliest mention of the appointment of elders (Num. 11:16, 24, 25), the laying on of hands (Deut. 34:9), and the role of women in the exercise of ministry gifts. For the latter, note the example of Miriam who worships with song, musical instrument, and dance at the Red Sea (Exod. 15:20, 21). All of the above concepts and emphases are built upon in the New Testament.

After the time of Moses, others among our Hebrew grandparents added further to what has come to be understood as the Hebraic heritage of Christianity. For example, Israel saw herself as a witnessing community to outsiders, as did the early church (Isa. 43:10, 12; Jonah 1:2; 3:2; see also Acts 1:8). The use of poetry set to music, as found in the Book of Psalms, plays prominently in ancient Israel. This practice is continued by the Qumran community as seen in the *Hodyoth* or Thanksgiving Psalms. During King

Hezekiah's day (eighth to seventh century B.C.), singers sang in the Temple as the offerings were made (2 Chron. 29:25-30). The Book of Ezra makes special mention of 128 Levitical singers (descendants of Asaph) and two hundred men and women singers who returned from Babylonian captivity under Zerubbabel to be on hand for the rebuilding of the Temple (Ezra 2:41, 65). The important place of music in Israel clearly influenced the use of psalms, hymns, and spiritual songs in the apostolic church (1 Cor. 14:26; Eph. 5:19; Col. 3:16; also Mark 14:26). In addition, the biblical, Hebraic use of liturgy and liturgical formulas such as "Amen" and "Hallelujah," the public reading of Scripture (Josh. 8:30-35; Neh. 8:1-3), the practice of interpreting or explaining Scripture (Neh. 8:8; also Acts 8:30-35), and use of a raised platform or pulpit (Neh. 8:4) all find parallels in early Christianity.

In addition to claiming the same grandparent — although not in identical ways — Christians and Jews also share the same *parent*. After the close of the Old Testament, the grandparent faith underwent certain modifications in response to a changing political, social, and cultural climate. After the time of Ezra (fifth century B.C.) in the Intertestamental Period and also into New Testament times, this emerging religion was referred to as Judaism (see 2 Macc. 2:21; 8:1; Gal. 1:13, 14). Between the testaments, the Jewish community produced a Greek translation of the Hebrew Scriptures (the Septuagint) for Jews outside the land of Israel and also established synagogues where Jews could study, pray, and find community support. Modern biblical scholars use several terms for the Judaism from which the church was parented. These include Biblical Judaism, Second Temple Judaism, or pre-70 Judaism. During the first century, Judaism was hardly monolithic; it was largely sectarian. It was comprised of a mosaic of many different "Judaisms." Some of the groups known from the New Testament and/or other writings include the Pharisees, Nazarenes, Sadducees, Herodians, Zealots, and Essenes.

Paul indicates he was a Pharisee and came from a family of Pharisees (Phil. 3:5; Acts 23:6). Though the New Testament does not explicitly state that Jesus belonged to the party of the Pharisees, he had considerable contact with Pharisees, and in many areas his teachings paralleled those of the Pharisees. For example, Jesus and the Pharisees drew heavily upon the Law, Prophets, and Writings of the Hebrew Bible. By contrast, the Sadducees primarily taught from the Law of Moses. Like the Pharisees, Jesus emphasized prayer, fasting, good deeds, demons and angels, rewards and punishment, and the resurrection of the dead.

In the first century, Judaism was very diversified and sectarian. Only two of the main sects of Judaism survived the year A.D. 70, the date Jerusalem and its Temple were overthrown by Rome. One group was the Pharisees, the other the Nazarenes. Each of these Jewish sects was part of Second Temple Judaism. The Pharisees and Nazarenes were scrapping siblings locked in an intramural debate. At times heated and emotional, this rivalry has been present for nearly two millennia as synagogue and church have continued to define their relationship to each other.

The Pharisees found themselves without a Temple, priesthood, or sacrificial system. Out of necessity, the Pharisees began to reformulate Judaism so it could function in the diaspora under the leadership of scholar-teachers known as rabbis. These rabbinic sages continued to develop Judaism through a particular emphasis on Oral Law and commentary, through *halakhah* and *aggadah*. Today, Modern Judaism, in its various expressions, is a further development of Rabbinic Judaism.

The Nazarenes, the other Jewish sect to survive the year 70, were originally comprised of the Jewish followers of Jesus. Like the pharisaic movement, this Jesus movement was an outgrowth of Second Temple Judaism. For at least the first twenty years of the church, one could not belong to the church unless one was a Jew by birth or a convert to Judaism. The rise of Jewish Christianity was accompanied by a rapid influx of non-Jews into the church (see Acts 15). With non-Jewish believers rapidly coming into positions of church leadership, especially in the diaspora, the church experienced a gradual falling away from many Jewish practices such as circumcision, Sabbath observance, and the keeping of dietary laws.

Shallow or Rotted Roots

Modern Christians study the Bible from a variety of different perspectives. Some read the Bible through denominational eyes. For example, they give preference to a Baptist or a Catholic or a Methodist or other denominationally approved theological perspective on Scripture. To be sure, different denominations are useful in highlighting certain emphases of the biblical text that otherwise might be muted or lost. When seeking to achieve an accurate understanding of the text, however, it is this writer's conviction that one's highest allegiance should not be to defend a particular denominational slant or perspective. Why? Every denomination has its blind spots and limitations. In addition, many denominations originally came into being to counteract error or to reform the perceived faulty teachings or omissions of other groups. Thus, some denominations may be somewhat theologically lopsided and not sufficiently nuanced as to reflect a healthy, well-rounded biblical perspective in their theological statements.

Other Christians may read or understand the Bible through the eyes of a favorite theologian, a particular Reformer or some prominent Christian writer or preacher. All thinking Christians, to be sure, will be influenced by the works or voices of those theologians they read and respect the most. It can be an exceedingly valuable experience to delve into the writings of various theological greats. The Augustines, Luthers, Calvins, Wesleys, Barths, and others certainly have an important place among the masters of theological literature and the history of Christian thought. However, we must always remember that every theologian — with no exception — is *human* and therefore fallible and subject to theological blind spots. Also, no theologian — as brilliant as he may be — has said it all. Thus a theologian may be limited in perspective and capability and may miss certain important nuances of scriptural teaching.

Still other Christians may approach the Bible through the lens of some overarching theological system or orientation. They may take a Covenantal or Dispensational approach to biblical interpretation. Their orientation may be strongly influenced by a fundamentalistic, existentialist, neo-orthodox, or other perspective. They may view the Bible through the eyes of process theology or liberation theology or other systems of thought. There is much to learn from many of the above points of view. However, if the Bible has system, it is preferable to discover that system inductively, from the phenomena of the biblical text, rather than trying deductively to impose a particular perspective or orientation on the Bible. The Word of God should not become a slave to any system. It is always preferable to shape system by Scripture rather than Scripture by system.

The above paragraphs raise a question: How deep do our roots as believers really go? Many Christians claim to be "biblical" Christians. Their understanding of the Christian faith, however, may in the end be shaped far more by a denominational creed, a Reformer, a church father, a theological system, or some other perspective than it is shaped by a personal grappling with the biblical text. Again, this is not to say the above perspectives are wrong in themselves. There is much that may be useful about each. They are limited, however, in what they can do. A preferable approach is to return whenever possible to the biblical text as the primary source. When the biblical Hebraic roots of the Christian faith are uncovered, we have a preventative against leaning too heavily on theological systems or denominational loyalties, or pitting personal preferences of one theologian over another. The goal of the biblical interpreter should not be to dismiss *a priori* all denominations, theologians, or theological systems of thought. Rather the goal should be to test these against the Hebraic context of Scripture, the main cultural background in which the Bible was written and from which the concepts of biblical theology arise. A biblical Christianity that does not reflect the influence of Israelite religion and Second Temple Judaism upon that faith may be defective and not truly biblical.

Irreconcilable Differences?

The history of Christian-Jewish relations reveals a very turbulent and rocky past. Bad attitudes often lead to bad language, and bad language frequently leads to bad actions. Throughout the centuries, each group has hurled stones at the other. In the Christian-Jewish encounter, faulty theology by some Christians has led to faulty behavior toward Jews. Paying no attention to Paul's warning about boastfulness and arrogance (Rom. 11:18-20), certain professing Christians, in or nearby the church, have unfortunately accounted for much ill-treatment of the Jewish people.

Jews sometimes responded to these assaults out of self-defense. More often, however, once Christianity became the dominant religion with strength in number and political power, especially from the fourth century on, the Jewish people became very marginalized by the church. Anti-Judaism led to increasing acts of hostility and hatred directed toward Jews. Christianity had begun as a movement within Judaism, but Christianity, the younger sibling, had turned against its elder sibling Judaism. In 1965, the Second Vatican Council issued a document, *Nostra Aetate,* which called for some revolutionary changes in Roman Catholic theology pertaining to Jews and Judaism. Especially in the decades immediately following this historic Vatican Council, many mainstream Protestant denominations likewise began to issue constructive and conciliatory statements concerning the church and the Jewish people. Our debt to the Jewish people is great. If the church takes ownership of the spiritual heritage of its past, the church must also face up to the ignominious actions of its past.

While we cannot change the largely negative history of earlier generations, it should be the desire of every Christian to work at building more positive Christian-Jewish relations in the future. Reconciliation is a process. It begins with the restoration of the church to its Jewish roots. Restoration involves recovery, and recovery is the process of getting well. When the church gets to know its Hebraic family roots and truly acknowledges and accepts its place within that family, new life and vigor will begin to flow from the church's withered and rotted roots. In this process, the Jewish people are a living reminder of the faithfulness of God and his purposes in history. For as David affirmed, God established his people Israel as his "very own forever" (2 Sam. 7:24).

Restoration to the church's Hebraic heritage is an important first step if the church is to move on to the next step and begin to be reconciled to the Jewish people. Christians and Jews have too long passed as ships in the night. Christians are never called to force their religion on other people; rather they do have an obligation to provoke others to holy envy (Rom. 10:19; 11:11, 14). The history of Christian-Jewish relations painfully reveals that Christians can convert no one; only God can change a human heart. Tragically, Christians have often provoked Jews to anger through actions not befitting the message spoken with their "Christian" lips. Accordingly, as Richard Booker has sagely pointed out, "While we understand that Christians and Jews have theological differences, we do not have to agree on theology in order to love one another. And if we cannot love one another, what good is our theology?"[9]

Unless God the Ultimate Reconciler directly intervenes, Christians and Jews will continue to live with theological differences and tensions until the *eschaton* fully dawns. Everyone wants to be right and see the beauty and power of his own religion vindicated in the eyes of the world. The Hebrew Bible again and again speaks of the expectation of the vindication of the God of Israel and the people of Israel before the nations of the earth. During biblical times, Israel was involved in a "battle of the gods." So too the church, since its inception, sees itself finally triumphant with Jesus as messiah and savior of the world. The church has received a mandate from its savior to proclaim God's good news to the entire world (Matt. 28:19, 20; Acts 1:8; Rom. 10:13-15).

Herein lies the ultimate tension. Who would want to hold to a set of religious beliefs and practices that, in the end, were the result of deception or untruthfulness? Certainly, a religion that is mainly intended to be meaningful to its practitioners and to make them feel good would, in the final analysis, be little more than a healing fiction. Many Christians and Jews also feel it is important that a religion reflect truth and the reality of divine

9. Quoted from Richard Booker, "Ten Commandments of Christian-Jewish Relationships," at Institute for Hebraic-Christian Studies, Houston, TX, www.rbooker.com.

revelation in history. Did the one eternal God speak to Abraham in Ur or was he just a product of a superstitious age and, accordingly, did Abraham merely experience some unknown voice in his head? Christians and Jews will not always agree on what revelation is, but it is more honest to live with theological tensions in relation to each other than to change one's theology or renounce core distinctives out of compromise. Without mutual respect, the process of reconciliation cannot advance.

What is needed is a measure of humility and modesty amidst theological claims. As for Christians, according to the New Testament, God sovereignly permitted Israel's "blindness," and only he can remove it (see Rom. 11:8-11). But Israel's lack of an overwhelming response to the church's position on Messiah was in God's plan intended to bring riches to the Gentiles. We are dealing with a mystery (Rom. 11:33-36). Christians and Jews must therefore reconcile as far as is possible, knowing that no human can remove the final darkness that separates us. Only when the Reconciler comes will the perfect achievement of this hope be realized.

UNDERSTANDING CHAPTER FOUR

1. What is the Table of Nations (see Genesis 10)? How might it communicate the idea of completeness in relation to the command given by God to Noah and his sons in Genesis 9:1?

2. From which son of Noah did Abraham descend?

3. In the author's opinion, who is the one to live "in the tents of Shem" in Genesis 9:27? Why? What does the concept of living in someone else's tent entail? In your opinion, what are the implications of this concept for a modern-day Christian exploring his or her Semitic roots?

4. What is often the first inclination of many Christians when articulating their spiritual identity? In contrast, what does the author point out regarding the origin of New Testament theology in answering the question, Who joins whom?

5. With whom do Christians find their *earliest* spiritual identity? What is one passage cited from the letters of Paul that succinctly illustrates this relationship? For additional consideration, review Galatians 3:16 and the surrounding context. With a group or partner, explore what it means to share in the identity of that *one* seed.

6. By what mysterious process do Gentiles join Israel? Review Romans 9–11 (particularly 11:11-24; see also Eph. 3:6) for the apostle Paul's ar-

ticulation of the mystery. What are some implications of this point of connection that the author lists in terms of family history? What additional implications come to mind for you?

7. What is one reason, concerning the perspective of the early church, that Abraham is appealed to again and again in the New Testament?

8. In what way may Abraham be seen as crucial to both the beginning and the end of the New Testament story? According to Manfred Gorg's observation on Luke 16:22, what biblical figure of speech during the time of Jesus is used for the place of honor where the righteous Jewish dead were thought to lean and rest?

9. In a group or with a partner, explore the idea of historical connectedness. How much attention has been given to the concept in your own church tradition or background? Do you think it should be a priority to sharpen this sense amidst the many expressions of Christianity today? Why or why not?

10. In light of numerous social and personal considerations, what particularly must be a critical priority in motivating Christians to be part of the church family and why?

11. What emphases characterized the process of self-definition for the synagogue and church in the early Christian centuries? How did these contribute to the disappearance of the Hebraic face of the church at large?

12. In what ways are many Christians semantically preconditioned to understand the role of the "new covenant"? How might the term "new" be better understood when exploring the relationship between the "new" and "old" covenants?

13. Who is the grandparent shared by Jews and Christians? The roots of which important concepts integral to both Judaism and Christianity lie in the Writings of Moses?

14. Trace the importance of music in Judaism and Christianity back to its Hebraic roots. Identify some examples of biblical texts in which we find testimony to its early prominence and purpose.

15. In addition to a common grandparent, modern-day Judaism and Christianity also share which *parent*? Around what point in history did it emerge, and what are three interchangeable names used to designate this parent?

16. What were the two main sects of Judaism that survived after A.D. 70? In what ways did these two groups fall away from one another as each continued to refine its identity?

17. What are three lenses through which the Bible is commonly approached by modern Christians? What are some benefits and dangers of each lens? What does the author suggest is the best approach? How would you balance these (and/or other) elements for a proper approach?

18. In what way did the Second Vatican Council serve as a model concerning Christians' relations to Jews in the modern world? What year did this landmark event occur, and what happened in other Christian denominations in the decades immediately following?

19. In the final section of this chapter, in the view of the author, what are the two important first steps in the recovery process involving restoration and reconciliation?

20. Discuss the following statement of Richard Booker: "While we understand that Christians and Jews have theological differences, we do not have to agree on theology in order to love one another. And if we cannot love one another, what good is our theology?" In the above context, how does love relate to truth? In your view, is one of these words superior to the other? Why?

CHAPTER 5

Abraham: The World's "First Jew"

In the previous chapter we emphasized that Christians find their deepest spiritual identity in an Abrahamic family. Through faith we are grafted into the family of our father Abraham. According to Scripture, Abraham is an honored father figure in our spiritual family portrait. Accordingly, it behooves us to make a rather careful study of the person of Abraham to discover the profound influence he has exerted upon Jews and Christians. Such will be our focus in this and the following chapter.

Abraham may be deceased, but he is not dead; he lives on in both Judaism and Christianity. How so? In Judaism, Abraham is not a principle or an idea to be comprehended but an exemplary life to be continued. In the words of A. J. Heschel, "The life of him who joins the covenant of Abraham continues the life of Abraham. For the present is not apart from the past. . . . Abraham endures forever. We are Abraham."[1] Regarding Christianity, Karl-Josef Kuschel makes a similar observation about Abraham, but in relation to the apostle Paul: "Anyone who reads Paul will immediately note that for him, as any Jew, Abraham is not a memorial of faith from distant, past times, but a living reality."[2] To be sure, the Abrahamic legacy has endured nearly four thousand years. Judaism and Christianity each look to Abraham as father.[3] The biblical phrase, "our/your father Abraham" (Isa. 51:2; Luke

1. Abraham J. Heschel, *God in Search of Man* (New York: Farrar, Straus & Giroux, 1955), p. 201.

2. Karl-Josef Kuschel, *Abraham: Sign of Hope for Jews, Christians and Muslims* (New York: Continuum, 1995), p. 82.

3. As a monotheistic religion, Islam considers Abraham (Ibhraim) to be father of Muslims. He is mentioned frequently in the Qur'an. However, the Qur'an states, "Abraham was neither Jew, nor Christian; but he was true in faith, and bowed his will to Allah" (3:67). Abra-

1:72; James 2:21) expresses the family relationship that every person of faith has with "the man of faith"; it also emphasizes the deep spiritual link every Christian has with the Jewish people (see Gal. 3:29).

In the shared Judeo-Christian tradition, Abraham is a major figure; references to him abound from antiquity to the present. One would expect therefore that Jews and Christians find considerable common ground and a convergence of their respective traditions in their discussion of Abraham. Looking at this issue historically, Jon Levenson has correctly observed that "[t]he community of Torah [Judaism] and the community of the Gospel [Christianity] would appeal to the same Scriptures . . . and seek to practice virtues that overlap to a high degree. . . . This is as we should expect from traditions that each revere the memory of Father Abraham."[4] Certainly, Abraham is an inspiring figure around whom Jews and Christians find many areas of agreement. The biblical narratives about him contain many foundational theological themes and ethical teachings, which have shaped the core of Judaism and Christianity.

On the other hand, Jews and Christians diverge in a number of ways in their understanding of Abraham. Just as the New Testament writers and church fathers took the Jewish Scriptures and developed a Christian theology regarding Abraham, so the rabbis of the post-biblical era had their own distinct Jewish take on those same Scriptures. In terms of interpretation and emphasis, this has resulted in some significant areas of difference between the two faiths. In the end, Judaism and Christianity claim one father, Abraham. But as rival siblings, synagogue and church have understood and related to their father from different perspectives. Strong family resemblance and ties? Yes. Identical points of view? No.

I have divided this chapter into two main sections. The first emphasizes the importance of Abraham in Jewish tradition. The second sets forth the importance of Abraham in Christian tradition.

The Significance of Abraham in Jewish Tradition

Abraham is father of the Jewish people (Isa. 51:2). Hence he is often referred to as the first Jew, the founder of the faith.[5] The annual Torah reading cycle

---

ham is identified with the Kaaba, a cubical building in the courtyard of the mosque at Mecca containing a sacred black stone. A mosque in Hebron marks his burial place.

4. Jon D. Levenson, *The Death and Resurrection of the Beloved Son* (New Haven: Yale University Press, 1993), p. 219.

5. Abba Hillel Silver, *Where Judaism Differed* (New York: Macmillan, 1956), p. 81.

places particular focus on Abraham in the narrative of Genesis 11:26–25:11. In Ur of the Chaldees, God reveals himself to Abraham and leads him out of an idolatrous way of life (see Josh. 24:2).[6]

A Person of Character and Faithful Obedience

Abraham keeps responding to God in faithful obedience. God promises Abraham numerous descendants, a land, and that the nations will be blessed through him. God sovereignly enters into a covenant relation with Abraham and establishes circumcision as a sign of that bond. Abraham faithfully walks with God, obeys him, and trusts him. God tests the depth of Abraham's commitment to him by telling him to bind his only son Isaac and prepare him for sacrifice, and Abraham willingly obeys. At the last moment, however, God dramatically intervenes to save the life of Abraham's beloved son. Abraham passes this ultimate test. Consequently, the Jewish Scriptures sum up the life of Abraham by stating that God "found his heart faithful *(ne'eman)*" (Neh. 9:8).

Abraham is the first person in the Bible to be called a Hebrew (Gen. 14:13) and the first to bear the title "prophet" (Gen. 20:7; also Ps. 105:15) and is given the title "anointed one" (see Ps. 105:15).[7] In an address to all Israel, Joshua refers to the patriarch as "your father Abraham" (Josh. 24:3). In the prophets,[8] God calls Abraham "my friend"*(ohabi)* (Isa. 41:8). The Psalms speak of Abraham as God's "servant" (Ps. 105:42) and refer to the Israelites as "the descendants of Abraham" (Ps. 105:6) and "the people of the God of Abraham" (Ps. 47:9). Centuries later the Jewish sages succinctly summarized their great esteem of Abraham and his unique place in Jewish religion: "Five possessions has the Holy One, blessed be He, made especially his own. These are: the Torah, Heaven and earth, Abraham, Israel, and the Holy Sanctuary" (Abot 6:10).

6. For two important essays on the historical and theological background to the life of Abraham see Edwin M. Yamauchi, "Abraham and Archaeology: Anachronisms or Adaptations?" in *Perspectives on Our Father Abraham*, ed. Steven A. Hunt (Grand Rapids: Eerdmans, 2010), pp. 15-32, and John N. Oswalt, "Abraham's Experience of Yahweh: An Argument for the Historicity of the Patriarchal Narratives," also in Hunt, ed., *Perspectives on Our Father Abraham*, pp. 33-43.

7. For a stimulating discussion of Abraham in Psalm 105 and the title "anointed one," see the essay of Ted Hildebrandt, "A Song of Our Father Abraham: Psalm 105," in Hunt, ed., *Perspectives on Our Father Abraham*, pp. 44-67.

8. Cf. Abraham J. Heschel, *The Prophets* (New York: Harper & Row, 1962), p. 311.

A Compassionate Soul

In the Talmud, God is referred to as *Rachmana,* "The Compassionate." Like father Abraham, children of Abraham are to show compassion, mercy, and kindness to others. "Whoever is merciful to his fellow-man is certainly of the children of our father Abraham, and whosoever is not merciful to his fellow-men is certainly not of the children of our father Abraham" (Babylonian Talmud, Bezah 32b; see also Yebamot 79a). Humaneness, sensitivity to hurt, and hospitality to strangers are hallmarks of the Jewish tradition. In Genesis 18:1-15, Abraham, with the help of Sarah, warmly welcomes and entertains three visitors. It is therefore apropos in the Psalms that God twice characterizes Abraham as "his servant" (105:6, 42).

The actions of Abraham found in the narrative of Genesis set a standard in Jewish tradition for the practice of hospitality built upon Abraham's example of servanthood to strangers. In Jewish tradition, hospitality, *hakhnasat orḥim,* literally "bringing in of guests" or "gathering in of travelers," became one of the most important functions of the home.[9]

Man of Justice

Abraham also shows great concern for justice. In Genesis 18:16-33, Abraham, moved with justice and compassion over Sodom, engages God in dialogue. Appropriately, Martin Buber has characterized religious faith in terms of dialogue, an "I and Thou" relationship.[10] Abraham's passionate pleading with God to spare human life results in "one of the most famous and boldest intercessory prayers in all of Scripture."[11] What is all the more remarkable about Abraham's concern is the fact that he intercedes for an evil place inhabited by a people with whom he has no personal ties. Abraham is concerned that justice be tempered with mercy; hence he argues with God that he not bring

9. For additional development of this same theme see Marvin R. Wilson, *Our Father Abraham: Jewish Roots of the Christian Faith* (Grand Rapids: Eerdmans, 1989), pp. 219-20. Also note the recently discovered synagogue mosaic (fifth century A.D.) at Sepphoris in Galilee, which may contain some of the earliest-known Jewish art of the three angelic visitors to Abraham and Sarah. See Zeev Weiss, "The Sepphoris Synagogue Mosaic," *Biblical Archaeology Review* 26, no. 5 (2000): 48-61, 70.

10. See Martin Buber, *I and Thou,* trans. Ronald Gregor Smith (New York: Scribner's, 1937, 1958); trans. Walter Kaufman (New York: Scribner's, 1970).

11. Ronald Youngblood, *Faith of Our Fathers* (Glendale, CA: Regal Books, 1976), p. 43.

destruction if ten righteous ones can be found. God repeats his willingness to be merciful for the sake of the righteous. Abraham's nobility of character emerges with his anguished cry for justice. All human beings are his brothers, and he wants the Judge of all the earth to do right (Gen. 18:25). Abraham's dialogue with God sets a historic tone. As Abraham displayed God's attributes of justice and mercy, so the actions of Abraham's children must reflect the same.

First "Missionary"

Judaism considers Abraham the "first great missionary in the world."[12] Abraham breaks with the deities of ancestral paganism and embraces the monotheistic ideal. The biblical record indicates Abraham was a rich merchant-trader who roamed across the Fertile Crescent. Called to be a blessing to humankind, Abraham, through his journeying from place to place, bore the message of only One God (see Gen. 12:2-3). Commenting on a midrashic parable about Abraham, Chaim Pearl points out that because Abraham was a "wandering Jew," Abraham could reach a wider population and so have greater influence.[13]

According to Samson Raphael Hirsch, the Israelites might have perished like their idolatrous neighbors had they not "received from Abraham the courage to be a minority."[14] Males who convert to Judaism recall Abraham through the covenant of circumcision, which God instituted with the patriarch. The rabbis taught, "If a proselyte wants to become a Jew, he should not say: I am an old man. At this stage I am not becoming a Jew. Let him learn from Abraham, who performed circumcision when he was ninety-nine years old" (Tanhuma, Buber, Lekh-Lekha, Gen. 17:24). Over the centuries, many converts to Judaism have chosen for themselves the Hebrew name, Avraham, as part of their conversion.

Merit of the Fathers

In the liturgy of the synagogue, Abraham is remembered in the *Amidah* or *Shemoneh Esrai* prayer, recited in the three daily prayer services. The first

12. Cf. Solomon Schechter, *Aspects of Rabbinic Theology* (New York: Schocken, 1961), p. 84.

13. Chaim Pearl, *Theology in Rabbinic Stories* (Peabody, MA: Hendrickson, 1997), p. 70.

14. Quoted in Paul Carlson, *O Christian! O Jew!* (Elgin, IL: David C. Cook, 1974), p. 14.

paragraph of the prayer begins, "Blessed are you, Lord our God, and God of our fathers, God of Abraham, God of Isaac, and God of Jacob." The paragraph ends, "Blessed are you, God, shield of Abraham" *(magen avraham)*. Why is Abraham singled out among the three forefathers? Abraham was the person responsible for creating an "indestructible spiritual inheritance of love of God for his descendants."[15] Jacob Neusner sums up this quality of Abraham as the "heritage of virtue."[16] In Jewish tradition, the name of Abraham is connected with the concept of *zekhut abot* ("merit of the fathers"), the belief that supernatural grace, favor, or mercy will be shown to the Jewish people for generations to come on account of the goodness of their ancestors.[17] *Zekhut* is about the grace of God, not the human manipulation of God. Indeed, "*zekhut* is not coerced and does not coerce, but forms a gift freely given, to which God, the ultimate recipient, freely responds."[18] *Zekhut* does not absolve individual Jews of moral responsibility based on the good deeds of the founding fathers. *Zekhut*, however, is a reminder that patriarchs such as Abraham, and indeed the righteous few of any generation, can impact those who will follow them.[19]

Assurance of God's indissoluble covenant with Abraham and his descendants provides the theological context for *zekhut*. Resting in covenant grace and the compassion of a merciful God, Israel, like father Abraham, was exhorted to live a life of confident trust in God and the performing of good deeds. In this connection, Elaine Phillips calls attention to an "ongoing tension between expressing the assurance of *zekhut abot* and exhorting the current generation to obedience . . . for the Sages recognized that dependence on merit, whether of the ancestors or one's own good deeds, was incomplete."[20] Prophetic literature may allude to the concept of *zekhut* in the phrase, "turning the hearts of the fathers to their children" (Mal. 4:6; see Luke 1:17).

Like all human beings, Abraham had imperfections and weaknesses.

15. Yitzchok Kirzner, *The Art of Jewish Prayer* (Northvale, NJ: Jason Aronson, 1991), p. 62.

16. See Jacob Neusner, *Questions and Answers: Intellectual Foundations of Judaism* (Peabody, MA: Hendrickson, 2005), p. 204.

17. See Talmud, Shabbat 30a where God instructs Israel to appeal to the merit of the patriarchs in the pleading of their cause to him.

18. Jacob Neusner and Bruce Chilton, *Jewish-Christian Debates* (Minneapolis: Fortress Press, 1998), p. 174.

19. Simon Glustrom, *The Language of Judaism* (Northvale, NJ: Jason Aronson, 1988), pp. 203, 204.

20. Elaine Phillips, "'They Are Loved on Account of the Patriarchs': *Zekhut Avot* and the Covenant with Abraham," in Hunt, ed., *Perspectives on Our Father Abraham*, pp. 218-19.

Yet in assessing the measure of the man, most of the biblical and extra-canonical writings that reflect back on the Genesis narratives do not dwell on Abraham's failures. Rather, Abraham stands out as a man of virtue, devout in faith, a model of piety to be emulated.[21] The early rabbinic traditions put particular emphasis on Abraham's response to God's command to bind and sacrifice Isaac, his greatest test. Abraham's obedience becomes a model to follow in times of testing. Indeed, the rabbis held that Abraham had ten trials of faith, each resulting in miraculous benefits for his descendants.[22] In the Jewish wisdom literature of the early second century B.C., Ben Sira, in his "Praise of the Elders," sums up the significance of this great patriarch and righteous forebear of the Jewish people:

> Abraham was the great father of a multitude of nations,
>   and no one has been found like him in glory;
> he kept the law of the Most High,
>   and was taken into covenant with him;
> he established the covenant in his flesh,
>   and when he was tested he was found faithful. (Sir. 44:19, 20)

Children of Abraham

God's election of Abraham was that he might impact the world, an awesome task considering the grip that polytheism had upon his environment. Abraham was to bring the teaching of ethical monotheism to all his children after him. God says of the patriarch, "I have chosen him, so that he will direct his children and his household after him to keep the way of the Lord by doing what is right and just" (Gen. 18:19). Josephus sums up the importance of

21. Kabbalism, the mystical tradition of Judaism, sometimes employs gematria, a seemingly subjective method of biblical exegesis based on the numerical value of Hebrew words. Kabbalists point out that the gematria of Abraham's name (i.e., the numerical sum of the five Hebrew consonants that comprise "Abraham") totals 248, equal to the positive commandments in the Torah. Thus, in Jewish mysticism Abraham is viewed as the one who perfectly fulfilled God's will. This exegetical technique of gematria was known to the Greeks (cf. Greek, *geometria*) and the Babylonians. It is found in the literature of Jewish sages and rabbis, especially in homiletical settings. Many scholars see the number fourteen (the sum of the three consonants in the name David) in Matthew 1:17 as a play on David's name and a form of New Testament gematria.

22. See Edward Kessler, *Bound by the Bible: Jews, Christians and the Sacrifice of Isaac* (Cambridge: Cambridge University Press, 2004), pp. 64-67.

Abraham as one who had a wise and righteous sense of calling: "Abraham, endowed with great sagacity, with a higher knowledge of God and greater virtues than all the rest, was determined to change the erroneous opinions of men."[23] Judaism and the Jewish people would not be as they are today without the revolutionary, groundbreaking influence of father Abraham.

The Significance of Abraham in Christian Tradition

Christian Beginnings

The earliest Christian documents link the origin of the church to Abraham and his seed. The New Testament mentions Abraham by name seventy-two times. Only the name Moses, among Old Testament characters, appears more frequently. Thus for Christians, "he [Abraham], not Moses, is the real progenitor of the Hebrew people, the founder of the Church."[24] The opening words of the New Testament include the name of Abraham: "A record of the genealogy of Jesus Christ the son of David, the son of Abraham" (Matt. 1:1). In the verses that follow, Abraham is the starting point for Matthew's telescoped version of the ancestry of Jesus (Matt. 1:2-17). The descent of Jesus from Abraham was an important point in the church's teaching and preaching concerning Jesus as Messiah.[25] According to Paul, the blessing promised through Abraham to the people of Israel was particularly realized in Christ. In Paul's words, "the promises were spoken to Abraham and to his seed. The Scripture does not say 'and to seeds,' meaning many people, but 'and to your seed,' meaning one person, who is Christ" (Gal. 3:16; see Acts 3:25).

New Testament Epistles

Paul writes to the church in Galatia, "If you belong to Christ, then you are Abraham's seed" (Gal. 3:29). In Paul's view, the church is made up of Jews and Gentiles in one body, and Abraham is father of all (Rom. 4:11, 12, 16; Eph. 2:11-18). In Paul's letter to the Romans he uses the metaphor of an olive

23. Josephus, *Antiquities* 1.7.1.

24. Stuart Blanch, *For All Mankind: A New Approach to the Old Testament* (New York: Oxford University Press, 1978), p. 82.

25. See H. Seebass, "Abraham," in *New International Dictionary of New Testament Theology,* ed. Colin Brown, vol. 1 (Grand Rapids: Eerdmans, 1968), p. 989.

tree to symbolize Israel (Rom. 11:16-24). Gentiles are grafted into this tree and are nourished by its root (vv. 16-20). From the context of Romans 9–11, the root most likely represents the patriarchs, Abraham the deepest of those roots.[26] As stalwart founder of the original people of God, Abraham had an enduring faith. Through Abraham and his ancestors comes a faith-filled, deep-rooted channel of blessing for Gentiles, one not decayed or uprooted through the years of time.[27]

In Jesus' day, Jews considered it an expression of honor to be termed "children of Abraham" (Matt. 3:9; Luke 3:8). He was "God's friend" (James 2:23), a man whose "faith was made complete by what he did" (v. 22). Abraham's life of faithful obedience from the moment God called him serves as an inspiring witness to all believers (Heb. 11:8ff.; 12:1). In addition, the Book of Hebrews makes the point that the Levitical priesthood is descended from Abraham (Heb. 7:5).

The Gospels and Abraham

In Luke's Gospel, Abraham has a prominent part to play in the story of The Rich Man and Lazarus (16:19-31). At the time of Jesus, Jewish tradition held that Abraham and other patriarchs remained alive with God and had the powers of intercession (see Gen. 18:16-33). In this Lukan story, however, Abraham refuses to intercede for the rich man. Rather, the account tells of judgment and torment of the rich man but the exaltation of Lazarus, a poor beggar, who is carried by angels to "Abraham's bosom" (Luke 16:22; NIV, "Abraham's side"). The expression "Abraham's bosom" apparently refers to a place of blessedness, honor, and repose for the righteous dead. Abraham refuses to hear the plea of the rich man, perhaps because the rich man did not apply the teachings of the Jewish Scriptures and hence live a life of faithful obedience like the patriarch did (see Luke 16:29). Lazarus, in contrast, finds himself in a place of "tranquil intimacy with great father Abraham."[28]

The Gospels also portray Abraham as an eschatological figure. The patriarchs Abraham, Isaac, and Jacob appear together at a heavenly banquet,

---

26. See James D. G. Dunn, *Romans 9–16*, Word Biblical Commentary (Dallas: Word, 1988), p. 672; C. Maurer, *Theological Dictionary of the New Testament*, vol. 6 (Grand Rapids: Eerdmans, 1968), p. 989.

27. See my discussion in *Our Father Abraham*, pp. 14-16.

28. John Nolland, *Luke 9:21–18:34*, Word Biblical Commentary (Dallas: Word, 1993), p. 829.

sitting at a table with the righteous, feasting in the kingdom of God (Matt. 8:10, 11; Luke 13:28, 29). Jesus states, "People will come from east and west and north and south and will take their places at the feast" (Luke 13:29). This statement seems to allude to the "Apocalypse of Isaiah" where the Lord prepares a future banquet of rich food "for all peoples" (Isa. 25:6; also 2:2-3). The Gospel writers thus emphasize the universality of the gospel message by opening the banquet door to include righteous Gentiles, those who at one time had no table fellowship with Jews but now are allowed to share in the eschatological banquet with Abraham and the other patriarchs. In a profound sense, "everything has been turned upside down."[29] To be sure, the promise to Abraham was that "all peoples on earth" will be blessed through him (Gen. 12:3).

Taking the High Road

The New Testament writers tend to take the high road in their theological and historical reflection upon the character of Abraham as set forth in the Genesis narratives. That is, in passages such as Acts 7:2-8 and Hebrews 11:8-19, it is the good and righteous qualities of Abraham the writers choose to emphasize. They are not particularly interested in writing about the questionable or debatable aspects of Abraham's life, the so-called low road.[30] In rather stark and provocative language, Philip Davies calls attention to this other side of Abraham: "For centuries Abraham has been regarded as a paradigm of how a good Jew or Christian should behave — although moving house all the time (Genesis 12:4, 10; 13:1, 18; 20:1; etc.), pimping off your wife (Genesis 12:10-16) and agreeing to slaughter your child (Genesis 22) are not usually highlighted as examples to be followed. . . . Alas, family values are not his [Abraham's] strong point."[31] While Davies's language may come across as very crude, it does underscore that the Hebrew Bible does not seek to whitewash its characters.

Certainly, virtually every Bible character has flaws and failures, whether reported or unreported in the text. In my mind, the fact that the Bible records such incidents makes the message of the Bible more believable. These

29. Kuschel, *Abraham*, p. 75.

30. See Alden Thompson, *Who's Afraid of the Old Testament God?* (Grand Rapids: Zondervan, 1989), pp. 18-21.

31. Philip R. Davies, "Abraham and Yahweh: A Case of Male Bonding," *Bible Review* (August 1995): 24-25.

are the stories of real men and real women coming to know God. Revelation of God's will, however, is progressive. It is extraordinary when one considers how well characters like Abraham did in view of how little light most of them had. True, there is a selectivity of Old Testament materials on the part of the New Testament authors, and Abraham is a case in point. But the overall purpose of these authors is to give hope and build faith in the promises of God by showing how God has faithfully guided various individuals in the history of his people (Rom. 15:4; Heb. 11:39, 40).

Lifestyle of a Pilgrim

One aspect of Abraham's character that is important to the New Testament writers is his pilgrim-like lifestyle.[32] Even when Abraham dwelled in the Promised Land, "like a stranger in a foreign country, he lived in tents, as did Isaac and Jacob" (Heb. 11:9). Abraham said to the Hittites, "I am an alien and a stranger among you" (Gen. 23:4). He accepted his status as a pilgrim. In the Promised Land, God gave him no inheritance there, "not even a foot of ground" (Acts 7:5).[33] According to the writer of Hebrews, the true homeland of Abraham and the other patriarchs is a heavenly country, a new Jerusalem (see Heb. 11:10, 16; 12:22). "The earthly Canaan and the earthly Jerusalem were but temporary object lessons pointing to the saints' everlasting rest, the well-founded city of God."[34]

The above theme of God's people viewing life as a pilgrimage, and living it as Abraham and the patriarchs did, is picked up in an early Christian document, the *Epistle to Diognetus*: "[Christians] dwell in their own countries, but only as sojourners; they bear their share of all responsibilities as citizens, and they endure all hardships as strangers. Every foreign country is a homeland to them, and every homeland is foreign. . . . Their existence is on earth, but their citizenship is in heaven."[35]

Many centuries later in England, the Pilgrims strongly identified with the memory of Abraham. The Pilgrims thought of themselves as "all the chil-

---

32. Cf. D. J. Wiseman, "They Lived in Tents," in *Biblical and Near Eastern Studies,* ed. Gary A. Tuttle (Grand Rapids: Eerdmans, 1978), pp. 195-200.

33. For a helpful discussion of this passage in the context of Stephen's speech in Acts 7, see Elaine Phillips, "The Tomb That Abraham Had Purchased (Acts 7:16)," in Hunt, ed., *Perspectives on Our Father Abraham,* pp. 110-25.

34. F. F. Bruce, *The Epistle to the Hebrews,* rev. ed. (Grand Rapids: Eerdmans, 1990), p. 299.

35. *Epistle to Diognetus* 5:5-9.

dren of Abraham" and thus under the covenant of Abraham, fleeing "Egypt" (England), crossing "the Red Sea" (the Atlantic Ocean) and emerging in their own "promised land" (New England).[36]

Abraham and Catholic Christianity

In Catholic Christianity, Abraham is a key figure in the liturgy. In the Offertory of every Mass for the Dead ("Requiem Mass") a prayer is included that the dead may come "into the holy light which Thou didst promise to Abraham and to his seed." At the end of the prayer are these words: "Grant them, O Lord, to pass from death unto life, which Thou didst promise to Abraham and to his seed." Furthermore, in the Canon of every Catholic Mass (that part of the Mass between the Sanctus and the Communion), the priest makes reference to "the sacrifice of our Patriarch Abraham."[37] In addition, the Vatican II document *Nostra Aetate* ("In Our Time"), which is a statement dealing with the relation of the church to the Jewish people, opens with the mentioning of Abraham: "As this Sacred Synod searches into the mystery of the Church, it remembers the bond that spiritually ties the people of the New Covenant to Abraham's stock." In the next paragraph it states, "She [the church] professes that all who believe in Christ — Abraham's sons according to faith — are included in the same Patriarch's call. . . ."

Disinherited Children?

In the early Christian controversy with Judaism, the church gradually distanced itself from appealing to Abraham as the father of Jew and Gentile alike. Instead, Christian theology "moved increasingly toward the portrayal of a Christian Abraham who has abandoned and disinherited his children, the Jews."[38] Gradually, a largely de-Judaized and Gentile-dominated church claimed to be the true heir; it arrogantly began forcing Jewish people to the

---

36. Henry L. Feingold, "The Jewish Role in Shaping American Society," in *A Time to Speak: The Evangelical-Jewish Encounter,* ed. A. James Rudin and Marvin R. Wilson (Grand Rapids: Eerdmans, 1987), p. 46.

37. Cf. Walter M. Abbott et al., eds., *The Bible Reader* (New York: Bruce Publishing Co., 1969), p. 23.

38. Jeffrey S. Siker, *Disinheriting the Jews: Abraham in Early Christian Controversy* (Louisville: Westminster/John Knox, 1991), p. 27.

margin and thereby sought to remove them permanently from salvation history. In short, Jews began to be read out of their own story.

Tragically, this exclusion of the Jewish people, the proclamation that God has canceled his *berit olam* ("eternal covenant") with Abraham (see Gen. 17:7), has, over the centuries, contributed greatly to the general malaise and indifference of the church concerning the Jewish people. Not only have Jews faced spiritual extinction through Christian insistence of their theological illegitimacy, but millions of Jews also faced physical extinction through crusades, the Inquisition, and the church's deafening silence during the infamous Holocaust years.[39]

This dark side of the Abrahamic story — a story in which theology brought destruction rather than life — is still in the process of being rewritten. Tragic but true: sometimes political reasoning is more humane than theology. A disinherited people is a superseded people. It is our contention in this book that the Abrahamic covenant continues and Abraham's family continues, for the God of Abraham yet lives.

UNDERSTANDING CHAPTER FIVE

1. In what way does Abraham still live on in Judaism and Christianity? Review the words of A. J. Heschel and Karl-Josef Kuschel cited on the opening page of this chapter. In your opinion, on what grounds might Heschel write that "[w]e are Abraham" and why might Kuschel assert that for the apostle Paul Abraham is a "living reality"?

2. In Judaism, how does the annual reading cycle of the Torah place particular focus on Abraham?

3. What was the ultimate test that Abraham passed? How does Scripture speak of Abraham's life as viewed by God because of this?

4. Abraham is the first person in the Bible to be called by what label and to bear what title? What additional designation is given to him in the Psalms? Cite Scripture references for each instance.

5. What does God call Abraham in the prophets?

6. What two titles is Abraham given in Psalm 105? Review the contents of the psalm and discuss ways in which Abraham is granted honor through these titles as well as through his indispensable role in the birth of God's people.

39. Kuschel, *Abraham*, pp. 128-29.

7. According to the Jewish sages, what "five possessions" did God make especially his own? Discuss the importance of each term for understanding the foundation of Judaism and Christianity. From a Christian perspective, if you were asked to add any two additional "possessions" to this list of five, what would you want to include? Why?

8. What is the meaning of *Rachmana,* a Talmudic word for God and also a virtue meant to be embodied by all descendants of Abraham? In the context of Hosea's marriage and birth of three children, each child bearing a name symbolic of Israel (see Hosea 1–3), what additional light do the cognate terms *(lo) ruhamah* (Hos. 1:6) and *rahamim* (Hos. 2:19) shed on the person and nature of God?

9. What do the actions of Abraham found in Genesis 18:1-15 set a standard for in Jewish tradition? How does the Hebrew *hakhnasat orhim* translate literally, and what significance did it acquire in Jewish tradition?

10. What is particularly remarkable about Abraham's intercession for Sodom in Genesis 18:16-33?

11. Why is Abraham considered the "first great missionary" in Jewish tradition? How did God's call and Abraham's subsequent faithfulness contribute to his participation in that role? Compare and contrast the "missionary" travels and message of Paul the apostle, about two millennia later, to that of father Abraham. Discuss.

12. What sign of a covenant did God institute with Abraham? How do the rabbis' teachings bear witness to the prominence given to this rite?

13. With what concept concerning grace is the name of Abraham associated in Jewish tradition? Be familiar with the Hebrew, the English translation, and meaning of the phrase.

14. What provides the theological context for *zekhut?*

15. What does Elaine Phillips mean by her comment that *zekhut* results in an "ongoing tension"? Explain the tension referred to. Is the teaching "merit of the fathers" *(zekhut abot)* compatible with biblical Christianity? Discuss. What did the Sages recognize about dependence on merit?

16. In the mystical tradition of Judaism, how does the gematria of Abraham's name contribute to his status as a model of obedience to God (see note 21)?

17. Which second-century B.C. writer honored Abraham, and in what piece of literature?

18. What "awesome task" was Abraham given in relation to his surrounding polytheistic environment? How does Josephus envision Abraham's capacity for and commitment to this task?

19. How many times is Abraham mentioned in the New Testament? Only what other Old Testament personal name appears more frequently in the New Testament?

20. In terms of Jesus' identity, why is it significant that the Gospel of Matthew opens by tracing Jesus' lineage back to Abraham?

21. Given the context of Romans 9–11, what does the "root" (see 11:16-20) most likely represent?

22. How is Abraham, along with Isaac and Jacob, an eschatological figure in the Gospels? In this context, why is table fellowship particularly poignant in relation to Jews and Gentiles?

23. What does the author mean by writing that the New Testament authors tended to take the high road in their reflections on Abraham? In contrast, what would the low road be? How do you regard Philip Davies's bold statement about Abraham in this section? What are your feelings about the fact that the Bible records both sides of the story?

24. How is Abraham's pilgrim-like lifestyle highlighted by the New Testament writers? In a more modern context, how was this line of thought embedded in the Pilgrims' journey from England to North America? As Jews or Christians, do you consider it important to balance a "pilgrim-like" attitude with a sense of this earth being our home? Why or why not?

25. What early Christian document made use of the theme of pilgrimage? In your own words, what does it assert about the Christian life?

26. In Catholic Christianity, how is Abraham honored in both the Requiem Mass and the standard Mass? What subject did Vatican II's *Nostra Aetate* explore, and how did it also honor Abraham?

27. As the church continued to define itself, how did Jews begin to be "read out of their own story"? Historically, what have been some related repercussions for the Jewish people?

CHAPTER 6

Thinking Theologically about Abraham

In the previous chapter we discussed the person of Abraham, the world's first Jew and father of Jews and Christians. Within that chapter we sought to highlight aspects of the character of Abraham and the consequent influence this looming figure has exerted within Judaism and Christianity. In this present chapter, we will explore the question of how Scripture theologically interprets the life of Abraham. We have organized this chapter around five themes central to the Abrahamic narratives.

Election: Chosen or Choosing?

Abraham marks a pivotal point in the history of biblical revelation. "A new start for humanity began with Abraham."[1] He lived in what the rabbis called an "age of chaos."[2] Yet God called Abraham to carry out his mission in the world. In Genesis 12:3, what appears at first sight to be particular (God chooses one man Abraham) is ultimately a call with the universal in view (all peoples on earth will be blessed through him).

Scripture continually emphasizes that God is the source of Abraham's call. Abraham Heschel calls attention to the importance of divine election as a foundational pillar in Jewish theological thought: "We have not chosen God; He has chosen us. There is no concept of a chosen God but there is the

---

1. Bernard J. Bamberger, *The Story of Judaism,* 3rd ed. (New York: Schocken, 1970), p. 292.

2. See Abraham Heschel, *God in Search of Man* (New York: Farrar, Straus & Giroux, 1955), p. 303.

idea of a chosen people."[3] In Genesis, God says to Abraham, "Leave your country . . . and go to the land I will show you" (12:1), and so he left (12:4). God confirms to Joshua and the people of Israel the fact of Abraham's call: "I took your father Abraham from the land beyond the River and led him throughout Canaan" (Josh. 24:3). Nehemiah states that God "chose Abram and brought him out of Ur of the Chaldeans" (9:7). In the Book of Acts, Stephen, a Hellenistic Jew, states that "[t]he God of glory appeared to our father Abraham while he was still in Mesopotamia . . ." (Acts 7:2). The writer of Hebrews says, "when called to go . . . [Abraham] obeyed and went, even though he did not know where he was going" (11:8). According to Thomas Cahill, the simple sentence "Abram went" *(wayyelekh Abram),* found in Genesis 12:4, sums up the enormity of Abraham's act of obedience to God's call, for these are "two of the boldest words in all literature. They signal a complete departure from everything that has gone before in the long evolution of culture and sensibility. . . . [His was] a journey of no return."[4]

The main emphasis in Genesis and the rest of Scripture is that God takes the initiative in reaching Abraham; the initial call comes from God.[5] Indeed, "Abraham's life is a life impregnated throughout with an extraordinary sense of God's presence and God's will, for which there is no rational explanation nor ever can be; God speaks, and listening, the dead receive new life."[6]

But it is important to ask to what degree human reason may have come into play in the establishing of Abraham's relationship with God. Does God find Abraham or does Abraham find God? Certainly the question can be argued from both perspectives. Throughout Scripture there is a tension between human reason and divine revelation, between free will and divine sovereignty. In post-biblical Jewish religious thought, however, there is an emphasis that Abraham came to know God by reason. The Talmud states that Abraham kept not only the 613 commandments of the written law (Kiddushin 82a) but also the Oral Law (Yoma 28b). This knowledge of revelation was not supernaturally given to Abraham but deduced from his own reason. Accordingly, Samuel Sandmel bestows the epithet "philosopher-king" on Abraham.[7]

3. Heschel, *God in Search of Man,* p. 425.

4. Thomas Cahill, *The Gifts of the Jews* (New York: Doubleday, 1998), pp. 62-63.

5. See Christoph Barth, *God with Us* (Grand Rapids: Eerdmans, 1991), pp. 38-55; also William LaSor, *Great Personalities of the Old Testament* (Westwood, NJ: Fleming H. Revell, 1959), pp. 13-21.

6. Stuart Blanch, *For All Mankind* (New York: Oxford University Press, 1978), p. 81.

7. Samuel Sandmel, *Judaism and Christian Beginnings* (New York: Oxford University Press, 1978), pp. 291, 294.

He explains: "By means of introspection, Abraham discovered within himself a *logos,* and reasoning by analogy, concluded that there must be a Divine *Logos* in the universe."[8] Shlomo Riskin sums up the rabbinic discussion on Abraham's reasoning ability by concluding that "the Torah is eminently reasonable and logical, and that a profoundly intelligent and sensitive human being can arrive at an understanding of the Biblical theology and legal structure by means of his reason, and even without revelation. This is the axiom which lies behind the Mishnaic insistence that Abraham performed all of the commandments."[9] While Abraham was obedient to God and of unusual character, most Christians would question the rabbinic conclusion concerning the degree of Abraham's reasoning ability and also the perceived perfection of Abraham in keeping all the (yet to be formally given) commandments.

Given the tension or paradox of Abraham either being sought by God or reasoning his way to him, this writer sides, in the end, with the former. While father Abraham is doubtless one of the most gifted people of Scripture, human reason, when all the theological dust settles, is not equal to God or capable of fully knowing him; neither can reason find him unless God by his grace assists the human. In the overall scheme of Scripture, divine-human relationship (i.e., "walking with God," see Gen. 17:1) takes precedence over human reason (i.e., personal, intellectual quest to reach and understand God). This is an overarching perspective of Scripture in general and of the biblical Abrahamic materials in particular. Accordingly, we agree with the conclusion that "Israel's religion originated in the initiative of God rather than in the efforts of man. It was not an invention of man but a creation of God; not a product of civilization, but a realm of its own. Man would not have known Him if He had not approached man. God's relation to man precedes man's relation to Him."[10]

Covenant: Permanently Bound to the Other

In the Old Testament, the most important metaphor to express God's relationship to his people is the covenant *(berit).*[11] In Genesis 15 and 17, God

8. Sandmel, *Judaism and Christian Beginnings,* p. 288.

9. Shlomo Riskin, "Keeping the Commandments," *The Jewish Advocate,* October 14-20, 1994, p. 16.

10. Heschel, *God in Search of Man,* p. 198.

11. See Frederic W. Bush, "Images of Israel: The People of God in the Torah," in *Studies in Old Testament Theology,* ed. Robert Hubbard, Robert Johnston, and Robert Meye (Dallas: Word, 1992), p. 100.

establishes a covenant with Abraham and his descendants. The New Testament writers, however, speak of a "new covenant" (Luke 22:20; 1 Cor. 11:25; Heb. 8:8). The theme of covenant thus becomes a significant issue of both convergence and divergence for Judaism and Christianity as Abrahamic religions.

In Genesis 15:9-21, through a mysterious covenantal ceremony, God establishes an enduring bond with Abraham and his descendants. God initiates this covenant and, by oath, confirms his promise to Abraham. The divine presence is symbolically manifested by a smoking firepot with a blazing torch passing between split animals (v. 17). The ceremony thus solemnizes the covenant; the parties, God and Abraham, are united by a bond of blood. Only God passes between the pieces of the animals. Abraham merely looks on, passive beneficiary of the covenant promise. "On that day the LORD made a covenant (*karat berit*, literally 'cut a covenant') with Abram" (v. 18). The unilateral, unconditional character of the covenantal agreement assures Abraham and his posterity that God's relationship with his people is permanent. The covenant with Abraham is sealed in blood. As Jeremiah 34:18, 19 indicates, in a covenant ceremony the slaughtered animals dramatically serve as a type of self-maledictory oath for the parties involved. In essence, each partner in covenant is saying, "May I be cut off and dead like these animals, should I renege on the terms of this agreement."

In Genesis 17:10, 27, circumcision is instituted as an external sign of the covenant. Circumcision is the oldest rite in Judaism. The commandment of circumcision is the first *mitzvah* in Torah specifically given to Abraham and his offspring. Indeed, it is intended "for the generations to come" (v. 12). God said to Abraham, "My covenant in your flesh is to be an everlasting covenant" (v. 13). Thus, circumcision is referred to as "the covenant of Abraham."[12] God expects an active response from those binding themselves to the terms of the covenant. Anyone unwilling to have the foreskin cut off would be cut off from God's people; such refusal amounts to a breach of the covenant. Although from God's perspective his covenant is everlasting, never to be broken, from the human standpoint the covenant could be broken by disobedience, and its benefits lost (Gen. 17:7, 13, 19). As God establishes the covenant with the shed blood of animals (Genesis 15), so circumcision, a sign of that covenant, involves blood, a reminder of the seriousness of the obligation.

---

12. See George Foot Moore, *Judaism*, vol. 2 (Cambridge, MA: Harvard University Press, 1955), p. 18.

Circumcision binds one to the covenant and is a sure mark of Jewish identity both within the Jewish community and without.[13] Circumcision is far deeper, however, than signaling religious, cultural, or national identity; its meaning is more profound than an outward mark on a physical body. Indeed, as Irving Greenberg has emphasized, "Because Abraham's covenant is built on values and concepts — transcendence, redemption, justice — Abraham's is more than a biological family."[14] In short, circumcision is a "symbol of the Jew's consecration and commitment to a life lived in the consciousness of that covenant."[15]

In the New Testament, Paul, in a number of ways, begins to tailor Judaism for Gentiles. One of these ways is by turning circumcision into a metaphor, a spiritual concept. He speaks of a "circumcision of the heart," a term first employed by Moses (Deut. 10:16; 30:6) and the prophets (see Jer. 9:26). As a biblical figure of speech, "circumcision of the heart," as most Christians understand the expression, is an inward spiritual seal of righteousness through faith, accomplished through the indwelling work of the Holy Spirit (Rom. 2:29). It is a circumcision not "done by the hands of men" but "done by Christ" (Col. 2:11) and is based on faith in Christ (Gal. 5:6). In Paul's view, those spiritually "circumcised" are those who have put their faith in Christ; they have an inward "badge," but it is that of the Holy Spirit; they have confidence, but not by trusting in the flesh (sinful human nature) or in an outward physical identity that cannot save (Phil. 3:3-9).

The Council of Jerusalem convened about A.D. 49 (see Acts 15). The assembly met to decide the issue of whether Gentiles are required to be circumcised and observe the entire Law of Moses for salvation (v. 1). The decision of the council was that circumcision is not a requirement for Gentiles (v. 10). In making its ruling, the council emphasized that salvation was a free gift of God; one cannot obtain it by mere conformity to a ceremonial ritual. The ruling began to send a strong message to the Jewish community. By not requiring the ritual practice of circumcision, a basic teaching of the Torah, the church was understood by the Jewish community to be saying it no longer considered itself part of traditional Judaism but rather apart from it. The old covenant, focused on *torah,* had been modified; a new covenant,

13. Robert L. Wilken, "The Christians as the Romans (and Greeks) Saw Them," in *Jewish and Christian Self-Definition,* ed. E. P. Sanders, vol. 1 (Philadelphia: Fortress Press, 1980), p. 103.

14. Irving Greenberg, *The Jewish Way* (New York: Simon & Schuster, 1988), p. 72.

15. Nahum M. Sarna, *Genesis,* JPS Torah Commentary (Philadelphia: Jewish Publication Society, 1989), p. 125.

focused on faith in Christ, and which interpreted the Hebrew Bible through Christian eyes, had now emerged.

In order for Gentiles to belong to the church for the first decade or two of its existence, it was necessary to convert to Judaism and uphold the Law of Moses. Once the church loosened the command of circumcision as a rite incumbent on Gentiles, however, it opened the door for a more rapid growth of Christianity. During the time the church was exclusively Jewish, if a Gentile male considered converting to Judaism, the thought of going through circumcision did not have a particularly pleasant connotation; many adults did not want to undergo the physical pain that was involved.[16]

After the Council of Jerusalem, things began to change significantly in regard to Gentiles and the Law. Gentile response to the gospel message began to increase. Among Jews, however, response to the gospel began to decrease. In light of Paul's special calling to reach Gentiles, from the church's historic perspective the Jerusalem Council's decision was a critical move. The decision would result in significantly advancing the Abrahamic promise that "all peoples on earth will be blessed through you" (Gen. 12:3; Gal. 3:8, 9).

Faith: Believing God and Acting on That Belief

For Christians, Abraham is probably best known for his faith; many would call him a paradigm of faith.[17] Accordingly, those who believe God, as Abraham did, are "children of Abraham" (Gal. 3:7). The Abrahamic narratives in Genesis emphasize the patriarch's strong trust in God and his prompt obedience to every request God made to him (Gen. 12:4; 17:23; 21:14; 22:3). The New Testament epistles particularly characterize Abraham as a man of faith (see Romans 4; Galatians 3; Hebrews 11; James 2). His commitment and trust in the promises of God allowed him to venture into the unknown with the full expectation that God would meet him there. It is almost incomprehensible for us to grasp the extraordinary way Abraham's faith operated. He had "no tangible object in which to trust: he believed the bare word of God, and acted upon it."[18] In Thomas Cahill's words, "Out of an age of tall tales of warriors and kings, all so like one another that they are hard to tell apart,

16. Stephen Wylen, *The Jews in the Time of Jesus* (New York: Paulist Press, 1995), pp. 32, 33, 90, 91.

17. Ronald Youngblood, *The Heart of the Old Testament,* 2nd ed. (Grand Rapids: Baker, 1998), p. 92.

18. F. F. Bruce, *The Book of Acts,* rev. ed. (Grand Rapids: Eerdmans, 1988), p. 135.

comes this story of a skeptical, worldly patriarch's trust in a disembodied voice. This is becoming, however incredibly, the story of an interpersonal relationship."[19]

In the story of this deepening relationship of trust, Genesis states, "Abram believed the LORD, and he credited it to him as righteousness" (15:6). God considers Abraham's trust in his promises as righteousness. That is, Abraham relies upon God and fully puts his confidence in him. God is pleased and considers him righteous. Righteousness in the Bible centers on one being faithful to a relationship, acting the right way to please another. Thus the meaning of the above text (see Rom. 1:16-17; 4; Gal. 3:6-9) seems to be that "a person's righteousness in relation to God is fulfilled when that relationship is characterized by faith."[20] In brief, Abraham's behavior is consistent with the nature of the relationship established; his covenant fidelity renders him righteous before the Almighty.[21]

Jewish scholarship, while certainly not unanimous, tends to understand Genesis 15:6 differently from the above. One such perspective is clarified by the Tanakh (Jewish Publication Society, 1985) and its rendering of this verse: "And because he [Abram] put his trust in the LORD, He reckoned it to his merit." Hebrew Bible scholar Nahum Sarna comments on the above translation: "Hebrew *tzedakah,* usually 'righteousness,' sometimes bears the sense of 'merit.' The idea is that Abram's act of faith made him worthy of God's reward, which is secured through a covenant."[22] In brief, faith itself is seen by God as an act of merit. God credits or adds this meritorious act to the other good works of Abram's life. In contrast to the above view, in the sixteenth century, Christian Reformers like Martin Luther took a strong stance against any position that may suggest a person can acquire a right standing before God based on human merit.

In Pauline literature, Abraham becomes a prime illustration of one justified by faith.[23] For Paul, faith is the means by which God declares all sinners righteous, and Abraham is Paul's example (Rom. 4:3; Gal. 3:6). In

19. Cahill, *The Gifts of the Jews,* p. 70.

20. William LaSor, David Hubbard, and Frederic Bush, *Old Testament Survey* (Grand Rapids: Eerdmans, 1982), p. 114.

21. William J. Dumbrell, *Covenant and Creation: A Theology of Old Testament Covenants* (Nashville: Thomas Nelson, 1984), p. 54.

22. Sarna, *Genesis,* p. 113.

23. For a helpful essay on Paul, Abraham, and faith, see Gordon D. Fee, "Who Are Abraham's True Children? The Role of Abraham in Pauline Argumentation," in *Perspectives on Our Father Abraham,* ed. Steven A. Hunt (Grand Rapids: Eerdmans, 2010), pp. 126-37.

Paul's understanding, through faith God forgives Abraham — no human, including Abraham, is without sin — and Abraham thereby is enabled to stand in a new and right relationship before God. Abraham does not earn God's merit in the sense of works righteousness, but he trusts God who justifies.[24] According to James Dunn, the key to understanding "credited to him as righteousness" (Rom. 4:3), lies in the Jewish theology of Paul's day which linked the covenant promise made to Abraham to Abraham's faithfulness under testing in regard to the binding of Isaac.[25] Such testing gave Abraham confidence before God. Paul is not attacking Judaism for belief in merit or reward or for human effort to achieve salvation by good works. Rather, in quoting Genesis 15:6, in regard to Abraham's faith, Paul is arguing against the language of "payment due," for "the righteousness is surely reckoned in terms of grace, not of payment due."[26]

The epistle of James (2:23) also cites Genesis 15:6, and removes it from the faith-works polarity that, unfortunately, certain Christian interpreters have mainly focused on in their particular reading of Paul. For James, the question is not "either/or" but "both/and." In short, "faith without deeds is dead" (James 2:26). James refers to Abraham as one God considered righteous for what he did in offering Isaac on the altar (v. 21). Abraham's "faith and his actions were working together" (v. 22). So, concludes James, "a person is justified by what he does and not by faith alone" (v. 24).

While certain Christian interpreters want to place faith and deeds worlds apart, some Jewish interpreters hold that "they [faith and works] are one and the same."[27] In a Christian reading of the Scripture, James must not be hastily dismissed as if he is in conflict with Paul. A full reading of the New Testament reveals that faith involves both attitude (trust) and action (deeds). Faith is the basis of a relationship with God. Yet faith, to be genuine, must produce good works to demonstrate it is a living faith.

Abraham's faith and devotion to God are tested to the limit in the *Akedah,* the "binding" of Isaac. The climax of Abraham's story is "the Mountain Experience,"[28] that moment when God summons Abraham to "give

---

24. See Daniel Fuller, *The Unity of the Bible* (Grand Rapids: Zondervan, 1992), pp. 255, 256.

25. James D. G. Dunn, *Romans 1–8,* Word Biblical Commentary (Dallas: Word, 1988), pp. 201.

26. Dunn, *Romans 1–8,* p. 204.

27. See Burton L. Visotzky, *Reading the Book* (New York: Doubleday, 1991), p. 93.

28. Cahill, *The Gifts of the Jews,* p. 83.

up his entire future."[29] In James's reference to the *Akedah* (2:21), one is reminded that the Bible is not a work of reason but one of history and faith.[30] As for Abraham, "Whatever the cost, [he] is ready to carry it out because his faith is so strong and immovable."[31] The *Akedah* remains an important word in Jewish life. It represents a willingness to sacrifice what is most cherished, dearest, or best in life, even life itself.[32] On occasion, during medieval times, parents willingly killed their own children as an act of martyrdom rather than submit them to baptism and forced conversion.[33] With utter abandonment to their faith, they saw themselves as repeating the test of Abraham, even being more faithful than he was. The Epistle of James is strong on the actions of Abraham. James emphasizes that Abraham was "considered righteous for what he *did*" (James 2:21, italics mine), not for what he *thought*.

In the Abrahamic narratives, all too frequently the question of faith becomes a matter of extreme divergence for Christianity and Judaism. Many are too easily prone to accept the oft-repeated stereotype: "Christians are only interested in creeds (faith — what one believes and the one in whom they believe), Jews are only interested in deeds (works — how one lives and how many *mitzvot* they perform)." Some of this thinking about the other is understandable given the overall Christocentricity of the New Testament narratives. Nonetheless, James is valuable for Christians and Jews in that with this epistle we come close to converging or "meeting in the middle." James is perhaps the least Christocentric book in the New Testament. For James (*Ya'akob,* or Jacob, his Hebrew name), there is no great divide or major conflict between faith and deeds. If there are differences, they are more on emphasis than substance. Both faith and deeds are essential to the teaching of Judaism and Christianity. Both complement each other in the biblical narrative.

29. John H. Marks, "The Book of Genesis," in *Interpreter's One-Volume Commentary,* ed. Charles M. Laymon (Nashville: Abingdon, 1971), p. 18.

30. See the discussion of this point in Paul Johnson, *History of the Jews* (New York: Harper & Row, 1987), p. 18.

31. Chaim Pearl, *Theology in Rabbinic Stories* (Peabody, MA: Hendrickson, 1997), p. 58.

32. In parallel Christian tradition, in the Church of the Holy Sepulcher in Jerusalem, on a wall near the traditional location of Jesus' crucifixion, is a large Old Testament scene depicting Abraham's sacrifice of Isaac, a picture that in Christian theology illustrates the sacrifice of Jesus as God's beloved Son.

33. Joseph Telushkin, *Jewish Literacy* (New York: William Morrow & Co., 1991), p. 37.

"Look to the Rock . . . Abraham Your Father"

More than a millennium after Abraham and Sarah had walked the Fertile Crescent, a cry comes from the prophets; it is a call to look back to father Abraham. The text reads:

> Listen to me, you who pursue righteousness,
>   and who seek the LORD.
> Look to the rock from which you were cut,
>   and to the quarry from which you were hewn.
> Look to Abraham your father. (Isa. 51:1-2)

The prophet begins his message with a sense of urgency. He employs three imperatives: *shim'u,* "listen" or "hear," and twice he uses *habbitu,* "look" or "focus intently upon." He calls for "maximum attention (v. 1), the concentration of both the literal ear and also the eye of the imagination."[34] His audience is composed of those who "pursue righteousness" *(tzedek),* as the Torah commands (Deut. 16:20), those who seek to lead a righteous life through a right relationship with God and by just actions towards others.

In this passage, God's people are called to reflect on their origin, and Abraham is the name synonymous with origin. In this context it appears the author may be intentional in linking Abraham to both his descendants and righteousness (Isa. 51:1-2; Gen. 15:6). Accordingly, as covenant people founded on Abraham, the calling of the children of Abraham is to reflect the way of the Lord, which is also the way of their father; it is *la'asot tzedakah,* "to do righteousness/justice" (see Gen. 18:19).

The admonition is, "Look to the rock *(tzur)* from which you were hewn." Abraham represents the human platform upon which the covenant community is built. A midrash on this verse reads, "When God looked on Abraham who was to appear, he said, 'See, I have found a rock on which I can build and base the world,' therefore he called Abraham a rock *(tzur):* Look to the rock from which you were hewn."[35] Why is Abraham called a "rock"? The metaphor implies someone solid, steady, reliable, and enduring. The Lord himself is many times called a Rock (e.g., Deut. 32:4; 1 Sam. 2:2).

---

34. Geoffrey Grogan, "Isaiah," in *Expositor's Bible Commentary,* vol. 6 (Grand Rapids: Zondervan, 1986), p. 294.

35. Hermann L. Strack and Paul Billerbeck, *Das Evangelium nach Matthaus,* vol. 1 (Munich: C. H. Beck'sche, 1992), p. 733.

So Abraham's descendants, quarried from Abraham the rock, are to reflect his faithfulness, his likeness.

There are some intriguing similarities between Abraham and Peter that raise the possibility of Peter being a "second Abraham."[36] Briefly, let us turn to some of the imagery that may relate Peter to Abraham. On the occasion of Peter's confession at Caesarea Philippi, Jesus says to Peter, "You are Peter" (Greek, *petros*) and on this rock *(petra)* I will build my church" (Matt. 16:18). Jesus may have pointed to himself as that rock on which he would establish his church, the rock may be Peter's confession that Jesus was the Messiah, or the rock may be Peter himself. If it is the latter, then from Peter, like Abraham the rock, a new but enduring community of faith will be built. Peter was one of those reputed to be a "pillar" in the early church (Gal. 2:9). Paul states that the church is "built upon the foundation of the apostles and prophets, with Christ Jesus himself as the chief cornerstone" (Eph. 2:20). The word "foundation" *(themelios)* implies something solid or rock-like used to support a structure. In this interpretive scenario, the church is built upon the apostles (represented by Peter) and the prophets (represented by Abraham), Christ being the cornerstone.[37]

Further, it is of interest to note that both Abraham and Peter undergo changes of name[38] to indicate the coming into being of the people of God (Abram to Abraham; see Gen. 17:4-5) and the birth of the church (Simon to Peter; see Matt. 16:18; John 1:42). Both Abraham and Peter are associated with a new work of God promising to have worldwide influence: Abraham is to be "father of many nations" (Gen. 17:4, 5) and a blessing to all people on earth (Gen. 12:3). On Pentecost, at the birthing of the church, Peter declares that God would pour out his Spirit "on all people" (Acts 2:17). Likewise Peter states that "God accepts men from every nation who fear him and do what is right" (Acts 10:35). In addition, as all members of Abraham's extended family in the flesh (Israel) are individuals cut from the rock (Abraham), so all members of the reconstituted and expanded Israel (the church) are individually likened to "living stones being built into a spiritual house" (1 Pet. 2:5; also Isa. 51:1-2).

The Gospels connect stones to Abraham. John the Baptist says, "Produce fruit in keeping with repentance. And do not begin to say to yourselves,

---

36. J. Massyngberde Ford, "Thou Art 'Abraham' and Upon This Rock . . . ," *The Heythrop Journal* 6 (1965): 289.

37. For the designation of Abraham as a prophet, see Genesis 20:7; Psalm 105:15.

38. W. D. Davies and Dale C. Allison, *The Gospel According to Saint Matthew*, International Critical Commentary, vol. 2 (Edinburgh: T. & T. Clark, 1991), p. 624.

'We have Abraham as our father.' For I tell you that out of these stones God can raise up children for Abraham" (Luke 3:8; also Matt. 3:8-9). The Baptist's concern is that Jews not rely on their physical descent or ethnic privilege as protection from the wrath of God (Luke 3:7; Matt. 3:7).[39] The blessing of Abraham had become "Israel's pride and boast."[40] When the Baptist alludes to stones giving rise to "children of Abraham" (see Isa. 51:1-2), he is addressing his fellow Jews. The "children" the Baptist seems to have in mind, however, may not be Abraham's physical seed. Rather, he holds forth the possibility that God can reconstitute Israel of old and bring forth a new people of God, "hewed not from the rock Abraham but instead founded on the rock Peter."[41] The Baptist's emphasis, however, is on an inward change of heart, not an outward mission to the Gentiles.

Our Father Abraham: Continuity, Discontinuity, and Hope

The expression "our father Abraham" increasingly becomes a theological "hot potato" as the church moves farther from the confines of the Jewish womb that gave it birth. The right to claim Abraham as "father" becomes more and more defined by faith rather than descent. Whereas John the Baptist seems to hint at this (see Matt. 3:8-9; Luke 3:8, quoted above), in the Fourth Gospel, Jesus brings this controversy to the fore (see John 8:31-59).[42] Abraham is mentioned ten times within the above literary unit. In the debate between Jesus and his Jewish opponents, Jesus argues that the claim, "Abraham is our father," is really a hollow presumption unless one performs deeds like Abraham did (v. 39). Not genetic descent, but believing Jesus' word determines the true "children of Abraham." Jesus points out to his opponents that they are not like Abraham because they try to kill him (vv. 37-40). Jesus says they are children of the devil because they do not accept the truth he teaches (vv. 41-47). The debate is brought to a head over the question of his

39. Nancy Calvert, "Abraham," in *Dictionary of Jesus and the Gospels* (Downers Grove, IL: InterVarsity, 1992), p. 4; also see Jeffrey S. Siker, *Disinheriting the Jews: Abraham in Early Christian Controversy* (Louisville: Westminster/John Knox, 1991), pp. 80, 84, 108-10.

40. Joseph A. Fitzmyer, *The Gospel According to Luke, I–IX*, The Anchor Bible (New York: Doubleday, 1981), p. 468.

41. Davies and Allison, *The Gospel According to Saint Matthew*, p. 624.

42. For a stimulating discussion of this section of the Fourth Gospel, see Steven A. Hunt, "And the Word Became Flesh — Again? Jesus and Abraham in John 8:31-59," in Hunt, ed., *Perspectives on Our Father Abraham*, pp. 81-109.

eternal existence (vv. 58-59). In sum, the true "children of Abraham" are recognized by their "belief in and witness to Jesus as the Christ" within the Johannine controversy with Judaism.[43]

In Paul's letters to the Romans and Galatians, a distinction is made between children after the flesh and children according to faith. There are children of Abraham by birth or natural descent and children who are spiritually his children through faith (see Rom. 4:1-24; 9:6-9; Gal. 3:6-29). In Romans 4, Paul focuses his attention on the inclusion of the Gentiles in God's plan of salvation. Paul emphasizes the similarity of Christian faith to Abrahamic faith; "Paul did not assert that Abraham had faith in Christ, but Paul did assert that faith in Christ is like Abraham's faith on this side of the resurrection."[44] All who believe in Christ (Jew and Gentile) are children of Abraham (Gal. 3:7, 29). "Through faith in Christ this divine blessing [of being children of Abraham) becomes really universal. It no longer remains limited to Israel but becomes truly comprehensive. God's promise of the blessing of the nations to Abraham has achieved a dimension that really spans the world.[45]

Does the above Christian vision of Abraham blessing the world diverge from or converge with that of the Jewish vision? Isadore Twersky insightfully comments on the Jewish vision: "Messianism may be described as the ultimate triumph of Abraham, when true belief will be universally restored. The beginning and end of history are interwoven. The task of Abraham was to form a nation that knows God."[46] This, Twersky concludes, will mark "the end of history and the ultimate vindication and victory of Abraham's struggle."[47] Indeed, in the end, there is a bringing together of the Jewish and the Christian visions. To be sure, as we have pointed out in this chapter and the preceding one, there is a difference in the way Jews and Christians understand and relate to Abraham. But the "victory of Abraham's struggle" is a common vision shared by both.

Thus, the expression "our father Abraham" expresses more than some historic remembrance of a virtuous biblical character or present spiritual ties to a family of faith. The expression is ultimately an eschatological statement.

43. Siker, *Disinheriting the Jews*, p. 143.

44. Siker, *Disinheriting the Jews*, p. 196.

45. Karl-Josef Kuschel, *Abraham: Sign of Hope for Jews, Christians and Muslims* (New York: Continuum, 1995), p. 85.

46. Isadore Twersky, *Introduction to the Code of Maimonides* (New Haven: Yale University Press, 1980), p. 451.

47. Twersky, *Introduction to the Code of Maimonides*, p. 451.

Abraham is a symbol of hope; he binds Christians and Jews together with a common vision of the outworking of the kingdom of God: Abraham, "All peoples on earth will be blessed through you" (Gen. 12:3).

UNDERSTANDING CHAPTER SIX

1. How is the declaration in Genesis 12:3 both particular and universal? With a group or partner, consider: In what capacity did Abraham witness the unfolding of these promises throughout his own lifetime? How do the writings of the New Testament bear witness to a continued unfolding of the process?

2. What does Scripture continually emphasize as the source of Abraham's call? Review Abraham Heschel's words about divine election on the opening page of the chapter. Do you agree or disagree? Why?

3. In addition to the account in Genesis, what other instances in Scripture reference Abraham's call? What additional light do these referents shed on Abraham's journey and relationship with God?

4. What does Thomas Cahill call "two of the boldest words in all literature"? Why?

5. In post-biblical Jewish religious thought, what is emphasized in terms of Abraham's coming to know God? How is this emphasis manifest in the Talmud?

6. What axiom, according to Shlomo Riskin, lies behind the Mishnaic idea that Abraham performed all of the commandments? What are your thoughts about Riskin's assertion concerning the potential of human reason to understand biblical theology and legal structure without revelation?

7. Given the tension between a divine call and human reasoning, what is the author's opinion concerning how Abraham came to know God and why? What is your opinion? In your view, are reason and faith compatible or are they enemies? Explain and discuss. In your personal faith journey, did *you* find God or did *he* find you? Discuss. In light of history, why do you think some modern Jews have had trouble embracing the expression "the chosen people"? Discuss. Does God have only one "chosen" people (see Deut. 7:7; 1 Pet. 2:9)? Discuss.

8. What is the most important metaphor in the Old Testament to express God's relationship to his people? In what way do the New Testament writers both modify and retain the metaphor?

9. How does the covenantal ceremony in Genesis 15:9-21 unfold? With what is the covenant sealed? What is the function of the slaughtered animals?

10. In Genesis 17, what else signifying the covenant between God and Abraham occurs? How was this foundational for the generations who were to come?

11. In what way is circumcision more than an outward mark on a physical body? On a deeper level, what does it signify? For the Christian, is baptism fully the equivalent of circumcision? Discuss.

12. From what biblical figures of the past does Paul acquire the concept of "circumcision of the heart"? How do most Christians understand the expression? In the context of interfaith discussion, from a Christian perspective, how does increased understanding of the role of circumcision in the Abrahamic covenant enhance your understanding of "circumcision of the heart"? From a Jewish perspective, what are your thoughts about Paul's emphasis on circumcision as a metaphor, an inner condition available to both Jews and Gentiles?

13. When and why was the Jerusalem Council held? What was the outcome, and how did Jewish and Gentile responses to the gospel begin to change after the decision? From a Christian perspective, how was the Council's decision critical in relation to the Abrahamic promise in Genesis 12:3?

14. What was it about Abraham that God considered as righteousness? What does righteousness in the Bible center on? How do Nahum Sarna's comments in this section provide another lens through which to interpret Genesis 15:6? How do you understand this critical verse?

15. Of what is Abraham the prime illustration in Pauline literature?

16. According to James Dunn, which critical manifestation of Abraham's faithfulness is key to understanding the phrase "credited to him as righteousness"? What do you think about this suggestion?

17. How does the epistle of James fail to accommodate the sense of faith-works polarity that has sometimes permeated Pauline interpretation? How does the epistle use Abraham as an example in this sphere?

18. What is the *Akedah*? In Jewish life, how does the word continue to remain important? How did devotion to the concepts associated with the *Akedah* occasionally become manifest in the lives of Jews in medieval times?

19. In what ways is James an epistle through which Jews and Christians come close to "meeting in the middle"? Regarding the oft-perceived

divide between faith and deeds, what does the author seek to communicate by writing that for James, "If there are differences, they are more on emphasis than substance"?

20. Which Hebrew imperatives does Isaiah employ to call for maximum attention in the opening verses of chapter 51? What are God's people called to do in 51:1-2?

21. Who is called a rock many times in Scripture? How might this contribute to our perception of Abraham as a rock in Isaiah 51:1-2?

22. In what ways might Peter be viewed as a "second Abraham"? Discuss the multiple points of connection that lead to the suggestion. Do you see Peter as a "second Abraham"?

23. In Luke 3:8, what is John the Baptist's concern, and what does he seem to envision with the phrase "children of Abraham"?

24. In John 8:31-59, what does Jesus argue regarding his opponents' claims to "father Abraham" and their understanding of what it means to be "children of Abraham"?

25. In Paul's letter to the Romans, what distinction is made between children after the flesh and children according to faith? Consider Jeffrey Siker's words that "Paul did not assert that Abraham had faith in Christ, but Paul did assert that faith in Christ is like Abraham's faith on this side of the resurrection." Explore the rich possibilities of connections between Christian and Abrahamic faith. Do you find yourself in agreement with Siker? Why or why not?

26. How does Isadore Twersky link Abraham with the concept of Messianism? How do you understand "Abraham's struggle"?

27. The opening paragraph of this chapter anticipated five themes central to the Abrahamic narratives. What are these themes? Form an understanding of the significance of each.

PART III

God and His Ways

CHAPTER 7

Who Is the God of Israel?

At the heart of any Jewish theology is the doctrine of God. Jews and Christians are theists. Theists hold that God is both transcendent and immanent; that is, God is above and beyond us, but he is also present in and around us. Deism, on the other hand, holds that God is only transcendent while pantheism says God is only immanent. Scripture affirms that God is an eternal, all-wise Creator and Revealer, whose nature is holy, just, and wholly good.[1] God proclaims many of his attributes to Moses as he passes before him: "The LORD, the LORD, the compassionate and gracious God, slow to anger, abounding in love and faithfulness, maintaining love to thousands and forgiving wickedness, rebellion and sin" (Exod. 34:6-7a).

For Christians, it is essential to have a correct understanding of God, his attributes, his ways, and his teachings. According to Scripture, before there was anything else in this world, there was only God (Gen. 1:1; John 1:1-3). Therefore, the subject of God is where theological studies must begin. Jews and Christians worship the same God, the Infinite One to whom both Moses and Jesus prayed. He is the God "who watches over Israel and does not slumber nor sleep" (Ps. 121:4).

Christians, however, frequently have a greatly diminished and shallow picture of God. This is largely due to their unfamiliarity with the Old Testament. But it is also a result of how many Christians come to, and then are nurtured in, the Christian faith. Their starting point is usually the teachings of Jesus and Paul. While these major figures of the New Testament were Jews and thus had their teachings largely grounded in Judaism, Christians often miss the rich context of the Jewish Scriptures out of which their teachings emerge.

---

1. See Louis Jacobs, *A Jewish Theology* (New York: Behrman, 1973), p. 15.

By way of example, every word in the Lord's Prayer, spoken by Jesus to his disciples, has an Old Testament origin (Matt. 6:9-13). Similarly, Paul's teaching in Romans 4 and Galatians 3 about the significance of Abraham cannot be properly grasped without a careful reading of Genesis 12–25. If Christianity starts with the God of Abraham and the patriarch's believing response to that God, every Christian should be driven back to the Old Testament where their theology and faith are firmly rooted (Gal. 3:29). Thus, they may exclaim, "Abraham's God has become my God!" Before we uncover more about who the God of Israel is, let us briefly turn to the question of his existence.

Scripture and God's Existence

The first great presupposition of theology is that God exists. The second is that this God has revealed himself in his inspired Word, the Bible. The Bible does not argue God's existence; it assumes it. Scripture does not debate his ultimate reality and power; it simply declares it: "In the beginning God created the heavens and the earth" (Gen. 1:1). A Christian believer accepts by faith the existence of God (Heb. 11:6). It is not a blind faith, however, but one informed by reason and the evidence of nature, history, experience, and especially the written Word of God (see Ps. 19:1-4).

Human intellect alone is not sufficient for one to find God and believe in his revealed Word. Neither does such knowledge and illumination come purely by education or sophisticated research. Neither logic nor science can prove or disprove the existence of God. One may contemplate the wonders and complexity of the universe, including the existence of human life and conscience, and yet fail to accept the existence of God. Further, to subscribe personally to God's existence is more than passive acceptance of an abstract concept "packaged" within one's family religious tradition.

In the end, to believe in God requires a step or "leap of faith." But faith itself is a gift, not a blind "whistling in the dark" or a mere "hoping against hope." For the Christian, the Holy Spirit graciously engenders faith within the human heart so one is able to perceive spiritual realities (1 Cor. 2:14-15). In short, God and his Word are truths that cannot be *taught;* they must be *caught.* They are grasped ultimately by inward persuasion, not by outward proofs or by some unique demonstration of empirical evidence. Those holding that there is no God are often described as atheists; those disclaiming any knowledge of God are said to be agnostics. But those claiming to know God are often described as "believers" (Heb. *ma'aminim,* Greek *hoi pisteuontes*). To define oneself as a believer is to make a personal statement of faith about God and his Word.

Monotheism

The world of ancient Israel was one of polytheism. Ancient Near Eastern deities and idolatrous practices were ubiquitously present around the Fertile Crescent, from Mesopotamia to Canaan to Egypt. In the call of Abraham at Ur, a revolutionary truth was revealed. The God of Abraham was alive, invisible, and one. Indeed, as John Oswalt puts it, "The Israelite concept of God is unique, there is nothing like it anywhere else. No place else is God thought to be a transcendent Person, utterly different from his creation."[2]

Throughout their history, Jews have maintained a rather strict adherence to the teaching of monotheism, a teaching that Moses first clearly declared in the Shema, "Hear, O Israel: The LORD our God, the LORD is one" (Deut. 6:4). Anything that might compromise the unity and oneness of God was usually eyed with great wariness. The Ten Commandments forbade idols, images, and other deities (Exod. 20:3-6). The ethics of pagan gods found in the mythologies of Israel's neighbors often left a lot to be desired. There was quarreling, conniving, blaming, and irrational behavior among the gods. The actions and judgments of gods were often undignified, whimsical, or capricious. For example, in the Babylonian Epic of Gilgamesh, the gods sought to blame each other for the deluge: the gods were frightened by the deluge, cowering like dogs; after the deluge, at a sacrifice, the gods crowded like flies around the sacrifice.[3] The nature of the God of Israel, however, was of a different moral order. Covenantally, he demanded exclusive obedience to him and his revealed will. In short, he "wrote the Book" on ethics. As the actions and ways of the God of Israel were merciful and just, his people were to follow suit in their relation one to another.

The claim that Jesus is God incarnate is foundational to traditional Christianity but is one of the most difficult concepts for Jews to understand. Going back to early Israelite history, Jews have had a fundamental theolog-

---

2. John N. Oswalt, "Abraham's Experience of Yahweh," in *Perspectives on Our Father Abraham,* ed. Steven A. Hunt (Grand Rapids: Eerdmans, 2010), p. 41.

3. See "The Epic of Gilgamesh," Tablet XI, in *The Ancient Near East: An Anthology of Texts and Pictures,* ed. James B. Pritchard (Princeton: Princeton University Press, 1958).

ical resistance to the idea of God becoming a man. The command to make no image or physical likeness of God has generally led Jews to prefer keeping the worship of God as an abstraction. Jews usually avoid concrete representations or physical symbols of God. It is held that to believe in such would be a departure from the idea of pure monotheism and would compromise the teaching of God's incorporeality. Christians, however, point to theophanies in the Old Testament. These temporary physical manifestations of God, they claim, indicate that God did occasionally choose to manifest himself in human form to his people. At the end of the day, however, both Jews and Christians subscribe to monotheism. Though paradoxical and mysterious to many, most Christians in the creedal tradition would be comfortable describing themselves as Trinitarian monotheists.

Coming to Know an Infinite God

One of the most important reasons why Christians need the Old Testament is to gain a broad perspective on how God has worked through hundreds of years of history. Unfortunately, when Christians largely limit their knowledge of Scripture to the New Testament documents, they often have a rather truncated view of God. Virtually all of the New Testament books were written during the last half of the first century. They record events limited to the first century. When one studies the Old Testament, however, one gains a historical perspective on how God worked among his people for nearly fifteen hundred years, the approximate time from Abraham to Malachi.

The Old Testament is not the story of Israel's discovery of God but the story of God's revelation of himself to Israel. God initiates revelation and individuals respond. From God's first encounter with Adam and Eve in the garden (Gen. 2:15–3:24), God has been in search of humankind.[4] God calls Abraham and says, "Leave your country," and he does (Gen. 12:1ff.). God calls Moses from the burning bush and says, "Go, I am sending you to Pharaoh to bring my people the Israelites out of Egypt" (Exod. 3:10). Though reluctant at first, Moses goes. God calls Amos from tending his flock and says, "Go, prophesy to my people Israel," and he obeys (Amos 7:15). There is a great spiritual mystery here. In this divine-human encounter, God initiates and a person completes. God speaks and an individual answers. When all is said

---

4. See Abraham J. Heschel, *God in Search of Man* (New York: Farrar, Straus, & Giroux, 1955), pp. 136-44.

and done, the message of the Bible is either theocentric, of divine origin, or it is anthropocentric, of human origin.

The discipline of theology largely concerns itself with the study of God, his attributes, and his relation to the world. Our ignorance about God far outweighs our knowledge of him. According to Scripture, God is an infinite, all-powerful, all-knowing Spirit. God is not an idea or blind force; he is a person. The God we serve is not a dead concept but a living reality. God is not an abstract philosophical assertion but a dynamic force. He reveals himself in history with deep pathos toward his creation. The God of the Hebrew Bible is not Aristotle's "Unmoved Mover" but is what Abraham Heschel called "the Most Moved Mover."[5]

Knowledge of God (*da'at elohim*) is more than learning about him cognitively as an object of exegetical inquiry. In the biblical Hebraic view, to "know" God means to experience him. God is subject and acts within history. His presence may be known relationally through intimate personal encounter. In Hebrew, *yada* ("to know") is not simply the ability to grasp abstract concepts. Rather, "knowing" often denotes "an act involving concern, inner engagement, dedication, or attachment to a person."[6] Thus, to know God is be aware of him; it is to be deeply committed in solidarity to him so that his concerns are our concerns.

Though God is fully in control and immutable in his nature, he responds sovereignly in relation to the actions of his people. This dynamic aspect of God is seen in Scripture in the conditional nature of much biblical prophecy. God says through Jeremiah, "If at any time I announce that a nation or kingdom is to be uprooted, torn down and destroyed, and if that nation I warned repents of its evil, then I will relent and not inflict on it the disaster I had planned" (Jer. 18:7-8). This passage indicates that God's sovereignty is not a static immobility but is conditioned on man's actions. When people repent, God responds by changing his course of action from one of judgment. It would be a mistake to view biblical prophecy as simply a unilateral pronouncement of God regarding human destiny. Far from it! Prophetic literature reminds us that God is caring and dynamically responsive to his people. Accordingly, "the word of God never comes to an end. For this reason, prophetic predictions are seldom final. No word is God's final

5. Quoted in Fritz A. Rothschild, ed., *Between God and Man* (New York: Free Press, 1959), p. 24, and in Edward K. Kaplan, *Spiritual Radical: Abraham Joshua Heschel in America, 1940-1972* (New Haven: Yale University Press, 2007), p. 196.

6. Abraham J. Heschel, *The Prophets* (New York: Harper & Row, 1962), p. 57.

word. Judgment, far from being absolute, is conditional. A change in man's conduct brings about a change in God's judgment."[7]

Our frail, human attempts to capture God systematically in formulas or to "box him in" via theological statements is, in the end, far too limiting and confining. One must confess there is a sovereign unpredictability about God and his ways. Mystery surrounds the vastness of God and his universe. The psalmist confesses, "Great is the LORD and most worthy of praise; his greatness no one can fathom" (Ps. 145:3). Finite Israel could never fully fathom the greatness of God; neither can we. So, the Infinite One reminds his people, "As the heavens are higher than the earth, so are my ways higher than your ways and my thoughts than your thoughts" (Isa. 55:9).

Names We May Trust

In the modern world a name may be used as a label for identification purposes or to express a preference. Sometimes names are given to single one out or to distinguish one individual from another. Today, when a name is chosen for a child, parents may be influenced in their choice for reasons such as: "It sounds so pretty"; "It's uncommon and really cute"; "It's my husband's first name"; or "It looks so distinguished in print." In Old Testament times, however, the right to name was an indication of power or ownership. Hence naming was in the hands of a superior or authority such as a parent, a ruler, or God himself. For example, Adam exercises dominion over the animals by naming them (Gen. 2:19-20).

A name was significant, for it was often chosen to denote the essence of the one to whom it was given. The name might signify a character role or reveal a certain destiny that person was intended to fulfill. The selection of the names of Isaiah's two sons are clear illustrations of this point. One son is named Maher-Shalal-Hash-Baz, "quick to the plunder, swift to the spoil," and the other Shear-Jashub, "a remnant will return" (Isa. 8:1; 7:3). Both these names carried direct prophetic significance concerning the history and destiny of the nation of Judah.

Sometimes one in authority changed the name of one subservient to him. God changed Abram's name to Abraham (Gen. 17:5). Jesus changed Simon's name to Peter (Mark 3:16). To know a person's name is to have a relationship with that person. God-fearing Israelites were "called by the name

---

7. Heschel, *The Prophets,* p. 194.

of the Lord" and hence had a special relationship of accountability to him (Deut. 28:10; see 2 Chron. 7:14). "To be called by the same name as your name-giver meant unity with him."[8] The prophets of Israel spoke in the name of the Lord as his divinely appointed representatives (Jer. 26:9, 16). To speak in another's name is to speak with that person's authority. "Thus says the Lord. . . ."

The names of God give us sacred glimpses into various aspects of God's character. They also reveal the close relation God has with his people. A very close relation exists between God and his names. They remind us that God is personal. He alone, because of his unchanging nature, perfectly embodies the true meaning of the names originated by him. His names also reflect the social and religious setting of the ancient Near East within which the Hebrews lived. Let us consider the four most common names for God in the Old Testament.[9]

Elohim: The Powerful God of Creation

The common Hebrew name for God is Elohim. It is found more than 2500 times in the Hebrew Bible. The related name El, a common, generic Semitic word for deity, carries the idea of force, power, might, or strength. Hence the Hebrew names *El Elyon,* "God Most High" (Gen. 14:18-22); *El Shaddai,* "God Almighty" (Gen. 17:1); and *El Olam,* "Eternal God" (Gen. 21:33). The name El is frequently combined in proper names: e.g., Bethel, "house of God"; Daniel, "God is my judge"; Ezekiel, "God strengthens"; and Michael, "Who is like God?"

Elohim may occur as an ordinary plural referring to pagan gods (Gen. 35:2; Exod. 20:3), supernatural beings or spirits (1 Sam. 28:13), or human rulers or judges (Ps. 82:1, 6). But when the name Elohim is used of the one true God of scriptural revelation, it regularly takes a singular verb. More than 90 percent of all uses of *Elohim* in the Old Testament fall into this category.

Some Christian writers have argued that the plurality of *elohim* is a definite indication of the Trinity. This writer, however, believes this is more a result of "reading back" into the text, a conclusion in search of an exeget-

---

8. Douglas Sanders, "The Names of God," *Eternity,* October 1983, p. 26.

9. For a recent discussion of the names of God, see Douglas A. Knight and Amy-Jill Levine, *The Meaning of the Bible: What the Jewish Scriptures and Christian Old Testament Can Teach Us* (New York: HarperCollins, 2011), pp. 139-47.

ical base. In a world of polytheism in which the need was to disabuse Israel of the idea that a plurality of deities existed rather than one God, it seems exceedingly unlikely that a triune understanding of God is being suggested by the plural. *Elohim* appears to be a plural of majesty or an intensive plural, suggesting the One who completely expresses the divine attributes, much as italics sets a word off by emphasizing or heightening its meaning.

In the first verse of the Bible we encounter Elohim, "In the beginning God *(elohim)* created the heavens and the earth" (Gen. 1:1). In exalted splendor, majesty, and power Elohim brings the world into being. By his power he actively preserves every creature he brings to life. Gordon Wenham wisely observes, "Elohim is not simply synonymous with the English word 'God.' Thanks to secularism, God has become for many people little more than an abstract philosophical concept. But the biblical view avoids such abstractions. . . . His reality is seen in his acts."[10]

In addition to creation, we may point to other mighty acts revealing the power of God. For example, in Exodus 15:2, when the Israelites experience the power of God and are delivered from the Egyptians at the Red Sea, Moses exclaims, "He is my God" *(zeh eli)*. Later in Israel's history, the boldness of the shepherd boy David that led to the mighty defeat of Goliath and the Philistine army required a display of the power of the living God so that, in David's words, "the whole world will know that there is a God *(elohim)* in Israel" (1 Sam. 17:46).

The opening verses of the Old Testament remind us that Elohim is not a localized deity of a primitive tribal people but the sovereign Creator of all that is in heaven and earth. Seven, the number of completeness or totality, is prominent in the creation narrative of Genesis. This is the case not simply in the number of days of creation but also in regard to the very frequent use of *Elohim*. In the opening account of creation that features "seven days" (Gen. 1:1–2:3), *Elohim* occurs thirty-five times (five times seven), an obvious poetical touch built around this divine name.

Adonai: Lord of the Submitted

Like *Elohim, Adonai,* meaning "my (great) lord," is a plural of majesty, lending an intensification to its meaning. *Adonai* derives from the singular, *adon*

---

10. Gordon Wenham, *Genesis 1–15*, Word Biblical Commentary (Waco, TX: Word, 1987), p. 15.

(Heb. "lord," "master"). Also, like *el/elohim*, the term *adon* is used in proper names — for example, Adonijah, "my lord is Yahweh"; Adoniram, "my lord is exalted"; and Adonizedek, "my lord is righteous." In the Old Testament, *adon* is used in various earthly contexts of a subordinate to one in charge, to one of higher status, or to one responsible for supervising another in some social relationship. For example, *adon* is used of a servant to his master (Isa. 24:2), of a wife to her husband (1 Kgs. 1:17, 18, 20), or of a daughter to her father (Gen. 31:35). Normally, one who addresses another as *adon* is subject to that person in a submissive or dependent relationship. Lordship implies ownership or the right to exercise authority over another.

In reference to God, the title Adonai is usually rendered into English as "Lord." The term points to the Ruler of the universe to whom all creation is dependent and subject. In sum, "the title indicates the truth that God is the owner of each member of the human family, and that he consequently claims the unrestricted obedience of all."[11] As Adonai, he is Master and his people are under his direction and guidance. Thus, Israel is to be in a submitted relationship to him in all avenues of life. Why? The God of Israel is *adone ha-adonim*, "Lord of lords" (Deut. 10:17).

In a similar vein, we who acknowledge his lordship as the spiritual children of Abraham are asked to submit to the divine will. Contrary to some contemporary popular "god concepts," the Adonai of Scripture does not serve us; but we serve him. As Master of the universe, he lovingly rules over all his creation. One is called to submit to Adonai out of love, not compulsion. In the Hebrew Scriptures, God emphasizes the priority of love before specific commandment keeping. The call to love God with the totality of one's being is to be heeded before adhering to other commands (Deut. 6:4-9). According to Jesus, the first and greatest commandment is to "love the Lord your God with all your heart and with all your soul and with all your mind and with all your strength" (Mark 12:30). This emphasis upon a relationship of love with the sovereign ruler of the universe is crucial in understanding the call to obedience implicit in the term "Lord." The loyal love and service of Israel to her Maker was to be a response to God's covenant love toward Israel. Love begets love. Accordingly, submission of will is not slavery if it flows from a heart of love.

Lordship thus reminds one of the paradoxes of Christianity: through loving submission to another (Christ) comes true freedom as a child of God;

---

11. R. B. Girdlestone, *Synonyms of the Old Testament* (repr. Peabody, MA: Hendrickson, 2000), p. 34.

to find one's life one must lose one's life; one must lovingly commit to a Person before one joyfully desires to do that Person's will. Relationship comes before rulership. Adonai is more than a name; it is the revelation of humans' humble standing before their Owner.

YHWH: The Ineffable Name of God

In the Old Testament, God has a four-lettered Holy Name (the Tetragrammaton). The four Hebrew consonants are *yodh* (Y), *he* (H), *waw* (W), and *he* (H), or YHWH. The name YHWH is the hidden or mysterious name of God. Arthur Green asks and answers, "What is its mystery? First, it has no vowels. Without vowels . . . it is impossible to pronounce a word. But Y-H-W-H also has no real consonants! Y, H, and W really are blowing sounds, rushings of air through the mouth. . . . The point is one of *elusiveness* or abstraction. The name of God is so subtle it could slip away from you. Y-H-W-H is not a God you can grab hold of and be sure you've got it in your mental 'grasp.'"[12]

This divine title is often referred to as the *Ineffable Name*.[13] To set the name apart, it is usually rendered into English by the four capital letters LORD. No one knows for sure how the Tetragrammaton was pronounced in Hebrew. However, the consensus of scholarship agrees that it was probably close to "Yahweh" (but see paragraphs below). There is a degree of mystery here. The Mishnah states that anyone who pronounces the Ineffable Name will have no share in the world to come (Sanhedrin 10:1). According to rabbinic sources, apart from the priests in the Temple, the name was rarely pronounced in Bible times.

An attempt to pronounce the name was probably avoided to protect the name from irreverence in light of several pointed warnings in the Torah. Exodus 20:7 states, "You shall not misuse the name of the LORD your God, for the LORD will not hold anyone guiltless who misuses his name." The words of Leviticus 24:16 are even stronger: "Anyone who blasphemes the name of the LORD must be put to death. The entire assembly must stone him. Whether an alien or native-born, when he blasphemes the name, he must be put to death." It should be observed that the TANAKH translation

---

12. Arthur Green, *These Are the Words: A Vocabulary of Jewish Spiritual Life* (Woodstock, VT: Jewish Lights Publishing, 1999), p. 3.

13. See Abraham J. Heschel, *God in Search of Man* (New York: Farrar, Straus & Giroux, 1955), pp. 64-65.

of the Jewish Publication Society renders these words of Leviticus 24:16 in this way: "If he also pronounces the name LORD, he shall be put to death." The sense of this passage seems to be that when anyone shows contempt and dishonor of God's name, failing to subordinate his will to God's will, this leads to anti-social behavior that makes it most difficult for society to function properly. To be sure, human peace and harmony must flow from an individual's desire to be controlled and guided by God's law.[14]

Today, in theological literature and ecumenical discussion, the Tetragrammaton is usually pronounced "Yahweh." Whether this pronunciation is exact, or not, must remain uncertain. The lengthy tradition — from Second Temple times — of not taking this sacred name on one's lips resulted in its pronunciation becoming lost. To avoid possible misuse of the name in synagogue liturgy and Scripture reading, Jews began to render the Tetragrammaton "Adonai," a tradition that has continued to this day.

Today, in addition to Adonai, sometimes other expressions are used in addressing God. These names include Ha-Shem ("The Name"), Ha-Makom ("The Place"), Ha-Kadosh Barukh Hu ("The Holy One, Blessed Be He"), Shekinah ("Divine Presence"), Ribono shel Olam ("Master of the World"), Ein Soph ("Infinite One"), and others. Many Christian scholars, when reading Hebrew texts, usually pronounce the Tetragrammaton "Adonai," out of respect for the Jewish tradition. The New Testament indicates that by the first century a type of circumlocution had developed in the matter of divine names in general. Matthew, for example, writing mainly to a Jewish audience, regularly chooses the less offensive term "kingdom of heaven" as opposed to the term "kingdom of God" employed by Mark and Luke.

The four capital letters LORD distinguish the name of Yahweh from Adonai, "Lord" (see above). They remind the reader that this is God's personal name, his name par excellence. The name occurs over 6800 times. Unlike *Elohim* and *Adonai*, Yahweh is exclusive; the name is not used of any being other than Israel's God. The name Yahweh is employed in many proper names, which have the familiar *iah* or *jah* ending. (The name "Yah" is an alternate or shortened form of Yah[weh], as in Ps. 68:19.) Examples of biblical names that incorporate God's personal name are Obadiah, "servant of Yah[weh]"; Zechariah, "Yah[weh] remembers"; Hezekiah, "Yah[weh] strengthens"; and Abijah, "Yah[weh] is my father." This divine name may also be recognized in English through the prefix "Jo" (Heb. "Yah") in such

---

14. See the commentary on "Parashas Emor" in *The Chumash*, The Artscroll Series/Stone Edition (Brooklyn, NY: Mesorah Publications, 1994), p. 693.

proper names as Joel, "Yah(weh) is God"; Jonathan, "Yah(weh) has given"; and Joshua, "Yah(weh) is salvation."

The name Jehovah is a hybrid proper name that combines the consonants YHWH with the vowels of Adonai. The Masoretes, Jewish scholars from the early Middle Ages who established the basic text for the Hebrew Bible and standardized its pronunciation, inserted the vowels of Adonai into the Tetragrammaton. They did this to remind readers to avoid saying the sacred name Yahweh and to substitute instead the name Adonai. In the late Middle Ages, and especially at the time of the Reformation, a Christian misunderstanding of the (vocalized) Masoretic text resulted in the expression Jehovah finding its way into common Christian usage. Though the creation of the name Jehovah is non-biblical and has no pretense to be correct, the name has been perpetuated through various hymns, Christian literature, and certain English translations of the Bible such as the American Standard Version (1901).

Ehyeh Asher Ehyeh, "I AM WHO I AM"

The noun Yahweh is related to the Hebrew verb *hayah,* meaning "to be, become, happen." The verb "to be" means more than mere existence or a state of being. It also often connotes the idea "to be actively present." Moses is the greatest Old Testament prophet. God calls him at the burning bush (Exodus 3). On that occasion, God assures Moses that his presence will be with him when he goes to Pharaoh and frees the Israelites. God says, *ehyeh immakh,* "I will be with you" (Exod. 3:12). In the verses that follow, Moses asks for the name of the God who is to send him forth. God replies, *ehyeh asher ehyeh,* "I AM WHO I AM" or "I WILL BE WHAT I WILL BE" (v. 14). The *ehyeh,* "I am," of verse 12 links directly with the divine name, *ehyeh,* "I AM," in verse 14. The Hebrew consonants YHWH, translated "LORD" in verse 15, derive from the root *hayah,* the same root word of *ehyeh,* "I AM," of verse 14. In Hebrew literature, the third person imperfect of the verb "to be" is *yihyeh,* "he will be." The imperfect is used for an open, incomplete, or future action and here links with the first person imperfect *ehyeh,* likely suggesting the preferable rendering, "I WILL BE WHAT I WILL BE."

In regard to the above, Martin Buber makes the point of emphasizing the dynamic quality of the name *ehyeh asher ehyeh.* Buber says this verb used at the burning bush does not denote existence in the static sense. Rather, the verb means "happening," "coming into being," "being there," or "being present." Hence the sense of the phrase is, "I will be there as I will be there," emphasizing the promise of his presence, as one open, willing, and able to respond to the human situation.[15]

The name Yahweh thus is comprised of the consonants of the Hebrew verb, "he will be, become." As the book of Genesis indicates, God revealed himself as YHWH prior to the period of the Exodus. But in the deliverance from Egypt, and in other mighty acts to follow, Israel would come to know the depth of his character revealed in his name (Exod. 7:5; also 6:3). In Joseph Telushkin's words, "[God] reveals Himself through His actions: 'I shall be as I shall be' means therefore 'I shall be as I shall *act*' (in contradistinction to the 'Unmoved Mover,' Aristotle's description of God)."[16] Thus, it would come to pass *(yihyeh),* through the unfolding of covenantal history, that Israel would increasingly experience and understand Yahweh's power, faithfulness, and presence in the deepest personal way. Writing about the "common hope" of Jews and Christians, Jewish scholar Pinchas Lapide makes this sage comment related to the "I AM" passage of Exodus 3:14: "No one is permitted to anticipate or know in advance the forms of God's appearance. Still less is it possible to claim to determine what God will do in the future or will allow."[17]

Yahweh, the God of the burning bush who was about to free Israel from Egypt, is the same One who revealed himself to the earlier patriarchs Abraham, Isaac, and Jacob. God said to Moses, "Say to the Israelites, 'The LORD, the God of your fathers — the God of Abraham, the God of Isaac and the God of Jacob — has sent me to you.' This is my name for ever, the name by which I am to be remembered from generation to generation" (Exod. 3:15). The name Yahweh affirms God's all-sufficiency and unchangeableness toward his people. This actively present Spirit would fulfill his covenant promises to all future generations, dynamically intervening on their behalf.

In his classic work *The Doctrine of God,* Herman Bavinck summarizes the significance of the name Yahweh: "[The name] is so rich and so full of meaning: He will be what He has been for the patriarchs, what He is now, and what He will remain: for His people He will be everything. The One Who appears to Moses is not a new or a strange God, but is the God of the fathers, the Unchangeable, the Immutable One, the Faithful One, the eternally Self-consistent One, the One Who never leaves or forsakes His people but

---

15. See the discussion of Buber in Johanna W. H. van Wijk-Bos, *Making Wise the Simple: The Torah in Christian Faith and Practice* (Grand Rapids: Eerdmans, 2005), pp. 241-42.

16. Joseph Telushkin, *Biblical Literacy* (New York: William Morrow, 1997), p. 101.

17. Karl Rahner and Pinchas Lapide, *Encountering Jesus — Encountering Judaism: A Dialogue,* trans. David Perkins (New York: Crossroad, 1983), p. 73.

ever seeks His own and ever saves them, Who is unchangeable in His grace, in His love, in His succor, Who will be what He is, since He ever remains Himself."[18] The name Ehyeh Asher Ehyeh thus mysteriously points to the future; the term suggests an anticipation of events to come. These happenings, encounters, interventions, and more will further disclose the nature of this divine Being. Progressive revelation is thus at the heart of biblical faith.

In the Christian tradition, the "I AM" who lights up the narrative of the burning bush also shines forth in the pages of the New Testament. One should especially note the importance of the "I am" *(ego eimi)* sayings in the Fourth Gospel. Jesus provoked controversy in applying these words to himself: "Before Abraham was born, I am" (John 8:58).[19] The Book of Revelation makes hundreds of allusions to the Hebrew Bible. One of the most striking is the introductory greeting, "Grace and peace to you from him who is, and who was, and who is to come" (Rev. 1:4; also 4:8). Here the author of Revelation calls attention to the divine name Yahweh by making a periphrastic expansion of the "I AM" of the burning bush (see Exod. 3:14-15). In addition, the letter to the Hebrews, a Christocentric work addressed to Jewish believers, also builds on the above theme: "Jesus Christ is the same yesterday and today and forever" (13:8).

In sum, names matter because God matters. If theology proper is the study of God himself, including his nature, his attributes, and his names, then the terms we have discussed in this chapter associated with God's self-revelation provide valuable windows into his personhood. Who is the God of Israel? He is Elohim, Adonai, Yahweh, Ehyeh Asher Ehyeh, and more.

UNDERSTANDING CHAPTER SEVEN

1. What are the basic differences between deism, pantheism, and Jewish and Christian theism?
2. Some of God's most important attributes are summed up in Exodus 34:6-7a. Name at least six of these.
3. The author states that Christians frequently have a greatly diminished and shallow picture of God. What are some reasons for this?

---

18. Herman Bavinck, *The Doctrine of God* (Grand Rapids: Eerdmans, 1951), pp. 105-6.

19. For a thoughtful and extensive treatment of this "I am" passage, see Steven A. Hunt, "And the Word Became Flesh — Again? Jesus and Abraham in John 8:31-59," in Hunt, ed., *Perspectives on Our Father Abraham,* pp. 81-109.

4. Each of the words of which prayer in the New Testament has an Old Testament origin?

5. What are the first two great presuppositions of Jewish and Christian theology? How does the Bible treat the topic of God's existence?

6. According to the author, in the end, to believe in God requires what? How is faith not blind or a mere "hoping against hope"? Do you agree?

7. What "revolutionary truth" was revealed about God through the call of Abraham? What particular uniqueness about the Israelite concept of God does John Oswalt bring to our attention?

8. At what point in Jewish history and in Scripture was the teaching of monotheism first clearly articulated? In moral comparison to the God of Israel, how did the gods of Israel's neighbors "leave a lot to be desired"? How does the Babylonian Epic of Gilgamesh illustrate this point?

9. Why is the foundational Christian claim that Jesus is God incarnate one of the most difficult concepts for Jews to understand? In response, what is the traditional Christian perspective? Is the expression "Trinitarian monotheist" an oxymoron? Discuss.

10. What length of time do the writings of the Old and New Testaments encompass respectively? In terms of knowing God through history, what is a clear consequence of Christians limiting their knowledge of Scripture to the New Testament? What is the rich benefit of studying the Old Testament?

11. If the Old Testament is not the story of Israel's discovery of God, what is it? Identify examples in Scripture in which God initiates revelation and individuals respond. Do you see this as a hard-and-fast rule, a general pattern, or no rule at all? Defend your position.

12. Rather than an idea or a dead concept, what is God and how does he reveal his nature in history? As an optional additional exercise, research Aristotle's articulation of the concept of the "Unmoved Mover." Consider why Abraham Heschel might have chosen to play on these words to emphasize God as the "Most Moved Mover."

13. What is *da'at elohim?* How does the meaning of the Hebrew verb *yada* help define the concept of the "knowledge of God" beyond simple cognitive understanding? In essence, what is it to "know God"?

14. How does prophecy remind us that God is dynamically responsive to his people? How does Jeremiah 18:7-8 reinforce this notion? What does it mean to say that "[n]o word is God's final word"? Do you agree with Heschel?

15. In contrast to the modern world, in Old Testament times, what did the right to name signify? Why were names themselves significant? As one of many examples, how did the names of Isaiah's sons function?

16. Give two examples of instances in which someone in authority changed the name of someone subservient to him. Beyond mere acquaintance, what did it mean to know a person's name?

17. How do knowing the names of God aid us in knowing him more deeply? List the four most common names for God in the Old Testament.

18. How many times is *Elohim* found in the Hebrew Bible? What does the related name *El* mean? How do the names *El Elyon, El Shaddai,* and *El Olam* translate into English?

19. As an ordinary plural, what can *elohim* refer to in the Old Testament? What grammatical distinction occurs when the term is used for the God of scriptural revelation? What percentage of all uses of *elohim* fall into this latter category?

20. Why does the author not uphold the view that *Elohim*, when used of God, is indicative of the Trinity? What alternative perspective does he present?

21. Reflect on Gordon Wenham's statement that "Elohim is not simply synonymous with the English word 'God.' . . ." Recall the ideas that accompany the word *El*. How is God's nature illumined when a simple one-to-one semantic correlation is refuted?

22. Identify three instances in which *Elohim* (or *El*) is used in a context that displays God's power and might. How do his actions and the words of his people work together to highlight this aspect of his character?

23. Numerically speaking, what does the author perceive as an "obvious poetical touch" regarding the use of *Elohim* in the creation narrative? Why?

24. What is the meaning of *adonai?* In what contexts is *adon* used in the Old Testament? In reference to God, how is the term *Adonai* usually rendered in English? What does the title indicate about the status of God in relation to his creation?

25. What important emphasis is crucial to understanding the call to obedience implicit in the term "Lord"? Provide scriptural support.

26. In Christianity, how does submission paradoxically lead to true freedom?

27. What is the Tetragrammaton? In your own words, summarize Arthur Green's analysis of this title. How might Green's emphasis be helpful in underlining the human need to grasp the invisibility of God as op-

posed to the physicality of pagan idols? Discuss. Do you find Green's perspective — a phonetic lens of interpretation — insightful?

28. How is the divine title often referred to? How is it usually rendered in English?

29. What does the Mishnah state about pronunciation of the Ineffable Name? What light do rabbinic sources shed on the history of its pronunciation? Why was an attempt to pronounce the name probably avoided? Cite Scripture passages in your response.

30. Note the Jewish Publication Society TANAKH translation of Leviticus 24:16 in comparison to traditional Christian translations. To what degree, if any, do you think Christians should honor their Jewish roots by exercising precaution in pronouncing "Yahweh"? From a Christian standpoint, do you think a casual or more frequent vocalization of the name of "Yahweh" (e.g., in contemporary worship songs) brings more honor to God or dissolves the sense of unique power and essence that the name carries? Are both effects possible? Why or why not?

31. When did the tradition of not taking the sacred name on one's lips come about? Alternatively, how did Jews begin to render the Tetragrammaton in speech?

32. In addition to *Adonai,* what are some other expressions used to address God in Judaism today? What is one New Testament example that indicates that a type of circumlocution had developed around divine names in general? Does Christianity have comparable circumlocutions for God? From a Christian standpoint, does the ability to address God intimately ("Abba, Father"; Gal. 4:6) eliminate the need for circumlocution, or is there a need for and benefit of both manners of addressing God?

33. How many times does *YHWH* occur in the Old Testament? How is the title exclusive?

34. Identify some examples of the name *Yahweh* employed in proper names, both as a prefix and a suffix.

35. Explain the development of the hybrid name "Jehovah."

36. To which Hebrew verb is the name *Yahweh* related? What does it mean?

37. In what historical context does God declare, *ehyeh asher ehyeh?* What does the author suggest as the preferable rendering into English?

38. How does Martin Buber understand the name Ehyeh Asher Ehyeh as denoting a dynamic existence?

39. In relation to Exodus 3:14, what does Pinchas Lapide write about the "common hope" of Jews and Christians? In the context of interfaith dialogue, in what areas in particular do you think his grounding statement should spur us to humility and admission of finite knowledge?

40. Review Exodus 3:15 as well as Herman Bavinck's summary of the significance of the name Yahweh. In what ways was and is God both unchanging and dynamic?

41. In what instances does "I AM" appear in the New Testament? (Cite the Gospel of John, Revelation, and the epistle to the Hebrews in your response.) From either a Jewish or Christian perspective, how does knowledge of the Old Testament foundation of the name "I AM" enrich your understanding and interpretation of its use in the New Testament?

CHAPTER 8

Reputation and Renown: Yahweh in His World

In the previous chapter, our main focus was upon the existence of God and the various names used for God in the Hebrew Bible. Not a force of nature, God is personal. As vehicles of revelation, the names of God display his essence, character, and aspects of the relationship he sustains with his people.

Our discussion in this present chapter will mainly look at how Yahweh, the "Holy One of Israel" (Isa. 30:11, 12, 15; 41:14, 16, 20), stands out in biblical society, especially among competing deities. In the experience of Israel, what is there about Yahweh that draws people's attention? What is remarkable about him, attracting singular devotion, obedience, and loyalty? What is especially noteworthy about the God of Israel in their Scriptures that gives them "bragging rights" among the nations? Again and again, Yahweh reveals himself in concrete, real-life situations. While Yahweh's abode is in heaven, his reputation and renown are established on earth, before a great "cloud of witnesses" *(nephos martyron)* (Heb. 12:1). How did his presence — especially in divine "visitations" — distinguish him in the wider "battle of the gods"? Finally, how did some of the metaphors applied to the God of Israel in Old Testament times influence the authors of the New Testament?

False Gods Cannot Act

The Old Testament boldly declares, "I am the Lord, and there is no other; apart from me there is no God" (Isa. 45:5). Israel was shown "great and awesome deeds" so that they "might know that the Lord is God" (Deut. 4:34, 35). When the biblical prophets wished to dismiss the reality of pagan deities and idols, they ridiculed their lifelessness. They showed how false gods were unable to act; they were lifeless, unresponsive to their worshipers' cries. Elijah mocked the prophets of Baal, for Baal was unable to meet the challenge to send fire down on the altar as the Lord was able to do (1 Kgs. 18:16-45). Jeremiah states, "Every goldsmith is shamed by his idols. His images are a fraud; they have no breath in them. They are worthless, the objects of mockery" (Jer. 10:14-15).

Psalm 115 provides another effective commentary on the phoniness of the idols of the nations: "But their idols are silver and gold, made by the hands of men. They have mouths, but cannot speak, eyes, but they cannot see; they have ears, but cannot hear, noses, but they cannot smell; they have hands, but cannot feel, feet, but they cannot walk; nor can they utter a sound with their throats. Those who make them will be like them, and so will all who trust in them" (vv. 4-8).

In a similar vein, Habakkuk debunks idols as lifeless: "Of what value is an idol, since a man has carved it? Or an image that teaches lies? For he who makes it trusts in his own creation; he makes idols that cannot speak. Woe to him who says to wood, 'Come to life!' Or to lifeless stone, 'Wake up!' Can it give guidance? It is covered with gold and silver; there is no breath in it" (Hab. 2:18-19). In contrast to idols, however, the God of Israel is alive and about to judge, and so Habakkuk exhorts, "let all the earth be silent before him" (v. 20).

A Supernatural "Battle"

The above passages delegitimize pagan deities and idols because they are unresponsive, fake, and hence useless. On the other hand, how did the Israelites go about establishing the validity of their claim to know (experientially) and worship the one true God? The claim was in action, not inaction. Their claim was in a God who had come to them in history, revealing himself and his will, often in extraordinary ways. They often appealed to the One who speaks and delivers, the living God able to do the awesome and miraculous. Such displays of divine action were sometimes supernaturally given in a "secular" or pagan environment in order to discredit the false gods of the foreign nations and to manifest the divine power of the true God.

In the Hebrew Bible, three great outpourings or clusters of miracles occur. As alluded to above, each takes place in the midst of a foreign nation and its gods. Consequently, polytheistic religion is attacked, demythologized, or rendered impotent in the face of the miraculous power of Yahweh. His mighty acts accredit his divinely appointed messengers, the prophets, and the truth of their words, including revelations about things to occur immediately or in the distant future. Jeremiah predicts the death of the false prophet Hananiah within a year. And it happens (Jer. 28:15-17). Yahweh intends to establish his reputation in all the earth, not simply within *eretz yisrael*, "the land of Israel." This is a "battle of the gods" over who is the supreme God.

The "Battle" with Egyptian Gods

The first cluster of miracles took place in Egypt at the time of the plagues. Would Re, the sun god of Egypt, or Yahweh, prove more powerful? Most of the plagues (Exod. 7:14–11:8) prove to be an attack on Egyptian idolatry, climaxing with a three-day eclipse of the sun god Re, the chief deity of the land. In the midst of the plagues, the Lord told Pharaoh to let his people go or else Egypt would receive the full force of the plagues (Exod. 9:13, 14). In Egyptian culture, the Pharaoh was considered divine. But Pharaoh would not get the last word. Yahweh the God of Israel did. The Lord informed this "divine ruler" of the purpose of the plagues: "so you may know that there is no one like me in all the earth" (Exod. 9:14).

In the defeat of Pharaoh and his pride came a "chink in the armor" of the impotent idols of Egypt. On the other hand, there was placed a "feather in the cap" of the living God of Israel. The Exodus from Egypt is a powerful story that illustrates the "battle of the gods." Which deity will prove superior through a victory gained for his people? After Israel has safely passed through the waters of the Red Sea, Moses sang a song of victory celebrating Yahweh's kingly power (Exod. 15:1-21). Biblical scholars call this paean, *shirat ha-yam*, "The Song of the Sea." Moses concludes the song with the victorious words, "The LORD will reign for ever and ever," sung in praise of Yahweh, the "warrior" of the Israelite people (Exod. 15:3, 18).

The "Battle" with Canaanite Gods

The second cluster of miracles came during the Divided Kingdom, at the time of Elijah and his disciple Elisha. God raised up these prophets to check the rise of Canaanite religion and Baal worship, briefly alluded to above. Especially on the northern borders of Israel, Baalism was a serious problem. King Ahab's wife Jezebel, the daughter of the King of Tyre, was a fanatic for

Baal worship. She particularly promoted Baalism in the Northern Kingdom of Israel where Ahab ruled. Baalism was detestable to the prophets of Israel because it was a form of nature worship that involved sacred prostitution and child sacrifice. Baal was the Canaanite god of fertility and nature.

The cult of Baalism particularly thrived on verdant Mount Carmel overlooking the Valley of Jezreel, the largest fertile region in northern Israel. According to the Canaanite religion, Baal brought pregnancy to the womb and life to the parched soil so crops could grow. Baal also controlled the weather; he sent rain to make the wadis flow. From the Canaanite perspective, the prophet Elijah appeared to meddle in Baal's domain because he forecast a drought in the land (1 Kgs. 17:1). This resulted in a severe famine (1 Kgs. 18:2). One of Baal's epithets is "Rider of the Clouds." Canaanite reliefs sometimes depict Baal with a thunderbolt in his hand.

The account of Elijah's (literally) breathtaking encounter with 450 prophets of Baal on Mount Carmel is dramatic (see 1 Kings 18). Baal did not answer the cries of his followers. They were unable to get Baal, the weather god, to bring down fire or lightning to ignite the sacrifice (vv. 18-29). Elijah prays, however, after this blatant intrusion into Baal's territory, "O LORD, answer me, so these people will know that you, O LORD, are God" (v. 37). Fire then descended, burning up the sacrifice, the wood, the stones, and the soil, and also licking up the water in the trench (v. 38). When all the worshipers of Baal saw this, they fell prostrate and cried, "The LORD — he is God! The LORD — he is God!" It is important to note that Elijah's name means "My God is Yah(weh)."

The above confrontation is a powerful example of poetic justice. The God of Israel miraculously demonstrated his aliveness in the presence of hundreds of devotees of the god of fertility and nature. Among other materials, his fire consumes wood, soil, and water, all of them important aspects of nature worship. The Canaanites and other ancient peoples addressed the world of nature as a "Thou." The Hebrews, by contrast, never confused deity with nature; theirs was not a pantheistic religion. The Hebrews saw "Thou" only in the Eternal God, Creator of life and nature, the One who personally revealed himself to Abraham, Moses, Elijah, and others.

The "Battle" with Babylonian Gods

The third group of miracles in the Hebrew Bible occurred while the Jewish people were in Babylonian exile. The Book of Daniel tells of the false gods in the kingdom of Babylon and the pagan worship practiced there. The chief god of Babylon was Marduk. When Jerusalem was sacked in 586 B.C., trophies were removed from Solomon's Temple in Jerusalem and placed in the shrine to Marduk in Babylon. It might have been natural to deduce from this event that the true God was Marduk. Why? The God of Israel did not intervene to deliver Jerusalem and his "chosen" people. Jeremiah, however, had warned that unless Judah repented of her idolatrous ways, exile to Babylon would come (Jeremiah 44). God's silence in not delivering Judah from this threat may have been to remind Judah that God is not a cosmic talisman to be touched at will to offer divine protection for any situation. Though longsuffering and compassionate, he is a God of justice and thus could not overlook Judah's sins. But despite the national disaster of a temple in ruins and the disgrace of being led captive to a foreign land, God's people came to reaffirm, *rabbah emunatekha,* "great is your faithfulness" (Lam. 3:23). While in captivity, God demonstrated his power to Daniel and his companions in extraordinary ways. The Lord revealed to Daniel the meaning of Nebuchadnezzar's dream (Daniel 2). He delivered Shadrach, Meshach, and Abednego from the fiery furnace totally unharmed (Daniel 3). He rescued Daniel from the den of lions, the very place a pagan king addressed this prophet, "Daniel, servant of the living God *(elaha hayya)*" (Aramaic of Dan. 6:20).

El Chai, "The Living God" of Israel

The above three groupings of miracles demonstrate the failure of false gods and the illegitimacy of idols. Yahweh, on the other hand, had a different reputation throughout the ancient world. The appeal to the legitimacy and genuineness of the God of Israel is seated in his aliveness; this set him apart from the others in a dynamic and caring way. At the time of Joshua and the conquest of Canaan, Scripture says *ted'un ki el chai beqirbekhem,* "you [Israel] will know [experientially] the living God is among you" (Josh. 3:10). How so? This was made clear when God showed his aliveness and power in bringing Israel safely across the waters of the flooded Jordan as he did previously at the Red Sea, also through the exercising of his lordship over the idolatrous inhabitants residing in his land, the land then known as Canaan.

Abraham Heschel comments on the above, attention-arresting God concept of our Hebraic heritage: "The living soul is not concerned with a dead cause but with a living God. Our goal is to ascertain the existence of a Being to whom we may confess our sins, of a God who loves, of a God who is not above concern with our inquiry and search for Him; a father, not an absolute. . . . This, then, is the minimum of meaning which the word God holds for us: *God is alive.*"[1] In his application of biblical thought for today, Heschel rightly concludes, "The problem of religious thinking is not only whether God is dead or alive, but also whether we are dead or alive to His realness."[2]

Indeed, the Old Testament understanding of God is not rooted in chilly abstractness but reflects the prophetic tradition of a God who is "warm, vivid and concrete."[3]

This is the God of Israel. He is *el chai,* "the living God." But he is also the God of the pages of the New Testament and there, likewise, is praised: "to the only God our Saviour be glory, majesty, power and authority" (Jude 25), for he "gives all men life and breath" (Acts 17:25).

Different from the Others: The Uniqueness of Yahweh

Personal vs. Impersonal

In the Jewish tradition, the first of the Ten Commandments is simply this: "I am the LORD your God" (Exod. 20:2). As Israel's suzerain and lawgiver, Yahweh, up front, identifies himself; he is personal. The consensus of Jewish scholarship takes these opening words to be "the positive commandment to believe in the existence of Hashem [the LORD] as the only God."[4] Israel lived four hundred years in a polytheistic environment within Egypt. In stark contrast, this first word of the Decalogue undergirds the exclusivist monotheism proclaimed in the Shema, "Hear, O Israel: The LORD our God, the LORD is one" (Deut. 6:4). In this connection, Daniel Block has observed, "[the Shema] is a cry of allegiance, an affirmation of covenant commitment in response to the question, 'Who is the God of Israel?' The language of the Shema is 'sloganesque' rather than prosaic: 'Yahweh our God! Yahweh alone!' or 'Our God is Yahweh, Yahweh alone!' This was to be the distinguishing

---

1. Abraham Heschel, *God in Search of Man* (New York: Farrar, Straus & Giroux, 1955), p. 126.

2. Heschel, *God in Search of Man,* p. 127.

3. J. H. Hexter, *The Judaeo-Christian Tradition,* 2nd ed. (New Haven: Yale University Press, 1995), p. 30.

4. *The Chumash,* Stone edition, The Artscroll Series (Brooklyn, NY: Mesorah Publications, 1994), p. 407.

mark of the Israelite people; they are those (and only those) who claim Yahweh alone as their God."[5]

In further comment on Exodus 20:2 above, we should carefully observe that God speaks to his "firstborn son" in the first person. Thus he identifies himself in a concrete way: "I am the LORD your God who brought you out of Egypt, out of the land of slavery" (Exod. 20:2; see Exod. 4:22-23; Jer. 31:9; Hos. 11:1). To be sure, "Yahweh has a personal relationship with his people, as shown by the personal pronouns employed. This is an 'I-thou' relationship of person with person; Yahweh is not some impersonal, cosmic force."[6] The Lord redeemed his people from Egypt fifty days prior to their arrival at Sinai (Exod. 19:1). The Lord alone was the Great Liberator. Here was the Lord's claim why Israel should recognize his authority, worship him exclusively, and keep his commandments. The God of Israel, by his action in delivering his people, "earned his right to be heard" from atop Sinai. He alone was Israel's Redeemer and hence worthy of their wholehearted obedience and allegiance. Belief in one Eternal God, the personal God of the Exodus and covenant at Sinai, has remained a core teaching of both Judaism and Christianity (see Mark 12:29; 1 Tim. 2:5).

Invisible vs. Visible

In addition to the above features, the God of Israel was distinct in other ways. Yahweh had an invisible presence; he was pure spirit (John 4:24). On occasion, however, he manifested himself in visible form. Appearances of the angel of the LORD, and the pillar of smoke by day and the fire by night in the wilderness, were external manifestations of the presence of God. God himself is an incorporeal being; he does not have a body. But the Old Testament often describes God in anthropomorphic and anthropopathic language. When Scripture speaks metaphorically of God as having human form and human emotions, it is a reminder that God is personal and relational, as emphasized above.

In that God is a Spirit, he is a sexless being; he is neither male nor female. This characteristic of Israel's God is in stark contrast to other ancient

---

5. Daniel I. Block, "How Many Is God? An Investigation into the Meaning of Deuteronomy 6:4-5," *Journal of the Evangelical Theological Society* (June 2004): 211.

6. D. W. Baker, "God, Names of," in *Dictionary of the Old Testament Pentateuch*, ed. T. Desmond Alexander and David W. Baker (Downers Grove, IL: InterVarsity, 2003), p. 363.

religions in which gods had consorts or goddesses. Especially in nature religions, pantheons were filled with a variety of deities whose activities made them popular through elaborate mythologies. The God of Israel, however, had no pantheon. The perpetuity of Israel's religion was not dependent upon the cohabitation or regeneration of gods. Israelite religion was not a nature religion. The Creator of the natural order always stood above his creation and acted into it. God and nature were never one.

Ancients often conceived of their deities personifying and controlling various aspects of the natural order. There were gods of the sun, moon, stars, thunder, sea, grain, plagues, sexual fertility, and death. In Israel, however, there seems to have been a direct effort to avoid equating nature in any way with divinity. Deryck Sheriffs points out that a "radical demythologization" takes place in the creation account (Gen. 1:14-18) and in Psalm 104, in that these passages "demote the sun and moon. No longer are they deities. They are timekeepers for humankind."[7] The rain, agriculture, and crops were not gifts of Baal but gifts of Yahweh. The myth is broken. It is Yahweh who reigns and "brings rain." So that no confusion or conflation would be made between Yahweh and nature, the metaphors used for him tend to be taken from the realm of everyday life and society rather than the natural world. Accordingly, his names include those of warrior, shepherd, lord, king, husband, father, potter, judge, refiner, builder, and redeemer. Yahweh, in his self-designations within Scripture, kept himself separate and distinguished from the world of nature that was characteristically worshiped by Israel's neighbors.

Prohibition of Images vs. Embrace of Images

In the ancient world, many nations saw foreign invaders destroy their pantheons and smash their idols. Such catastrophic experiences demoralized nations. The very gods — those to whom they brought gifts and from whom they anticipated tangible benefits — were destroyed. The ancient Near East was an iconoclastic world. By contrast, Yahweh could not be bribed by gifts (Deut. 10:17-18). In Israel, ritual was intended to be an expression of love, not an opportunity to manipulate or appease Yahweh through costly presents brought to a shrine or altar. Unlike Canaanite practice, the religion of Israel was not established on the terms of *quid pro quo*, tit for tat, or one tangible gift for another. Israel had already freely experienced Yahweh's grace and

---

7. Deryck Sheriffs, *The Friendship of the Lord* (London: Paternoster Press, 1996), p. 331.

was held secure in his covenantal love; what he wanted was their loyal love in response. (See chapter 10 in this book, "A Life of Worship," for further discussion of this theme.)

A distinguishing mark of Israelite religion was its prohibition of images or physical likenesses representing the divine. Israel's religion was very different; it required worshiping a God they could not see or visually represent. In drawing a comparison with the broader culture of the ancient world, Peter Schafer comments, "The notion of a God who is unique and by definition excludes the possibility of other gods besides him is mirrored in most of the pagan discussions about Judaism and its customs and beliefs, mediated to us by a wide range of reactions: from admiration through curiosity and amazement to disapproval and satirical contempt. What clearly most strikes the Greek and Roman authors is the aniconism of the Jewish God, the evident fact, contrary to all the customs of the Greco-Roman world, that he is invisible and wants to remain invisible, that is, that he does not allow any image to be made of him."[8] The Torah strictly forbids images and idols of Israel's God (Exod. 20:3-6). Yahweh could not be represented in material form. Since Yahweh was incorporeal, Israel's religion could not be destroyed. When the Romans destroyed the Second Temple in A.D. 70, Judaism was not destroyed. Judaism simply became a religion of the home, a new "temple in miniature."[9]

Throughout Israel's history, it was God's intention that his people grasp that he was different from other deities. He was an infinite, invisible, transcendent Being, not some local, destructible, concrete entity shaped by human hands. Divine Presence was not to be equated with physical form or works of art. Yahweh could be worshiped at the Temple in Jerusalem or he could be worshiped away from the Temple. When Israel worshiped by the waters of Babylon in captivity, God was there. The prophet Ezekiel writes of the glory *(kabod)* of the Lord, which is the living presence of God. In 3:23 he states that the glory of the Lord was standing before him like the glory he saw by the River Kebar when the heavens opened and he saw the living creatures and wheels.[10] Thus Israel was forced to think of her God in spiritual or meta-

---

8. Peter Schafer, *Judeophobia: Attitudes toward the Jews in the Ancient World* (Cambridge, MA: Harvard University Press, 1997), p. 34.

9. See Marvin R. Wilson, *Our Father Abraham: Jewish Roots of the Christian Faith* (Grand Rapids: Eerdmans, 1989), pp. 214-17.

10. Note the excellent study of this theme in John Kutsko, *Between Heaven and Earth: Divine Presence and Absence in the Book of Ezekiel* (Winona Lake, IN: Eisenbrauns, 2000). Kutsko concludes, "The dispersion of members of the Jewish community to regions outside the parameters of Judah required Israel's God to become limited by neither Temple nor land.

physical terms, beyond and above what the eye could see. Such was central to Yahweh's renown: he was a universal God; his presence filled the universe. He was not confined to a locale or a geographical area as were all other ancient Near East gods. The realization of this teaching "stretched" Israel. It stretches us also. Israel is called to obey an invisible, unseen God. Like Israel, Christians must learn to live by faith, not by sight (2 Cor. 5:7; Heb. 11:1-2).

Metaphor and Yahweh's Reputation

It is a truism, that when God spoke and gave the holy Scriptures, he did so in "baby talk." What this statement means is that much of the language of Scripture is figurative; the language of analogy or what is really understatement.[11] In order to communicate truths from the realm of the purely spiritual to that of time and space, God needed to "put the cookies on a lower shelf" so people could reach them. There is a language of grandeur in the Bible; its words point in a direction. They often remind us in the end that there is more, not less, to the meaning we are able to perceive. What we often grasp is by analogy to the world around us; but often it is but a tip of the iceberg.

Let us illustrate by example. When the Bible says, "The LORD is a warrior" (Exod. 15:3), the meaning is profound, but it is not to be taken literally. The expression does not mean God is on guard in heaven with his chariot, dressed in full armor, sword and shield in hand. Rather the words speak of a God who is involved in every aspect of Israel's existence; this includes the sovereign ability to overthrow earthly tyrants in order to deliver his people from their enemies. In context, the words are a metaphor for the Almighty God, who by his power defeated Pharaoh, his army, and best chariots at the sea (Exod. 15:1-21). The poetry of the Song of Moses is a reminder that the Lord fights for his people, and he will fight until he triumphs and all his foes are vanquished. The central theme of the last book of Scripture, the Apocalypse of John, sums this story up in two words: "He wins!" In making this point, note how the New Testament author picks up the Exodus theme of the Lord as warrior. He depicts Christ as the Warrior-King riding on a white horse accompanied by the armies of heaven. He is victor over all (Rev. 19:11-16).

Ezekiel presented a vision of a God who could make his revelations known and his power felt beyond the previous borders — both physical and ideological. It was only if the presence of God could be perceived in exile that they could have hope" (pp. 155-56).

11. See Heschel, *God in Search of Man,* pp. 176-83.

In order to understand who God is, the Bible uses a variety of metaphors or verbal pictures to describe the roles he fulfills in relation to his people. From a human perspective, there is an inherent inability to grasp fully who the Infinite One of Israel is. Metaphor is thus one of God's gifts in Scripture to help us expand our understanding of the reputation of Yahweh in his world. In addition to our brief discussion above of the Divine Warrior motif, we shall discuss in greater length two other figures, each taken from the social life of ancient times: God as Shepherd and God as King.

Shepherd of Israel

The ancient New East was a highly pastoral society. The life of a shepherd and his relation to the sheep provides considerable insight into the relation that God sustains with his people. Indeed, "[sheep] herding was not only important economically as a way of life, it was also Israel's way of understanding Yahweh."[12] One of the most comforting psalms for Jews and Christians is Psalm 23, the "Shepherd Psalm." "The LORD is my shepherd" — these words have provided people assurance of God's presence, even in the darkest times of life. Among the metaphors for Israel's God, the shepherd metaphor is particularly rich and meaningful, for it gives us confidence in our Ultimate Spiritual Leader.

Shepherding in Bible Times

From an early date the term "shepherd" was used not only of a herdsman but also was often used of a ruler, king, or deity. In the prologue to the Law Code of Hammurabi, the king refers to himself as "shepherd." Many of the patriarchs of Israel were shepherds. Abraham (Gen. 13:7), Isaac (Gen. 26:20), Jacob (Gen. 30:36), and the sons of Jacob cared for flocks (Gen. 37:12ff.). Some of Israel's greatest leaders were shepherds. Moses was one of them. A fascinating midrash of the rabbis teaches that the personal way Moses cared for sheep is what caught God's attention to make him leader of Israel: "[When Moses shepherded the flocks of Jethro], he used to stop the bigger sheep from grazing before the smaller ones, and let the smaller

---

12. Victor H. Matthews and Don C. Benjamin, *Social World of Ancient Israel* (Peabody, MA: Hendrickson, 1993), p. 66.

ones loose first to feed on the tender grass; then he would let the older sheep loose to feed on the grass of average quality; lastly he let the strong ones loose to feed on the toughest. God said, 'Let . . . him who knows how to shepherd the flock, each according to its strength, come and lead my people.'"[13]

The leaders of Israel were often referred to as "shepherds" (Jer. 10:21; 23:1-4). This is the Hebraic background to the New Testament Greek term *poimen*, "pastor." In Ephesians 4:11, the word *poimen* means "pastor-teacher," an important office in the early church for helping to equip God's people for works of service. Paul builds on this shepherding theme when he commands the Ephesian elders: "Keep watch over yourselves and all the flock of which the Holy Spirit has made you overseers. Be shepherds *(poimainein)* of the church of God" (Acts 20:28).

The Bible indicates that the life of a shepherd was very demanding, for it carried great responsibility in the guidance, nourishment, and safety of each member of the flock. Sheep need constant supervision, for they wander (Isa. 53:6; 1 Pet. 2:25), are non-aggressive (Isa. 53:7), and are virtually defenseless (Mic. 5:8). Daily, the shepherd sought the best grazing land available for the flock (1 Chron. 4:39, 40). He led his sheep to pasture (Ps. 77:20; 78:52) and had to provide water for them at least once a day (see Ps. 23:2; Isa. 49:10).

A skilled shepherd was required to know his flock well (John 10:14). The sheep also know their shepherd; they recognize the shepherd's voice and follow him (John 10:4). The shepherd was always on the lookout for the injured or weak and occasionally bore those sheep back to the pen on his shoulders (Luke 15:5). One of the most frequently found depictions in the Christian catacombs of Rome is that of Jesus, the good Shepherd of the sheep, with a lamb slung over his shoulder.

David and the Divine Shepherd

In Ezekiel, the Lord, divine leader of Israel, is figuratively depicted as a shepherd (34:11-24). He searches for his sheep and looks after them and rescues them (vv. 11, 12). Under his guidance "they will feed in a rich pasture on the mountains of Israel" (v. 14). The Lord binds up the injured and strengthens

---

13. Exodus Rabbah 2:2, quoted in Rabbi Joseph Telushkin, *Biblical Literacy* (New York: William Morrow, 1997), p. 337.

the weak (v. 16a). He says, "I will shepherd the flock with justice" (v. 16b). The Lord also promises, "I will place over them one shepherd, my servant David, and he will tend them" (v. 23). The reference in Ezekiel 34:23 is to a messianic leader, an ideal figure like the shepherd king David, who someday would rule as prince under the Lord.

David, the shepherd from Bethlehem who became king, writes, "The LORD is my shepherd" (Ps. 23:1).[14] The language, however, is similar to the words of David's ancestor Israel (Jacob) who speaks of the Almighty as "[t]he God who has been my shepherd all my life to this day" (Gen. 48:15). These uses of the metaphor of shepherd remind us that as Israelites, David and Jacob were very familiar with the job description of shepherding.

In Psalm 23, David's opening acknowledgment, "The LORD is my shepherd," makes the words of this psalm very personal. But these words have also proven reassuring for Jews and Christians over the centuries; they bring the Lord's living concern for his people very much down to earth. The heavenly shepherd of Israel is someone to whom David can relate. He borrows most of his imagery in the psalm from the life of a shepherd, a life he knows well (1 Sam. 17:15). As this psalm indicates, David places great confidence in his divine shepherd-king. He is completely dependent on him. Because of the constant care of his shepherd, David lacks nothing (v. 1). His shepherd-leader provides all he needs for guidance, rest, and renewal of life (vv. 2-3). Even in the deepest darkness, David has no fear because his shepherd is with him to protect and comfort him (v. 4). The psalm affirms that the Lord's steadfast love and active presence are with the psalmist throughout his life (v. 6). David's shepherd is the same God who cares for us. Indeed, as Psalm 95:7 likewise affirms, "He is our God and we are the people of his pasture, the flock under his care" (see Ps. 100:3).

The metaphor of a divine Shepherd is rich and comforting to Jew and Christian alike. In a world in which wolves often prey on the helpless and vulnerable of the flock, the vigilant and daily care provided in the imagery of Yahweh the Shepherd gives encouragement and hope. Earthly shepherds are imperfect. Sometimes they are more interested in "fleecing" the sheep than guiding, feeding, and protecting them. However, though a metaphor, the heavenly Shepherd personifies the very best of "shepherding." With him, says David, "I lack nothing" (Ps. 23:1).

14. For a valuable treatment of Psalm 23 through the eyes of a rabbi with a pastor's heart, see Michael Samuel, *The Lord Is My Shepherd: The Theology of a Caring God* (Northvale, NJ: Jason Aronson, 1996).

King of the Universe

Perhaps the most powerful metaphor for Yahweh in Scripture is that of king. Divine kingship is one of the key theological themes that links the First and Second Testaments. Human sovereignty is limited but God's kingship is eternal. Yahweh is the only true king, hence the superlative use of this royal metaphor is found in the Hebrew Bible and later, in rabbinic literature (see Deut. 10:17; Ps. 136:2-3; Dan. 2:47). While a human emperor might have the chutzpah to call himself "king of kings," God remained beyond him. In Jewish liturgy, he bears the title *melekh malkhe ha-melakhim,* "King over kings of kings."[15]

Kingdom of God in Jewish Thought

In Christianity, the kingdom of God, and the parallel expression, kingdom of heaven, is a dominant emphasis in the teaching of Jesus. Most Christians regularly pray the Lord's Prayer (Matt. 6:9-13). Unknown to many Christians, however, is the fact that the phraseology of this prayer is totally Jewish. The Lord's Prayer teaches how the followers of Jesus should pray (v. 9). Jesus says their prayer should include, "Your kingdom come." What did Jesus mean? "Your kingdom come" is an entreaty to God the Father to continue to bring into human life his eternal reign. This same theme is found in the Kaddish, a prayer originating during the time of the Second Temple and widely used in Jewish liturgy today. Like the Lord's Prayer, the Kaddish sanctifies God's name and beseeches, *yamlikh malkhuteh* (Aramaic, "May he establish his kingdom").[16]

Simply defined, therefore, the kingdom of God is the reign or rule of God. In Scripture, the expression is primarily an active or dynamic concept, not a sphere or geographical realm where God's sovereign rule is exercised. "Kingdom of God" refers to God's authority, his kingly power, taking charge in the lives of individuals and in the events of humanity. In the present, God spiritually exercises his kingdom through his reign in human lives; in the future, at the end of history, God will perfect his rule on earth, fully establishing his sovereignty over persons and nations.

---

15. See Arthur Green, *These Are the Words* (Woodstock, VT: Jewish Lights, 1999), p. 19.

16. See Lawrence A. Hoffman, "Jewish and Christian Liturgy," in *Christianity in Jewish Terms,* ed. Tikva Frymer-Kensky, David Novak, Peter Ochs, David Fox Sandmel, and Michael A. Signer (Boulder, CO: Westview, 2000), p. 176.

In Modern Judaism, following the text of daily Jewish prayers, we are reminded that divine kingship has remained from Bible times a major theological pillar in the history of Judaism. The standard rabbinic blessing formula acknowledges God as Ruler of the world, *Barukh atah adonai eloheinu melekh ha-olam,* "Blessed are You, O LORD our God, King of the universe." In regard to the phrase *melekh ha-olam,* "King of the universe," Hayim Donin observes, "When we relate to God as a Sovereign Ruler, we assume a more respectful role."[17] More than a hundred of these blessings, each giving praise to God as King, are recited daily by the observant Jew. Why in the Jewish tradition are so many blessings offered? Harvey Lutske explains, "In the biblical book of Deuteronomy, there are enumerated 100 curses which will befall Israel if the people ever fall into apostasy. Although the curses are national, for the nation as a whole and not for the individual, Israel's survival to this day is due to a 'righteous remnant' that has remained within the nation. Nevertheless, each individual, to do his or her part to offset the 100 curses, recites 100 benedictions daily."[18]

God's eternal rule is affirmed in the Hebrew Bible in texts such as Psalms 29:10 and 146:10. In the Bible, the emphasis is upon time, i.e., "the LORD reigns for ever," rather than place, but in rabbinic texts the meaning of *olam* is "both temporal ('eternity') and geographical ('the world')."[19]

The exact expression "kingdom of God" is not found in the Old Testament, but the idea of God's reign or kingship is found. God declares to his people, "I am the LORD, your Holy One, Israel's Creator, your King" (Isa. 43:15). After God demonstrates his kingly power in splitting the waters of the Red Sea, Moses sings, "The LORD will reign for ever and ever" (Exod. 15:18). In commenting on this text, biblical linguist Brad Young points out that the sense of the verb "reign" is that God *now* reigns eternally, for his kingship is established through his redeeming act of deliverance. Young further emphasizes that this interpretation is supported by Aramaic translations and also the Septuagint text, which uses a present participle *(basileuon)* for the verb "reign." Concludes Young, "The idea of God's Kingship is not connected with time. God reigns; . . . he is actively involved with his people and their redemption."[20]

---

17. Hayim Halevy Donin, *To Pray as a Jew* (New York: Basic Books, 1980), p. 66.

18. Harvey Lutske, *The Book of Jewish Customs* (Northvale, NJ: Jason Aronson, 1986), p. 278.

19. See Marc Brettler, *My People's Prayer Book: Traditional Prayers,* vol. 5: *Birkhot Hashachar* (Morning Blessings), ed. Lawrence A. Hoffman, Modern Commentaries series (Woodstock, VT: Jewish Lights, 2001), p. 59.

20. Brad Young, *The Jewish Background to the Lord's Prayer* (Dayton, OH: Center for

A Kingdom "Already, but Not Yet"

Throughout the Old Testament, God's reign was a present, dynamic reality, largely experienced in God's sovereign visitations of both deliverance and judgment. In the Gospels, the present in-breaking power of God's dynamic reign is seen in the ministry of Jesus as he exercises control over disease, demons, sin, nature, and death. In Jesus, God's sovereign, kingly rule is exercised. Those who bring their lives under God's authority, thereby submitting to the "yoke of the kingdom," experience his reign and become a part of his kingdom. According to the Mishnah, Berakhot 2:2, "to take upon oneself the yoke of the kingdom of heaven" was to acknowledge the One God and then to receive upon oneself the yoke of the commandments. Rashi, the most influential medieval Jewish commentator, has noted, "a *yoke* represents complete subjugation without thought or reasoning."[21] In the New Testament, the present spiritual dimension of the kingdom is manifest in the lives of individuals transformed by the power of the gospel and who live in faithful, active obedience to God's ways.

In Old Testament texts, God's present reign is not limited to his people Israel. The Scriptures also teach that God reigns over the entire world. God is actively involved in history, but all people have yet to acknowledge his sovereignty. The Psalms declare, "How awesome is the LORD Most High, the great King over all the earth!" (Ps. 47:2). "Say among the nations, 'The LORD reigns'" (Ps. 96:10), and "The LORD reigns, let the earth be glad" (Ps. 97:1). In the Hebraic perspective of Scripture, there are only two ages: "this age" *(olam ha-zeh)* and "the age to come" *(olam ha-ba)*. The kingdom of God is already, but not yet. There is a tension between the present and the future. The kingdom is partially realized in the present age, yet not perfectly achieved. God's kingdom is here, and can be experienced, but it is also a future hope. Thus, in both Judaism and Christianity, there is an "inaugurated eschatology." In Christianity, however, the power of the age to come is proclaimed as having dynamically arrived as a spiritual (non-political) kingdom. The presence of this kingdom is demonstrated in the life and ministry of Jesus and comes to those who submit to him.

Judaic-Christian Studies, 1984), pp. 12-13. See also Joseph Frankovic, "The Kingdom of Heaven," in *Roots and Branches: Explorations into the Jewish Context of the Christian Faith*, ed. John Fieldsend, Clifford Hill, Walter Riggans, John C. P. Smith, and Fred Wright (Bedford, UK: PWM Trust, 1998), pp. 147-62.

21. See Pinchas Doron, *Rashi's Torah Commentary* (Northvale, NJ: Jason Aronson, 2000), p. 199.

"Yahweh Will Reign": Consummation of the Kingdom

The prophets anticipate a future day when the kingdom of God will be fully consummated on this earth. The prophets frequently associate this perfect achievement of the Old Testament hope with the term "the day of the LORD" *(yom YHWH)*, or a shorter phrase, "in that day." The "day of the LORD" is frequently used of God's intervention in Israel's history whereby he promises to bring destruction or blessing in accordance with the word of his messengers, the prophets. More often, however, the term carries an eschatological meaning; it points to the end of the age and the time when God intervenes in history to redeem his people, to judge the nations, and to purge evil from the earth. Such is the spiritual goal of history, the time when God's ultimate rule will be established in the hearts of all humanity. Righteousness, justice, and peace will cover the earth. This is the prophetic moment humanity now awaits, the moment when "the kingdom *(ha-melukhah)* will be the LORD's (Obad. 21).

The prophet Zechariah sees on the distant horizon a day when "[t]he LORD will be king over the whole earth" (Zech. 14:9). So significant are these words that they form the climax of the *Aleinu*, the closing prayer to a group of prayers that observant Jews pray three times a day, every day of the week. The Aleinu appears to be pre-Christian in origin and has as its central theme the kingdom of God.[22] The words are profoundly biblical in the Hebraic tradition. All life begins with God the Creator and longs for the day when he will be the Consummator. The Aleinu expresses "the fervent hope for the coming of the kingdom of God."[23] An English translation of the prayer follows:

> We therefore hope in You, O Lord our God, that we may soon behold the glory of Your power, as You remove the abominations from the earth and heathendom is abolished. We hope for the day when the world will be mended as a kingdom of the Almighty, and all flesh will call out Your name; when you will turn unto Yourself all of the earth's wicked ones. May all the earth perceive and understand that only unto You should every knee bend, and only unto You every tongue vow loyalty. Before You, O Lord our God, may they bow in reverence, giving honor only unto You. May they all accept the yoke of Your sovereignty. Rule over

22. See Joseph H. Hertz, ed., *The Authorized Daily Prayer Book*, rev. ed. (New York: Bloch, 1948), p. 209.

23. "Aleinu Le-shabbe'ah," in *Encyclopedia Judaica*, vol. 2 (Jerusalem: Keter, 1972), p. 557.

them speedily and forever more. For dominion is Yours and to all eternity will You reign in glory; as it is written in Your Torah: The Lord shall reign for ever and ever. And it has also been foretold: The Lord shall be King over the whole earth; on that day the Lord shall be known as One, and only One.[24]

Psalm 95:6 exhorts, "Come, let us bow down in worship, let us kneel before the LORD our Maker." In Jewish religious practice today, during the high holidays at the point when the cantor sings the Aleinu in the Musaf (Heb. "additional service"), the cantor kneels down to the floor and says, "We bend the knee and prostrate ourselves before the King of Kings." While Jews have tended to see kneeling or "bending the knee" as a Christian practice and thus something generally inappropriate for Jewish worship, this gesture associated with the words "King of Kings" is a fitting reminder of the One before whom humanity stands when engaged in humble worship.[25] The Book of Revelation, the last book of the New Testament, builds on this same Hebraic theological emphasis. The Lamb of God is declared the ultimate supreme ruler, the "KING OF KINGS AND LORD OF LORDS" (Rev. 19:16; also 17:14).

In this chapter we have looked at some of the ways the Hebrew Bible presents the story of how Yahweh went about building a reputation among his own people Israel and among the nations of the earth. During Old Testament times, rulers inside and outside of Israel took the title of "king." However, many kings were only a shadow of what they could be because they could not handle pride, fame, riches, or power. These and other human weaknesses and lusts often consumed them and contributed to their downfall. The prophet Samuel warned about the dangers of having a king (see 1 Samuel 8). His wisdom largely proved right. Few were the truly "great" and "godly" kings of the Jewish people.

Among all the kings of the Monarchy and Divided Kingdom, the name of the last ruler of the kingdom of Judah was Zedekiah. The Bible tells us quite a bit about the final years of Zedekiah and the Southern Kingdom, the fall of Jerusalem, and the toppling of the Davidic dynasty (2 Kings 25; 2 Chronicles 36; Jeremiah 52). Perhaps the most interesting point about Zedekiah, however, is the meaning conveyed in his name. His is perhaps

24. Translation of the Aleinu by Rabbi Stuart E. Rosenberg, *The Christian Problem: A Jewish View* (New York: Hippocrene Books, 1986), pp. 201-2.

25. Simon Glustrom, *The Language of Judaism* (Northvale, NJ: Jason Aaronson, 1988), pp. 237-38.

the ultimate theological meaning in a biblical name; Zedekiah *(tzidqiyahu)* means, "Yahweh is my righteousness."

It is sad that on a personal level King Zedekiah failed to live up to his own name. The good news, however, is that a King will reign in the Messianic Age and his name is "Yahweh (is) Our Righteousness," *YHWH tzidqenu* (Jer. 23:5-6). He will perfectly embody on this earth what a "righteous reign" will be (Isa. 9:7; 11:4-5). His reputation and renown will be from sea to sea and "his kingdom will never be destroyed" (Dan. 7:14).

UNDERSTANDING CHAPTER EIGHT

1. What was Israel shown so that they might know that the Lord is God? In contrast, what was ridiculed about pagan deities? Why specifically did Elijah mock the prophets of Baal?

2. According to Jeremiah (10:14-15) and Habakkuk (2:18-19), there is no *what* in idols? How does the God of Israel stand in contrast?

3. How did Israel go about establishing the validity of their claim to know and worship the one true God?

4. In what context does each of the three great outpourings of miracles in the Hebrew Bible occur? What does this indicate about Yahweh's intention to establish his reputation? What about his "reputation" do you think Yahweh specifically aimed to communicate to other nations during these encounters?

5. Which Egyptian god in particular was in competition with Yahweh during the plagues reported in Exodus? How did the final and climactic plague reveal who the victor was? How was the Pharaoh viewed in Egyptian society and why is this significant?

6. After Israel had passed through the Red Sea, what song did Moses sing (cite both the Hebrew and the English titles)? How is Yahweh viewed as both a king and a warrior? (A review of Exod. 15:1-21 may be helpful.) From a Christian perspective, are you comfortable with the idea of God as a warrior? Why or why not?

7. With what deity did Yahweh compete during the second great outpouring of miracles? Why was the worship of this deity a particularly acute problem at this point?

8. Describe the realm of Baal according to the ancient Canaanite perspective. What was his role? How did the Israelite prophet Elijah present an unwelcome threat?

9. Briefly summarize the encounter on Mount Carmel involving Elijah and the prophets of Baal. What does Elijah's name mean? How did the God of Israel dramatically illustrate his own aliveness in contrast to the Canaanites' perception of Baal?

10. During what phase in Jewish history did the third major outpouring of miracles occur? Who was the chief god of Babylon, and how might the sacking of Jerusalem have been perceived in a religious context in which a nation's defeat signaled the defeat of its god? What words had Jeremiah penned, however, that are significant? How does the book of Daniel illustrate God's faithfulness and power in the midst of Babylonian captivity? Provide specific examples.

11. How does *el chai* translate into English? How did God identify with this title at the time of Joshua and the conquest of Canaan?

12. In the words of Abraham Heschel, what is the "minimum of meaning" that the word "God" holds for us? What would you choose as the "minimum of meaning" of the word "God"?

13. How is the declaration "I am the LORD your God" (Exod. 20:2) largely understood in Jewish scholarship to be a positive commandment? Review Daniel Block's observations about the Shema (Deut. 6:4). How does the claim of the Shema likewise function as a distinguishing mark of the Jewish people?

14. What do the pronouns in Exodus 20:2 indicate about the nature of God and his relationship to his people?

15. What kind of presence does Yahweh have? What are some examples from the Old Testament of visible manifestations of his presence? Should the Old Testament's anthropomorphic and anthropopathic language be understood literally? What does it remind us of concerning God's nature?

16. How does God as a sexless being stand in stark contrast to the deities of other ancient religions? Explain the significance of the fact that Yahweh did not have a pantheon. How do your own perceptions of God in a masculine and a feminine light compare with one another?

17. How did ancients often conceive their deities in relation to the natural order? How was Israel different? In your own words, explain the "radical demythologization" that Deryck Sheriffs sees in the creation account of Genesis, and comment on its significance.

18. The author points out that, in ancient Israel, metaphors for Yahweh tended to be taken from what realms rather than what other realm? Provide examples of some of the names given to him. In terms of com-

ing to know God through metaphor, do you think that analogies drawn from nature would be less or equally dangerous in various contexts of the modern world than they were in the ancient world? Why or why not?

19. In what sense was the ancient Near East an "iconoclastic world"? How were Israel and her God unique in the midst of this? For additional discussion or research: How was Israel's practice of ritual both similar to and different from that of her neighbors?

20. What prohibition was a distinguishing mark of Israelite religion? What does Peter Schafer emphasize as the most striking characteristic of the Jewish God in the eyes of ancient Greek and Roman writers? How did Judaism's belief in an incorporeal God allow it to survive even after the destruction of the Second Temple in A.D. 70?

21. What experience of the Israelites in Babylonian exile indicated that God was not a localized deity? Rather than reigning over a particular geographical area, how far does Yahweh's presence extend?

22. What does the author mean by stating that God gave the Scriptures in "baby talk," or that God needed to "put the cookies on a lower shelf"?

23. How does the description of God as a warrior in Exodus 15:3 function metaphorically? How does the New Testament author of the Apocalypse of John build upon this metaphor?

24. From an early date, the term "shepherd" was used not only of a herdsman but of what else? In what ancient Near Eastern document does a king refer to himself as a shepherd?

25. In your own words, summarize the content and meaning of the midrash that the rabbis used to explore why God appointed Moses as the leader — the shepherd — of his people.

26. What is the Hebraic background to the New Testament Greek term *poimen,* meaning "pastor"? How does this inform your understanding of the role of pastors at large? Beyond the traditional Protestant Christian expectation of preaching, what do you see as a pastor's responsibilities toward his flock?

27. On a practical level, what did shepherding entail that made it a demanding lifestyle?

28. What is one of the most frequently found depictions in the Christian catacombs of Rome? What aspect of responsibility in a shepherd's life lays the foundation for this image?

29. How is the Lord figuratively depicted as a shepherd in the book of Ezekiel? How is shepherding explicitly linked to the Messiah in the same book?

30. In your own words, explain how the concept of shepherding makes Psalm 23 a personal and reassuring piece. Has the metaphor of a divine Shepherd played a role in your own life? If so, in what way?

31. In what ways is kingship a powerful metaphor for Yahweh throughout Scripture? What royal title does Yahweh bear in Jewish liturgy?

32. The concept of God's coming kingdom is present not only in the Lord's Prayer but in what other Jewish prayer? When did this prayer originate?

33. How is the kingdom of God primarily expressed in Scripture? How does God exercise his reign in the present, and how will he in the future?

34. What is the standard rabbinic blessing formula that reminds us that divine kingship remains a major theological pillar in Judaism? How does Harvey Lutske explain the number of blessings recited daily by some Jews? From a Christian perspective, review the blessing formula. Noting that God often remains the object of blessing in the Orthodox and Catholic liturgies, in what ways have some forms of Christianity strayed from declaring God himself the object of blessings? Do you think the church would do well to "revise" some of her blessings (e.g., in prayers or worship songs)? Why or why not?

35. What interesting distinction exists between the sense of God's rule in the Hebrew Bible and in rabbinic texts? What is your sense of the spheres included in the reign of God, and why?

36. What insights does Brad Young offer in regard to God's kingship as expressed in Exodus 15:18? What does he point out about Aramaic translations and the Septuagint?

37. How is God's kingly rule exercised through Jesus in the New Testament? Explore how the areas in which Jesus worked transformatively mirror areas in which Yahweh worked in the Old Testament. Which connections come to mind?

38. How do the Mishnah and Rashi each describe the concept of a yoke (in the context of the "yoke of the kingdom")? Are these helpful in your own perception of the yoke of the kingdom of God? Why or why not?

39. In the Hebraic perspective of Scripture, what two ages exist (cite both the Hebrew and the English titles)? How is the kingdom of God "already but not yet"? In Christianity, how in particular is the age to come proclaimed as having arrived, and how is it demonstrated?

40. Comment on the use of *yom YHWH* in the Old Testament: How does it translate and what kind of meaning does the term most often carry?

From a Christian perspective, what do you think Jesus' role was and is in the anticipation of *yom YHWH*? How can an "already but not yet" kingdom fit into this framework of thought?

41. What Jewish prayer has the kingdom of God as its central theme? What seems to be its origin, and which words of Zechariah are included in it?

42. From a Christian perspective, do you think the *Aleinu* would be a meaningful addition to Christian liturgy or worship? Why or why not? How does your theology compare with the theology contained in the prayer? How does this prayer remind us of the strong "common ground" shared by Jews and Christians?

43. How have Jews tended to view kneeling or the "bending of the knee" historically? When, however, does it play a part in Jewish worship, and with what purpose and effect?

44. Who was King Zedekiah? What does his name mean, and what did his life demonstrate in relation to it? What does the future King's name, *YHWH tzidqenu*, mean?

CHAPTER 9

The Image of God and Idols of Humanity

The Bible is a wrestling match between a sovereign, infinite, faithful God and flip-flopping, sinful, ephemeral man. Scripture opens with God creating humankind and taking great pleasure and satisfaction with his work. Viewing all that he had made, God saw that "it was very good" (Gen. 1:31). But soon a power play, a battle of the wills, begins. It will continue throughout the rest of Scripture. In this chapter we will briefly look at several aspects of this endless struggle between God and humanity, the unique pinnacle of his creation.

The first struggle with God comes right after his work of creation. God places the man and the woman in a garden. He commands them on what they are allowed to do and forbidden to do. The Creator takes a risk; he gives the couple freedom of choice. They wrestle with the choice of following God's instructions or yielding to the beguiling words of the serpent. The man and the woman disobey God's command, fall under his judgment, and are expelled from the paradisiacal garden. God states that their choice, as representatives of the human family, will be but the very first episode in a divine-human power struggle for centuries to come. The entire Bible is a commentary on the human struggle to know God and to submit to the divine will; further, it concerns the ongoing narrative in which, by human effort and divine assistance, despair and absurdity will be conquered, and, if humans hold onto the promise, good will eventually prevail over evil (Gen. 3:15).

The Divine Image: Something Sacred at Stake

The image of God in man is one of the most important teachings of Judaism set firmly in the foundation of Christianity. Its implications have had great effect in such disciplines as theology, psychology, sociology, medicine, and other fields.

During the first two centuries, the sages of Israel gave thought to the question of the greatest principle of the Torah. The great Rabbi Akiba argued that "love your neighbor as yourself" is most important (Lev. 19:18). Akiba's disciple Ben Azzai, however, argued from Genesis 5:1 that there was a greater principle, namely, "When God created man he made him in the likeness of God." By placing a higher emphasis on the likeness of God in man, Ben Azzai was expressing a concern about potentially shaming a neighbor. If this were done, said Ben Azzai, you would be shaming one created in the likeness of God (see Sifra, Kedoshim 4:12). The sense of Ben Azzai's argument is this: "If you cannot respect the Divine image that you are made in, the odds are that you will not be able to respect the Divine image in others."[1]

Toward Defining "Image" and "Likeness"

Within the Tanakh, only the book of Genesis contains explicit statements about humanity's creation in the image of God. The first reads, "Then God said, 'Let us make man in our image *(tzelem),* in our likeness *(demut)'*" (1:26; also see 1:27; 5:1; and 9:6). The first person plural, "Let us," may be a plural of majesty or an address to the heavenly court, but clearly the author intends no Old Testament *"vestigium Trinitatis."*[2]

Scholars have debated much about the meaning of the words *tzelem* (image) and *demut* (likeness). *Tzelem* is normally rendered in the Septuagint by *eikon* (icon). The word *tzelem* is usually used in a derogatory sense of idolatrous images either to be destroyed or avoided. But the term can also be used of things less concrete, implying what is empty or lacking reality or substance. For example, in the Psalms, *tzelem* is used parallel to *hebel,* "futility," "vanity," "breath," or "shadow."[3]

The word *demut* is translated by *homoiosis* in the Greek of the Septuagint. *Demut* usually means "to resemble," "to represent," or "to be something like" (by means of comparison). According to William Dyrness, *demut,* "likeness," is more a "verbal abstraction" as in words such as "appearance,"

---

1. Michael L. Samuel, *Birth and Rebirth through Genesis: A Timeless Theological Conversation,* vol. 1: *Genesis 1–3* (Coral Springs, FL: Aeon, 2010), p. 356.

2. See D. J. A. Clines, "The Image of God in Man," *Tyndale Bulletin* 19 (1968): 62.

3. See Victor P. Hamilton, *The Book of Genesis 1–17,* New International Commentary on the Old Testament, vol. 1 (Grand Rapids: Eerdmans, 1990), pp. 134-36.

"analogy," or "similarity." Taken together, *tzelem* and *demut* appear to be descriptive of the whole person and thus "complementary rather than competing meanings."[4] The expression is a figure of speech in that man is no physical copy of God. The combined terms are to be "understood as a joint description of a single idea."[5]

In ancient Mesopotamia and Egypt, kings or other notable officials were often considered the living "image of God." For example, in Egypt, King Thutmose IV is termed "the likeness of Re." A statue of the pharaoh was believed to be where the deity dwelt. "The king puts his statue in a conquered land to signify his real, though not his physical, presence there."[6] In a similar manner, though God is absent, he is present in man who is his image. While man is not divine, he bears corporeal witness to God's presence in the world by how he lives and the good he does. As theologian J. I. Packer points out, we as image-bearer should display a "representative likeness" to God, "reflecting at our creaturely level, what Genesis 1 shows God is and does . . . [one who] generated value by producing what is truly good; so should we."[7]

The dignity of man, according to Abraham Heschel, comes not from his achievement or talents; it is inherent in his being created in the image of God. Observes Heschel, "Man is man . . . *because of what he has in common with God. . . . The image is not in man; it is man.*"[8] As opposed to secular humanism, Heschel developed a theology of "sacred humanism" emphasizing reverence for humanity. When pain is inflicted on man, it simultaneously hurts God.[9] In the words of Heschel, "Man, every man, must be treated with the honor due to a likeness representing the King of kings."[10] In creating man in the image of God, "the intention was for man to be a *witness for God,* a symbol of God. Looking at man one should sense the presence of God."[11]

4. William A. Dyrness, "The *Imago Dei* and Christian Aesthetics," *Journal of the Evangelical Theological Society* 15, no. 3 (1972): 161-62.

5. James I. Cook, "The Old Testament Concept of the Image of God," in *Grace upon Grace: Essays in Honor of Lester J. Kuyper,* ed. James I. Cook (Grand Rapids: Eerdmans, 1975), p. 86.

6. Clines, "The Image of God in Man," p. 87.

7. J. I. Packer, "Reflected Glory: What Does Genesis Mean by Man Being Made in the Image of God?" *Christianity Today,* December 2003, p. 56.

8. Abraham Joshua Heschel, "Sacred Image of Man," in *The Insecurity of Freedom: Essays on Human Existence* (New York: Schocken, 1966), pp. 152-53.

9. See the discussion of Edward K. Kaplan, *Spiritual Radical: Abraham Joshua Heschel in America, 1940-1972* (New Haven: Yale University Press, 2007), pp. 229-34.

10. Abraham Joshua Heschel, "Religion and Race," in *The Insecurity of Freedom,* p. 95.

11. Heschel, "Sacred Image of Man," p. 164.

As an ancient Near Eastern king is the image of a divine being, so man is created to be God's image. Humans are God's regal representatives on earth, granted authority to "rule over" God's creation (see Gen. 1:28). The royal description of man in Genesis 1:26 is echoed in Psalm 8:5, 6. The psalm states that God "crowns him with glory and honor" and makes him "ruler," putting "everything under his feet." In sum, "Just as the might of the god, his brilliance, and his splendor are present in the image (see Ps. 8:6) and radiate from it, so divine authority, divine 'lord-ship,' is granted humans."[12] Such biblical teaching about God's image is inclusivistic. Not just the king (of Egypt) represents God; Scripture implies that every human being by reason of the divine image is envisioned in royal terms. Man is God's image by the very fact that he is man. Each human visibly embodies the invisible God. We must remember, however, that "to be in the image of God cannot mean equivalence between deity and humanity, but only an analogous or corresponding relationship between the two."[13]

Meaning for Today

The image of God impressed on all human beings is the first and perhaps most fundamental sign of God's love of humankind.[14] Through creation in God's image, human beings are endowed with certain intrinsic dignities such as uniqueness, equality, and value, which evoke human love toward others.[15] We have the obligation to try to imitate God through an exercise of free will in concrete deeds toward God's human representatives on earth; this is how the divine image is manifest.[16] As God is love, we love; as he is merciful, we show mercy; as he is just, we pursue justice. The challenge is to make one's own life an image of his will. This is best done relationally, in community, through respectful treatment of others that demonstrates genuine kindness, dignity, equality, and a sense of worth.[17]

12. H. Wildberger, "Selem," in *Theological Lexicon of the Old Testament,* ed. Ernst Jenni and Claus Westermann, trans. Mark E. Biddle, vol. 3 (Peabody, MA: Hendrickson, 1997), p. 1084.

13. E. H. Merrill, "Image of God," in *Dictionary of the Old Testament: Pentateuch,* ed. T. Desmond Alexander and David W. Baker (Downers Grove, IL: InterVarsity, 2003), p. 443.

14. See Michael Wyschogrod, *Abraham's Promise: Judaism and Jewish-Christian Relations* (Grand Rapids: Eerdmans, 2004), p. 171.

15. See Irving Greenberg and Shalom Freedman, *Living in the Image of God* (Northvale, NJ: Jason Aronson, 1998), pp. 31-33.

16. Gordon J. Wenham, *Story as Torah* (Grand Rapids: Baker Academic, 2000), p. 107.

17. Dan Cohn-Sherbok, *The Jewish Heritage* (New York: Blackwell, 1988), p. 72.

The image of God finds some of its most meaningful practical expression when the international human family is relationally engaged, living in *shalom,* and when the Creator and Owner of the world's natural environment is honored through careful stewardship of its resources. In addition, the image of God also has cross-cultural and eschatological implications. Christians see the image of God marred or distorted due to the fall of man and his consequent propensity to sin. Man is free to choose, yet he is finite; his potential is subject to human limitations. In Christ, however, through the work of the Spirit, a process of restoration begins, never reaching the full image of godliness in this life. Richard Mouw creatively challenges Christian thinking about the image of God and the future of the church:

> We might think of the Creator as having distributed different aspects of the divine likeness to different cultural groups, with each group receiving, as it were, a unique assignment for developing some aspect or another of the divine image. Thus, it will only be in the eschatological gathering-in of the peoples of the earth, when many tribes and tongues and nations will be displayed in their honor and glory in the New Jerusalem, that we will see the many-splendored *imago dei* in its fullness.[18]

Thus, as part of a gospel of renewal and total transformation, Christians must await the fullest expression of God's image in the pan-national eschatological ingathering of the New Jerusalem. The image of God in this life, blunted by the self-centeredness of sin in the human heart, will eventually be fully restored, by his grace, so we may live as we are meant to live as part of a new humanity.

In this present age, Christians must seek for a biblical balance in their understanding of the image of God. On the one hand, some have an unhealthy preoccupation with inherent sinfulness and the bleakness of the human condition, which has led to a kind of cosmic pessimism and hopelessness among many Western Christians concerning the future of humanity. On the other hand, others have an unrealistic optimism about human nature and too high a view of human potential to perfect the world, which has led to a false theological conclusion that the human may be divine and the ultimate redeemer of this world.

An authentic Christian humanism will emphasize freedom of the will

---

18. Richard J. Mouw, "The Imago Dei and Philosophical Anthropology," *Christian Scholar's Review* 41, no. 3 (Spring 2012): 265.

and human potential. However, one must realistically ground any notion of utopian idealism in the blunt reality of Scripture that includes many examples of human failure due to pride, greed, self-will, narcissism, and lust for power. Certainly, if the concept of the image of God teaches us anything, it is this: one of our highest ideals is to become more and more like God in our character and actions (see Lev. 19:2). It is to show the power of God in the potentialities of life. Accordingly, Leo Baeck points out that because man is created in the image of God "the highest may be demanded of him" and he can be "the preserver and renewer of the world."[19] In the words of Hillel, "In a place where no one behaves like a human being, strive to be a human" (Mishnah, Abot 2:7). In other words, be a humane leader, a person of noble character and true substance, by taking the initiative and assuming responsibility.[20] Such are worthy goals if both feet are planted solidly on the ground, and if one is "grounded" in Scripture with a realistic understanding of both the possibilities and the foibles of human nature.

The Hebraic concept of the image of God is a place where Jews and Christians can come together, reflect, and be inspired to positive joint action. Unlike certain other parts of the Bible, quite literally, on the first page of the Bible we can meet together and find considerable agreement. How is this possible? Christians and Jews have value and significance not because one's dialogue partner deems the other worthy of such recognition but because the Creator himself grants this through making all people in his image and likeness. When we remember we are created in the image of God it is a striking reminder of how to treat each other; every human is my brother or sister. Indeed, our neighbor is "the face of God" in the world. Something sacred is at stake.

False Images and Idolatry

The prohibitions against having other gods and making idols for worship are near the "top of the list" of the Ten Commandments (Exod. 20:3-6). During the biblical period, an intense war was waged by the prophets against idolatry. Jeremiah and Ezekiel were among the most vociferous voices calling the people of God back to covenant fidelity and the worship of the one true God.

---

19. Leo Baeck, *The Essence of Judaism* (New York: Schocken, 1948), pp. 123, 154.
20. See Judah Goldin, ed., *The Living Talmud: The Wisdom of the Fathers* (New York: New American Library, 1957), p. 92.

Their oracles and teachings reveal that idolatry was probably the most significant cause resulting in the fall of Jerusalem and exile to Babylon in 586 B.C.

Hear the scathing, stinging words of Jeremiah: "For you have as many gods as you have towns, O Judah" (Jer. 2:28). "You have scattered your favors to foreign gods under every spreading tree" (3:13). "For the customs of the people are worthless; they cut a tree out of the forest, and a craftsman shapes it with his chisel. They adorn it with silver and gold; they fasten it with hammer and nails so it will not totter . . . they are all senseless and foolish; they are taught by worthless wooden idols. . . . But the LORD is the true God; he is the living God, the eternal King" (10:3, 4, 8, 10).

Ezekiel also has a strong polemic against idols. In his valuable study of God's presence and absence in the Book of Ezekiel, John Kutsko points out Ezekiel's "scorching mockery" in linking idols with dung. In his prophecy, Ezekiel employs the word *gillulim*, "idols," nearly forty times. Kutsko notes how Ezekiel exploited the "double entendre" conveyed by *gillulim*, a pungent term meaning (idol-)stone and excrement (literally, turds that "roll"), implying the loathsomeness and impurity of pagan idols.[21] At an earlier period, in much the same scathing manner, the followers of Yahweh spoke with mocking ridicule of Baal-zebub, "lord of the flies," the Caananite god worshiped at the major Philistine city of Ekron (2 Kgs. 1:1-16). In Canaanite texts the name appears as Baal-Zebul, "Baal the prince," a term of high honor and respect (see Matt. 10:25; 12:24). By making a deliberate distortion or alteration of Baal-Zebul to read Baal-Zebub, "lord of flies," the Israelites equated this pagan god with dung or excrement, the stinky, detestable substance around which flies congregate and "buzz" (note the onomatopoeic *zebub*, "flies"). Little wonder that the rabbis concluded: "The essence of Judaism is the denial of false gods."[22]

At least until Babylonian exile, idolatry was a major problem in Israel. The images of Baal, the Ashtoreths, and other deities competed for Israel's affection. In the midst of the temptation to forsake the living — yet invisible — God of Abraham to follow the dead — yet visible — idols of the nations, Israel was engaged in a battle for the very vitality of her spiritual existence.

Israel was far from successful in her efforts. Though theoretically monotheistic, Israel was far from consistent in "following the script." When the nation would go through cycles of decline, they usually ended with a

21. See John F. Kutsko, *Between Heaven and Earth,* Biblical and Judaic Studies, vol. 7 (Winona Lake, IN: Eisenbrauns, 2000), pp. 32-34.

22. See Joseph Telushkin, *Jewish Wisdom* (New York: William Morrow, 1994), p. 277; cf. Babylonian Talmud, Megillah 13a.

forsaking of idolatry accompanied with repentance, renewal, and reform. Despite Israel's many failures and the spiteful mockings heard from those of neighboring nations, God's living presence and loving acts continued to assure Israel of her election. Indeed, the message of the prophets was consistent: "Yahweh alone is God and idols are impotent; though not physically present, Yahweh makes himself known by his actions."[23] Conversely, in the polemics of Israel directed to the nations, Israel frequently sought to invalidate pagan idols and gods by poking fun at their lifelessness and inability to act (see 1 Kgs. 18:18-40; Ps. 115:1-8). Michael Wyschogrod explains the great challenge of Israel living among the nations:

> Just as Israel's record is mixed, so is that of the nations. Instead of accepting Israel's election with humility, they rail against it, mocking the God of the Jews, gleefully pointing out the shortcomings of the people he chose, and crucifying it whenever an opportunity presents itself. Israel's presence is a constant reminder to them that they were not chosen but that this people was, and that this people remains in their midst as a thorn in the flesh. Minute by minute, the existence of Israel mocks the pagan gods, the divine beings who rise out of the consciousness of all peoples but which are gentile gods because they are deifications of humanity and the forces of nature rather than the true, living God of Abraham.[24]

For the prophets of Israel, idolatry destroyed the very foundation of covenantal loyalty. Unlike the surrounding nations' gods, the invisible God of Israel could not be chiseled, carved, molded, or shaped into a concrete or material form of an animal, a bird, a fish, or anything in the created world. Such an image would, in effect, be a call to reverse the Exodus and return to the bondage of an idolatrous land with a god as its king, serving other gods. As Wyschogrod alludes to above, pharaoh was one of the "deifications of humanity." In the Hebrew text of the Ten Commandments, the expression *bet 'abadim*, "house of bondage," is placed directly next to the commands that forbade having other gods and making idols (Exod. 20:2-4). The word for "bondage" and the word for "worship" come from the same root, *'abad*, "to serve" or "to worship" (a master or god that one is subservient or subject to).

Israel is not to "bow down" to idols or to "worship" them because Yahweh is *el qanna*, "a jealous God" (Exod. 20:5). The Jewish Publication

---

23. Kutsko, *Between Heaven and Earth*, pp. 4, 5.
24. Wyschogrod, *Abraham's Promise*, p. 182.

Society (JPS) TANAKH translation renders *qanna* ("jealous") with the word "impassioned," seeking to underline how strongly and passionately Yahweh feels. The root of *qanna* seems to carry the idea of "becoming extremely red" out of rage, envy, passion, jealousy, or some other emotion intensely felt. In human situations, the term likely alludes to the face area, which may change color — hence the expressions "red with envy" or "red with rage." Here, then, is a powerful anthropomorphism as Yahweh, "red-faced" with passionate envy, desires ardently that his bride Israel maintain her exclusive relationship with him and not be attracted to other images of worship competing for her affection.

Idolatry and the New Testament

The New Testament has a deep concern about idolatry. But it sometimes appears in a different cultural and social context than found in the Old Testament. For approximately the first twenty years of the church, one had to be a Jew to be part of the church. The original church was fully a movement within Judaism. At the Council of Jerusalem in A.D. 49, however, concerns about idolatry began to surface. The council was an event that focused on the inclusion of Gentiles as well as Jews in the early Jewish church. How would these two groups meld into one body? Several of the decisions of the Council of Jerusalem related to pagan or idolatrous practices of the Gentile world.

The first issue decided by the council forbade Gentiles — those joining Jews in this all-Jewish entity, the church — from eating food polluted by idols (Acts 15:20, 29; 21:25; see also 1 Cor. 8:1-13; 10:19). The Jerusalem apostles supported Jewish-Gentile fellowship in the church but wished to respect the conscience of their Jewish brothers and sisters. In the first century, the term "Gentile" was virtually synonymous with "idol-worshiper." Thus the avoidance of food that may previously have been placed on pagan altars would remove something offensive to Jewish scruples.[25]

The overall position of the New Testament is clear: "There is one God" (1 Tim. 2:5) and thus believers are enjoined to heed such deeply rooted Hebraic commands as *pheugete eidololatrias*, "flee from idolatry," and *phylaxate eauta apo ton eidolon*, "Keep yourselves from idols" (1 John 5:21). This strong New Testament apologetic against idolatry is especially found in Paul, "the

---

25. See Marvin R. Wilson, *Our Father Abraham: Jewish Roots of the Christian Faith* (Grand Rapids: Eerdmans, 1989), pp. 22, 48-50.

apostle to the Gentiles" (Rom. 11:13). Paul spent much of his life in the diaspora of the Mediterranean world where idolatry was rife. In Athens he was "greatly distressed to see that the city was full of idols" (Acts 17:16). In Ephesus (Western Turkey) Paul is quoted as saying, "man-made gods are no gods at all" (Acts 19:26). Paul points out to the Corinthians that they were once "led astray to mute idols" (1 Cor. 12:2). Similarly, in a style reminiscent of the Old Testament prophets, the Book of Revelation dismisses the reality of idols by attacking their lifelessness: "idols of gold, silver, bronze, stone and wood — idols that cannot see, or hear or walk" (9:20). In contrast, the Thessalonians are commended for their wide reputation for having turned from idols to serve "the living and true God" *(theo zonti kai alethino)* (1 Thess. 1:9). In New Testament terms, sexual immorality and greed may hold such a strong grip upon a person so as to interfere with his relation to God. Accordingly, such attractions are viewed as "idolatry" (Col. 3:5).

In the post-biblical period, the rabbis declared there were seven Noahide laws, the first of which prohibits idolatry. These ethical and moral teachings were binding on the descendants of Noah (Gentiles), on all humanity. The rabbis taught that Jews, however, were bound by "TaRYaG mitzvot," the 613 commandments found in the Law of Moses (TaRYaG, an acronym using the four letters of the Hebrew alphabet that are the numerical equivalent of 613). The Babylonian Talmud states that under duress, to save one's life, a Jew is allowed to break any commandment of the law except idolatry, adultery, and murder (Sanhedrin 74a). These three prohibitions, at the heart of the Ten Commandments, have a striking resemblance to both the Noahide laws and the areas prohibited by the Jerusalem Council (see Acts 15:20, 29). Extending from antiquity to modernity, the prohibition of idolatry is one of the strongest teachings held in common by the three monotheistic Abrahamic religions: Judaism, Christianity, and Islam.

The Disguise of Modern Idolatry

Modern Judaism has much to teach Christians about the dangers and folly of idolatry. As a people, Jews have always considered themselves iconoclasts, those who fight against idolatry. This built-in propensity to stay away from idols is doubtless related to the fact that idolatry is one of the three cardinal sins for which a person should be willing to lay down his life rather than to succumb. In addition, one of the tractates of the Mishnah, Avodah Zarah, "Idolatry," is devoted to the prohibition of pagan worship in any form whatsoever.[26] Further, the long memory of such disturbing events as the dance before Aaron's golden calf in the wilderness and the placing of Jeroboam's golden calves at Dan and Bethel during the start of the Northern Kingdom long haunted Israel's history (Exodus 32; 1 Kgs. 12:25-33). Göran Larsson places the golden calf event in significant context:

> The sin in Exodus 32 seems to be more serious than the fall in Genesis 3. First of all, the worship of the golden calf is idolatry of the worst kind. But the most serious is that it takes place *after* the Lord has demonstrated so much love toward the people. God has saved them from slavery and oppression through unprecedented miracles. The children of Israel have come closer to God than any other people. And they have not only accepted the first of all his commandments, "You shall have no other gods before me" but also have promised to do all that the Lord has commanded (24:7). Obviously, they know what they are doing. . . . Nevertheless, we should not look at their precipitous fall in a judgmental or smug way. . . . How many people today willingly give up God to make money and achieve earthly success?[27]

For ancient Israel, the prohibition against idolatry was not limited to earthly images. It also included worship of "anything in heaven above" (Exod. 20:4). Thus, to believe that stars or constellations control someone's fate or determine his destiny is idolatry. Jeremiah was critical of those who worshiped the "Queen of Heaven," probably a reference to the Babylonian goddess Ishtar, symbolized by the Morning Star (Jer. 7:18; 44:17-19, 25).

As stated above, idolatry is often far more subtle and disguised than publicly bowing down to images. Idolatry can occur when a person makes anything of greater importance or of higher value than God. Such a temptation is always before human beings. It is insidious. For example, Abraham Heschel calls attention to "disguised polytheism," an inner attitude of idolatry. According to Heschel, this inward expression of idolatry occurs "if in performing a religious act one's intention is to please a human being whom he fears or from whom he hopes to receive benefit[;] then it is not God whom he worships but a human being."[28]

---

26. See Adin Steinsaltz, *The Essential Talmud* (New York: HarperCollins, 1976), p. 91.

27. Göran Larsson, *Bound for Freedom* (Peabody, MA: Hendrickson, 1999), pp. 246-47.

28. Abraham J. Heschel, *God in Search of Man* (New York: Harper & Row, 1955), p. 392, and also *A Passion for Truth* (New York: Farrar, Straus & Giroux, 1973), pp. 37-38.

Today, especially in the Western world, materialism has become one of the most obvious forms of idolatry. Materialism places an excessive emphasis on physical matter or stuff one acquires, but the spiritual and intellectual realms are of diminished importance. God created man to love people and use things; materialism pursues things and, in the end, tends to "use" individuals and ignore God. All reality is not confined to the personal pursuit of wealth or the amassing of things. To live with such values is idolatrous. Solomon Schimmel explains the deception of such modern idolatry: "The premise is that unrestrained pursuit of wealth will eventually [make] us happier, because the more money we accrue the happier we will be. But in so worshiping money, placing our hope and trust in it — a form of idolatry — we blind ourselves to the social and personal costs of greed."[29]

Narcissism or self-love may be another modern expression of idolatry. It is true that if we do not accept and love ourselves, it will be exceedingly difficult to express meaningful love to others. However, when we have an honest estimate of ourselves, value who we are, and possess a healthy sense of self-esteem, we are more likely to love, respect, and see the worth and beauty of our neighbor. Love begets love. To be sure, extreme self-love often leads to pride, arrogance, and selfishness. A mature, aware, and balanced love, however, often expresses itself in reciprocity, mutuality, and sharing with others. This is *agape* love. Paul lists some of its characteristics: "Love is patient, love is kind. It does not envy, it does not boast, it is not proud. It is not rude, it is not self-seeking" (1 Cor. 13:4-5a).

A humble heart will not be solely absorbed inwardly with self-worship and self-importance; it will not be gripped by an "I'm-the-only-one-who-matters" mentality. Rather, such a heart will look outward to care about one's neighbor and most of all will look upward in worship of the one true God from whom all earthly gifts flow. While the ego of most humans is fragile and may be rather easily damaged, modern education may be contributing to the "I am the greatest" or "idolatrous self" concept by having to send every child home with a trophy and pronouncing everyone "special," for there are no "losers" in life. Perhaps a better (Hebraic) strategy is that of corporate solidarity, in which an individual is always part of a larger group or body: "If one part suffers, every part suffers with it; if one part is honored, every part rejoices with it" (1 Cor. 12:26).

Modern idolatry may take other shapes and expressions from those

---

29. Solomon Schimmel, *The Seven Deadly Sins: Jewish, Christian, and Classical Reflections on Human Nature* (New York: Macmillan, 1992), p. 166.

mentioned above. It is often subtle, insidious, unwitting, and deceptive. For example, one may highly value any number of things including education, a spouse, a spiritual leader, a piece of art, or even a holy book. However, if one ascribes ultimate or supreme value to any of these they turn into gods. Some turn from worshiping the God of Scripture into a rigid biblicism that may be described as an "idolatry of the book."[30] In short, paper and ink may be exalted to a position higher than the Ultimate Authority inspiring it. Others today seek to elevate a political cause over a basic moral sensitivity and respect for human rights. Thus, despite issues that are very complex and often daunting, it may be idolatrous for either Jews or Christians to believe that the Land of Israel holds a greater holiness than the human beings living in that land.[31] Often difficult to detect, the blind worship of a thing, person, or cause over the One Supreme God who claims the right to be first in all things is idolatry. "There will be terrible times in the last days. People will be lovers of themselves, lovers of money . . . lovers of pleasure rather than lovers of God" (2 Tim. 3:1, 2a, 4b).

Israel and the Divine Presence

Although in Babylonian exile the Jewish people lost their political independence, they gained their religious soul. The departure of the abiding Presence from the Temple in Jerusalem left the city open to invasion and destruction (Ezek. 10:1–11:15). To be sure, "The misrepresentation of God's image, the illegitimate expression of his presence — resulted in the removal of God's presence and the destruction of his symbolic dwelling place. . . . Humans, not idols, are the image of the divine."[32] Paradoxically, "by emphasizing God's absence (his lack of physical representation) Ezekiel enabled his audience to perceive God's presence in exile."[33]

In connection with the above, one of the most important terms in the Hebrew Bible is *kabod*, "glory." The word *kabod* comes from a Hebrew root meaning "to be heavy" or "to be weighty." When *kabod* is used of God, it usually has reference to the presence of God in the world. When we say a person "has presence" we are referring to something more than outward and

---

30. Christian Smith, *The Bible Made Impossible* (Grand Rapids: Brazos, 2011), p. 124.

31. See David S. Ariel, *What Do Jews Believe? The Spiritual Foundations of Judaism* (New York: Schocken, 1995), pp. 127-28.

32. Kutsko, *Between Heaven and Earth*, pp. 76, 150.

33. Kutsko, *Between Heaven and Earth*, p. 76.

physical. When a person of considerable wisdom, brilliance, or intellectual reputation is said to carry "weight," it is not a reference to how many pounds that individual weighs on a scale. Rather, that person's "presence" suggests an indwelling power, a sense of impressiveness, weightiness, or greatness that may be inexpressible, but nevertheless, commands honor and respect. The *kabod* or "living presence" of God is often associated with an awareness of grandeur and indescribable awe. The outward setting for God's glory may be fire, cloud, whirlwind, or lightning. God's glory was often concealed. However, when revealed, its appearance came at set moments, especially to the prophets.

Further, God's awesome presence is not a concrete substance but an overwhelming power that descends to guide; it is a power acting in nature and history reflected in goodness and truth.[34] To the Israelites, "the glory of the Lord looked like a consuming fire" on the top of Sinai (Exod. 24:17). On another occasion, as Moses sought to enter the Tent of Meeting, "the glory of the Lord filled the tabernacle" and the cloud, in which God's presence was manifested, had settled upon it, so he could not enter (Exod. 40:34, 35). Centuries later, at the dedication of Solomon's Temple, "the priests could not perform their service because of the cloud, for the glory *(kabod)* of the Lord filled his temple" (1 Kgs. 8:11).

In Scripture, the glory of God must not be solely thought of as a localized phenomenon whereby the divine presence is limited to certain holy precincts such as those described above. In Isaiah's inaugural vision, the seraphim declare, "the whole earth is full of his glory *(kabod)*" (Isa. 6:3b). In this and other texts is a "great universalizing" of God's presence in the world.[35] Indeed, the psalmist also speaks of nature, "God's other book," singing an ineffable song of the presence of God: "The heavens declare the glory of God . . . their voice goes out into all the earth" (Ps. 19:1a, 4a). In contemporary Judaism, the Hasidic community places considerable emphasis on the manifestation of God's presence everywhere, especially the celebration of his immanence within the created order.

In the post-biblical period, the rabbis used the term *shekhinah* to refer to God's indwelling presence in the world. The Hebrew root *shakhan* means to "dwell," "stay," "settle," "inhabit." While the Shekhinah had a special attachment to the Temple in Jerusalem, the presence of God may be revealed and embraced anywhere. The Shekhinah could be experienced in the stillness

---

34. See Heschel, *God in Search of Man,* pp. 80-87.
35. See Arthur Green, *These Are the Words* (Woodstock, VT: Jewish Lights, 1999), p. 15.

of a moment contemplating the beauties of nature or in the exuberant joy of performing a sacred deed. The rabbis particularly emphasized that the Shekhinah is present when two people come and sit together to study Torah (Mishnah Abot 3:2, 6). In a similar way, Jesus assured his followers, "For where two or three come together in my name there am I with them" (Matt. 18:20; see also Col. 1:19). As one rabbi observes, "The Shekhinah is always associated with God's nearness. . . . God cannot live together in the same environment with sinfulness. The presence of one excludes the presence of the other."[36] Belief in the living God and confidence in his nearness is a hallmark that set Judaism apart from the mythological teachings of other ancient religions (see Deut. 4:7). The mythology of polytheism leads to a belief in chance, caprice, or fate, the very antithesis of Jewish teaching regarding the closeness of God.[37]

Perhaps the most familiar term used in Scripture for the presence of the living God is *ruaḥ ha-kodesh,* "the Holy Spirit." In the Hebrew Bible, the Spirit's activity is often displayed outwardly as he manifests his power in special situations or comes upon specific people to enable them to perform certain tasks. For example, God is dynamically present at creation as "the Spirit of God . . . hovering *(meraḥephet)* over the waters" (Gen. 1:2). The term used for "hovering" is a participial form taken from the world of ornithology; it conveys the idea of the Spirit's ceaseless and lavish loving care over creation as a mother bird attentively hovers over her young in the nest. The Spirit empowers or enables people to perform various skills or acts of service. This includes Bezalel's ability in craftsmanship (Exod. 31:2-5), Gideon's prowess in leadership against the Midianites (Judg. 6:34), and Samson's physical strength to tear a lion apart with his bare hands (Judg. 14:6).

Theologically speaking, the most important work of the Spirit emphasized in the Hebrew Bible is that of the divine inspiration of the prophets. The Spirit enabled them to speak the word of God with power and divine authority (see 2 Pet. 1:20-21). Prophecy was not a matter of pure human genius; rather, God was speaking through the words of the prophets. Again and again, this is the testimony of the Hebrew Bible. Ezekiel says, "Then the Spirit of the LORD came upon me, and he told me to say . . ." (Ezek. 11:5). Micah says, "As for me, I am filled with power, with the Spirit of the LORD" (Mic. 3:8). Nehemiah states, "By your Spirit you [God] admonished them

---

36. Simon Glustrom, *The Language of Judaism* (Northvale, NJ: Jason Aronson, 1988), p. 171.

37. Leo Baeck, *The Essence of Judaism* (New York: Schocken, 1948), pp. 88-91.

[Israel] through your prophets" (Neh. 9:30). It was the *ruaḥ ha-kodesh* that came upon Jeremiah that compelled him to speak forth, for the prophet declares, "his word is in my heart like a fire, a fire shut up in my bones. I am weary of holding it in; indeed, I cannot" (20:9).

Moving away from the prophetic period of Bible times, Judaism today understands the work of the Spirit somewhat differently. In what ongoing way is the presence of the Spirit primarily manifest in today's world? Jewish scholar Aaron Singer defines the *ruaḥ ha-kodesh* as the "palpable presence of God," and then Singer comments further about the term:

> God's revelation is now the responsibility of the sage, the religious virtuoso, to preserve and interpret. The manifestation of *ruaḥ ha-kodesh* . . . is evidence of the active involvement within and without the framework of halakhah. The concept demonstrates a consciousness of God's nearness and uninterrupted concern for his creatures. . . . The assertion of God's immanence together with his transcendence in rabbinic teaching reflects, concretizes, and completes the worldview of the Bible. "I dwell on high, in holiness, yet with the contrite and lowly in spirit — reviving the spirits of the lowly, reviving the hearts of the contrite" (Isa. 57:15).[38]

In similar yet contrasting language, the New Testament emphasizes that the presence of God, through the Holy Spirit *(to pneuma to hagion)* indwells believers. However, in traditional Christianity, there is the understanding of the Holy Spirit as a distinct person within the Godhead. John's Gospel states that the Holy Spirit "lives with you and will be in you" (John 14:17). The Spirit usually works relationally through such activities as convicting of sin, illuminating truth, guiding people, comforting them, producing his "fruit" in them, and filling them with his presence (John 14:16; Gal. 5:22; Eph. 5:18). Likewise, one finds the role of the Holy Spirit in teaching and testifying to truth (John 14:26; 15:26). In sum, the historic creeds of the church affirm that the Spirit of God is more than an influence in the world for good. Rather, the Holy Spirit is a separate person within a Trinity and is synonymous with God himself.

Throughout this chapter we have explored the meaning of the image of God in man. Life is sacred, for people are sacred. All bear his image and

---

38. Aaron Singer, "Holy Spirit," in *Contemporary Jewish Religious Thought*, ed. Arthur A. Cohen and Paul Mendes-Flohr (New York: Free Press, 1987), pp. 413-14.

likeness. Sadly, however, the idols of humanity never cease vying for human allegiance. Such was true in ancient Israel's experience and is likewise true in our modern world. Today, however, idolatry is often more subtle. Self-centered attitudes are an easy first step that can lead to the dethroning of God in the human heart and the defacing of his image. As an antidote, believers are urged to rely on the power and presence of the living God around them and within them. The Lord gave these empowering words to the patriarchs and to Moses: "I will be with you" (see Gen. 26:3; Exod. 3:12). David, likewise, knew the Spirit was always with him: "Where can I go from your Spirit? Where can I flee from your presence?" (Ps. 139:7). These words reverberate into the pages of the New Testament and into the hearts of believers. In Acts 2, the Spirit comes on the Jewish festival of *Shabuʿot*, "Weeks" or Pentecost, filling believers with his powerful, indwelling presence.

Finally, the First Letter of John teaches that inwardly believers "have an anointing from the Holy One" and so should confidently live with the assurance: "the one who is in you is greater than the one who is in the world" (1 John 2:20; 4:4). The Spirit's indwelling presence is needed to counter the power of the opposition or adversary (*satan,* in the Hebrew Bible), "the one who is in the world." The living and true God alone deserves full allegiance and complete trust. Thus, when all is said and done, John's last word is the first word of the Ten Commandments; it concerns false gods: "Dear children, keep yourselves from idols" (5:21; see also Exod. 20:3-6).

UNDERSTANDING CHAPTER NINE

1. The author states that the entire Bible is a commentary on what, and concerns what ongoing narrative?

2. When asked what the greatest command in the Torah is, how did Rabbi Akiba and his disciple Ben Azzai answer? What was the reasoning behind Ben Azzai's response? How do their answers demonstrate the interconnectedness of respecting God's image and loving one's neighbor?

3. Which Hebrew words in Genesis 1:26 are typically translated into English as "image" and "likeness"? What sense does each word usually carry, and how is the sense of *tzelem* obviously different in Genesis 1:26? From your perspective, does knowledge that *tzelem* is sometimes paralleled with the Hebrew *hebel* clarify or cloud your understanding of God's image in Genesis 1:26? How do the terms *tzelem* and *demut* seem to work together in the description of man?

4. In ancient Mesopotamia and Egypt, what figures were often considered the living "image of God"? Why might a king place a statue of himself in a conquered land? How can humans be seen as functioning similarly in relation to God? What is your reaction to the conceptual connection between a truthful assertion of Scripture (the image of God contained in the human) and an erroneous assertion of humanity (a deity contained in a statue)? How does Christian theologian J. I. Packer say that we, as image-bearers, should reflect a "representative likeness" to God?

5. According to Abraham Heschel, from where do human beings receive their dignity? Explain Heschel's idea of "sacred humanism."

6. How does Psalm 8 illustrate humanity's role as God's regal representative on earth? In what way is Scripture's teaching about the image of God inclusive?

7. What is the first and perhaps most fundamental sign of God's love for humankind? How is the divine image manifest?

8. What practical expressions of living in the image of God does the author list? What would you add to the list? How has the "fall" (Genesis 3) affected Adam's descendants in relation to the fact that each is created in the image of God (see Rom. 5:12-19)?

9. How do Richard Mouw's comments about the image of God and the future of the church suggest an interdependence among people groups in regard to living in God's image? Do you think that the church typically operates within this mindset or not? In your opinion, how does a "chosen people" fit into the picture?

10. What tension does the author allude to when he states that "Christians must seek for a biblical balance in their understanding of the image of God"? What will "authentic Christian humanism" both emphasize and acknowledge? Toward which side do you see yourself personally leaning? Do you feel a need to balance the two sides?

11. What did Hillel mean by the words, "In a place where no one behaves like a human being, strive to be a human"?

12. Which two prophets mentioned by the author particularly fought against idolatry? How might their words be understood to reveal the relationship between idolatry and the fall of Jerusalem and subsequent exile to Babylon?

13. How does the prophet Ezekiel exploit the double entendre conveyed by the Hebrew *gillulim* to characterize idols? How did earlier followers of Yahweh similarly exploit the name of a Canaanite god? For additional discussion: From a Christian perspective, how much of a priority do

you think the church should place not only on exploring the Hebrew Bible in the native tongue of her members but also in Hebrew? In what ways could the church empower her members to enhance their understanding of the Hebrew Bible by becoming familiar with the ancient language? How could interfaith projects help to fulfill this vision?

14. According to Joseph Telushkin, the rabbis pithily sum up the essence of Judaism as "the denial of false gods." Can Christianity be reduced to one expression about something (most) Christians *deny*? What would it be? Why? What does Israel's journey reveal about the character of Yahweh, her God?

15. What is the meaning of the Hebrew phrase *bet 'abadim*? Where is it placed in the Ten Commandments, and why is this significant? Interestingly, which two different concepts share the root *'abad*? What does *'abad* itself mean?

16. What does the title *el qanna* mean? How does the JPS TANAKH render it? What anthropomorphic sense does this evoke?

17. How is a deep concern about idolatry evident in the first issue decided upon by the Jerusalem Council?

18. What clear-cut commands against idolatry in the New Testament reveal a strong concern about the subject? Where especially is a strong teaching against it found? How did various New Testament contexts allow for strong commentary about and against idolatry? How does the Book of Revelation particularly mirror Old Testament condemnations of idols?

19. In the post-biblical era, which two major groups of laws did the rabbis identify, and to which people groups did they apply? What does the Babylonian Talmud allow concerning the breaking of commandments? How do the three prohibitions mentioned demonstrate a striking unity of thought among the Ten Commandments, the Noahide laws, the Jerusalem Council, and post-biblical Judaism?

20. To what is tractate Avodah Zarah of the Mishnah devoted?

21. In what ways does Göran Larsson see the sin in Exodus 32 as more serious than the fall in Genesis 3? Do you agree with his assessment?

22. Beyond earthly images, what did the prohibition against idolatry extend to for ancient Israel? In what way was this command pertinent in an ancient Near Eastern context? How might Jeremiah's words make this evident? In your opinion, should modern Jews or Christians have any serious interest in the signs of the Zodiac?

23. What does Abraham Heschel mean by the phrase "disguised polytheism"?

24. Which two major modern forms of idolatry does the author discuss? How do you perceive each one in yourself or in the contexts in which you live? Can you think of other forms of idolatry that are as pervasive in the modern world?

25. How does the author describe *agape* love? What are some of the characteristics of *agape* love that Paul lists in one of his letters to the Corinthians? How do the qualities of this love enable it to triumph over idolatry?

26. Regarding the ego and self-absorption, what critique does the author offer of modern education? What alternative mindset does he suggest? Do you agree with him? Why or why not?

27. What does the phrase "idolatry of the book" refer to? For additional discussion: In what ways are some traditions of Christianity more susceptible to this form of idolatry than others? How might ecumenical dialogue be beneficial in creating a more balanced sense of the role of Scripture for the church?

28. Review the author's statement that "it may be idolatrous for either Jews or Christians to believe that the Land of Israel holds a greater holiness than the human beings living in that land." Unpack the statement with the concept of political idolatry in mind. In your opinion, what should political action itself be guided by in order to avoid idolatry and, in relation to previous material in the chapter, maintain respect for the image of God in all humanity?

29. Though the Jewish people lost their political independence through Babylonian exile, what did they gain? What did Ezekiel emphasize that led — paradoxically — to a sharpened perception of God's presence?

30. What does the Hebrew *kabod* mean? What does it usually mean when referring to God? What kind of awareness is it often associated with?

31. In what outward manifestations did God appear to the Israelites at Sinai, to Moses at the Tent of Meeting, and at the dedication of Solomon's Temple? In your eyes, what do these particular "mediums" communicate or reveal about God's glory?

32. In what ways does Scripture reveal that God's presence is universal throughout the world? Which community within contemporary Judaism pays special attention to this? Do you know of any comparable Christian communities?

33. In the post-biblical period, what term did the rabbis use to refer to God's indwelling presence in the world? What does its Hebrew root

mean? How was this presence understood, and how did Jesus' words communicate a similar concept?

34. What is the *ruaḥ ha-kodesh?* Briefly summarize Aaron Singer's thoughts on the presence of God in the world. How do you understand his statement that the rabbinic view of God's immanence and transcendence together *completes* the worldview of the Bible?

35. What does the New Testament emphasize about the Holy Spirit? How does the Holy Spirit relate to God in Christianity? How does he usually work, and for what purposes? Taken together, do you think that Jewish understandings of the *ruaḥ ha-kodesh* and Christian understandings of the Holy Spirit offer a more complete understanding of the Spirit of God?

36. In what ways can Jews and Christians alike find strength in the battle against idolatry by reflecting on God's presence as experienced by foundational figures such as Moses and David? In what passages of the New Testament is such encouragement continued, and how so?

PART IV

On Approaching God

CHAPTER 10

A Life of Worship

In today's church, misinformation about worship abounds. The biblical basis of worship is theological, not anthropological. Worship was never designed to make people feel better. In Scripture, worship is directed to the God of Israel. It is in his honor. There is a trend in certain churches today to equate worship with an entertainment type of mentality. People come with a view to "enjoying" the service. To worship is for the audience to feel good or feel happy or feel "blessed." A main question of concern of some who come to "worship" is, "What am I going to get out of it?"

Yet others approach worship much like spectators at a public event. Their primary intention is to watch some paid religious professional perform certain rituals on their behalf. There is an expectation of decorum and the proper comportment and set formula of a robed functionary to ensure a genuine worship experience. Biblical worship, however, is focused upon neither the worshiper nor the one leading in worship. Praise is directed to the God of Israel. He is the object of worship. True worship focuses on him. Worship involves paying awesome devotion and reverent service from the human heart to the King of the universe. His pattern for Israel is the same as it is for us. We serve him; he does not serve us.

People of Praise

The worship that Christians render must be shaped by an appreciation of how the Jewish community has understood and practiced worship through the centuries. First, at the heart of worship is praise. The word "Jew" *(yehudi)* is traced back to Jacob and Leah's son, Judah *(yehudah)*.[1] The name Judah is derived from the Hebrew root *yadah*, to "praise," to "give thanks." According to Genesis 29:35, Leah says on the occasion of Judah's birth, "'This time I will praise [Heb. *'odeh*] the LORD.' So she named him Judah *(yehudah)*." In Jacob's blessing of Judah in Genesis 49:8, a memorable play is made on the word "praise." Jacob says, "Judah *(yehudah)*, your brothers will praise you *(yodukha)*; your hand *(yadekhah)* will be on the neck of your enemies."

After the conquest of Canaan, the name Judah referred to the members of his tribe living in the territory assigned to Judah, the large hilly region running directly west of the Dead Sea (Josh. 15:1-12). From the time of the United Kingdom, the tribal area of Judah must have had a particular appreciation for praise and worship through music. David, a musician from Bethlehem, composed many songs of praise in the Judean hills. In addition, songs of praise by Levitical choirs flowed from the courts of the Temple in Jerusalem built by David's son Solomon. King Hezekiah, for example, "ordered the Levites to praise the LORD with the words of David and of Asaph the seer. So they sang praises with gladness and bowed their heads and worshipped" (2 Chron. 29:30).

After the kingdom split North and South, the term "Judah" was used for all residents of the Southern Kingdom, which also included the tribe of Benjamin (see 1 Kgs. 12:16-21). Once the Northern Kingdom was destroyed (721 B.C.), the term "Jews" *(yehudim)* gradually became applied to all the descendants of Jacob, whatever their tribal origin.[2]

The rabbis, with etymological interest, built upon the above meaning of Judah's name. Indeed, they taught that to be a Jew is to be a person of praise, one who thanks God for everything. Jews were to do more than to sing songs of praise to the Almighty. Rather, as one Orthodox rabbi once described his calling to me, "I am to be and my life is to be a song of praise to the living God." Accordingly, one of the greatest sins is that of

---

1. In the Jewish mystical tradition the name *Yehudah* carries special significance. According to Benjamin Blech, "Of the twelve sons of Jacob, Judah would be the one destined to become the ancestor of the Davidic dynasty as well as the Messiah. The role of the Messiah is to bring about the universal recognition of God. Within the name YeHUDaH we find the four-letter name of God, YHVH, together with a dalet. Dalet [the Hebrew letter 'd' and fourth in the alphabet] is four because it would be the task of the seed of Judah to make the nations in the four corners of the world acknowledge the four-letter name of God." See Benjamin Blech, *The Secrets of Hebrew Words* (Northvale, NJ: Jason Aronson, 1991), p. 182.

2. See Yehoshua M. Grintz, "Jew," in *Encyclopedia Judaica* (Jerusalem: Keter, 1971-72), vol. 10, pp. 21-22.

ingratitude. Traditional Jews, in a given day, praise or bless the Almighty upwards of a hundred times. Praise starts upon awakening. The first prayer a Jew prays is the Modeh Ani, literally, the "I give thanks" prayer. The great nineteenth-century Talmudic scholar Yitzchak Meir pointed out that Jews came to be called Yehudim, after Jacob's son Judah, because one of the hallmarks of being Jewish is to be continually grateful to God in that God has given Jews more than their rightful share.[3] Prayer and praise go together. In the Jewish tradition, "The primary purpose [of prayer] is to praise, sing, to chant."[4]

Psalms is the largest book in the Bible. The Hebrew title for this collection of poetry is *Tehillim*, "praises." The Hebrew root *hll* means "to praise." The Book of Psalms is a work containing dozens of songs of praise. Throughout the history of the Jewish people, one of the keys to their survival has been the ability to sing in the dark experiences of life, particularly in those times of adversity when faith seeks understanding. The singers of Israel were able to proclaim the goodness of God irrespective of life's circumstances. One of the great praise psalms in Jewish liturgy is Psalm 136. Verses 1-3 read,

> Give thanks *(hodu)* to the LORD, for he is good.
> *His love endures for ever.*
> Give thanks *(hodu)* to the God of gods.
> *His love endures for ever.*
> Give thanks *(hodu)* to the Lord of lords:
> *His love endures for ever.*

Psalm 150 serves as the "Grand Finale" of the collection; it is the "praise psalm" par excellence. It concludes, *kol ha-neshamah tehallel yah hallelu-yah,* "Let everything that has breath praise the LORD. Praise the LORD" (v. 6). In the beginning, God breathed the "breath of life" *(nishmat ḥayyim)* into man and he became a living being (Gen. 2:7). From man's first breath till his last, his calling in life, according to the psalmist, is to give praise to his Creator (see Job 1:20).

---

3. See the Stone edition of the *Chumash* (New York: Mesorah Publications, 1994), p. 153.

4. Abraham Joshua Heschel, *Moral Grandeur and Spiritual Audacity,* ed. Susannah Heschel (New York: Farrar, Straus & Giroux, 1996), p. 397.

Paul's View of Who Is a Jew

In Romans 2:28-29, Paul defines who is a Jew. His answer is different from most contemporary definitions. As "apostle to the Gentiles" (see Acts 9:15; Gal. 1:16), Paul takes his argument beyond the "outward and physical" (Rom. 2:28) and focuses upon the inward and spiritual (v. 29). A real Jew, in Paul's view, is one vitalized by the renewing gift of the Spirit within the heart, one whose "praise is not from men, but from God" (v. 29). By employing this spiritual metaphor from the Hebrew Bible, Paul emphasizes the need for one to have a circumcised heart, for this is what God especially cites as exemplary. Such a person is the object of God's praise in that this "circumcising" work focuses on inward transformation through the Spirit of God. Inwardly, through a sincere faith, one spiritually consecrates oneself to God and thereby rolls away any impediment or obstacle that may block God's genuine and deep work in the human heart (see Deut. 30:6; Jer. 4:4; Ezek. 36:26-27; also Josh. 5:9). For Paul, the ritual cutting of flesh is not enough. All outward ceremonial acts are intended to point beyond themselves to a deeper spiritual meaning. As the Scriptures of Israel teach, "Man looks at the outward appearance, but the LORD looks at the heart" (1 Sam. 16:7; also Ps. 51:10, 17).

In the above verses from Romans that emphasize inward spiritual identity rather than the purely physical, Paul is apparently playing on the Hebrew word for "Jew," *Yehudi*. According to Joseph Fitzmyer, "In popular etymology [*Yehudah*] was often explained as the passive of *hodah*, '(someone) praised.' Thus the person with the circumcised heart is the one 'praised' in God's sight, the real Jew. Cf. Gen. 29:35; 49:8."[5] So, for Paul, praise cuts both ways as a kind of spiritual reciprocity: those who are recipients of God's praise are those who have come to know God inwardly through the Spirit (Rom. 2:29). Their response, in return, is a life of active praise. Energized by God's Spirit within, such believers are exhorted to "pray in the Spirit on all occasions" (Eph. 6:18). Paul also instructs, "Sing and make music in your heart to the Lord, always giving thanks to God the Father for everything" (Eph. 5:19-20).

Praise is a thematic pillar of Hebraic heritage; it is a key to spiritual self-definition. As the psalmist declares, "I will extol the LORD at all times; his praise will always be on my lips" (Ps. 34:1). Christians, like Jews, are to be people of praise. In Christian hymnology, a fitting reminder of this task is the song "The God of Abraham Praise," a hymn of the church whose tune, sung

---

5. Joseph A. Fitzmyer, *Romans,* The Anchor Bible, vol. 33 (New York: Doubleday, 1993), p. 323.

in a minor key, is derived from a synagogue melody. Furthermore, the words of the Book of Common Prayer leading into the Eucharist are instructive for all Christians. They call believers to enter Israel's vocation as people of praise: "It is indeed right; it is our duty and our joy at all times and in all places to give you thanks and praise."

Paul's emphasis above in defining who is a Jew not only as a matter of physical descent or ethnicity but of spiritual circumcision of the heart was an important teaching for the apostle to the Gentiles to communicate to Rome and other young churches of the Mediterranean world. However, the language must have been difficult — if not threatening or subversive — to the larger Jewish community around him; it meant some serious rethinking about the oldest rite in Judaism, God's everlasting covenant in the flesh (Gen. 17:13).

At the Council of Jerusalem — several years before Paul penned his Letter to the Romans — a watershed decision had previously taken place concerning Gentiles and circumcision. The question before church leaders pertained to whether Gentiles were required to be circumcised according to the Mosaic Law in order to be saved (Acts 15:1). The decision rendered for this newly constituted community of faith was that circumcision was not a requirement. The appeal was to the inward, not the outward, person; salvation comes by grace through faith (Acts 15:11).

Gentiles could now be part of the expanding Abrahamic family without having to become (physically circumcised) Jews and uphold all the ritual requirements of Judaism (Gal. 3:8, 9, 29). Abraham believed God and was declared "righteous" *before* he was circumcised; this occurred hundreds of years before the giving of the Mosaic Law (see Gen. 15:6 and Romans 4). Gordon Fee sums the matter up: "For Paul, therefore, Abraham became the key to all Gentile acceptance with God — on the basis of their trusting God, not on the basis of 'doing the law,' just as was the case with Abraham."[6]

Paul's appeal to the faith of Abraham, and the point in time when Abraham believed, are crucial points for understanding Paul's emphasis on inward spirituality over outward ritual. Paul was a Jew, so he appeals to father Abraham to open the door for Gentiles in a church whose origins were in the Nazarenes, a Jewish sect within Second Temple Judaism. Thus, following Paul's exegesis, Abraham, the first Jew, gets the last word on defining who is a Jew.

---

6. Gordon D. Fee, "Who Are Abraham's True Children? The Role of Abraham in Pauline Argumentation," in *Perspectives on Our Father Abraham,* ed. Steven A. Hunt (Grand Rapids: Eerdmans, 2010), p. 129.

Toward Redefining Worship

In worship, God and his people meet. Sometimes a specific place was set aside for such an encounter. However, the worship of the God of Israel was never confined to a building. The Temple of Solomon was a magnificent structure, a "house of worship" that had no peer in Israel. The Temple — as did the synagogue in Second Temple Judaism and beyond — had an important role to play in corporate or community worship. But God's presence was never synonymous with physical structures or so-called holy precincts. The Holy of Holies that contained the Ark of the Covenant, the atonement cover ("mercy seat"), and the cherubim pointed beyond themselves to a higher metaphysical reality. The earthly temple was more than aesthetic delight. It led the sincere worshiper upward to a heavenly temple and the throne room of the King of kings. The Jerusalem Temple was but the earthly counterpart of that eternal abode. God's presence filled the universe. Accordingly, Solomon's prayer at the dedication of the Temple states, "But will God really dwell on earth? The heavens, even the highest heaven, cannot contain you. How much less this temple I have built!" (1 Kgs. 8:27).

There is a rhythm to worship, especially experienced in the biblical liturgical calendar. Through much of biblical history, worshipers communally assembled for scheduled times of daily prayer and the celebration of various festivals and holy days that recalled God's gracious provisions for his people. However, as emphasized below and elsewhere in this book, God's presence could be experienced everywhere; worship was not simply confined to designated areas. "The whole earth is full of his glory" (Isa. 6:3). Whether individually or corporately at worship, people could spontaneously, or at set times, render to the King of the universe honor, devotion, and humble service in their daily lives.

To understand worship is more than knowing about sacrifices and sacred pilgrimages; rather, it is to have an attitude and lifestyle of responsiveness, awe, love, and active obedience rooted in the heart. Indeed, the New Testament emphasizes that we are to "worship God acceptably with reverence and awe" (Heb. 12:28). Likewise, worship is more than mechanically attending mandatory meetings to seek external validation of piety by the religious establishment. Israel served God. This was a twenty-four-hour responsibility, whether at the tabernacle, temple, or synagogue, or outside in the community. The people of Israel dedicated themselves to a life of worship. Yes, cultic acts of sacrifice and other rituals and ceremonies were expected. Indifference to the teaching of Torah was not an option. But faithful, loving obedience to God and ethical, just relations with one's neighbor, in every dimension of life, were foundational to everything else.

The community of faith was to identify inwardly with the attributes and ways of their Creator and Redeemer. Motivated by love and gratitude for his many gifts, as God's children, Israel was to imitate the divine qualities of their Father. Thus, acts of compassion, mercy, and justice were at the core of godly worship. Ritual without ethics is heartless, a meaningless charade (Isa. 1:10-17; Joel 2:13; Amos 5:21-24; Matt. 5:23-24). God's *hesed,* his covenantal love for Israel, begets Israel's *hesed,* their loyal, steadfast love for God. Worship cannot be coerced; it is prompted in response to God's gracious acts in behalf of the worshiper. In the concluding words of Samuel's farewell speech, "Be sure to fear the LORD and serve him faithfully with all your heart; consider what great things he has done for you" (1 Sam. 12:24).

Israel had many of the same challenges to a life of worship that we have in the modern world. It was tempting, for example, to put one's trust in government or politics or a particular leader such as the king to be the defender and savior of the people. Others might rely and hope in the power of armies or the strength of city walls to protect their lives. The Hebrew Scriptures, however, clearly teach that one's ultimate reliance and security are not in rulers, armies, or defensive barriers, as strong and necessary as these may be. Rather, God must be the object of our ultimate trust, hope, and worship.

In the Hebrew Bible, the term *bitaḥon* means "trust." This word, according to Abraham J. Heschel, is "perhaps the most characteristic quality of Jewish existence . . . our faith is trust in Him."[7] The psalmist speaks again and again of placing full confidence, hope, and trust in God (Ps. 37:3; 56:4). To emphasize this point, Jeremiah employs a chiasm (an A-B-B-A poetic structure) using the verb *bataḥ,* "to trust," that we accordingly may translate: "Blessed is the man who trusts in the LORD and the LORD is his trust" (Jer. 17:7). Thus, a lifestyle committed to worship requires trusting God every day. In sum, *bitaḥon* is "placing your life in God's hands with the understanding that God alone knows what is best for you."[8]

---

7. Abraham Joshua Heschel, *Israel: An Echo of Eternity* (New York: Farrar, Straus & Giroux, 1969), p. 94.

8. Arthur Green, *These Are the Words* (Woodstock, VT: Jewish Lights Publishing, 1999), p. 121.

Changing Patterns of Worship

The pattern of worship practiced by the early church was modeled after the synagogue. It should not be forgotten that for the first two decades of church life (c. A.D. 29-49), the church was totally a movement within Judaism. The Jewish followers of Jesus, the sect of the Nazarenes, were part of the diverse religious mosaic of Judaism (see Acts 24:5). In the first century, hundreds of synagogues dotted the many hillsides and villages surrounding the Temple in Jerusalem. According to early Jewish tradition, ten or more families were needed to comprise a synagogue. In these places of assembly, the sacred Scriptures were read, psalms were sung, liturgical selections recited, and sermons or homilies presented that interpreted and explained the biblical text. One of the most important and lasting contributions of the synagogue to Christian worship is this emphasis upon textual exposition in sermons.

Christianity began as a "house church" movement. By the fourth century, however, during the reign of Constantine, change began to take place. Constantine was the first Roman emperor to convert to Christianity, and the effects were widely felt across the empire. Instead of Christianity being a persecuted minority, Christianity was now *religio licita,* a "legal religion," that would soon dominate the empire. Thousands of new converts joined the church. Rapid growth required large church buildings or basilicas to accommodate the crowds. Under Constantine the Great, the church of the East expanded in different directions. For example, in the Land of Israel, two of the oldest and most famous church structures in the world, the Church of the Nativity in Bethlehem and the Church of the Holy Sepulcher in Jerusalem, were built to provide worship space for groups of Christian pilgrims.

From the time of the Byzantine period of the fourth century, the Eastern half of the Roman Empire through its emerging "Orthodox" expression of Christianity had retained certain emphases of the synagogue. These included a high respect for tradition, the conducting of worship in the vernacular of the (New Testament) Scriptures, and emphasis on a life of prayer, periodic fasting, and use of incense. In addition, Eastern Orthodoxy, like Traditional Judaism, placed strong emphasis on lay participation in the liturgy and also usually maintained a separation of sexes in worship.

Christians in the East also continued to embrace oral tradition, and on a theological level Eastern expressions of worship continued to incorporate elements of thought such as mystical theology, a deep sense of the potential goodness of human nature, and the restorative relationship between God and man as an evolving process rather than a position founded on a discrete moment or moment of "justification," a term notably borrowed from Roman legal contexts. In sum, the Eastern churches manifested a unique blend of traits as they represented an emerging belief system — Christianity — which was still rooted in its Semitic origins on a geographical, cultural, and linguistic level.[9]

The rapid growth of Christianity under Constantine, however, led to certain changes within the church in the centuries to follow. One of the most obvious changes was a general departure from the relatively small and intimate type of worship that the synagogue and house-church model typically provided. As the church moved further to the West, change also began to take place in church leadership. An increasing division of roles was developing between laity and formal clergy. The strong influence of the synagogue upon the early church had undergone significant change as church leadership fell into the hands of non-Jews. Correspondingly, this brought about a more "de-Judaized" expression of Christianity. The so-called "democracy of the synagogue," which strongly encouraged each layperson to be a virtuoso in Torah, became significantly altered. Instead, religious learning and teaching became more and more the work of church leaders whose influence came mainly from their office. In the ensuing centuries, a rather sharp distinction between clergy and laity was drawn. Unlike the synagogue model in which the rabbi — though learned as a scholar-teacher — was considered a layperson, a new and different hierarchical approach to leadership had emerged.

The Danger of *Quid Pro Quo* Worship

If today's church is to adopt a model of worship closer to its Hebraic roots, it must remain vigilant to protect itself from the ever-present danger of viewing worship as a mere *quid pro quo.* During Old Testament times, Canaanite worship was largely based on the concept of *quid pro quo,* an equal exchange of something for something. The Canaanites and other pagan religions believed the gods granted tangible benefits to worshipers. These included such desirables as fertility, longevity, good health, and an abundance of possessions. Gods, accordingly, needed to be bribed through gifts. Worshipers gave in order to get. Gods could be manipulated through favors conveyed in

---

9. For further reading on the Orthodox Church, see these two useful works by Kallistos Ware: for a standard historical and theological introduction, *The Orthodox Church* (London: Penguin, 1997); and on general doctrine, theology, and worship, *The Orthodox Way* (Crestwood, NY: St. Vladimir's Seminary Press, 1995).

ritual. The offerer gave a gift. If sufficiently generous, the god in return gave fertility within the family, an abundant harvest, or multiplication of livestock. In "*quid pro quo* religion," a thing (of value) is taken in return for something else (of value). In this scheme, among the Canaanites, the greatest gift was the offering of one's firstborn, the fruit of one's own body (see Mic. 6:7).

The prophets of Israel were opposed to *quid pro quo* religion. Among the people of Israel, ritual was to be an expression of love, not an opportunity to bribe. Israel's religion was not based on something for something. Israel could not earn or buy God's blessing. Israel already was secure in a covenantal relationship with the living God who asked for loving obedience to his will and complete trust in him. Israel's one response was to serve God out of loving devotion, not out of a sense of demand or dread concerning an angry deity. God was to be loved for who he was in himself, not for any anticipated benefits one believed God should convey in exchange for various human tokens of worship. In biblical religion, there was no need to equalize. Since when have God and any individual been equals? Israel receives freely from God's hand, by grace alone. God owes nothing back to his worshipers. People worship because God is worthy, not people.

When God gives, he gives simply because he is gracious, merciful, and loving — not because worshipers are able to get his attention through gifts. As part of a fertility or nature religion, the Canaanite farmers believed their success in the fields was tied to giving gifts to please deities, to get on their good side. The religion of Israel, however, was radically different, for Israel's God could not be bribed or manipulated by presents. The invitation to God's table is always open; no spiritual admission fee is required. No one has to give in order to get. To be admitted to God's table, and to dine, costs nothing: "Come, all you who are thirsty, come to the waters; and you who have no money, come, buy and eat! Come, buy wine and milk without money and without cost" (Isa. 55:1).

The great twentieth-century rabbi Joseph B. Soloveitchik points out the danger of this wrongheaded *quid pro quo* philosophy and how it affects the modern world of religious thought:

> Western man diabolically insists on being successful. Alas, he wants to be successful even in his adventure with God. If he gives of himself to God, he expects reciprocity. He also reaches a covenant with God, but this covenant is a mercantile one. In a primitive manner, he wants to trade "favors" and exchange goods. The gesture of faith for him is a give-and-take affair and reflects the philosophy of Job which led to ca-

tastrophe — a philosophy which sees faith as a *quid pro quo* arrangement and expects compensation for each sacrifice one offers.[10]

What is one's motivation for serving God? In the book of Job, Satan suggests loyal love and commitment to God himself can be bought: "Does Job fear God for nothing?" (Job 1:9). Material and physical prosperity is not a simplistic reward for human piety, nor is its loss conclusive evidence of one's moral failure. As a very wealthy person who was also a God-fearer of upright moral character, throughout the narrative — even in the face of severe suffering — Job maintains his innocence. Characteristic of this man's spiritual integrity, even after experiencing great personal loss Job affirms, "The LORD gave and the LORD has taken away; may the name of the LORD be praised" (Job 1:21).

In the Western world many Christians have bought into the formula that a successful church is a megachurch — large attendance, large budget, and large facilities equal success. A "successful" pastor is one who is rewarded by personal prosperity for his "godly" efforts. The teaching simplistically holds that whatever you plant is what you reap. However, in terms of success in ministry, bigger is not always better; also the blessing of spiritual successfulness is not always measured one-for-one in financial prosperity. There are many pastors who have served small, struggling churches in difficult neighborhoods or in non-Christian cultures. They do not worship in large churches or have large budgets. In fact, some continue to struggle after decades of work with very little growth to show; if judged by earthly business standards of success, many would be judged a "failure," not a "success."

Quid pro quo philosophy assumes what you put in is what you are entitled to get out. In Job's world, the philosophy of Job's comforter "friends" was rigidly to uphold a widely held ancient formula: "piety equals prosperity." In short, the message of Job's friends was, "Look, Job, you became a wealthy and successful man because you were a pious, God-fearing person; you have lost everything, however, because you have sinned and have lost your moral integrity and righteous, godly character." In other words, in life, you always get what you deserve. To the contrary! One must read the whole Bible. Some sufferers in Scripture are saints. Wealth, physical blessing, and prosperity are not always tied to degrees of spiritual piety and personal righteousness. The simplistic success formula of *quid pro quo* has so many exceptions that it is seldom — if ever — an accurate gauge for judging others or oneself.

Success, in God's eyes, is measured more accurately by faithfulness

10. Joseph B. Soloveitchik, *The Lonely Man of Faith* (New York: Doubleday, 1965), p. 104.

than through quantification of performance. Sincere servants of the Lord are not always compensated for each sacrifice made, each deed performed, each soul rescued. Indeed, in biblical service, God calls us to faithfulness and selfless love, not success by statistical self-satisfaction. God's definition of success is different from that imposed by the secular world around us. God is usually more interested in quality than impressive numbers. After all, if you have numbers to show, who do you think gave you those numbers? In some Christian circles, Jesus himself might have been judged somewhat of a failure for attracting only 120 followers by the time he left this earth (Acts 1:15).

The primary reward for service is the joy of being called by the King of the universe into his work; it is primarily spiritual satisfaction, reward, and contentment; it is humbling delight that comes through the consciousness that one is unworthy, yet the Master has named you one of his servants. Servanthood and Judaism go together. Israel was the 'ebed YHWH, "servant of the LORD" (Isaiah 42; 49). This role of servanthood is at the foundation of the church's calling, too. Authentic worship and service to the living God allow no bragging rights. He "made himself nothing, taking the very nature of a servant" (Phil. 2:7).

Where Is God Found?

People investigating faith sometimes ask the question, "Where is God found?" Answers may vary, but certain Christians will aver that God is mainly found in the Bible, in history, in human experience, and most significantly in the incarnation. While some or all of these answers may prove helpful, there are other ways of asking about the presence of God. For example, does God exist in heaven or on earth? The answer can be polarizing. Is God a transcendent being or an immanent being? Or does the teaching of Scripture affirm that all of the above are correct? The latter answer seems to be the right one, and more.

Christians and Jews have much to learn from each other in this important area of theological reflection. Theologically conservative Christians can especially profit from Jewish reflection on divine immanence, spirituality, and spiritual awareness. In the church, much of Reformed theology has tended to emphasize God's transcendence, sovereignty, and control over the entire universe. As the supreme and all-powerful Ruler of individuals and nations, he is above everything. God is self-existent and totally independent of his creation and the material order (see Acts 17:23-25). But there is a paradox here, for God is also immanent. According to Paul, God is "over all and through all and in all" (Eph. 4:6). God is present within his creation. Such is the reality and mystery of God.

Some Christians are fearful of emphasizing the immanence of God because Scripture draws a very clear distinction between Creator and creature (Rom. 1:25). In addition, nature worship is idolatrous; God and nature are never synonymous. Thus, it is sometimes held, for Christians to celebrate God's presence in the natural order may lead to a pantheistic understanding of God. Yet, the "silent" heavens do lavishly testify of God; all nature sings his praise (Ps. 19:1). There is a difference between God speaking through nature, and nature speaking as God. In the words of musical artist Frankie Laine, "Every time I hear a newborn baby cry, or touch a leaf, or see the sky, then I know why I believe." If God is alive, his presence may be intuited in the natural order. As an omnipresent spiritual being, God is in us, among us, and around us, and he works through us. Nature reveals his glory. Accordingly, Psalm 104 is a hymn that celebrates the Creator and his creation: "How many are your works, O LORD! In wisdom you made them all" (v. 24).

Like each of us, the rabbis were concerned about God's presence in this world and where he may be found. Rabbi Joshua ben Karhah was once asked by a non-Jew, "Why did the Holy One, blessed be he, speak to Moses out of a thornbush?" The rabbi replied, "To teach you that there is no space free of the Divine Presence, not even a thornbush" (Exodus Rabbah 2:9). As an invisible spirit, God is not limited to any set locale; he hears the cries of his people wherever they may be. In Samaria, across a religious divide, Jesus said, "God is spirit, and his worshipers must worship in spirit and in truth" (John 4:24).

At Bethel, Jacob had a dream with angels going up and down a stairway that led to heaven. The dream marked Jacob as God's chosen one through whom the Abrahamic promises concerning land, numerous descendants, and worldwide blessing would be fulfilled. Jacob awoke from his dream and he thought, "Surely the LORD is in this place, and I was not aware of it" (Gen. 28:16). The great Jewish commentator Rashi explains, "If Jacob had known this he would not have dared go to sleep."[11] Here is a type of "preaching from an unexpected pulpit." Sometimes even the greats of Scripture are not awake and aware of God's presence. Jacob had to learn the lesson that God can reveal himself anywhere, day or night. Such an experience may prove "awesome," indeed, even "the gate of heaven" (Gen. 28:17).

---

11. The *Chumash*, Stone Edition, p. 146.

What is one of the lessons of the experience of Jacob that is useful for believers today? It is this: God is continually speaking, but people are not always listening. Our ears may be deaf and our eyes may be blind to God's presence all around us. To be "attention deficit" is to thwart spirituality. Abraham Heschel says spiritual alertness and faith are cultivated by a sense of awe, radical amazement, mystery, and surprise. Miraculous and beautiful things are constantly happening around us, each worthy of a brief blessing or prayer of thanksgiving to the Giver. However, without an appreciation of "sacred humanism," celebration of holiness in the commonplace things of life, we may be oblivious to his presence. Thus, as spiritual beings, we must be daily mindful of this truism: "Spirituality is life lived in the continuous presence of the divine."[12]

A distinctive emphasis of Hasidic Judaism is to bring spirituality right down to earth. The Hasidim teach that God's life is able to shine forth in every area of human activity and bodily function. Proverbs 3:6 states, "In all your ways acknowledge [or "know" *(da'ehu)*] him." The verb "acknowledge" is an imperative, a command. Hasidic Jewry emphasizes that this verse means one must daily serve God through corporeality or the physical dimension. All dimensions of life are thus consecrated to the Almighty. This includes such bodily functions and activities as eating, studying, sex, walking, and dancing. So, by emphasizing the immanence of God in human behavior, Hasidism looks at each human and says, "God dwells wherever man lets Him in."[13]

In the Hebrew Bible, the verb *qarab* means "to come near" or "to draw near." In Modern Hebrew, *qerobim* are "relatives," those near to you. In the Bible, in certain contexts, the word *qarab* is translated "to approach" and may be used as a euphemism for sexual intercourse, thus implying a very close relationship (Gen. 20:4). The verb is also used in the Old Testament in the context of worship and means "to bring (an animal) near" or "to offer" a sacrifice. The noun *qorban* means "offering" (Lev. 1:2; Mark 7:11). In Hasidic teaching about spirituality, when two human beings draw near to each other God is present, just as in Temple times an offerer would draw near *(qarab)* the altar in worship of the living God. Further, when an individual is *qereb,* literally, "in the midst of" or "the middle of" another, such closeness has the potential to be a profound spiritual experience, a face-to-face relationship of

---

12. See Abraham Joshua Heschel, *God in Search of Man* (New York: Harper & Row, 1955), pp. 73-79; also Lawrence Kushner, *Jewish Spirituality* (Woodstock, VT: Jewish Lights, 2001), p. 9.

13. See Aryeh Rubinstein, ed., *Hasidism* (New York: Leon Amiel, 1975), p. 34.

intimacy and personal involvement that reflects the love of God. In the Bible, worship is relationally focused; one comes into the presence of the Other.

Martin Buber, a great twentieth-century Jewish philosopher, wrote about the Hasidim and the Hasidic quest for closeness to God. Buber held that nothing is of greater importance to God than a relationship between two people. Lawrence Kushner sums up the spirituality of relationship found in Buber's thought: "When two individuals realize, for even just a moment, that they depend on each other, that they are fully present for one another then they have come closer to God. Buber called this an I-Thou experience and imagined that the invisible lines of relation joining them to one another also join them to God."[14] Distance, separation, and miscommunication between people often foster aloofness, alienation, and pain. God is present whenever the human family draws nearer to each other in bonds of friendship, respect, and love. In every personal encounter, to the one who draws near, the image of God is at stake (Gen. 1:26-27). The Gospels emphasize a similar theme found in the teachings of Jesus: "For where two or three come together in my name, there am I with them" (Matt. 18:20).

Clinging to God

Many traditional Jews consider "clinging" or "holding fast" to God to be one of the most important commands of Scripture (Deut. 10:20; 11:22; 30:20; Josh. 22:5; 23:8). The Hebrew verb *dabaq*, "to cling" or "to cleave," is used of physical objects such as the tongue sticking to the roof of the mouth (Ps. 137:6), bones cleaving to the skin (Ps. 102:5), and a waistcloth clinging to the loins of a man (Jer. 13:11). The verb *dabaq* is used figuratively of two people "clinging" or "sticking" to each other in a close relationship such as a man cleaving to his wife (Gen. 2:24), Ruth leaving Moab and sticking with her mother-in-law Naomi (Ruth 1:14), and Ruth sticking close by the workers in the field (2:21).[15] The above idea of attaching, adhering, or sticking together is carried forward into modern Hebrew by the noun *debeq*, "glue."

The theological use of *dabaq* carries the idea of an individual clinging to or binding oneself to God in love and loyalty. To worship God is to have close fellowship or communion with God. Joshua's farewell words to Israel

---

14. Kushner, *Jewish Spirituality*, p. 33.

15. See G. Wallis, "dabhaq, debheq, dabheq," *Theological Dictionary of the Old Testament*, vol. 3 (Grand Rapids: Eerdmans, 1978), pp. 79-84.

to "hold fast" to God were a call for Israel not to be separated from him by pursuit of false gods but to pursue him and to serve him exclusively with their entire being (see Joshua, chapters 22 and 23). Joined in a covenantal bond with God, Israel was given a sense of security and blessing from the command to stick close to God. By not wandering away or getting separated, but by placing complete trust in the Lord, fearing him, walking in his ways, and keeping his commands, Israel would remain firmly attached in an indissoluble relationship. But the call to "cling" and to "worship" is a matter of the will, a decision that requires renewing each day. Accordingly, Joshua reminds his generation and ours, "Choose for yourselves this day whom you will serve" (Josh. 24:15).

A definitive "life's verse" for many observant Jews is Psalm 16:8 (see Acts 2:25): "I have set the LORD always before me" ("I am ever mindful of the LORD's presence"; JPS TANAKH translation). In accord with the command of Torah, all Jews are encouraged to strive for and aspire to attain *debequt*, "cleaving" or "clinging," at all times. To be sure, in the Talmud, the rabbis cite Deuteronomy and how Israel's "cleaving" to God had kept Israel alive: "All of you who held fast *(ha-debeqim)* to the LORD your God are still alive today" (4:4). But the rabbis ask, "Is it possible to 'cleave' to the divine presence concerning which it is written in Scripture: 'For the LORD thy God is a devouring fire'?" (Deut. 4:24; Babylonian Talmud, Kethuboth 111b). These passages underscore the paradox of "cleaving." How close can an individual come in seeking to become intimate with, be absorbed into, or joined with the divine presence? What does God mean, "No one may see me and live" (Exod. 33:20), and "No one has ever seen God" (John 1:18)? How do physical individuals cling to the invisible God?

Judaism has understood the word *debequt* or *devekut* ("cleaving" or "clinging") in a number of ways. The rabbis debated what constituted *debequt* and how it was to be achieved. In general, the term has carried the simple meaning of attachment or devotedness to God.[16] Accordingly, traditional Jews mainly have understood this to mean that they are to pursue consistent study of Torah, intensive prayer, and meditation. These are the main avenues of expressing the sincerity and depth of one's love for God and pursuit of him. Others have emphasized that *debequt* includes seeking to imitate God by embodying his attributes.[17]

---

16. See Gershom G. Scholem, "Devekuth, or Communion with God," *Review of Religion* 15 (1950): 115.

17. Josef Dan, "Devekut," in *Encyclopedia Judaica*, vol. 5, p. 1598.

In the thirteenth century, Jewish mystics began to understand *debequt* as close communion with God. Some Jewish teachers argued that there were different levels of *debequt*. In the mystic tradition, for example, many Kabbalists argued that *debequt* is the highest rung on the ladder of spirituality and only very few are able to climb to that level of spiritual ascent.[18] This state of *debequt,* taught the Kabbalists, was mainly achieved through attentive direction of the soul through prayer and meditation. The goal of this "clinging" was a willingness to lose oneself in the divine presence. This state of mind was usually brought about through intense concentration, resulting in the adhesion of the soul to God. For example, Nahmanides (Ramban), a thirteenth-century Spanish Jew, Bible scholar, and Kabbalist, taught that through *debequt* one could achieve a rank among the immortals, for the person himself was an abiding place of the *Shekhinah*. Nahmanides goes on to define *debequt* in his commentary on Deuteronomy 11:22 as a state of mind in which "You constantly remember God and His love, nor do you remove your thought from Him . . . to the point that when [such a person] speaks with someone else, his heart is not with them at all but is still before God."[19]

In the eighteenth century, the rise of the Hasidic movement brought about a change in the Kabbalistic understanding of *debequt*. The Baal Shem Tov or "Besht," founder of the movement, joined by his followers, brought spirituality right down to earth, accessible to commoners and scholars alike. Gershom Scholem explains how Hasidism brought change to the meaning of *debequt*:

> Hasidic *Devekuth* is no longer an extreme ideal, to be realized by some rare and sublime spirits at the end of the path. It is no longer the *last* rung in the ladder of ascent, as in Kabbalism, but the *first*. Everything *begins* with man's decision to cleave to God. *Devekuth* is the starting point and not the end.[20]

Now, with Hasidic Jewry, *debequt* becomes "democratized"; all Jews are potentially active participants.

A fundamental teaching of Hasidism is that God pervades everything. He is immanent in all creation. Hasidism emphasizes that God is an intimate

18. See Ada Rapoport-Albert, "God and the Zaddik as the Two Focal Points of Hasidic Worship," *History of Religions* 18, no. 4 (1979): 297, 305.

19. Quoted in Gershom G. Scholem, *Kabbalah* (Jerusalem: Keter, 1974), p. 175.

20. Scholem, "Devekuth, or Communion with God," p. 120.

friend whose presence fills the universe. To the Hasid, all of life has to be hallowed, dedicated to God. The outer world is not a barrier to the worship of God; it becomes a means for joyful service of the Almighty. In the view of the Baal Shem Tov, physical acts (e.g., eating, drinking, sexual relations) are considered religious acts if a person intends to worship God and is performing them in a state of *debequt*.[21] This daily mindset of worship in the actions of everyday life helped to overcome the fundamental separation of the spiritual and the profane or secular. It also prevented retreat from the real world and helped address the ever-present challenge of "spiritual schizophrenia." Martin Buber described this Hasidic life of worship through the corporeal and worldly dimensions as "pan-sacramentalism."[22]

In a parallel vein, today's church must insist that all of life is a "sacrament." Indeed, the act of being alive is a call to be holy before the Holy One of Israel (Lev. 19:2; see Isa. 6:3; Rev. 4:8). "You are a chosen people, a royal priesthood, a holy nation, a people belonging to God, that you may declare the praises of him who called you out of darkness into his wonderful light" (1 Pet. 2:9).

Faith on Fire

In addition to "pan-sacramentalism," the Hasidic quest for close communion with God sometimes assumed a joyful and ecstatic character, especially in prayer. The Baal Shem Tov taught that Israel's God is not a somber being. One should not worship in a depressed state of mind. So a person must serve God with emotion and joy out of love for the world (Ps. 100:2). Hasidism emphasized that a consciousness of the nearness of God will of necessity make one happy and give one a joyful spirit. Unlike various other religions and philosophies, Judaism has affirmed human emotion. Stoicism valued emotional detachment; it taught indifference to pleasure or to pain. Rooted in Torah, Judaism saw human emotion as a lubricant of the soul as one sought to navigate the various mood swings of life. Gordon Wenham explains how feelings are part and parcel of the narrative of Genesis:

> From Adam's shout of joy as he is introduced to Eve, "This at last is bone of my bones . . ." to Joseph's tears at his brothers' fears, the leading

21. Rubinstein, ed., *Hasidism*, pp. 19, 32.
22. Rubinstein, ed., *Hasidism*, p. 108.

characters all seem very ready to express their feelings (2:23; 50:17). The birth of children is the occasion of joy and laughter, most often encapsulated in the name given at birth. . . . At the end of life mourning is equally vigorous.[23]

In accord with this emphasis in Torah, the Hasidic community has especially emphasized Jewish religion as a gospel of joy as God is served from the heart. The Torah teaches one to serve the Lord joyfully and gladly (Deut. 28:47). Worship of God is to be an exciting adventure, not a monotonous routine of repetitious acts.

Accordingly, Hasidic prayer often includes an ecstatic reaching that brought a kind of thrilling intensity to prayer as worshipers sought to ascend to the presence of God. For the Hasid, prayer involved awareness and aspiration, a directing of the inner self to God. Hasidism often describes such enthusiastic worship as *hitlahabut,* "burning enthusiasm," an inflaming feeling of rapture of the soul as the individual seeks envelopment or *debequt* in God.

Abraham Heschel grew up in the Hasidic community of Poland before the war years. In his final work, *A Passion for Truth,* Heschel explains the Baal Shem's teaching of *hitlahabut,* "being aflame," and how this affected Hasidic thought and practice:

> Faith was fire, not sediment. . . . The Baal Shem stirred the fervor that slumbered in the ashes. . . . [he] drew people along in a stream of enthusiasm. . . . [he] awakened the zest for spiritual living, expressed in *hitlahabut* . . . the experience of moments during which the soul is ablaze with an insatiate craving for God. . . . Exaltation may last for an hour, but its flower, joy, the jewel that wins the hearts of all men, lasts forever. . . . A Jew should serve God with ardor. It was necessary, vital, to have fire in the soul.[24]

Heschel goes on to point out, however, that the flaming intensity within, the "holy fire" of *hitlahabut,* should not be a phenomenon of Hasidic worship whereby a person is swept away and loses total control. Rather, each individual needs to be sensitive to others around him. Heschel also observes how the Hasidic movement, over the years, has undergone change:

---

23. Gordon J. Wenham, *Story as Torah* (Grand Rapids: Baker Academic, 2000), p. 97.

24. Abraham Joshua Heschel, *A Passion for Truth* (New York: Farrar, Straus & Giroux, 1973), pp. 47-48.

Fire is by nature indiscreet; it tends to show off. But nothing is as obnoxious as demonstrative piety. This is why the Hasidic norm underwent modification. No worship without concealment. A flame there must be, but it should burn chastely and privately, deeply hidden within the individual. Let there be no outward show of ardor. When you are carried away by enthusiasm, veil it.[25]

Heschel's description of the flaming intensity, fervor, and enthusiasm of Hasidic Judaism illustrates for us that *debequt* may indeed involve one's emotions. At the same time, Heschel's emphasis on the need in worship to "conceal" emotions is worth noting.

In the passionate pursuit of *debequt* among the Hasidim, moments of extreme ecstasy were cherished. However, these "flashing fires" of God's presence, momentarily experienced on top of one's personal "Sinai," still left the worshiper with the daily need to attend to the mundane and practical affairs of life "down in the valley." No one lives forever on the mountain. *Debequt* also demanded a constancy of daily living characterized by deep commitment to God and his ways. Arthur Green points out that any intense moments of rapturous reaching for God were, for the Hasidim, only "steps on the road toward the much cooler but longer lasting goal of *debequt,* an attachment to God in which one may live and act."[26]

Debequt and the Church

In the modern world, the worship of Hasidic Jews, especially their practice of *debequt,* has contributed to a larger conversation on spirituality. Therefore, we conclude this chapter by briefly commenting on some of the valuable lessons and also cautions that Christians might take from an understanding of Hasidism and *debequt.*

First, clinging/holding fast to God is not an optional matter. "You are to hold fast *(tidbaqu)* to the LORD your God" (Josh. 23:8). Here is a scriptural imperative that every biblical theist must take seriously. The question is not about whether one should cling to God but how this should be understood and best carried out. This is a starting point for all serious believers, not a luxury of a lifetime for a few spiritual "elites." Certainly this is in keeping

25. Heschel, *A Passion for Truth,* p. 49.
26. Green, *These Are the Words,* p. 128.

with the New Testament command for all believers to be continually filled with the Spirit (Eph. 5:18).

Second, the emphasis on the immanence of God in Hasidic worship is also commendable. Christians sometimes miss the fact that God is constantly all around them. Whatever one's view of divine transcendence, Christians must be careful their view of God is not one-sided, a God who is only far above them, beyond and "out there." God is also here. While nature worship is idolatrous and sinful, nature does bear witness to the Creator in unusual ways. The Hasidic movement began with the discovery of God in the out-of-doors, in the country among common folk, not simply in the study centers of the scholarly and erudite engaged in rarified debate over sacred texts. The Hasidim taught that nature — in country villages, close to the natural world of ponds, frogs, birds, and animals — was a spiritual realm for "listening to the world as the song of God."[27] Thus, nature was an avenue for communion with God.

Third, theologically speaking, *debequt* is a form of reciprocal love. God's love for us elicits a response of love. In love, God is searching for us. We, in return, seek to express our love by communing with God. We best understand *debequt* by analogical theology. What we know to be true in the physical realm God uses to instruct us in the spiritual realm. As the Book of Proverbs points out, "There is a friend who sticks closer *(dabeq)* than a brother" (18:24). We come to know the invisible through the visible. In the physical realm, the opposite of "clinging" and "holding fast" is to exercise one's own freedom of the will to let go and to choose an alternate object of affection and commitment. As in any lasting relationship of love or close friendship, every day one chooses anew to cling, to stay close, and not to stray. To "cling" to God is a metaphor for a close spiritual relationship. But there is reciprocity in the paradox of faith. If it is true that God in election love holds firmly on to Israel, then it is likewise true that Israel responds with reciprocal love by holding on to God. Thus, in the paradox, there are two sides to the "coin of faith." We are called to "cling"; our lives depend on it. But God at the same time is "holding us fast."

Fourth, Christians must beware of any prescribed "magic formulas" or concentration techniques that are guaranteed to lead to an ecstatic encounter with the living God. A genuine life of faith requires constant concentration on God, not validation of one's own spirituality by seeking spiritual highs,

---

27. David S. Ariel, *What Do Jews Believe? The Spiritual Foundations of Judaism* (New York: Schocken, 1995), p. 82.

pursuing trances of dizzy rapture, or positioning oneself to be "slain in the Spirit." God can speak and work in any way he deems appropriate. God's people may place no limits on God. We should be open to a variety of biblical approaches that lead to God's holy presence. Our prayers must be with feeling and from the heart. In the midst of their quest for authentic worship, today's Christians must not forget, as James Dunn points out, that the earliest form of Christianity and one of its main strands is that of "enthusiastic Christianity," a stream characterized by vision and ecstasy, miracles, and inspired speech.[28] One may draw certain parallels between Hasidic Judaism and various expressions of Charismatic and Pentecostal Christianity. In this vein, consider the Hebrew New Testament rendering of the command of Romans 12:11: "Be fervent/aflame in spirit" *(hitlahabu ba-ruah).*

Finally, the Jewish concept of *debequt* is a constant reminder to Christians that God is more than an abstract concept; he is a powerful, living presence to whom God's people must cling for hope in this life and the next. The New Testament teaches that all Christians already possess the Spirit of God within them (Rom. 8:9). But perhaps the question is not so much a believer's possession of him as it is his full possession of the believer. In any sincere, lifelong pursuit of God there will be unusual moments of personal experience when the presence of God is overwhelmingly real. Yet, as in God's work of salvation and distribution of his ministry gifts, all is under his sovereign and supernatural control. *Debequt* teaches each believer to act on the hunger within to know God and his revelation. One's goal for today and tomorrow must remain that of being aflame with God's love in passionate service to him.

Simply put, "when all the theological dust settles," *debequt* is a "stick-to-it" reminder: each believer must hang in there, ever reaching toward God and clinging to him in trust, not letting him go. There is no attraction in this world of more value than that of laying hold of God and having a firm grasp of his Word. Put in New Testament imperatives, "Remain true to the Lord with all the heart" (Acts 11:23). "Cling to what is good" (Rom. 12:9). "Let us hold firmly to the faith we profess" (Heb. 4:14). In short, hold on, do not let go, for of such indissoluble commitment is a life of worship and discipleship forged.

---

28. James D. G. Dunn, *Unity and Diversity in the New Testament,* 2nd ed. (London: SCM Press, 1990), pp. 174-84.

UNDERSTANDING CHAPTER TEN

1. What tendencies of misguided worship mentalities exist in certain churches today? What is the true focus of biblical worship?

2. In what way linguistically is praise at the heart of worship? From where does the term "Jew" derive? List related Hebrew terms that shed light on this truth. What memorable play on words occurs in Jacob's blessing of Judah in Genesis 49:8?

3. What indicates that the tribal area of Judah must have had a particular appreciation for praise and worship through music? In what context did David compose songs of praise? In what context did Levitical choirs sing praise?

4. When the monarchy after Solomon split North and South, what two tribes comprised the Southern Kingdom? After what point did the word "Jews" come to be applied to all descendants of Jacob, regardless of tribal origin?

5. What did the rabbis teach by building upon the meaning of Judah's name? Accordingly, what is one of the greatest sins? What is the Modeh Ani, and how does its placement upon waking at the beginning of each day speak to you of its significance?

6. What is the Hebrew title for the Book of Psalms? What does the Hebrew root *hll* mean?

7. How are Psalm 136:1-3 and Psalm 150 demonstrative of the foundational commitment to faith that has often enabled Jews to uphold the goodness of God in both joyful and dark experiences of life?

8. How does Paul define a Jew (see Rom. 2:28-29)? Which powerful spiritual metaphor does he employ from the Hebrew Bible and how?

9. How do Joseph Fitzmyer's linguistic observations shed light on Paul's emphasis in defining a Jew? What kind of spiritual reciprocity is recognized in this train of thought?

10. Which specific examples of Christian worship does the author provide that reflect a focus of praise? From a Christian perspective, do you think church bodies that have adopted more contemporary forms of worship and praise have generally gained, lost, or merely shifted modes in this area of focus?

11. Why was Paul's message about circumcision of the heart an important teaching for the "apostle to the Gentiles" and his audiences? In what way, however, was it a challenge to the broader Jewish community of the time?

12. Be familiar with the decision of the Jerusalem Council regarding circumcision (see also earlier chapter 6, "Thinking Theologically about Abraham," for prior discussion). Review Gordon Fee's comment about Gentiles' acceptance with God; how was Abraham key in Paul's reasoning?

13. In Israel, which physical space was set aside for worshiping God? How was this space significant, yet at the same time merely a "counterpart" of something grander? Why was God not limited to such a space, and how do King Solomon's words in 1 Kings 8:27 attest to this?

14. Throughout biblical history, which various events contributed to the "rhythm of worship" of God's people? What are your thoughts on the value of repetition as a practice in worship?

15. What was at the core of godly worship for Israel? What did the concept of imitation have to do with it? How do Samuel's words in 1 Samuel 12:24 reinforce the idea of worship as a fitting response to God?

16. In what way did Israel face the same challenges in worship that we face today? Does this heighten your sense of historical connectedness to your ancestors in the faith? What term does Abraham Heschel suggest may be "the most characteristic quality of Jewish existence"? How does the chiasm that Jeremiah employs in Jeremiah 17:7 complement the notion?

17. The first two decades of the early church were totally a movement within what? Accordingly, the early church's practices of worship were modeled after what? Briefly describe the composition and activities of a typical first-century synagogue.

18. What events in the fourth century sparked changes in the church's original structure as a "house church" movement? Which two examples in modern-day Israel does the author cite as illustrations of this? What other significant changes occurred in the church during the time that Constantine reigned?

19. How did Eastern Orthodoxy retain certain emphases found in Judaism and synagogue life?

20. What is a "*quid pro quo* religion"? What Old Testament religion does the author cite as an example? In such belief systems, which tangible benefits were often sought after by offering gifts to the gods? How were the prophets of Israel opposed to such a mentality?

21. Which passage of prophetic Scripture is cited in conjunction with the idea that no spiritual "admission fee" is required to be admitted to God's table? How do you understand the invitation issued in Isaiah?

22. Review Joseph B. Soloveitchik's quote on pages 188-89. What does he

mean by the powerful statement that "Western man diabolically insists on being successful"? Do you think the motives of some Jews or Christians today are amiss in a similar manner? How are Job's words in Job 1:21 a valuable example of spiritual integrity after deep loss of prosperity?

23. Do you think that some Christians in the Western world have gone too far in buying into a *quid pro quo* philosophy? (Note the author's succinct description of the position — "what you put in is what you are entitled to get out" — with particular thought given to *entitlement*.) What do you think prompts the development of this mindset, and how do you think it can best be combated?

24. What was largely the position of Job's friends? In response to this formulaic mindset, what does the author seek to communicate by stating, "To the contrary! One must read the whole Bible"?

25. Regarding the modern world's interest in "quantity" (sometimes over quality), in what way might Jesus himself have been judged a failure in some Christian circles? What does this "humble" number remind us of concerning the mysterious ways in which God works?

26. What is the primary reward for service to God? What does *'ebed YHWH* mean, and what was the phrase's significance for Israel? In your own cultural context, is it ever considered an honor to be a servant? How might the concept of servanthood in today's Western world serve as an example of one area in which Christians would benefit from exploring the mindset of their Semitic roots?

27. What response does the author offer to the question, "Where is God found?" How do *you* respond?

28. In what area of thought about spiritual awareness does the author suggest that Christians can especially profit from Jewish thought? In the church, what has Reformed theology tended to emphasize? How do Paul's words to the Ephesians balance these notions by illustrating the "other side" of the paradox about God's presence?

29. Why are some Christians fearful of emphasizing the immanence of God? Why do they not need to be afraid? Are you personally more eager or more hesitant to embrace God's presence as manifested by nature? Why? For further discussion: How did some of the emphases of the American Transcendentalist movement championed by Ralph Waldo Emerson, Henry David Thoreau, and others differ from traditional Christian theological expression?

30. What truth about God's presence does Exodus Rabbah 2:9 illustrate? How did Jesus emphasize a similar point (see John 4:24)?

31. How did Jacob experience "preaching from an unexpected pulpit" at Bethel? What lessons did Jacob — and do we also — learn from this episode? What does Abraham Heschel say spiritual alertness and faith are cultivated by? Reflect on Heschel's statement, "Spirituality is life lived in the continuous presence of the divine." How would you describe what it means to *live in the presence of the divine?*

32. What is a distinctive emphasis of Hasidic Judaism? How does Hasidic Jewry interpret Proverbs 3:6?

33. What does the verb *qarab* mean in the Hebrew Bible, and in what contexts is it used? What do the Hasidim teach about drawing near? Explore what is meant by the statement that "[i]n the Bible, worship is relationally focused; one comes into the presence of the Other."

34. How does Lawrence Kushner sum up Martin Buber's thoughts about the spirituality of relationship? How do you understand Buber's term "I-Thou experience"? How do distance and closeness serve as measures of spirituality in relationships? Do you find this framework of thought helpful in seeking to better relate to God and others?

35. Many traditional Jews consider what command to be one of the most important in Scripture? What does the verb *dabaq* mean? In what literal and figurative senses is it used in the Old Testament? What idea does it carry on a theological level?

36. The call to "cling" and to worship requires what? How do Joshua's words in Joshua 24:15 reinforce this?

37. Why is Psalm 16:8 so definitive for many observant Jews? Jews are encouraged to attain *debequt,* but what did the rabbis ask regarding the possibility of realizing this aspiration? With the paradox in mind, how would you respond to their question?

38. Briefly describe the ways in which Judaism has understood the word *debequt* (1) in a general sense, (2) in the thirteenth century from the Kabbalist perspective, and (3) in the eighteenth century from the Hasidic perspective. Who was Nahmanides, and what did he teach about *debequt?* Who was the Baal Shem Tov, and how did he "reverse" Nahmanides' line of thought?

39. What characteristics of Hasidic Judaism enabled Martin Buber to aptly describe the Hasidic life of worship as "pan-sacramentalism"? Similarly, on what must today's church insist? How does the exhortation in 1 Peter 2:9 echo ancient Israel's call and remind us of the church's rich Hebraic heritage as well as her inherited responsibility?

40. How is Hasidism a prime example of the fact that Judaism is a religion

that has affirmed human emotion? How do Gordon Wenham's comments on the narrative of Genesis highlight that this was characteristic of God's people from the beginning? Accordingly, how was prayer often experienced in Hasidism? What Hebrew term is used to describe the enthusiasm involved?

41. How does Abraham Heschel describe the Baal Shem Tov's teaching of *hitlahabut* and its effect on Hasidic Judaism? What restraint, however, does Heschel himself posit? What is the reasoning behind his exhortation, "When you are carried away by enthusiasm, veil it"? Do you take one side or the other when thinking about proper worship, or do you find a balance of the two to be most appropriate? Why?

42. What five reflections on Hasidism and *debequt* does the author offer at the close of the chapter? List them and comment briefly on the significance of each.

43. Consider the statement that for the Hasidim, "nature was an avenue for communion with God." Do you see this as a universal truth concerning communion with the one true God, regardless of belief system? Why or why not?

44. Regarding *debequt,* what does the author mean by commenting that "[w]e come to know the invisible through the visible"?

45. The author stresses that we should be open to a variety of biblical approaches that lead to God's holy presence. How do you personally balance expectation of God's presence in a traditional or familiar sense with openness to God working in new and unexpected ways? Which areas or contexts of your life have demonstrated a diversity of ways in which God works?

46. How, when all the "theological dust" settles, is *debequt* a "stick-to-it" reminder? Note the New Testament references that the author cites concerning this spirit of devotion. How do these exhortations testify to the church's Hebraic heritage? How does this clearly reveal powerful areas of common ground between Jews and Christians?

CHAPTER 11

Entering His Gates: On Repentance and Prayer

In Bible times, the gate (Heb. *sha'ar*) of a city was strategic. The gate was the center of social and civic life, a place associated with rulers and power. To gain control of the "gate of one's enemy" was to have the power to occupy an entire city (see Gen. 22:17; 24:60). The rulings, judgments, and physical presence of kings, judges, and elders were directly connected to the main entranceway into a city. This was the "corridor of power." Thus, as Richard S. Hess puts it, "to possess the gate is to possess the city. To gain access to the gate of the sanctuary is to gain access to God."[1] In Israel's understanding, God's sanctuary was the Temple.

The gates to the Temple (or holy city) are dramatically personified in Psalm 24:7-10. The psalm depicts Yahweh as the powerful, victorious King. The King and gates go together; he returns from battle, and the palace gates symbolically open amid jubilant shouts: "Lift up your heads, O you gates . . . that the King of glory may come in" (v. 7). Accordingly, to enter his sanctuary and have access to his presence, God's people were to acknowledge his power through praise: "Acknowledge that the LORD is God. . . . Enter His gates with praise, His courts with acclamation" (Ps. 100:3-4, JPS TANAKH translation).

In Jewish tradition, repentance and prayer are closely intertwined spiritual disciplines. Each holds a central place in Hebraic heritage and the practice of a biblically rooted faith. Repentance and prayer are difficult, yet powerful and personally rewarding spiritual exercises. The Hebrew expressions *sha'are teshubah*, "gates of repentance," and *sha'are tephillah*, "gates of prayer," highlight the importance of these acts in entering the presence of the

---

1. Richard S. Hess, "Gate" [*Sha'ar*], in *New International Dictionary of Old Testament Theology and Exegesis*, vol. 4 (Grand Rapids: Zondervan, 1997), p. 210.

living God. According to the rabbis, God created repentance, and God himself opens the "gates of repentance."[2] The gateway is the avenue for accessing power and bringing oneself back into conformity to the will of the Almighty. *Teshubah*, or "repentance," allows one to engage in a process of honestly dealing with failure and sin, reversing direction, and returning home. A sincere facing up to one's failures, the personal decision to right the wrong, allows one with a pure heart, through prayer, to experience the gracious presence and powerful help of the King, Judge, and Ancient of Days (Ps. 47:7; Gen. 18:25; Dan. 7:13). Repentance and prayer go together. They are vital means for restoring and maintaining a healthy relation with the living God.

Water and Repentance

In the prophetic tradition of the Hebrew Bible, John the Baptist announced the coming of Jesus: "Repent, for the kingdom of heaven is near. . . . Produce fruit in keeping with repentance" (Matt. 3:2, 8). Rabbi Stephen Wylen suggests that John the Baptist be called "John the Mikvah-man" because of John's emphasis on Jewish ritual immersion and the deep spiritual significance it carried.[3] Indeed, the Gospels indicate that John's baptism was not a mere outward perfunctory ritual involving water; John had a deeper concern — purification of the heart. In Mark's words, "John came, baptizing in the desert region and preaching a baptism of repentance for the forgiveness of sins" (Mark 1:4). John's baptism focused on the inward "washing," the spiritual cleansing of the heart that came through forsaking sin and turning to God in forgiveness, renewal, and good deeds (see Isa. 1:16-17; Jer. 4:14).

For "John the Mikvah-man," the term *mikveh* may have served as a "spiritual" double entendre of sorts. The word carried two main meanings: "immersion pool" and "hope." The baptism associated with John in the Jordan River required candidates to do more than physically submerge in running water. These people were also called to turn away from their sin and come back to a restored relationship with the God of hope: "O LORD, the hope *(mikveh)* of Israel, all who forsake you will be put to shame . . . because they have forsaken the LORD, the spring of living water *(mayim hayyim)*" (Jer.

---

2. See Solomon Schechter, *Aspects of Rabbinic Theology* (New York: Schocken, 1961), pp. 314-15.

3. Stephen M. Wylen, *The Jews in the Time of Jesus* (Mahwah, NJ: Paulist Press, 1996), p. 90. Note that *mikveh* is the Hebrew term for an immersion pool for ritual cleansing; the water was required to come from a river or natural spring.

17:13; see John 7:37-39). Citing these words of Jeremiah, the Mishnah states, "O Lord the hope *(mikveh)* of Israel — as the Mikveh cleanses the unclean so does the Holy One, blessed be he, cleanse Israel" (Yoma 8:9). John's work was primarily focused on spiritual cleansing, purifying the person within.

In the primitive church, Peter links repentance with the use of water baptism (see Acts 2:38). According to Acts 2:41, three thousand Jews responded to his message on the Festival of *Shabu'ot* (Pentecost). Doubtless, the numerous *mikvaot,* "ritual immersion pools," uncovered by archeologists on the southern side of the Temple Mount, provided the main site where so many of these believers bathed (Acts 2:41). Later in the Book of Acts, Paul builds on this emphasis upon water and spiritual cleansing with the command: "Be baptized and wash your sins away" (Acts 22:16).

James exhorts, using a similar Jewish idiom, "Wash your hands, you sinners, and purify your hearts, you double-minded" (James 4:8). Likewise, 1 John emphasizes that if we acknowledge our sin before God "[he] will forgive us our sins and purify *(katharise)* us from all unrighteousness" (1 John 1:9). Thus, in the Hebraic prophetic tradition and in apostolic Christianity, outward washing was intended to be a symbol of inward cleansing of sin and a purified heart.

Divine and Human Interaction

Paradoxically, there is both a human and a divine side to repentance. Humans have the personal responsibility "to turn, go back, come back." Repentance requires the individual to initiate the process. God cannot impose it; repentance is impossible without a person willing it. The way of repentance calls those trapped in sin to turn away from their idolatry or sinful ways and to return to the living God. The Hebrew verb *shub,* "to (re)turn" (from which *teshubah,* "repentance," derives) "combines in itself the two requisites of repentance: to turn from evil and to turn to the good."[4] The action of repentance is synergistic. In keeping with the above emphasis, James states that spiritual renewal begins when individuals heed the command to make the first move: "Come near to God and he will come near to you" (James 4:8). To turn from sin is an invitation to God in seeking his forgiveness.

---

4. Victor P. Hamilton, "*Shub.* (re)turn," in *Theological Wordbook of the Old Testament,* 2 vols., ed. R. Laird Harris, Gleason L. Archer Jr., and Bruce K. Waltke (Chicago: Moody Press, 1980), vol. 2, p. 909.

God is thus present in the work of repentance. If the people of Israel fulfill their responsibility, God will fulfill his: *shubu elai ve-ashubah aleykhem*, "Return to me and I will return to you" (Mal. 3:7). In a similar prophetic emphasis, "Return *(shubu)*, faithless people; I will cure you of backsliding" (Jer. 3:22). The verb *shub* is frequently found in the causative *(hiph'il)* stem, meaning "to bring back," "lead back," or "restore." The Lord says to Jeremiah, "If you repent, I will restore you" (Jer. 15:19). If one chooses to redirect one's life, God graciously responds to that person's free exercise of the will. In that sense, there is a back-and-forth aspect to repentance, a type of reciprocity associated with the word *shub* (see Gen. 8:7). Such meaning ("if you return, I will bring you back") is especially evident in various contexts in which *teshubah* may be rendered "answer" or "response" (see Job 21:34; 34:36). Lawrence Kushner points out that *teshubah* can also mean "apology," and above all, it can mean "return" — as in "going back to who you were meant to be, returning home."[5] Restoration is the divine "response" to Israel's (re)turning.

This "divine-human" interaction of repentance — of human turning and of divine bringing back/restoring — is certainly not always evident in every text. However, there are various contexts in Scripture where this interaction is clearly implied. For example, Psalm 51 is a powerful picture of David or some other person who turns away from sin, seeks God's cleansing, and looks to God to restore and renew him. One may note the emphasis on spiritual "washing" and "cleansing" from sin (vv. 2, 7).

The Shophar: Call to Repentance

The *shophar* or "ram's horn" is one of the earliest symbols of Judaism. As decorative art, the shophar is found on ancient synagogues, tombs, and ritual items. The shophar recalls a variety of biblical events and themes. These include God's Kingship over all the earth, the Akedah or "binding" of Isaac by Abraham, the revelation at Sinai, the warning for battle in ancient Israel, and the reminder of the final Day of Judgment.

In regard to the calendar of holy days, the Hebrew Bible specifies that "[i]n the seventh month, on the first day of the month, you shall observe a sacred occasion: you shall not work at your occupations. You shall observe it as a day when the horn is sounded" (Num. 29:1, JPS TANAKH translation;

---

5. Lawrence Kushner, *Jewish Spirituality* (Woodstock, VT: Jewish Lights, 2001), p. 87.

see Lev. 23:24). The month (and new year) began with the sounding of the ram's horn on New Year's Day (sometimes called the Feast of Trumpets). The horn sounded again ten days later on *yom kippur,* "The Day of Atonement" (Lev. 25:9). The rabbis came to refer to the first day of the seventh month as Rosh Hashanah, the "New Year."

Today, on Rosh Hashanah, the shophar is played a hundred times to usher in the season of repentance, the ten Days of Awe. Its eerie sound can create spiritual shivers. On the first day of the New Year, the blowing of the shophar is a call to the assembled to take serious spiritual inventory: to look back with sadness and regret on obligations undone, but to look ahead with anticipation of change through a new beginning. In the words of the great Jewish thinker Joseph Soloveitchik, the most important aspect of repentance is that "the future has overcome the past."[6]

The sobbing and whimpering sound of the shophar thus pierces to the heart; indeed, it replicates the broken, repentant heart. The shophar speaks in human language; it speaks with deep feeling. But this is not the end. Even the most hard-hearted must not wallow in the despair of their past, but cling to hope. The Almighty assures every truly repentant one anew: "I will give you a new heart and put a new spirit in you: I will remove from you your heart of stone and give you a heart of flesh" (Ezek. 36:26; see 18:31).

Now Is the Day

From Bible times to the present, Judaism has maintained a strong emphasis on the need for continual repentance. Why? The wisdom of Koheleth is applicable for all humanity in every age: "There is not a righteous man on earth who does what is right and never sins" (Eccles. 7:20). The Mishnah states, "Repent one day before thy death" (Abot 2:10). The rabbis understood this to mean a person should repent every day, for one never knows the day of his death; thus daily repentance is necessary if one is to be prepared to meet his Maker.[7]

The call to repentance from the lips of Hosea to his unfaithful con-

---

6. Quoted in Ehud Luz, "Repentance," in *Contemporary Jewish Religious Thought,* ed. Arthur A. Cohen and Paul Mendes-Flohr (New York: Free Press, 1987), p. 790.

7. Shlomo P. Toperoff, *Avot: A Commentary on the Ethics of the Fathers* (Northvale, NJ: Jason Aronson, 1997), p. 118.

temporaries continues to echo through the corridors of time as a universal prophetic call: "Return *(shubah),* O Israel, to the LORD your God. Your sins have been your downfall! Take words with you and return to the LORD. Say to him: 'Forgive all our sins and receive us graciously' " (Hos. 14:1-2). In the Mishnah, Rabbi Jacob says, "This world is like a vestibule *(prozdor)* before the world to come: prepare thyself in the vestibule that thou mayest enter into the banqueting hall. Better is one hour of repentance and good works in this world than the whole life of the world to come" (Abot 4:16-17). This life is a "foyer," "passageway," or "ante-chamber" leading to the *ha-olam ha-ba,* "the age to come" or future age.

These words of Rabbi Jacob emphasize the urgency of the present. Now is the day to put one's life in order through repentance and good works. One should not wait for the age to come, the day of ultimate perfection and eternal bliss, for it will be too late and impossible to prepare oneself. There will be neither repentance nor good works in that future "banqueting hall." Therefore, one must live a godly life of repentance and good works. Now is the day of preparation, the "dress rehearsal" for the life to come.

The above emphasis on repentance and good deeds is likewise taught in the New Testament, especially in light of the coming of God's good news in Jesus. At Athens, Paul urgently proclaims, "now he [God] commands all people everywhere to repent. For he has set a day when he will judge the world with justice" (Acts 17:30-31). In Paul's witness before King Agrippa, he sums up his message proclaimed to both Jew and Gentile: "I preached that they should repent and turn to God and prove their repentance by their deeds" (Acts 26:20). Christianity strongly teaches that repentance and good deeds matter. Such are not the grounds of salvation but rather the byproduct and fruit of a godly and righteous life of faith.

The call to repent now is also a main theme in the Book of Revelation, especially in the letters to the seven churches (see 2:5, 16, 21, 22; 3:3, 19). As the Mishnah teaches that deeds performed in the *prozdor* or "vestibule" (the present age) do not go unnoticed in the life to come, so Revelation teaches a similar Hebraic concept: "Blessed are the dead . . . they will rest from their labor, for their deeds will follow them" (Rev. 14:13). The future age is an "eternal Shabbat" of rest and joy in the divine presence.

Steps of Repentance: Finding the Way Back

According to the rabbis, *teshubah,* "repentance," is a process of the whole self that requires serious reflection and action. To be effective, this spiritual exercise involves several concrete steps.[8]

Acknowledgment

The first step in *teshubah* is acknowledgment. Maimonides commends the biblical example of David who acknowledged to the prophet Nathan, "I have sinned" (2 Sam. 12:13). This initial step emphasizes that a person must confess wrongdoing and freely admit to past deeds and the guilt of any wayward actions. The individual agrees to tell the truth about oneself rather than covering over one's sins. One must give careful consideration and honest assessment to the direction of one's life and, accordingly, own up to offensive behavior. Through acknowledgment of wrong, any repentant person can take the first step to "come back home."

Regret

The second step is that of expressing regret. The rabbis taught that we must have an attitude of remorse about our sins. A deep and sincere sense of disgust and godly sorrow over personal actions, however, is far different from the attitude of "sorry I got caught." In true regret, the sinner is ashamed of his transgressions and despises his actions. The rabbis considered a penitent and contrite heart to be among the genuine signs of a remorseful sinner. God says, "This is the one I esteem: he who is humble and contrite in spirit and trembles at my word" (Isa. 66:2). Indeed, "A broken and contrite heart, O God, you will not despise" (Ps. 51:17).

---

8. For various rabbinic discussions of the steps of repentance, note the following works: Jacob Neusner, *Questions and Answers: Intellectual Foundations of Judaism* (Peabody, MA: Hendrickson, 2005), pp. 135-36; Seymour Siegel, "Sin and Atonement," in *Evangelicals and Jews in an Age of Pluralism,* ed. Marc H. Tanenbaum, Marvin R. Wilson, and A. James Rudin (Grand Rapids: Baker, 1984), pp. 192-93; Schechter, *Aspects of Rabbinic Theology,* pp. 335-43.

Resolve

Third, repentance involves a resolve not to repeat the action. The decision to turn from the wrong and redirect one's life demands a strong mental resolve. It is always a challenging task to renounce the rebelliousness of self-will and to bring oneself into conformity with God's will. One must change the mind and reverse one's thinking to prevent being a repeat offender. Though scars of the past may remain, the human will is powerful; when exercised wisely, it can affect destiny.

Such a resolve of the will requires inward strength with a determination to master the self and its decisions. The courage and firmness to be a new person will be tested when an occasion to revert to the particular sinful action arises. The resolve and ability to overcome temptation by saying No enables one to build character. "But Daniel resolved not to defile himself with the royal food and wine" (Dan. 1:8).

Reconciliation

The final step in repentance, according to the rabbis, is reconciliation with God and the birth of a transformed person. Change has occurred. The individual is restored to fellowship, the relationship repaired. Estrangement between God and the repentant one is now bridged. Reconciliation brings harmony. God's provision of forgiveness of sin makes the restoration of a broken relationship possible. Bonds are now renewed and appropriate reparations made. Through sincere *teshubah,* the changed person has turned his life around and come back home.

In the modern world of social and behavioral sciences and also long-term reparative therapy, the above four steps of repentance may appear simplistic, ineffective, and too spiritual. While some failures and sinful actions may be a direct offense to God himself, many concern character defects or actions that offend others. While God's help and strength are necessary if a repentant person is to be successfully restored, in many situations turning around and returning home permanently — especially from certain loathsome sins and addictions — would usually need to be combined with an ongoing support group and/or regular therapy with health professionals. Restoration and rehabilitation often involve a complex process; it is more than a person saying a quick prayer, gritting the teeth, and instantaneously arriving at wholeness of mind and body.

If genuine repentance is to have *lasting* results, a repentant individual will normally seek out a caring, resourceful, spiritually sensitive community or support system. Here the community may provide help to clarify the nature of the sin, weakness, or problem and give guidance in keeping a weak person from the source(s) of temptation and destruction. The community must also remind the repentant individual that success and victory in one's personal life have to be accomplished one day at a time. Certainly, repentance does not guarantee perfection. But it is expressive of an attitude of humility and desire to change, a move that makes greater maturity and perfection possible. Thus the importance of the first Beatitude: "Blessed are the poor in spirit"; indeed, they know they need God's help (see Matt. 5:3).

Acting on Repentance

As indicated above, this transforming work of repentance involves action both on the part of the sinner and on the part of God; it is synergistic, but the sinner must initiate the process. Jewish scholar Seymour Siegel explains: "[Repentance] comes through an act of will on the part of the sinner. Of course . . . the sinner is helped by God's grace. But this grace is extended only if the movement toward God has already begun. 'He who comes to cleanse himself,' say the rabbis, 'he is helped from above.'"[9] God's call of repentance "implies also a certain mutual repentance, so to speak, or returning on the part of God, who meets Israel half-way."[10] Solomon Schechter illustrates God's compassionate role in the return (repentance) of his children by citing this rabbinic story:

> It is to be compared to the son of a king who was removed from his father for the distance of a hundred days' journey. His friends said to him, "Return unto your father," whereupon he rejoined, "I cannot." Then his father sent a message to him, "Travel as much as it is in thy power, and I will come unto you for the rest of the way." And so the Holy One, blessed be he, said, "Return unto me and I will return unto you" (Mal. 3:7).[11]

9. Siegel, "Sin and Atonement," p. 193.
10. Schechter, *Aspects of Rabbinic Theology,* p. 327.
11. Cited in Schechter, *Aspects of Rabbinic Theology,* p. 327.

There are parallels in this story to Luke 15, the parable of the gracious father, often referred to as the parable of the prodigal son. Luke 15 also displays a clear emphasis on repentance as the lost are found (see vv. 7, 10).

In the Sermon on the Mount, Jesus, a rabbi, teaches his *talmidim,* "disciples," that reconciliation with one's brother or sister must be sought *before* reconciliation with God is possible. Estrangement or hostility in interpersonal relationships is to be corrected *prior to* the act of worshiping God. "If you are offering your gift at the altar and there remember that your brother has something against you, leave your gift there in front of the altar. First go and be reconciled to your brother; then come and offer your gift" (Matt. 5:23, 24).

The Mishnah, in a context dealing with sin and repentance, establishes a similar priority to the above: "For transgressions that are between man and God the Day of Atonement effects atonement, but for transgressions that are between a man and his fellow the Day of Atonement effects atonement only if he has appeased his fellow" (Yoma 8:9). Thus, as Jewish ethicist Louis Newman sums up the rabbinic position: "Even the Day of Atonement will not erase sins committed against others unless the offender first repents and achieves reconciliation with the offended party."[12]

How is it possible to know another is genuinely penitent? The rabbis believed that changed behavior, through consistency of life, was necessary to demonstrate this. Accordingly, the Talmud asks, "How is one proved to be a true penitent? Rabbi Judah said: If the opportunity to commit the same sin presents itself on two occasions, and he does not yield to it" (Babylonian Talmud, Berakhot 34b). The more important question, however, is how to avoid sinful situations that lead to sin and the consequent need for repentance.

Sage Advice on the Avoidance of Sin

The Tannaim, or, sages of the Mishnah, have no magic formula on how to resist sin. But they do provide some wise, preventative advice: "Consider three things and thou wilt not fall into the hands of transgression *(aberah):* know what is above thee — a seeing eye and a hearing ear and all thy deeds written in a book" (Abot 2:1). The language is figurative, but it conveys vital truth. One must contemplate or reflect on three things to avoid coming under the power of sin.

---

12. Louis E. Newman, *An Introduction to Jewish Ethics* (Upper Saddle River, NJ: Pearson Prentice Hall, 2005), p. 62.

First, "know what is above you — a seeing eye." The idols of the nations are inanimate objects of silver and gold; "they have eyes but they cannot see" (Pss. 115:5; 135:16). God, however, is alive; he looks down from the heavens and takes notice of his people. The language is anthropomorphic. The use of "theology by analogy" helps to bring God, an immaterial spiritual Being, closer to us. As the Hebrew Bible rhetorically asks, "Does he who formed the eye not see?" (Ps. 94:9). "Can anyone hide in secret places so that I cannot see him?" (Jer. 23:24). Just as a police officer stationed along the highway may make a driver aware of the reality of a speed limit by his physical presence, so the divine "seeing eye" is a reminder that God "always has us on his radar."

Second, God also has a "hearing ear." By contrast, idols "have ears, but cannot hear" (Ps. 115:6; 135:17). Eyes and ears are often coupled together in Scripture (see Prov. 20:12). Again, the language emphasizes divine knowledge of humankind. To be blind or deaf is to be lacking two of the most important sensory organs. That God sees and hears speaks of his providence and impartiality of judgment.

Third, God not only observes and "listens in" on all, he also keeps record of all human deeds in a book. Again, the language is not literal but richly symbolic. The biblical background for this imagery likely includes such texts as Psalms 40:7; 56:8; 69:28; 139:16; Daniel 10:21; 12:1; and Malachi 3:16. In Jewish tradition, this theme is picked up at Rosh Hashanah to open the ten "Days of Penitence." Using richly symbolic language, the Talmud says, "On Rosh Hashanah (when the world is judged), three books are opened in the heavenly court; one for the wicked, one for the righteous, and one for those in between. The fate of the righteous is inscribed and sealed then and there: Life" (Rosh Hashanah 16b). A contrasting Christian understanding of divine judgment of sin and the sinner is explained in the paragraphs immediately below.

Repentance, Faith, and Deeds in Christianity

In the New Testament Book of Revelation we also find the expression, "the book of life" (3:5; 13:8; 17:8; 20:12, 15). In the Christian system, for a believer to have his name "written in the Lamb's book of life" is to have entry to the Holy City, the New Jerusalem (Rev. 21:2, 27). As pointed out above, God is not the divine bookkeeper as we understand record keeping in the modern world. Rather, the idea that our actions are "written in a book" strongly suggests that God does not forget; he has perfect memory. Therefore, repentance, faith, and lasting good works should strongly motivate and characterize the life of every sincere believer. Each believer will be judged "for things done while in the body, whether good or bad" (2 Cor. 5:10; see 1 Cor. 3:10-15).

Though not always clearly understood or discussed, biblical Christianity, like classical Judaism, holds to belief in rewards and punishments according to personal deeds, at the end of the age (Rev. 20:12; 22:12). This perspective is grounded in a fundamental teaching of Torah, namely, God observes everything humans do and judges them justly according to their deeds (Gen. 6:5-8; 18:25).

In biblical Christianity, the New Testament emphasizes that salvation is by grace through faith; works are the outward living proof or fruit of an inner living faith rooted in love and obedience to Christ (Eph. 2:8, 9). Thus, for believers, deeds are not the grounds of salvation; rather, salvation comes freely and supernaturally through the mercy and grace of God. This redeeming work of God initiates a radical change, through Christ, in the repentant sinner's heart (Titus 3:5).

In Matthew 25:31-46 we find a pictorial description of the final judgment before the King of the universe. The King's separation of the sheep from the goats dramatically points out the great importance works of love and compassion hold for this Judge of the nations. While the "inheritance" of the kingdom granted by the King (v. 34), in canonical context, is not a reward for works of human kindness, the New Testament firmly proclaims that faith without deeds is dead (see James 2:14-26).

Atonement is a major focus in Christianity and Judaism; all people sin through thoughts or deeds (1 Kgs. 8:46; Rom. 3:23). Sin not only offends a holy God but often creates division between individuals and people groups. In historic Christian teaching, atonement for sin is centered in the death of Jesus. For Christian believers, Jesus is the one who freely bears the sins of the world by sacrificing his own life on the cross, thus taking upon himself the eternal consequences of sin's penalty. Christians are continually reminded of this emphasis in communal worship through the celebration of the Mass, Eucharist, or Holy Communion.

Among Jews, however, atonement is especially emphasized during the High Holy Days climaxing with the Day of Atonement *(yom kippur)*, the holiest day on the religious calendar. Unlike at the time of the Temple in Jerusalem when there were priests and animal sacrifices, Judaism came to develop a somewhat different understanding of atonement. In Modern Judaism, in matters such as unfulfilled vows, atonement is sought by the individual directly with God. When it comes to offenses against one's fellow human beings, a Jew is expected to go to the offended party and right the wrong. In this understanding of atonement, repentance, good deeds, and prayer are of central importance in the restoration of relationships.

Some Observations on Jewish Prayer

In the Hebrew Bible there are many different types of prayer. These include prayers of petition, intercession, imprecation, lament, and thanksgiving. But when an individual comes before God in search of forgiveness and restoration — important dimensions in the process of repentance — a prayer of confession is sometimes employed. For Jews, prayer is rooted in the assumption that humankind may have fellowship with a personal God. Sin often mars or breaks that communion or fellowship. But, according to the psalmist, for the one who acknowledges his sin, God covers over and forgives the guilt of the sin (Ps. 32:1-5).

Prayer and Moral Reformation

In keeping with the above emphasis, Joseph Soloveitchik reminds us, "prayer is always the harbinger of moral reformation."[13] Indeed, as God instructs Solomon after the Temple has been dedicated, "If my people, who are called by my name, will humble themselves and pray and seek my face and turn (ve-yashebu) from their wicked ways, then will I hear from heaven and will forgive their sin and will heal their land. Now my eyes will be open and my ears attentive to the prayers offered in this place" (2 Chron. 7:14-15). A similar invitation to confession is found in the New Testament: "If we confess (homologomen) our sins, he [God] is faithful and just and will forgive us our sins" (1 John 1:9).

We Are in This Together

As alluded to above, in contemporary Judaism the holiest day of the religious calendar is Yom Kippur, the Day of Atonement. This High Holy Day of fasting and prayer employs a corporate confessional. As emphasized in the

13. Joseph B. Soloveitchik, *The Lonely Man of Faith* (New York: Doubleday, 1965), p. 65.

paragraphs above, specific sins against one's neighbor may *not* be removed by a prayer of absolution; rather, an individual must go personally to one's neighbor, seek that person's forgiveness, and make any restitution to justice.

But the liturgy on the Day of Atonement especially focuses on collective responsibility; on this occasion one hears the cry of an entire community to the Father above. The emphasis is on *"we,"* not "I," for the failures and shortcomings of the past year. After naming various types of sin committed against God, the liturgy concludes, "For all these sins, O God of forgiveness, *selah lanu* 'forgive us,' *mehal lanu* 'pardon us,' *kapper lanu* 'grant us remission.'"[14]

What may we deduce from this? Jews are a family. From Bible times to the present, Jews see themselves as interconnected. What affects one, affects all. Jews share in the successes as well as the failures of each other. Accordingly, Jesus, a member of Israel, established for his disciples this pattern of daily prayer: *u-selah-lanu et-hobotenu,* "And forgive us our sins" (Luke 11:4; see also Matt. 6:12, *The New Testament in Hebrew and English*).

A Life of Prayer

It would be simplistic, misleading, and inaccurate, however, to reduce Judaism to a religion that features one "day of prayer," Yom Kippur. Rather, Judaism teaches the necessity of "a life of prayer." An examination of the biblical evidence indicates that prayers are spoken by a wide range of individuals: laypeople — both men and women — prophets, priests, kings, governors, and more. What distinguishes the nearly one hundred prayers recorded in the prose sections of the Hebrew Bible — whether confessions, petitions, benedictions, or curses — is that they appear to be "freely composed in accordance with particular life settings."[15] This implies that biblical prayer was continuous, as a wide range of people from various segments of society uttered numerous spontaneous prayers to God, prayers of petition as well as thanksgiving.

Judaism teaches we must come to appreciate the gifts of God through nature. Jews were outdoors people, shepherd-farmers who prayed for rain, planted seed, and harvested crops. We moderns, on the other hand — people

14. See Joseph H. Hertz, ed., *Daily Prayer Book,* rev. ed. (New York: Bloch, 1948), pp. 918-19.

15. Moshe Greenberg, *Biblical Prose Prayer* (Berkeley: University of California Press, 1983), p. 7.

who typically pick up a loaf of bread and agricultural produce at a supermarket — are more prone to curse the rain, be indifferent to it, or rarely consider it a blessing. Little wonder that petitionary prayer, including intercessory prayer, is the most often attested form of biblical prose prayer.[16]

Anytime, Anywhere

As stated above, we must not limit our understanding of prayer in Bible times to formal occasions, special events, or religious gatherings at sacred places of worship such as the Temple. Many prayers appear to be extemporaneous in reaction to real-life situations. For example, when Miriam the sister of Moses becomes leprous, with skin white "like snow," Moses passionately prays one of the shortest prayers of Scripture, a prayer of five monosyllabic words: *el na r(e) pha na lah*, "O God, please heal her" (Num. 12:13)! Equally charged with deep feeling, Moses prays prostrate for a long time — forty days and forty nights — following the episode of the Golden Calf (Deut. 9:18). Biblical men and women prayed anywhere: at home, at work, on a journey, on a mountain, in the fields, on a ship, and even in a pagan temple (see Judg. 16:28). In short, they invoked the name of God whenever they sensed a need. These prayers often appealed to God as merciful, compassionate, gracious, or loving.

The inclusion of such an emphasis in a petitionary prayer likely served as grounds, on the part of the one praying, for expecting God's sympathetic hearing and response. God expected utter sincerity and candor in prayer. Samuel tells the whole house of Israel that sincerity is measured by action. The prophet states that "returning *(shabim)* to the LORD with all your hearts" will mean ridding themselves of foreign gods (1 Sam. 7:3). Such a life-changing about-face or radical call for spiritual housecleaning is concrete evidence of the type of wholehearted sincerity God expects in prayer.

A Spirit of Thankfulness

According to the rabbis, thankfulness is a necessary response for anyone who has received God's benefits; otherwise, one would be like a thief. "Praise the LORD, O my soul, and forget not all his benefits" (Ps. 103:2). The rabbis further said that in the Messianic Age, when all sin is abolished, a certain

16. Greenberg, *Biblical Prose Prayer,* p. 9.

type of sacrifice would remain: "Though all sacrifices may be discontinued in the future . . . the offering of thanksgiving will continue . . . though all prayers may be discontinued, the prayer of thanksgiving will never cease" (Leviticus Rabbah 9:7). Rabbi David J. Zucker pithily sums up this midrashic text: "giving 'thanks' is timeless."[17]

This emphasis on gratitude and praise is in accord with Old and New Testaments. What is the best sacrifice one may give to the Lord? According to the psalmist, it is not one's livelihood — sheep, goats, bulls; rather, it is placing on God's altar a contrite heart and offering up one's lips in praise: "O Lord, open my lips and my mouth will declare your praise. You do not delight in sacrifice, or I would bring it . . . the sacrifices of God are a broken spirit; a broken and contrite heart" (Ps. 51:15-17). The continual attitude of giving thanks is also affirmed in Psalm 34:1: "I will extol the LORD at all times; his praise will always be on my lips," and in 1 Thessalonians 5:17-18: "Pray continually; give thanks in all circumstances, for this is God's will for you." Abraham Heschel sums up the importance of praise in the Jewish tradition: "The secret of spiritual living is the power to praise. Praise is the harvest of love. Praise precedes faith. First we sing; then we believe."[18]

Kavanah: On Praying with Intention

In the act of prayer — whether in ancient times or today — one may outwardly be mouthing words but not inwardly directing the heart. In memorable "A-B-B-A" (chiastic) style, the Lord describes those guilty of this type of verbal hypocrisy: "These people come near to me with their mouth and honor me with their lips, but their hearts are far from me" (Isa. 29:13; see also Matt. 15:8-9).

In Judaism, the rabbis address this concern about an "absent" or wandering mind. They call for the importance of directing one's soul in worship and other spiritual actions through *kavanah.*[19] *Kavanah* means "directed

17. David J. Zucker, *The Torah: An Introduction for Christians and Jews* (New York: Paulist Press, 2005), p. 131.

18. Quoted in *Abraham Joshua Heschel: Essential Writings,* ed. Susannah Heschel (Maryknoll, NY: Orbis Books, 2011), p. 155.

19. For useful Jewish works on *kavanah,* see Martin Buber, *Hasidism and Modern Man,* ed. and trans. Maurice Friedman (New York: Harper & Row, 1958) pp. 98-108; Abraham Joshua Heschel, *God in Search of Man* (New York: Harper & Row, 1955), pp. 314-19, 341-46; Max Kadushin, *Worship and Ethics: A Study in Rabbinic Judaism* (Evanston, IL: Northwestern University Press, 1964), pp. 185-98; C. G. Montefiore and H. Loewe, eds., *A Rabbinic Anthology* (New

intention," the concentration or attention of the mind during prayer or the performance of a deed. This term derives from a verbal root in biblical Hebrew, *kun,* suggesting the idea of "prepared," "set in order," or "made ready."[20]

The above meaning of *kun* is extended into Aramaic texts in which it carries the idea "to direct the mind, to pay attention, to do a thing intentionally."[21] Although the actual noun *kavanah* is rabbinic and not biblical, the root idea of "directing the heart (or mind)" in the sense of to *intend* or to *mean* to do something is found in the Hebrew Bible. For example, the prophet Samuel admonishes Israel, "If you mean to return to the LORD with all your heart, you must remove the alien gods . . ." (1 Sam. 7:3, JPS TANAKH translation; see also Ps. 78:8; 2 Chron. 20:33). The Talmud further builds on this theme of praying with intent: "He who prays must direct his heart toward heaven" (Babylonian Talmud, Berakhot 31a). Accordingly, "Kavanah in prayer is the very antithesis of the mechanical and perfunctory reading of words."[22]

By way of application, the sages were concerned that a person not attempt to pray in a place that may destroy one's *kavanah.* For example, the Mishnah states that a bridegroom is exempt from reading the Shema (the "Hear, O Israel" prayer and confession of faith in Deuteronomy 6) on his wedding night, for the circumstance would compromise proper concentration on the prayer (Berakhot 2:5). On the other hand, while not specifically using the verb *kun,* the prophet Ezekiel expresses the sense of this word — not the attentiveness of human prayer — but by underlining the need for full concentration of oneself regarding what God says: "The LORD said to me, 'Son of man, look carefully, listen closely and give attention to everything I tell you concerning all the regulations regarding the temple of the LORD'" (Ezek. 44:5).

Accordingly, in Jewish religious life, *kavanah* is about awareness and paying attention. It concerns the intention and redirection of the individual so the heart and soul are in sync with the action. Words and deeds may be routine, mechanical, and heartless; *kavanah* is about attentiveness to God; it focuses upon attitude that governs action. As one scholar succinctly ob-

---

York: Schocken, 1974), pp. 272-94; Jakob J. Petuchowski, *Understanding Jewish Prayer* (New York: Ktav, 1972), pp. 3-16.

20. See John N. Oswalt, *"Kun,"* in *Theological Wordbook of the Old Testament,* vol. 1, p. 433.

21. See Marcus Jastrow, ed., *A Dictionary of the Targumim, the Talmud Babli and Yerushalmi, and the Midrashic Literature,* vol. 1 (London: Luzac & Co., 1886-1903; repr. Peabody, MA: Hendrickson, 2005), p. 622.

22. Hayim Halevy Donin, *To Pray as a Jew* (New York: Basic Books, 1980), p. 19.

serves, "Prayer without kavanah is like a body without a soul."[23] *Kavanah* concerns more than words; it is "spiritual consciousness-raising."[24] *Kavanah* is awareness of what you are doing so that you are inwardly turned toward God's presence, offering your words or actions as gifts upon an inner altar.[25]

Praying and Living with Conviction

In prayer, the call to awareness of what a worshiper is doing is captured in the Talmudic command, "Know before Whom you are standing" (Berakhot 28b). Personal conviction about being in the presence of the living God is a *sine qua non* of effective prayer: "The primary presupposition [of prayer] is conviction. If such conviction is lacking, if the presence of God is a myth, then prayer to God is a delusion. If God is unable to listen to us, then we are insane in talking to Him. All this presupposes conviction."[26]

Traditional Judaism and historic Christianity hold to a glorious afterlife, a future age when the righteous of all ages will enter the gates of "God's banquet hall" and enjoy "his goodness and love forever" (Ps. 23:6; Isa. 25:6-9; 26:19; also Rev. 19:9). While many mysteries attend the age to come, there is a strong and secure belief in the inseparable and indissoluble relation God has with his people. Doubtless contemplating his own death, David speaks with great conviction about his future in Psalm 16:9-11: "My body will also rest secure because you will not abandon me to the grave. . . . You have made known to me the path of life; you will fill me with joy in your presence, with eternal pleasures at your right hand." In the New Testament, this passage is applied to Jesus and his resurrection from the dead (see Acts 2:24-28; 13:34-35).

These words of David from Psalm 16 anticipate the climax of all earthly utterances directed to the heavenly throne room. For when the language of prayer as God-directed words of the heart are finally stilled in his eternal Presence, the human heart will hear the humbling words of the Honored One, "You are because I am."[27]

---

23. Simon Glustrom, *The Language of Judaism* (Northvale, NJ: Jason Aronson, 1988), p. 221.

24. David R. Blumenthal, *God at the Center: Meditations on Jewish Spirituality* (Northvale, NJ: Jason Aronson, 1994), p. 187.

25. Arthur Green, *These Are the Words* (Woodstock, VT: Jewish Lights, 1999), p. 131.

26. Abraham Joshua Heschel, *The Insecurity of Freedom* (New York: Schocken, 1966), p. 258.

27. Michael Fishbane, "Prayer," in *Contemporary Jewish Religious Thought,* ed. Cohen and Mendes-Flohr, p. 729.

UNDERSTANDING CHAPTER ELEVEN

1. In biblical times, why were gates significant? What association did they have with ruling figures? In what way are gates personified in Psalm 24:7-10?

2. In Jewish tradition, how are repentance and prayer closely related? Which Hebrew expressions incorporating the concept of gates emphasize the importance of these acts? What are the "gates of repentance" that the rabbis speak of?

3. Which title did Rabbi Stephen Wylen suggest for John the Baptist and why? Beyond external immersion, what was John's concern in baptizing? In what way might the term *mikveh* have served as a "spiritual" double entendre of sorts for John? Which Old Testament and Mishnaic texts does the author provide as examples of the Lord being the *mikveh* of Israel, and what does this phrase mean?

4. Cite scriptural examples that communicate that in Hebraic tradition and apostolic Christianity, outward washing was intended to be a symbol of inward cleansing of sin and a purified heart. Which interesting archeological discovery does the author mention that would appear to corroborate the dramatic activity of Acts 2:41?

5. How is it that human beings must initiate the process of repentance, yet repentance is synergistic? Cite biblical passages in your response. What does the Hebrew verb *shub* mean, and what two requisites of repentance does it combine? What significance may lie in the fact that *shub* is often found in the causative *(hiph'il)* stem of the verb?

6. What is a shofar? Which major biblical events and themes does it recall?

7. What is the biblical background of the day that the rabbis came to call the "New Year"? What is the Hebrew title for this holiday? Today, how does the shofar play a role in the New Year? What is the purpose of the ten Days of Awe that follow? Accordingly, what does Joseph Soloveitchik state is the most important aspect of repentance?

8. Why has Judaism, from biblical times to the present, maintained an emphasis on the importance of continual repentance?

9. In the Mishnah, how did Rabbi Jacob emphasize the urgency and importance of the present? What is a *prozdor*? Is viewing "this age" as a foyer or antechamber to the "age to come" a helpful framework of thought for you? How do you understand and respond to his statement that "[b]etter is one hour of repentance and good works in this world than the whole life of the world to come"?

10. Briefly discuss the New Testament's emphasis on repentance in the work of Paul and in the Book of Revelation.

11. What is the Hebrew term for repentance? According to the rabbis, effective repentance includes which four major steps?

12. Concerning *acknowledgment* as a step in the process of repentance, which biblical character does Maimonides commend, and in what context did the character's acknowledgment take place? (Review 2 Sam. 12:1-13, if necessary.)

13. Why did the rabbis wisely consider a penitent and contrite heart to be so significant? How do you understand what it means to *despise* one's wrong actions?

14. Consider the author's statement that "the human will is powerful; when exercised wisely, it can affect destiny." Have you found this to be true in the lives of people you know or in your own life? What is the power of resolve?

15. How can the rabbis' four steps of repentance potentially be viewed in the modern world? While an individual will always need the direct aid of God's transformative Spirit, are other humans God's instruments of transformation as well? In your opinion, is there anything good about the fact that restoration and rehabilitation is rarely instantaneous? How is the first Beatitude (see Matt. 5:3) of immense value in the broader discussion?

16. Though repentance is synergistic, how does Seymour Siegel assert that the initiation must begin with the sinner? How does Solomon Schechter illustrate the same point by means of a rabbinic story? (Note the story's similarity with a particular New Testament passage.) From a Christian perspective, how do you view the synergy of God and man working together in the process of repentance? Must a sinner be the one to initiate? Does he do so according to his own initiative, upon God's prompting, or in response to a combination of both?

17. How do both Jesus and the Mishnah teach, in slightly different senses, that interpersonal reconciliation must precede worship of God? What do you see as the reasoning behind this? Is this always the order that should be followed? Explain your position. In the Talmud, how does Rabbi Judah answer the question of how it is possible to know whether another is genuinely penitent?

18. Who were the Tannaim? What three things did they exhort mankind to be aware of? Briefly discuss what is meant by each of these figurative images, and cite biblical passages that provide the foundations for the

idea of a book with human deeds recorded in it. How does the Talmud (see Rosh Hashanah 16b) portray the role of such books on the Day of Judgment?

19. Where in the New Testament is the expression "book of life" found? What does the imagery of having one's deeds "written in a book" communicate about God?

20. Though not always clearly understood or discussed, how does Christianity, like Judaism, hold to belief in rewards and punishments at the end of the age according to personal deeds? Of what significance is Matthew 25:31-46? How does its content communicate the same message as James 2:14-26?

21. Compare and contrast understandings of atonement in Christianity and Judaism. What practice continually reminds Christians of the centrality of Jesus in atonement? From a Christian perspective, do you think it matters whether this is a consistently frequent practice or a more occasional one? Why or why not? How do the Christian and Jewish perspectives on atonement together emphasize both God's graciousness in paving the way for atonement and humanity's remaining responsibility for sin?

22. Which various kinds of prayer are found in the Hebrew Bible? In Hebrew thought, what assumption is prayer rooted in? Cite a passage from the Old Testament and a passage from the New Testament that present invitations to confession. According to Joseph Soloveitchik, what is prayer always the harbinger of?

23. What is the holiest day of the religious calendar in contemporary Judaism? What does the liturgy on this holiday particularly center on? How did Jesus offer a similar expression in the Lord's Prayer (see Luke 11:4; Matt. 6:12)? From your knowledge, do Christians have comparable times reserved for a focus on corporate responsibility for sin?

24. What is significant about the fact that the nearly one hundred prayers recorded in the prose sections of the Hebrew Bible appear to be "freely composed in accordance with particular life settings"?

25. Provide examples of the occurrence of spontaneous prayer in the Hebrew Bible. In what sense do such occurrences remind us not to limit our perceptions of prayer?

26. According to the rabbis, if anyone who had received God's benefits was not thankful, what would he be like? Review Leviticus Rabbah 9:7. What does Rabbi David Zucker mean by his brief summary statement that "giving 'thanks' is timeless"? How is this emphasis in line with

what the Old and New Testaments have to say about the most fitting sacrifice one can give?

27. What is *kavanah*? What concern in prayer does it address? From what Hebrew root does it derive, and what sense does it carry in rabbinic thought and in its occurrence in Aramaic texts? How does the Talmud illustrate its importance? What example from the Mishnah reveals how the sages were concerned about preserving *kavanah*? Reflect on one scholar's observation that "Prayer without kavanah is like a body without a soul." Does this value placed on *kavanah* resonate with your own personal aspirations in prayer?

28. What does Berakhot 28b of the Talmud say? How does this function as a call to awareness? What does Heschel state is the primary presupposition of prayer, and in what way is this so? How does David demonstrate great conviction in Psalm 16:9-11? Note the passages of the New Testament in which these verses are applied to Jesus' resurrection.

CHAPTER 12

Israel's Struggle with God

Wrestling with God

Jacob encountered a mysterious supernatural being at the Jabbok River (Gen. 32:22-32). As poets powerfully make points by puns, so the storyteller revels in paronomasia. He engages the reader as God *ye'abeq* (wrestled) with *ya'aqob* (Jacob) at the *yabboq* (Jabbok).

According to the above text, Jacob had sent his family and possessions across the Jabbok. Jacob was left alone. An angel, in the form of a man, began to struggle with him through the night until daybreak (Gen. 32:24-26; Hos. 12:4). When Jacob's assailant saw he could not overpower him, he wrenched or strained the patriarch's hip. The unexpected visitor told Jacob to let him go. Jacob replied, "I will not let you go until you bless me" (Gen. 32:26). Rhetorically, the man asked him his name. After Jacob told him, the man said, "Your name will no longer be Jacob, but Israel, because you have struggled with God and with men and have overcome" (v. 28). Then the man blessed Jacob there (v. 29). In verse 30, after the blessing, Jacob named the place Peniel ("face of God") for he said he had seen God "face to face" (Heb., *panim el-panim*; Greek, *prosopon pros prosopon*). In only five places within the Tanakh do we find God encountering humanity "face to face" (see Gen. 32:30; Exod. 33:11; Deut. 34:10; Judg. 6:22; Ezek. 20:35).

In the world of Jewish thought, the above confrontation between Jacob and the angel is considered one of the "cosmic events" in Jewish history.[1] The interpretations and implications of this story of Jacob's wrestling with

---

1. *The Chumash*, Stone Edition, 4th ed. (Brooklyn, NY: Mesorah Publications, 1994), p. 174.

God are many. While the story raises numerous questions, the text says that Jacob struggled with God in the form of an angelic messenger. Especially during the era of the patriarchs and the time of the greatest Old Testament prophet, Moses, God temporarily appeared in human form. In that these human representations of the divine are often associated with the communication of a message, the term *mal'akh*, "angel," is frequently used for such mysterious manifestations (see Hos. 12:4).

Jacob's tenacity of struggle was related to his intense desire for blessing. Jacob said to the man, "I will not let you go unless you bless me" (Gen. 32:26). The combatant blessed Jacob. The Hebrew word for blessing is *berakhah*. Properly, *berakhah* means a "gift" or "present" given to another. The bestowed blessing to or upon someone can be in the form of concrete material substance or in the form of spiritual prosperity. In the ancient world, words were more than haphazard verbiage; words were influential in that they were believed to carry significance, power, promise of fulfillment, and the ability to affect the outcome of a person's life. Verbal blessings upon people were gifts of strength, encouragement, or consolation in the hope that what was spoken would come to fruition. Jacob's descendants, the people of Israel, have remained an "indestructible" people through history. Through struggle, pain, discouragement, defeat, and exile, Jews corporately have held on to that promise of blessing first bestowed on Abraham in Mesopotamia and now reiterated to Jacob in the trans-Jordan Jabbok (Gen. 12:1-3; 32:29).

In opening the lens of blessing further, especially as it applies to us today, it is important to point out the probable connection of *berakhah* to the word *berekh*, "knee." The idea of "bending the knee" or "kneeling" is likely associated with submission before a superior. When it comes to individuals blessing others, there is nothing magical about blessing. No one has the independent power to confer or withhold prosperity or success upon another. Only God can do this. "Bending the knee" is a reminder that all material and spiritual blessings come from the ultimate Source of blessing and everything good in the world. We submit to him. Tangible blessings such as health and wealth are not automatic or permanent. Accordingly, they are to be held loosely for they are fragile, temporary, and sometimes inexplicable. Only God is eternal. However, when we use our material gifts as a blessing to bless others and our spiritual blessings from Scripture to provide blessing and encouragement to the lives of those around us, we become a gift to others and receive God's blessing in the process. We are blessed to be a blessing. In short, reciprocity is a part of blessing: "I will bless those who bless you" (Gen. 12:3).

Jacob was alone. In an experience of profound intimacy, a supernatural being suddenly comes "face to face" with Jacob. In flesh and blood, this messenger reveals a new name that would characterize this heretofore "deceitful" one; he and his descendants would struggle with men and God and prevail.[2] The name Israel is a title of victory. The night challenged Jacob's tenacity and he won. Accordingly, J. H. Hertz says the title is larger than Jacob and would mark his descendants: "Israelites are champions of God, contenders for the divine, conquering by strength from above."[3]

Jews have much to teach Christians about "God-wrestling." As Arthur Green points out, the name Israel is a fitting and broad enough name for those who wrestle with the "Mighty One," for it includes challengers, doubters, deniers, and anyone engaged in struggling with God and questions of religious truth.[4] An alternate reading, going back to Philo (first century B.C.), suggests that the name Israel may come from a different root, meaning "the people who see God." Such a reading would imply those who stand directly in the presence of God and hence participate in a collective religious vision as Israel did at Sinai and thus see that God is with them.[5] Elie Wiesel points out how Jacob's struggle with God at the Jabbok underlined the patriarch's progress in understanding God's omnipresence: "Jacob has just understood a fundamental truth: God is in man, even in suffering, even in misfortune, even in evil. God is everywhere. In every being, not only in the victim. God does not wait for man at the end of the road, the termination of exile; He accompanies him there."[6]

In modern thought, piety is often associated with weakness, prudishness, effeminacy, passivity, social seclusion, and abandonment of the world. In the patriarchal narratives, however, piety is often associated with those, like Jacob, who are courageous, strong, possessing dogged persistence, and having physical and mental toughness.[7] Indeed, in Wiesel's words, "[Jacob] plunged into the fight and returned blow for blow. And there was nobody around to come to his rescue, or even to give him moral support, or even

2. See Mark D. Wessner, "Toward a Literary Understanding of 'Face to Face' in Genesis 32:22-32," *Restoration Quarterly* 42 (2000): 69-77.

3. J. H. Hertz, ed., *The Pentateuch and Haftorahs*, 2nd ed. (London: Soncino Press, 1975), p. 124.

4. Arthur Green, *These Are the Words* (Woodstock, VT: Jewish Lights, 1999), p. 188.

5. Green, *These Are the Words*, p. 189.

6. Elie Wiesel, *Messengers of God* (New York: Random House, 1976), p. 117.

7. See Gordon J. Wenham, *Story as Torah: Reading Old Testament Narrative Ethically* (Grand Rapids: Baker Academic, 2000), p. 90.

to admire him. The metamorphosis seems so incredible."[8] Drawing certain similarities to the persistent struggle of Jacob, Abraham J. Heschel makes these observations on true piety: it is "something unremitting, persistent, unchanging in the soul, a perpetual inner attitude of the whole man . . . piety is a life compatible with God's presence[;] . . . we have to conquer in order to succumb; we have to acquire in order to give away; we have to triumph in order to be overwhelmed."[9] Jacob did triumph, and he was assured face-to-face of God's presence. Jacob's piety has persisted through Israel, those determined descendants bearing his name.

At the burning bush, the Lord said to Moses, "I am the God of your father, the God of Abraham, the God of Isaac, and the God of Jacob" (Exod. 3:6; see Matt. 22:32; Mark 12:26; Luke 20:37). To us, the expression may sound repetitious or appear redundant, with the mention of God's name four times. The rabbis, however, considered the repetition of the word "God" before each of the patriarchs very important, for each patriarch experienced God differently. Yes, he was the same God, but the personal episodes of encountering this God varied. Orthodox Jewish scholar Pinchas Lapide summarizes the rabbinic discussion:

> Abraham experienced him as the God who leads the way, who calls to him in the uncertainty of the promised land; Isaac, his son, experienced him as the guardian, who delivered him on the mountain of Moriah from the sacrifice by the knife of his own father; Jacob, the grandson, on the other hand, experienced him as the combative angel who wrestled with him throughout the night until at dawn he could wrest his blessing from him and the new name Israel. . . . The Jew relies upon the three fundamental experiences of the God of his ancestors, to which in the course of history have been joined [to] so many others of different sorts that all attempts at a systematic classification evoke scorn. The prophets warn us repeatedly about the manufacturing of images of God: "To whom then will you liken God, or what likeness compare with him?" (Isa. 40:18).[10]

The God of the Bible will be experienced in different ways by God's people today. To use the words of Scripture concerning these two sides of the

8. Wiesel, *Messengers of God*, p. 108.

9. Abraham J. Heschel, "An Analysis of Piety," in *Moral Grandeur and Spiritual Audacity*, ed. Susannah Heschel (New York: Farrar, Straus & Giroux, 1996), pp. 307, 311, 317.

10. Karl Rahner and Pinchas Lapide, *Encountering Jesus — Encountering Judaism* (New York: Crossroad, 1987), pp. 31, 36.

"coin of faith," he is the "God of our fathers" (see Exod. 3:6) and "He is my God" (Exod. 15:2). The heritage of faith is not merely to be received passively as an heirloom from generations past but is to be personally encountered, won, and owned; the believer must also say, "This God and this faith are mine, not by hearsay but by my experience and choice." Thus, to know God must not be perceived as sluggishly receiving some musty souvenir of fate. Rather, with the patriarchs, it embraces a fresh, personal encounter of faith.

Questioning God

Part of being human is to struggle for meaningful answers. We struggle with ourselves, with our faith, with our world. We wish no passive understanding of God, one acquired as a hand-me-down relic. Thus, on occasion, we may be energized and sense that it is right to speak up and to engage, contend, and even argue for authentic answers. As believers we wish to make sense out of life, so we struggle intellectually and spiritually with our problems, questions, and even honest doubts.

Abraham Heschel writes that the greatness of a person is measured in how many deep problems that person is concerned with. But Heschel also paradoxically points out that even God has problems, noting that we need but only "[l]ook in the Bible. God is always wrestling with the problem of man."[11] Most believers desire to have an informed and "reasonable" faith, a faith that seeks greater understanding and depth through investigation, reason, and experience. We observe in the Hebrew Bible God's invitation to Israel to dialogue with him. Like Israel, we hear God's invitation, "Come now, let us reason together" (Isa. 1:18, NIV); or "Come, let us reach an under-standing" (JPS TANAKH translation). The verb used for "reason together" is *yakhah*, meaning "to argue out together" (see Isa. 1:18; also Mic. 6:2). God is the sovereign, omniscient Judge of the earth who gets the last word whether or not man fully understands or likes his judgment. Yet God encourages his people to accept his challenge to argue things out together. Believers who truly love God should not be afraid to question God.

Like Jacob, we also wrestle with God. We strive to know him and his ways. We struggle with his Word, often desiring to search deeper for answers. In segments of the Christian world, however, it is not considered proper or "spiritual" to question God. To question God is a sign of arrogance or

11. Heschel, *Moral Grandeur and Spiritual Audacity*, pp. 402-3.

downright unbelief. Who are we to question? Such may be the case. However, Moses did not know all God's ways of dealing with the perplexity of the human situation, so he asked him, "Teach me your ways so I may know you" (Exod. 33:13). God did not promise to Moses that he would have all the answers but he did assure him saying, "My Presence will go with you" (Exod. 33:14). The word for "my Presence" *(panai)* is the same word used above for the One Jacob wrestled with "face to face" *(panim el-panim)*.

Precisely, because of the above point that God's people have his presence, I would contend that questioning God can and should be a spiritually healthy exercise. Indeed, asking questions may be a profound expression of one's love for God, a genuine manifestation of the seriousness of one's faith and the closeness of one's relation to God.

Consider Israel of Bible times. Israel stood within a secure covenantal relationship. This, however, was not the case within the nations that surrounded Israel. The mythologies of these peoples indicate how insecure they were. Their fate was in the hands of capricious, whimsical, and conniving gods who could be ritually appeased and manipulated. Israel, however, knew where she stood. Torah was God's definitive contract with his people. Israel also knew through experience the Faithful One before whom she stood. This provided security and assurance to the nation. Like a spouse in a positive marriage, Israel knew she was loved. Even occasional questioning and disagreement with Israel's heavenly Bridegroom could not sever that love or destroy the permanency of the relationship. Indeed, God calls his bride Hephzibah, "my delight is in her," and her land Beulah, "married," for "as a bridegroom rejoices over his bride, so will your God rejoice over you" (Isa. 62:4-5).

Pointing back to Jacob's experience at the Jabbok, all generations of Jews are taught — indeed, each individual Jew is taught — to struggle personally to know God "face to face" (intimately) and to come closer to him through asking the most personal of questions. Part of the Jewish mystique and a hallmark of being Jewish from Bible times to the present is to be one who grapples with God. Sometimes this can get very passionate and accusatory; it may look like "God in the dock," or the "trial of God." But usually it is simply a candid and open investigation about scriptural teaching in relation to what is happening in one's personal life or in the world.

In today's church, many are told they must content themselves with traditional, preapproved Christian answers or learn to accept unquestioningly the "hand that is dealt them" from God. It is unacceptable to doubt, argue, or debate with God, for whatever is "not of faith" is sinful. This negative reaction about questioning is often spawned through a mentality that is characteristically looking for a one-word answer to truth rather than approaching truth as a living, dynamic, dialogical conversation with the text and the "Lord of the text." Frequently, Christians are told never to "rock the boat," thus being forced to settle for easy or pat answers to complex questions; Jews, on the other hand, typically answer questions by asking further questions.

Hermeneutically, Jews are usually bent toward an ongoing, timeless quest for truth. Without this, for example, the biblical law of *ayin tahat ayin,* "eye for an eye," would never have evolved into the more compassionate and rational requirement. Today, this law seeks to compensate for physical damage with money rather than to inflict additional bodily damage by retaliating against the perpetrator. Among Christians, so-called authoritative "biblical" teachings given by earlier generations to justify actions such as black slavery, the burning of witches, and the tyrannical submission of women are only a few examples of distorted practices in society that could have been modified or avoided had serious questioning taken place sooner.

There are numerous passages in the Bible that are not crystal clear in how they should be understood, interpreted, and applied in the modern world. A difficulty may arise when one teaching is in conflict with another. One sign of love for God and his Word is to seek sincerely to understand what is being said. God is all-knowing, but we are not. Thus, firmly held in God's loving grip, one may question God's sometimes not-so-loving ways.

There is a difference between insolence and innocence. God is pleased with a pure, honest, and open heart that is continually seeking to understand. Either faith seeks understanding, or it may not be a tried-and-true faith. The Christian mind is more than a repository of truth, a robotically generated font of right answers. The One who is faithful and true is patiently and lovingly holding us in his secure grip even as we are in the process of coming to understand his truth and his ways (see Isa. 55:6-9; Rev. 19:11).

Some Tough Questioners of God

A thorough understanding of our Hebraic roots should take most of the disrepute and stigma away from questioning God. Why? Some of the greatest figures of Scripture questioned God. Likewise, serious students of the Word should be able to take their problems, questions, and doubts to God, supposedly their closest and most understanding friend. What is the biblical precedence for this questioning? Abraham, "the friend of God," came back to God ten times, interceding and "bargaining" with him over his intention to destroy Sodom and Gomorrah, wicked cities that Abraham was convinced had at least ten righteous people within them (Gen. 18:16-33; James 2:23). Eventually, Abraham resolved to face God with a powerful rhetorical question: "Will not the Judge of all the earth do right?" (Gen. 18:25). In the meantime, Abraham and his descendants were to "keep the way of the LORD by doing what is right and just" (Gen. 18:19). Irving Greenberg sums up the significance of Abraham's protest to God: "Abraham learned one of the most daring implications of the reciprocity of covenant: God, too, should be held to the standard of justice and righteousness. Abraham initiated a signature Jewish expression of love for God by protesting to his Creator against injustice in the world."[12]

Moses questioned God's directions at the burning bush. Moses declared to God, "Who am I, that I should go to Pharaoh and bring the Israelites out of Egypt?" (Exod. 3:11). Decades later, in the wilderness of Sinai, Moses questioned God again. God had decided to destroy unfaithful and rebellious Israel with a plague and then start over again with Moses. Moses interceded and confronted God by appealing to God's reputation among the nations. God then decided to relent and he forgave his people (Num. 14:11-20).

Job, among the most righteous of Scripture, questioned why God should have allowed him to be born to a life of trouble and tragedy. Job asked God why he was not born dead: "Why did I not perish at birth, and die as I came from the womb?" (Job 3:11).

Jeremiah complained to God about the way he was running the universe. He confronted God with the problem of theodicy: How can a good, just, and righteous God permit evil in the world? Jeremiah arraigned God by citing a discrepancy between God's righteous and holy nature and his allowing evil people in society seemingly to prosper (Jer. 12:1). To paraphrase Jeremiah, "You are righteous, O LORD, but I have this problem with what I see around me!"

Like Jeremiah, the prophet Malachi complained, "Certainly the evildoers prosper, and even those who challenge God escape" (Mal. 3:15). Habakkuk, also deeply perplexed, asked a similar tough question on why a God of holiness and goodness seems indifferent and powerless in the face of human cries concerning violence, injustice, and evil in this world (Hab. 1:1-4). In addition, Jonah, with patriotic zeal, lodged his great displeasure in God's decision to show compassion on Nineveh and not to destroy the evil city

---

12. Irving Greenberg, *For the Sake of Heaven and Earth* (Philadelphia: Jewish Publication Society, 2004), p. 59.

after it repented (Jonah 3:10). In a somewhat confrontational, prophetic-like style perhaps fostered with a growing awareness of his unique mission, even Jesus at the tender age of twelve gently rebuked his parents with a question rooted in his own sense of loyal obedience: "Didn't you know I had to be in my Father's house?" (Luke 2:49).

Like the greats of Scripture, we must develop a comfort level in taking our questions, difficulties, and doubts to God. We may not always get the answer we are expecting. But if our intention is honest and pure, we may learn to live with the answers. Often we will have incomplete or partial answers; sometimes we may receive nothing but silence. While hanging on the cross, did Jesus get a direct answer when he questioned his Father, *"Eloi, Eloi, lama sabachthani?"* "My God, my God, why have you forsaken me?" (Matt. 27:46; Mark 15:34)? There was an apparent rupture in relationship; Jesus deeply felt the abandonment of his Father (see Ps. 22:1). By questioning his Father, there was a release from the depth of his being. No voice, however, could be heard from heaven. Only silence.

Paul wrote, "Now we see but a poor reflection as in a mirror; then we shall see face to face. Now I know in part; then I shall know fully, even as I am fully known" (1 Cor. 13:12). In powerfully alliterative style, Paul speaks of a future day when believers would be able to see *prosopon pros prosopon* "face to face." Perhaps Paul, master of Torah that he was, is alluding to the rare experiences of his spiritual ancestors, such as Jacob or Moses, who are said — in some real, yet mysterious way — to have seen God "face to face."

Collective Memory and the God of History

Memories quickly fade; thus they must be recalled from year to year and generation to generation. If Israel's faith was not rooted in the past in God's great deeds in history on its behalf, Israel would lack confidence and an expectant hope for its future. The importance of historical memory was thus critical in that the past was linked to both present and future. If Israel had its beginnings in God, surely it would find its ultimate eschatological meaning in him.

Destruction, despondency, and disbelief challenged Israel throughout much of its history. Yet ultimate despair and giving up were impossibilities to those who stubbornly believed and held to the promise among the righteous remnant. Even if God was seemingly silent and his love temporarily suspended from Israel's experiences as a people, the God of Israel was *emu-*

nah, "faithful." For Israel to survive the many grave challenges it has faced throughout its history, the Jewish people and religion have had to maintain continuity but have also had to be open to innovation, adaptability, and change. The events leading to the Exodus and the revelation at Sinai were foundational to Israel's spiritual identity. Yet Israel's faith continued to be shaped and reshaped by other biblical events such as the destruction of the Temple, the Exile, and the Restoration. These events, however, were never forgotten. From Rabbinic Judaism to Modern Judaism these narratives continue to be recalled and reflected upon in Bible reading, liturgy, and various festivals and holy days.

The above is a permanent reminder that Judaism is far more event-centered than place-centered. The same is true in Christianity, which largely focuses not on specific events of corporate Israel but on key events in the life of Jesus as the one who individually personifies Israel. Accordingly, the church recalls those redemptive activities in its life of worship, liturgy, music, and the celebration of the Eucharist. Israel was reminded again and again that their God was a God of history. So too the church recalls, recites, and responds to God's acts in history through Jesus.

Israel's collective memory that recalled the past provided hope for the future. Providentially, the Lord of history was guiding his people; he did not leave them to flounder and to wonder about the meaning of history. The prophets interpreted events and gave them divine significance. Thus, within the community of faith, history was not reduced to a stark randomness of events or something perceived to be willy-nilly. There was a divine scheme that set Israel's understanding of history apart. Israel had a theological view of history; through history God's hand — though sometimes hidden — was revealed. The words of John Macmurray strikingly grasp this point: "Jewish reflection thinks of history as the act of God. Where our historians say, 'Caesar crossed the Rubicon,' or 'Nelson won the Battle of Trafalgar,' the Jewish historian says, 'God brought His people up out of the land of Egypt.'"[13]

When God Is Silent

The narrative of Israel's survival throughout the centuries testifies to the presence of the living God past, present, and future. God's presence corpo-

---

13. Quoted in Tzvi Rabinowicz, *A Guide to Life* (Northvale, NJ: Jason Aronson, 1989), p. 109.

rately among his people is a sign that nothing can ultimately frustrate God's purposes and promises established with father Abraham and his descendants. In the penetrating words of Michael Wyschogrod, "[Israel] survives the mightiest nation-states, many of which have long disappeared from history, while Israel, against all human calculation, endures. Israel is thus a living witness that the God who chose it is the Lord of history and that his purpose will be achieved."[14]

The catastrophes and absurdities of life pose one of the greatest problems for human existence. The silence of God in the face of evil often becomes the reason for the defiance of God. Revealed religion, however, assures us there is meaning beyond absurdity and calamity. In the words of Abraham Heschel, "there is a meaning beyond mystery . . . holiness conquers absurdity . . . without holiness, we will sink in absurdity."[15] Heschel challenges his readers to defy absurdity. God, not imponderable evil, must have the last word.

In the second century, under the leadership of Bar Kokhba, Jews in the land of Israel conducted their second revolt against the Romans (A.D. 132-35). Bar Kokhba had laid claim to messiahship, and Rabbi Akiba (c. A.D. 50-135), one of the great sages of the day, supported Bar Kokhba's claim. There was great expectancy that the Jewish struggle against Rome, an enslaving and idolatrous nation, would bring about the freedom of the Jewish people. Was not the same God who delivered his people from their Egyptian oppressors on their side? The second Jewish revolt failed. During the revolt, in a most excruciating type of torture, Rabbi Akiba died a martyr at the hands of the Romans.

One of Rabbi Akiba's students was Rabbi Simeon ben Yochai. Simeon was one of the Tannaim of the Mishnah, a loyal *talmid* who remained with his master to the day of his death. Simeon had studied with Rabbi Akiba for thirteen years and was acknowledged for his saintliness and for being a miracle worker.[16] Simeon was distressed by the death of Akiba and the crushing defeat of his fellow Jews by Rome. Further, Simeon was appalled at the severe persecution of Jews by Emperor Hadrian after the revolt. Simeon, in accord with traditional Jewish theology, believed that God was all-powerful and good. However, in the face of so much Jewish suffering around him,

---

14. Michael Wyschogrod, *Abraham's Promise: Judaism and Jewish-Christian Relations* (Grand Rapids: Eerdmans, 2004), p. 182.

15. Heschel, *Moral Grandeur and Spiritual Audacity*, p. 398.

16. See Gershom Bader, *The Encyclopedia of Talmudic Sages* (Northvale, NJ: Jason Aronson, 1993), pp. 352-61.

Simeon decided to vent. In a rabbinic midrash, Simeon speaks up. The rabbi is critical of God's silence and failure to intervene in behalf of his people. Accordingly, Jewish scholar Chaim Pearl labels Simeon's midrashic parable "The First Holocaust Midrash." Why? Pearl sees Simeon crying in anguish to understand the ways of God, yet God is silent.[17] A whole literature of post-Auschwitz responses among theologians, scholars, and poets, in the same vein as Simeon, appeared in the decades immediately following the infamous Holocaust years (1933-45). This perplexing issue of the goodness of God in relation to human suffering constitutes one of the great ongoing enigmas of theists. Answers are far from easy.

Scripture does not provide a final resolution to the problem of evil. At the end of the day, there is an unsolvable mystery here. Theodicy seeks to address the vindication of the ways of God in a mixed-up world. It attempts to square a theology that teaches that God is good, just, and powerful, with human experience that reveals life is not always good. In fact, sometimes life is brutalizing and indescribably evil. According to Scripture, God is a moral and just being in control of this world. From our limited human perspective, however, people possess freedom of the will whereby they may act out of control. Is God responsible for the evil perpetrated by one human being upon another? Is the question raised by the Holocaust — where was God? — a proper question to ask? Why not the question, where was man? At the end of the day, God does not always provide a satisfying answer to the Why of all human suffering. Rather, he provides himself.

Jewish theologian Michael Wyschogrod sheds some useful light on this perplexing issue. He makes the point that Israel's faith has always revolved around the great saving acts of God such as election, deliverance, revelation, the Temple, and Messiah. The focus, especially in Jewish holy days, remains on redemption. In Wyschogrod's words, "The God of Israel is a redeeming God; this is the only message we are authorized to proclaim."[18] Further, he cautions, "There is no salvation to be extracted from the Holocaust. . . . If there is hope after the Holocaust, it is because to those who believe, the voices of the Prophets speak more loudly than did Hitler, and because the divine promise sweeps over the crematoria and silences the voice of Auschwitz."[19]

Indeed, the letter of the prophet Jeremiah, directed to the exiles in

---

17. Chaim Pearl, *Theology in Rabbinic Stories* (Peabody, MA: Hendrickson, 1997), pp. 64-65.

18. Michael Wyschogrod, *Abraham's Promise* (Grand Rapids: Eerdmans, 2004), p. 119.

19. Wyschogrod, *Abraham's Promise*, p. 120.

Babylon just before Jerusalem fell, brought encouragement and hope: " 'For I know the plans I have for you,' declares the LORD, 'plans to prosper you and not to harm you, plans to give you hope *(tiqvah)* and a future'" (Jer. 29:11). According to Scripture, not despair but optimism ultimately wins. In biblical theology, God, not Auschwitz, holds the last word.

UNDERSTANDING CHAPTER TWELVE

1. What creative play on words did the narrator of Genesis 32:22-32 employ? Briefly sum up what transpired in this narrative. What are the only other four instances in the Old Testament in which God is said to encounter humanity "face to face"? Where is Peniel? (Consult a map.) How is the meaning of this place name an important reminder to future generations of the uniqueness of Israel's beginnings and calling?

2. Which Hebrew term is often used to denote the mysterious manifestations of God during the time of the patriarchs and Moses? What is the English translation? What is the Hebrew word for "blessing"? What sense does it carry?

3. In the ancient world, how were words more than "haphazard verbiage"? Does this enhance your understanding of why Jacob desired blessing in his struggle at the Jabbok? Review Genesis 32:22-32. How was Jacob's change of name illustrative of his blessing through the event that had just transpired?

4. How is the Hebrew word for blessing probably connected to the similar word *berekh,* "knee"? What is the phrase "bending the knee" a reminder of? How is reciprocity a part of blessing, and what does the author mean by stating that we "are blessed to be a blessing"?

5. What did Jacob's name change signify? In what sense does J. H. Hertz understand the new title to be "larger than Jacob"? Historically, how has Israel's struggle with God proven to be a positive character trait of the Jewish people as well as an assuring word of promise and hope?

6. How do Jews have much to teach Christians about God-wrestling? What did Philo suggest about the meaning of Jacob's new name, "Israel"? What truth did Elie Wiesel point out that Jacob gained understanding of as a result of his experience at the Jabbok?

7. What kind of connotations does piety often have in the modern world? In contrast, what connotations did it have in the patriarchal narratives? How do Elie Wiesel's and Abraham Heschel's observations about piety

offer a renewed understanding of piety, especially as it relates to Jacob at the Jabbok? Prior to reading this chapter, how would you or someone from your church have defined a "pious" person? In your view, should piety be a trait of every Christian?

8. Read Exodus 3:6 and note the number of times God's name appears in the text. While a modern reader may perceive this as mere redundancy, how did the rabbis view it very insightfully? Review Pinchas Lapide's quote on page 231 and explain how each patriarch experienced God uniquely. Lapide writes that "[t]he prophets warn us repeatedly about the manufacturing of the images of God" (see Isa. 40:18). How is this exhortation significant both on an individual level and for a corporate body of believers? What are the two sides of the "coin of faith" that the author makes reference to?

9. In light of the truth that part of being human is struggling for meaningful answers, how does Abraham Heschel say the greatness of a person may be measured? Review Isaiah 1:18. What does the Hebrew verb *yakhah,* used in this verse, mean? How is this illustrative of the fact that God welcomes his people to "argue things out" with him?

10. How can we, as believers today, struggle or wrestle with God just as Jacob did? Do you tend to view such a struggle negatively or positively? Why? What notable connection exists between Jacob's words in Genesis 32:30 and the words God speaks to Moses in Exodus 33:14? What is the author's position in the broader conversation about "wrestling with God"?

11. How is Israel's relationship with God in the Bible helpful to review when considering what questioning and disagreeing with God can look like? How is a positive marriage a good framework of thought for exploring what it means to have security with and commitment to God, yet retain the freedom to question? How do traditional Jewish and Christian contexts often contrast in the way they approach the idea of questioning God?

12. Which serious historical misfortunes — either practiced or tolerated by people who identified with Christianity — does the author assert could have been modified or avoided if serious questioning had taken place sooner? Are there situations today that you think some "serious questioning" could have prevented or could be instrumental in improving?

13. Some of the greatest figures of Scripture questioned God. Briefly explain how Abraham, Moses, Job, Jeremiah, Malachi, Habakkuk, and Jonah serve as examples of "biblical precedence" for believers today

who would sincerely question. Are all of their questions admirable to you? Why or why not? Do any of the incidences leave you with more questions?

14. How does Paul provide reassurance of a future day in which believers will indeed see "face to face" (see 1 Cor. 13:12)? What allusions does Paul make by using such a phrase?

15. Sometimes the questions we present to God appear to remain unanswered. From a Christian perspective, is it comforting to you to ponder the fact that Jesus also experienced the pain of God's "silence" (see Matt. 27:46; Mark 15:34)?

16. How was the concept of historical memory critical to Israel? What are some of the major events throughout Israel's history that shaped her? How did — and do — these events continue to "live on" as a part of Israel's identity? Do you think that the church — particularly the Protestant church in the West — might benefit from and strengthen her relationship with God by gaining a deeper sense of church history?

17. Review Michael Wyschogrod's quote on page 238; in what way does Israel function as a "living witness" that her God is the Lord of history and his purposes will be achieved?

18. What does the "silence of God" in the face of evil often lead to? Review the author's discussion of the second Jewish revolt. Who was Bar Kokhba, who was Rabbi Akiba, and what was the end result of the revolt? How did Rabbi Simeon ben Yochai, one of Rabbi Akiba's students, handle this reality? How does Chaim Pearl label one of Rabbi Simeon's midrashic parables? In your opinion, do humans ever have the right to accuse God of failure? Why or why not?

19. The author acknowledges that, from our human perspective, God does not always provide a satisfying answer to the question Why? when it comes to evil and suffering in the world. What does the author state that God *does* provide, however? For additional research and/or discussion: How does the literature generated in the post-Holocaust years contribute to the wider conversation about theodicy? On a personal level, does it help you come to any conclusions about the matter?

20. What is the only message that Michael Wyschogrod states Israel is authorized to proclaim? What is the reasoning behind his statement?

PART V

Moving into the Future

CHAPTER 13

Has the Church Superseded Israel?

In this post-Holocaust era, I believe one of the positive things that has emerged is an attempt by the church to engage in some serious soul-searching and self-criticism. While I do not believe one can draw a direct line from the pages of the New Testament to Auschwitz, the way was certainly paved by hundreds of years of a history of contempt. Instead of a spirit of indebtedness and appreciation to the Jewish people for its biblical heritage, a spirit of apathy, indifference, and hostility characterized the church's attitude toward the Jews. Centuries of anti-Judaism and malicious stereotypes were allowed to fester and go unchallenged, providing an ethos within which Hitler's targeting of the Jewish people for extermination was made possible. Memory of the Holocaust and the overwhelmingly negative history of the Jewish-Christian encounter that led to the Holocaust is vastly important for our generation. Indeed, as the Yad Vashem Holocaust Memorial in Jerusalem boldly states, "In remembrance, there is hope."

The Teaching of Supersessionism

A spirit of triumphalism and arrogance on the part of the church has largely characterized most of the history of Christian-Jewish relations. Irving Greenberg explains: "Christians concluded that the Jews had to be spiritually deaf and dumb or willfully devilish to resist Christian understandings. From this conclusion it was not a big jump to medieval Christianity's demonizing and dehumanizing of the Jews and, from there, to the Holocaust. Thus a gospel of love — which often acted that way among Gentiles — turned into a sermon of hatred."[1] This long history of contempt culminating in the Holocaust is one of the darkest chapters of history. It is all the more painful with the realization that a religious body, a so-called "people of love," would foster hatred and largely remain indifferent, apathetic, and uncaring during this catastrophic event.

For much of its history, Judaism has had to deal with the claim that Christianity has superseded it. The term "to supersede" derives from two Latin words (*super* and *sedere*), literally "to sit upon" or "sit over." Hence, to "supersede" implies an action whereby "one person takes a seat that has been vacated by another, thus preventing that person from sitting there again."[2] One religion, Christianity, permanently displaces the other, Judaism. By sitting in the place of the other, supersessionism "absolutizes" the superseding religion, raising it to the "level of ultimacy."[3] Certainly, the story of Christian-Jewish relations reveals supersessionism as a phenomenon that is obstinate and intractable.

If supersessionism is the will of God, then the logical conclusion of such teaching is to call for the removal of the Jewish people and their distinct religious identity from the face of the earth. Thus, to "supersede" another may be dangerous when acted on; it allows no legitimate place for the other. We must point out, however, that it is not necessarily supersessionism to believe differently from one's co-religionists. For example, classic Christian belief upholds the teaching that Jesus loves the whole world and would desire everyone to come to know his grace, power, and forgiveness. To hold such a belief is not supersessionism, for it is a fundamental tenet of New Testament teaching, a *sine qua non* of New Testament theology. Such a historic Christian distinctive can be turned into a form of supersessionism, however, if a Christian attempts to denigrate a Jewish person by saying that he has no theological validity in the eyes of God and that all Jewish vocation ceased with the birth of the church. Such a Christian may hold to the above belief and then feel compelled to impose his view on the other. Thus a careful distinction must be made. For a Christian to hold that the Messiah has come and the gospel is real is not supersessionism. However, a Christian who takes this personal belief and specifically uses it to target, deceive, or coerce another to his point of view is unworthy of the name Christian.

---

1. Irving Greenberg, *For the Sake of Heaven and Earth: The New Encounter between Judaism and Christianity* (Philadelphia: Jewish Publication Society, 2004), p. 224.

2. Clark M. Williamson, quoted in Michael Shermis and Arthur E. Zannoni, eds., *Introduction to Jewish-Christian Relations* (Mahwah, NJ: Paulist Press, 1991), p. 26.

3. See Clark M. Williamson, *Has God Rejected His People?* (Nashville: Abingdon, 1991), pp. 90-91.

Supersessionist teaching was very pervasive during the patristic period, and it began to inflict great pain and misery upon the Jewish people. For example, the *Epistle of Barnabas* illustrates this "replacement theology," a feature of early *adversus Judaeos* literature. Barnabas declares that just as the Scriptures belong to the Christians, so too does the covenant. The epistle instructs its readers not to "heap up your sins and say that the covenant is both theirs and ours. It is *ours*" (*Epistle of Barnabas* 4:6-8).[4] If not held in check by other forces to counter such arrogant and destructive language, bad theology eventually leads to bad sociology. Sadly, the negative teaching during the early centuries of the church was to have dire consequences for centuries to come. It is one thing to be a "guest" in another's house; it is another thing to "evict" the owner and lay claim to his title deed.

According to Rabbi Gilbert Rosenthal, in starkest terms triumphalist doctrine has taught that "[t]he New Israel has superseded the Old; God has replaced the Old Testament with the New; the chosen people is now the Church. The national election of Israel has been replaced by the individual election to eternal life without regard to people, race or station. God has substituted the election of a faith community for the choice of a nation or people."[5] For the position of supersessionism, it is all too easy to give attention to but one side of the argument. In my understanding, each point of the triumphalist doctrine above has a complexity to it and thus needs discussion, analysis, and qualification based on a fair and open reading of all the biblical data. However, it is not in my purview to do so here as I have commented on most of these themes elsewhere in this chapter, in this volume, or in earlier publications.

Divine Covenant and Supersessionism

If one takes a historical look at the question of exclusivity and supersessionism, Christianity was not the only group to make such claims. Oxford scholar Geza Vermes points out a parallel between the Jewish community at Qumran and Christianity in seeing itself as the *true Israel*: "Each group believed in its own absolute and exclusive election; they alone formed the community

---

4. Also see Edward Kessler, *Bound by the Bible* (Cambridge: Cambridge University Press, 2004), p. 19.

5. Gilbert S. Rosenthal, *What Can a Modern Jew Believe?* (Eugene, OR: Wipf & Stock, 2007), p. 74.

of God's chosen. Each group was certain that it was the legitimate heir to all the divine promises made to the historical Israel, and that it, and it alone, was the participant of a new Covenant. The Qumran community describes itself as a 'house of truth.'"[6]

In Romans 9–11, Paul gives grave warnings to Gentile believers concerning arrogance, boastfulness, and exclusivity. The Gentile church has not replaced or displaced ethnic Israel in God's plan of world redemption. The failure of the church to heed these warnings has led to supersessionist theologies that have inflicted great pain on the Jewish community. Some scholars such as Rosemary Ruether and Roy Eckardt have spoken out against Christological confessions and creeds that seem to promote a sinful Christian triumphalism and a feeding into anti-Judaism and replacement theologies. In this regard, Christian theologian Isaac Rottenberg raised for the church an important question that it must return to again and again: "Can we proclaim a triumphant gospel without, in the process, producing a triumphalistic church?"[7] Must these two, of necessity, always go together?

While certainly difficult to do, there are sensitive post-Holocaust Christians who believe Christian distinctives can be upheld without a repulsive supersessionist spirit. A careful reading of Romans 9–11, which informs such thinking, reveals a type of paradox. God's covenant with Israel is irrevocable. Paul says, "to them [Israel] *are* [Greek, *eisin*, present tense] the covenants" (Rom. 9:4; see also 11:1, 16-18). The language about God's hardening of Israel is not the negation of their election (see Rom. 9:18). It seems that Paul is able to "hold in tension two realities that appear on the surface to be contradictory, namely, hardening and election."[8] In the above connection, the church must ask, "Does God break covenant with one to fulfill a promise with another?"[9] I think not. God does not renege on promises (see 1 Sam. 15:29).

Karl Barth, the great twentieth-century Swiss Protestant theologian, clearly emphasized the permanency of Israel's election. Barth wrote,

> Without any doubt the Jews are to this very day the chosen people of God in the same sense as they have been so from the beginning, according to the Old and New Testaments. They have the promise of God; and

6. Geza Vermes, *Jesus and the World of Judaism* (Philadelphia: Fortress Press, 1983), p. 117.

7. Isaac C. Rottenberg, *Christian-Jewish Dialogue: Exploring Our Commonalities and Our Differences* (Atlanta: Hebraic Heritage Press, 2005), pp. 103, 117.

8. David E. Holwerda, *Jesus and Israel* (Grand Rapids: Eerdmans, 1995), p. 166.

9. Brad Young, *Paul the Jewish Theologian* (Peabody, MA: Hendrickson, 1997), p. 139.

if we Christians from among the gentiles have it too, then it is only as those chosen with them; as guests in their house, as new wood grafted onto their old tree.[10]

In a similar vein, Jürgen Moltmann comments on Israel by noting that the plan and purposes of God for this world are incomplete without the inclusion of Israel:

> Ultimately, the ecumenical movement and ecumenical thinking always come back to the first schism, the one from which non-Jewish Christianity developed, i.e., the separation of the Church and Israel. This is where schismatic thinking began, and this is where it must finally end. In Jesus Christ, the Jew, it is not only the true God and the true man who looks at us non-Jewish Christians, but also Israel. Through him, we perceive Israel and are linked with Israel, because, through him, the promises of the God of Abraham, Isaac and Jacob come down to us; the ecumenical movement will not find its completion without Israel.[11]

In Moltmann's view, not only is the past history of Israel important, but the future of Israel is likewise crucial and indispensable to the program of God. Moltmann further emphasizes that if Christians do not grasp the significance of "Jesus Christ the Jew," they will miss their connection to the people of Israel from whom he came. Accordingly, a study of the Jewishness of Jesus must remain a priority of every knowledgeable Christian.

In addition to the need to reaffirm God's ongoing covenant with Israel, both Christians and Jews need to recognize how, at certain points in history, new claims to revelation created major challenges and resulted in differing responses. Most of these claims were radical; they vied for the modification, enlargement, or even displacement of previous teachings. For example, Abram received a revelation that caused him to break away from the idolatry of Ur. Moses and the prophets expanded their understanding of the one true God into an ethical monotheism. In the coming of Jesus, the New Testament proclaims a new revelation about Jesus centered on his teachings and the apostolic commentary on his death, resurrection, and ascension. Six centu-

---

10. Karl Barth, "The Jewish Problem and the Christian Answer," in *Against the Stream* (London: SCM, 1954), p. 200.

11. Jürgen Moltmann, address to the Faith and Order Conference in Lausanne, Switzerland, Pentecost Sunday, 1977, quoted in Rottenberg, *Christian-Jewish Dialogue*, p. 146.

ries later, Islam is born. This religion announces to the world a new prophet, Muhammad, and a new revelation, the Qur'an. Such religious developments point to a most probing fundamental question raised by David Klinghoffer: "Is religion important because it is useful? Or is religion important because it is true?" Says Klinghoffer, "We are confronted here with the choice between the instrumentalist theory of faith, and the truth theory. Is religion about man, or is it about God?"[12] Klinghoffer's question reminds us that, at the end of the day, the religion and calling of Israel have their origin either in the eternal council of God or in the changeable theories of man. If the permanence of Israel's election is in doubt, the trustworthiness of God's Word is likewise in doubt (Gen. 17:7; Deut. 7:7-9; 2 Sam. 7:24; Jer. 31:35-36).

Absolutes, Mystery, and Eschatology

In my view, it is grossly simplistic to attempt to reduce religion to such an either/or choice. But it does raise the issue of how competing theological absolutes and ideologies relate to supersessionism. Certainly, interfaith discussion should not move on reductionist impulses. As Geoffrey Widoger has pointed out, "Dialogue can discover but not reconcile fundamental theological differences."[13] One perspective, that of W. C. Smith, has argued that Christianity has been "idolatrous." Smith says, "Christians have equated their religion with God by making that religion final or absolute. Christianity itself has become the idol rather than the object of Christianity."[14] Irving Greenberg, however, offers a different point of view. He wisely argues for the need to keep absolute claims in check by "setting healthy limits on absolutes, valid or otherwise."[15] In agreement, Krister Stendahl notes, "There is an analogy between God's limiting his absolute power by respecting human freedom for purpose of a higher perfection and the need for 'healthy limits' to even valid absolute claims."[16]

12. David Klinghoffer, "God Is Not a Pluralist," in *The Role of Religion in Politics and Society*, ed. Harold Heie, A. James Rudin, and Marvin R. Wilson (New York: American Jewish Committee), p. 84.

13. Geoffrey Widoger, "Ecumenism," in *Contemporary Jewish Religious Thought*, ed. Arthur A. Cohen and Paul Mendes-Flohr (New York: Free Press, 1987), p. 152.

14. Quoted in E. David Cook, "Truth, Mystery and Justice," in *One God, One Lord in a World of Religious Pluralism* (Cambridge: Tyndale House, 1991), p. 185.

15. See Greenberg, *For the Sake of Heaven and Earth*, p. 265.

16. Stendahl, in Greenberg, *For the Sake of Heaven and Earth*, p. 265.

If Christians speak with conviction about a divine Redeemer who rose from the dead, such teaching may appear supersessionist to those outside the Christian community. Each faith community, however, understands and speaks with conviction and contrast — especially in the perception of those outside their community — concerning aspects of its own religious experiences. For example, during the Maccabean revolt, many Jews were thought obstinate by their Greek oppressors for having the conviction to hold on to their Torah scrolls and to practice circumcision, the mark of the covenant, even if it meant death by martyrdom. Concerning the relation between Jews and Christians, the teaching of Christians about the finality of redemption in Christ has sometimes led to conflict between Jews and Christians. In this connection, I believe Martin Buber was correct in stating that therein lies the "gulf which no human power can bridge . . . but we can wait for the advent of the One together, and there are moments when we may prepare the way before him together."[17]

It is a truism that much interfaith dialogue is nothing more than polite shadow-boxing rather than a sincere mutual quest for truth. Indeed, if dialogue is to be serious, more than a lesson in civility and politeness, participants must be willing to risk something. This side of the life to come, one must acknowledge that we have partial answers; mystery beclouds our search for full understanding of truth. As Christian scholar Amos Yong has observed, "Our finite minds do not know [God's] truth exhaustively. If all truth is God's truth, we can be open to learning from and being transformed . . . through open relationships with those in other faiths, rather than continue to foster fear of religious others."[18] There is a wideness in God's mercy that allows Christians to engage others with respect and reverence. It is not a Christian responsibility to resolve all differences or to impose the Christian faith on others. The anti-Semitic hatred and violence seen in the Crusades, the Inquisition, and the Holocaust are not expressions of Christianity. To be sure, especially in the Shoah, all manner of indescribable evil was perpetrated by many within the institutional church or those outwardly affiliated with it. Such horrendous and despicable actions, however, were a gross aberration or distortion of the Christian faith, not a valid expression of it.

In this twenty-first century, is there an "acid test" of Christian super-

---

17. Martin Buber, "The Two Foci of the Jewish Soul," quoted in *Disputation and Dialogue*, ed. Frank E. Talmage (New York: Ktav, 1975), p. 282.

18. Amos Yong, "Significant Turns in Contemporary Theology of Religions," *Theology News and Notes* (Fuller Theological Seminary) (Winter 2005): 22.

sessionism? I am intrigued with the position of Jewish scholar Michael Wy-schogrod that the Christology of the church need not entail or imply the replacement of God's promises to Israel. Rather, if there is an "acid test" — and in this, I think Wyschogrod is largely correct — it appears in the church's conduct toward Jews in their midst. According to Wyschogrod, "through faith in Christ gentiles become — not Jews — but associate members of Israel's covenant," joining Israel as adopted sons and daughters in the household of God.[19]

The teaching of Gentile believers "grafted into Israel" and being part of the spiritual "seed of Abraham" is an important piece of Paul's theology (see Rom. 11:11-24; Gal. 3:29). However, in contrast to Wyschogrod's use of the term "adoption," Christians usually view adoption differently, certainly not as "associate members" in the covenant, an expression that could imply secondary status. Rather, in keeping with New Testament usage, adoption designates the spiritual status of "sonship" granted through the Spirit to believers as they join the family of God through faith and become his spiritual children, thus enabling them to address him as "*Abba*, Father" (Rom. 8:15).

Dialogue and Theological Impasse

If conduct toward one another rather than lack of theological agreement is one of the real tests of supersessionism, then supersessionism seems very much rooted in attitude as well as action. Triumphalism often derives from a spirit of arrogance rather than humility. Christian witness and conversation with any people is always to be conducted in the spirit of "one beggar telling another where they have found bread." While historic Christianity has always had a universal witness to faith, it is never an individual Christian's prerogative to judge others as to the sincerity or validity of their relation with God, or to pronounce who is truly "righteous" in God's eyes and who is not. At the dialogue table, each individual has the right to share respectfully with others his personal story of faith, connecting it — if so desired — to any relevant sacred texts.

Interreligious conversation is not a place for angrily venting one's frustrations or blaming others for "damage" done by a particular faith or its adherents. It is also not a platform to exploit one's neighbor in order to promote

19. Michael Wyschogrod, *Abraham's Promise: Judaism and Christian-Jewish Relations* (Grand Rapids: Eerdmans, 2004), pp. 15-18, 236.

one's own religious agenda. Dialogue is not a setting to abolish one's enemy by making truth claims arrogantly. It is no place for seeking greatness for oneself. Further, interfaith conversation is not to convert one's partner from one faith tradition to another. Conversion is the work of God, not of human beings. In addition, the purpose of interreligious dialogue is not the seeking of reconciliation through theological compromise. Authentic dialogue is not to melt down Judaism and Christianity to their lowest common denominators. Genuine dialogue does not call for the building of some symbiotic world religion through the cross-fertilization of Judaism and Christianity. While possessing many similarities, each faith is different. The object of interfaith is not the homogenization of belief or the elimination of distinctives.

Rather, dialogue is an invitation to learn, to enhance personal growth and understanding through a mutual search for truth. No one has all the answers. Interfaith provides a context to broaden and enrich one's spiritual capacity without need to relinquish the uniqueness of one's core values and commitments. Conversation with the other provides a context to examine commonalities and subtle differences. It allows us to see something in the other that is beautiful and that tells us about God, his creation, or his will. That something is what Krister Stendahl has described as "holy envy," an opportunity to learn something new, to respect the other person and to celebrate the differences.[20]

Supersessionism and the Future of Church and Synagogue

Clearly, the New Testament sounds a strong messianic note: in the view of the early church, a new era has already begun; in Jesus is the establishment of a spiritual kingdom. On a theological level, this creates an impasse or tension between Christians and Jews. But on a more practical level, this teaching need not be a barrier that divides. Again, I return to the importance of Wyschogrod's point about attitude and conduct. If Christians and Jews experience disagreement, it is more likely *how* we look at our differences rather than the fact that we *have* differences; it is demeanor, not simply dogma; it is learning to disagree without being disagreeable; it is often more the person than the perspective.

We may not fully resolve differences; only the Spirit of God can do that

20. Krister Stendahl, study guide to the public television documentary, *Jews and Christians: A Journey of Faith*, ed. Marvin R. Wilson (Potomac, MD: Auteur Productions, 2000), p. 40.

in his gracious timing and way. None of us fully knows the details of what God has in store for Jew and non-Jew in the time to come. We both agree on a future redeemed society, but we have a theological impasse on how God will fully bring this about. However, in the meantime, we can learn to live respectfully with differences; we must be careful about using the label "triumphalist" for someone who possesses a "peacemaker's spirit," yet whose views may not be the same as ours.

For most Christians, theological truth matters, not simply the mantra, "Why can't we all just get along?" Christians can respect Judaism and the right of the Jewish people to live in peace within their ancient homeland. Certain tensions between Jews and Christians are probably not going to be fully resolved until the *olam ha-ba,* "the age to come." So we must learn to befriend and respect each other now, to cooperate as far as we can and still maintain the integrity of our own individual religious commitments. As for the Christian community, it needs to have a greater appreciation of the presence of God in practical deeds, not taking a glib satisfaction in the mouthing of theological creeds. A theology not applied with justice, compassion, and humaneness runs the risk of invalidating itself. Eschatological certitude must never trump justice; our perception of the future should not provide *carte blanche* endorsement of any obvious act of injustice.

Within our respective canons of Scripture, we cannot change sacred texts that are difficult to the ears of the other. However, what we teach about those texts in relation to the other can make a significant difference. In addition, Christians must examine their hermeneutic or principle of interpretation. I would contend that any hermeneutic that starts with the New Testament rather than the Jewish Scriptures potentially minimizes the importance of Judaism and may result in spiritualizing Israel right out of this flesh-and-blood world.

I believe Israel, a religious people, does have a future in the covenantal history of God. According to Paul, the destiny of Jew and Gentile is mysteriously, inextricably intertwined in the plan of God. Despite human failures and flaws, God's covenant with Israel is irrevocable (Rom. 11:28-32). The church has not displaced or permanently superseded Israel. To be sure, mercy and riches continue to flow to the Gentile because of the Jew (Rom. 11:11, 12).

God's ways, though often mysterious, are right and just. It is not for us to understand divine mystery, but to rejoice in God's covenantal faithfulness. God is not fickle; he is consistent, and his Word is trustworthy. He does not break covenant with one in order to fulfill a commitment to another.[21]

---

21. Young, *Paul the Jewish Theologian,* p. 139.

UNDERSTANDING CHAPTER THIRTEEN

1. What positive aspect of the church's life does the author point out emerged in the post-Holocaust years? While there is no direct line between the New Testament and the Holocaust, how did the history between the two contribute to the situation that gave birth to such an atrocity?

2. What kind of spirit has largely characterized the history of Christian-Jewish relations? How does Irving Greenberg very briefly review the development of this relationship throughout history?

3. What is the etymology of the word "supersede," and what literal sense does it carry? What is supersessionism, and how has Judaism been burdened by it? What is the danger of supersessionism? From a Christian perspective, had you previously given much thought to this aspect of Jewish-Christian relations? Why or why not?

4. In what period of the church's development was supersessionist thinking particularly pervasive? Which literary example of such "replacement theology" does the author cite, and what does it state? How does bad theology eventually lead to bad sociology?

5. Which other community during the time of the church's birth saw itself as the *true Israel*? How did the claims of Christianity and this group mirror one another? What warnings does Paul give to the Roman church in Romans 9–11, and what were the consequences of failing to heed these warnings?

6. Which pivotal question does Isaac Rottenberg raise concerning "triumphalism"? How does the author, citing support from Paul, respond? Review the insightful statements of Karl Barth and Jürgen Moltmann that lend similar commentary to the issue. In what way do both theologians illustrate the enduring vocation and unique honor of the Jewish people? Why must the study of the Jewishness of Jesus be a priority for every knowledgeable Christian?

7. From the time of Abraham forward, how did new claims to revelation create challenges and prompt differing responses? How is David Klinghoffer's question, "Is religion about man, or is it about God?" representative of the larger debate about revelation and truth?

8. Reflect on Geoffrey Widoger's statement that "[d]ialogue can discover but not reconcile fundamental theological differences." Do you agree? In your opinion, what is the ultimate purpose of interfaith or ecumenical dialogue?

9. How do you understand Irving Greenberg and Krister Stendahl's concept of "healthy limits" on absolutes? What is the purpose of such limits?

10. What central Christian teaching has led to disagreement and sometimes conflict between Jews and Christians? How did Martin Buber wisely describe both the challenge and opportunity presented by such a difference?

11. The author states that if ecumenical dialogue is to be serious, what must the participants be willing to do? Do you agree? How do you respond to Amos Yong's statement that "[i]f all truth is God's truth, we can be open to learning from and being transformed . . . through open relationships with those in other faiths"?

12. Citing Michael Wyschogrod, what acid test does the author suggest is useful for measuring supersessionism in the church today? What is it about *conduct* that is so critical and so telling? From a Christian perspective, what does it mean to be an adopted son or daughter in the household of God? Why might many Christians prefer to speak of themselves as adopted sons and daughters of God rather than "associate members" of the covenant?

13. Reflect on the statement that Christian witness and conversation with any people should always be conducted in the spirit of "one beggar telling another where they have found bread." Consider this in light of the first Beatitude (see Matt. 5:3). How is humility absolutely critical to the Christian life? For additional discussion: In what way should humility extend beyond ecumenical dialogue and into the sphere of Christian missions?

14. Briefly sum up the author's review of what interreligious conversation is *not* for. In contrast, what *is* such dialogue for? How would you personally describe the purpose of interreligious dialogue? Building upon Krister Stendahl's point, have you ever experienced a form of "holy envy" in the context of interfaith relations? Explain. For further discussion: How does Paul use the concept of envy in Romans 10:19?

15. The author states that Christian and Jewish disagreement more likely stems from what, rather than the simple fact that there are differences? What must we each be willing to admit about the resolving of such differences?

16. Reflect on the author's statement that "[a] theology not applied with justice, compassion, and humaneness runs the risk of invalidating itself." In your opinion, are there areas in which particular expressions

of contemporary Christianity need to reevaluate themselves in light of this powerful truism? Discuss with a partner or group.

17. The author contends that any hermeneutic that starts with the New Testament rather than the Jewish Scriptures has the potential to minimize the importance of Judaism. How do you respond to this assertion? In your opinion, does the church have the option to pursue a deeper understanding of the Jewish Scriptures (especially as a "starting point" for biblical interpretation), or does it have the *responsibility* to do so? Why?

18. What thoughts does the author provide in connection with his belief that Israel, a religious people, does have a future in the covenantal history of God? How does Paul's Letter to the Romans emphasize the mystery of God's redemptive work through both Jew and Gentile? Optional: Read Romans 9–11, paying special attention to the theme of *covenant* throughout. What conclusions about Christian-Jewish relations, if any, do you personally reach in reading this passage? What additional questions come to mind?

CHAPTER 14

Study of Scripture: Preserving the Flame

Scripture Study and the Rabbis

In ancient Israel, the priests and Levites were the educational backbone of community life. While the prophets and sages also had an important instructional role within society, the priests were the primary teachers of the law (Jer. 18:18). The heads of Israelite families learned the traditions of Israel as they were passed on from generation to generation within their respective clan. In addition, however, forty-eight Levitical cities, scattered throughout the land, served as teaching hubs within each tribal territory (Joshua 21).

After the Temple in Jerusalem was destroyed in the year 70, a major restructuring and reformulation of Judaism began to take place. The priesthood, a hereditary institution dating back to the time of Moses, became defunct. Individuals, within their own family units, became the "new priests." Torah study, deeds of loving kindness, and an emphasis on personal sacrifice rather than animal sacrifice became hallmarks of the new system. Instead of daily offerings in the Temple, offerings of praise from the lips of Israel ascended to the divine throne (see Dan. 6:10; Rev. 5:8; 8:3). In short, the rituals of the Temple were now relegated to the home. Lacking a central sanctuary and increasingly scattered among the nations, a reconstituted holy people — a lay kingdom of priests — emerged (see Exod. 19:6). The holy of holies would be in the sanctuary of the home and holiness diffused throughout the community by a life of sacred deeds.[1]

---

1. See Jacob Neusner, *An Introduction to Judaism* (Louisville: Westminster/John Knox, 1991), pp. 161-62.

A Supreme Commandment

One of the most important dimensions in the Hebraic heritage of Christianity is the necessity to cultivate the spiritual life through personal study of sacred texts. Spiritual growth was not to happen by proxy; no one was authorized to become the community virtuoso in spiritual matters so as to relieve others of that obligation. One's love for God was expressed by constant study of the commandments, "when you lie down and when you get up" (Deut. 6:7). No one was exempt from study of Torah, not even a king of Israel: "When he takes the throne of his kingdom, he is to write for himself on a scroll a copy of this law. . . . It is to be with him, and he is to read it all the days of his life so that he may learn to revere the LORD his God and follow carefully all the words of this law and these decrees" (Deut. 17:18-19).

Knowledge of the Scriptures was not an inheritance to receive passively, but a challenge to accept and win. The Bible has many layers of meaning to uncover and explore. Hence Jews saw this relationship to the Bible as a spiritual duty. In Jewish tradition, "it became a supreme commandment to 'study,' to explore the Scriptures."[2] This task was passed from generation to generation as Israel realized that her divinely imparted mission was to preserve the prophetic Word: " 'My words that I have put in your mouth will not depart from your mouth, or from the mouths of your children, or from the mouths of their descendants from this time on and forever,' says the LORD" (Isa. 59:21).

Why was study so important? One of the basic issues of theology is the question of how we know God. Judaism answered that question by teaching that one meets God and communes with him when studying Torah. In its narrowest definition Torah is the Five Books of Moses; but its meaning is also often extended to include the study of a wide range of related religious texts. The study of Torah is where God speaks. In the words of Jacob Neusner, "God is present when Israel takes up study of the Torah. . . . In study of the Torah, Israelites return to Sinai and replicate the encounter and make it their own."[3] This is Sinai revisited. Students of Scripture hear the word anew and vicariously take that word to themselves. In reflecting upon the heritage of Israel's Scripture, in meeting God, students are renewed in God's

---

2. Leo Baeck, *The Essence of Judaism* (New York: Schocken, 1948), p. 25.

3. Jacob Neusner, *Questions and Answers: Intellectual Foundations of Judaism* (Peabody, MA: Hendrickson, 2005), p. 31.

love and hear afresh the details of God's plan for justice and righteousness upon this earth.

Through the memorization of Torah and the constant repetition of its teachings, it was believed that Torah study imparted "supernatural power," allowing a "person of Torah" to do things an ordinary person could not do.[4] While the memorization and repetition of Torah was never given to be a type of "mantra" guaranteeing the learner supernatural abilities, the Tanakh is clear that God's Word is powerful when it goes forth and does not return to him empty (see Isa. 55:11). Perhaps the New Testament equivalent for this belief in the dynamic Word of God is found in Hebrews 4:12: "For the word of God is living and active. Sharper than any double-edged sword, it penetrates even to dividing soul and spirit, joints and marrow; it judges the thoughts and attitudes of the heart."

Not just in internalizing Torah did one come to know God through meditation on his ways. At least weekly, Israel was expected to ponder anew the power, wisdom, and grandeur of the Creator through his mysterious works of creation (Exod. 20:8-11). Creation was "God's other book" (see Job 38; 39). Through the wonders and marvels of his created order, he speaks (Ps. 19:1-4).

Studying "for Its Own Sake"

Toward the end of the first century, Rabbi Johanan ben Zakkai founded the academy *(bet midrash)* at Yavneh, west of Jerusalem. Regarding Torah, this important sage said, "If you have accomplished much in the study of the Torah do not take pride on that account, for it was to that end that you were created."[5] In short, the study of Torah was to be done *Lishmah*, "for its own sake." This was the Jewish ideal. In the words of Solomon Schechter, "The notion of *Lishmah* excluded even the intention of fulfilling a law with the hope of getting such rewards as are promised by the Scriptures.... Love pure and simple is the only worthy motive of the worshipper."[6] Accordingly, the Mishnah urges, "Be not like servants that serve their master with the view to receive reward" (Abot 1:3). One should seek to serve one's Master out of

---

4. Neusner, *An Introduction to Judaism*, p. 203.

5. Quoted in Jacob Neusner, *The Way of Torah*, 5th ed. (Belmont, CA: Wadsworth, 1993), p. 114.

6. Solomon Schechter, *Aspects of Rabbinic Theology* (New York: Schocken, 1961), p. 162.

delight, not dread; study of Scripture should be out of love and honest devotion, not necessity or compulsion.

Biblical Christianity seeks to balance the above emphasis on freely giving out of love as motivation for performance of good works with that of personal accountability. In the parable of the talents, Jesus commends the "good and faithful" servant for his work ethic and also asks that he share in his master's happiness and accept additional responsibilities (Matt. 25:21). The New Testament emphasizes divine reward for faithful service — not worthiness in regard to personal salvation — in the life to come (2 Cor. 5:10).

The rabbis debated whether study or deeds are greater. "Rabbi Tarfon said, 'Deeds are greater.' Rabbi Akiba said 'Study is greater.' All of them [the sages present] said, 'Study is greater for it leads to deeds'" (Kiddushin 40b). Joseph Telushkin points out several benefits that come from studying sacred texts: study enables us to acquire wisdom, study provides us with models of righteous behavior, study teaches us how to act ethically, and study gives us strength to resist temptation.[7]

One scholar has wisely stated, "Theology is not an intellectual parlor game but the articulation of a prior commitment. Observance of the commandments is an expression of that commitment. The Jewish theologian is not only obliged to *do* what he or she *believes,* but to *believe* what he or she *does.*"[8] The Talmud teaches, "The purpose of wisdom is to bring about repentance and good deeds" (Berakhot 17a). Hebraic heritage is grounded in an "action-faith." The commandment of God is "very near" *(qarob me'od),* namely, "it is in your mouth and in your heart so you may obey it" (Deut. 30:14). With the internalization of truth, "to know" is "to do."

"Turning It Over Again"

According to the sages, study of Torah is far from completing a "been there, done that" routine or accomplishing a once-and-done assignment. Rather, they insisted, "Make your study of Torah a fixed, habitual activity" (Abot 1:15). Study is a life calling; it requires a persistent examination of Scripture, wrestling with the text to find new insights. The treasure of Torah is inex-

---

7. Joseph Telushkin, *A Code of Jewish Ethics,* vol. 1 (New York: Bell Tower, 2006), pp. 508-11.

8. Byron Sherwin, "An Incessantly Gushing Fountain: The Nature of Jewish Theology," in *Contemporary Jewish Theology,* ed. Elliot N. Dorff and Louis E. Newman (New York: Oxford University Press, 1999), p. 8.

haustible. Rabbinic literature states, "The Torah has seventy faces" (Numbers Rabbah 13:15). The number seventy figuratively implies that a full or complete number of faces are reflected in the "multifaceted mirror" of Torah.[9]

In the prophecy of Jeremiah, the Lord says, "Is not my word like . . . a hammer that breaks a rock in pieces?" (23:29). The rabbis reflected on this text as meaning this: as a hammer splits a rock up into numerous splinters, so will a scriptural text yield many legitimate meanings (see Babylonian Talmud, Sanhedrin 34a). In short, the depth and breadth of the Word of God is limitless and inexhaustible for even the most diligent of students.

Nearly two thousand years ago a sage named Ben Bag-Bag insisted that students must go deeper, turning the biblical text over and over again: "Turn it over and over because everything is in it and reflect upon it and wax grey and old over it and do not leave it, for you have no better lot than that" (Abot 5:22). Every new generation discovers layers of deeper meaning in the text as it is "turned over and over again." For Ben Bag-Bag, superficial scanning of Scripture will not be sufficient to satisfy a starving soul. Review it. Go deeper, for "everything is in it." In this modern world, we understand that the Bible is not a textbook on science, nor was it written to function that way. However, in his work on Abot, *The Ethics of the Fathers,* Shlomo Toperoff comments on Ben Bag-Bag's expression, "everything is in it," by noting and illustrating, with examples, how much modern thought owes its origin to the Torah.[10] Indeed, the sages taught that all the wisdom in this world is found in the Torah (Babylonian Talmud, Erubin 54b). Well did William Lecky observe, "Hebraic mortar cemented the foundations of American democracy."[11]

Rabbi Michael L. Samuel suggests several intriguing, variant readings of Ben Bag-Bag's saying. One variant says the interpreter keeps turning over the text of Torah again and again "because everything is in it, *and all of you are in it.*" Another reading, found in the Kaufmann manuscript, states in chiasmic style, "because all of it is in you — and all of you is in it." These variants point to the truism that the Bible is a commentary on human nature. The full breadth of all human experiences and circumstances will be found in Scripture — if one studies long enough and hard enough. Thus, the command to the reader, "turn it over and over," implies that the text has flexibility rather than a strict rigidity. Indeed, "for the ancients," concludes Samuel, "the

---

9. See Sherwin, "An Incessantly Gushing Fountain," p. 11.

10. Shlomo P. Toperoff, *Avot: A Comprehensive Commentary on the Ethics of the Fathers* (Northvale, NJ: Jason Aronson, 1997), pp. 361-65.

11. Quoted in David de Sola Pool, *Why I Am a Jew* (Boston: Beacon Press, 1957), p. 185.

Word of God was dynamic, alive, and always communicative."[12] In a similar vein, H. G. M. Williamson, Regius Professor of Hebrew at Oxford University, comments on the flexibility of the biblical text: "While Scripture is not so open that it can mean whatever a reader chooses to find there, it is flexible to an inspiring extent in the range of human experience that it can address."[13]

As an expression of such flexibility, the rabbis speak of "PaRDeS," an acronym for the four different layers of exegetical meaning.[14] The first is "Peshat," the plain, simple, or literal meaning. The second is "Remez," hinting, alluding, the allegorical meaning. The third layer is "Derash," meaning to inquire, explain, search (for truth). The fourth is "Sod," the secret, mysterious, or mystical nuances of the text, normally understood only by the most advanced students. The rabbis insisted that a text should be rooted in Peshat before other meanings are explored. In like fashion, the Reformers normally insisted on the straightforward, natural meaning of the text, grounded in grammatical-historical exegesis.

In regard to the formation of the acronym PaRDeS, in Genesis 2:8, the Hebrew word *gan,* "garden," the scene for Adam and Eve, is rendered in the Greek of the Septuagint translation as *paradeisos* or "paradise." In the Greek world, *paradeisos* was used of a park, garden, or orchard. In the Garden of Eden God placed fruit trees, also *etz ha-ḥayyim,* "the tree of life" (Gen. 2:9). PaRDeS is a play on paradise. Rabbi Lawrence Kushner comments on PaRDeS, in an "Orchard of Words," a chapter from his book on Jewish spirituality. Kushner writes, "The Torah, the source book of Judaism, is like an orchard; it conceals many wonderful and delicious surprises. . . . Just as it says in the Book of Proverbs (3:18), 'It is a tree of life to those who hold on to it.'"[15]

"To Study, to Do, and to Teach"

Study is one of the most sacred obligations incumbent on God's people. At the heart of the biblical heritage of the church, Ezra sets a noteworthy example for all would-be students of the Word. Ezra was a skillful scribe, "a

12. Michael L. Samuel, *Birth and Rebirth through Genesis: A Timeless Theological Conversation* (Coral Springs, FL: Aeon, 2010), p. 31.

13. H. G. M. Williamson, "Abraham in Exile," in *Perspectives on Our Father Abraham,* ed. Steven A. Hunt (Grand Rapids: Eerdmans, 2010), p. 78.

14. Samuel, *Birth and Rebirth through Genesis,* pp. 38-40.

15. Lawrence Kushner, *Jewish Spirituality* (Woodstock, VT: Jewish Lights, 2001), p. 51.

teacher well versed in the Law of Moses" (Ezra 7:6). As leader of the second return of captives from Babylon to Jerusalem, Ezra had developed his study skills and scholarship during captivity in Babylon, a place of increasing importance for copying and editing biblical manuscripts. Over the centuries, the reputation of Babylon as a major center of Jewish learning continued to grow. Some one thousand years after Ezra left Babylon to return to Jerusalem, the academies of Babylon produced the Babylonian Talmud.

In Jerusalem, Ezra "devoted himself to the study and observance of the Law of the LORD, and to teaching its decrees and laws in Israel" (Ezra 7:10). In this verse, the three Hebrew verbs associated with Ezra's task are significant to note. First, Ezra devoted himself to study. The text says he "set his heart to study." The word *lebab*, "heart," conveys the idea of his unwavering steadfastness to the task, a commitment of his whole self. "Ezra thus concentrated his whole life on the study of the law."[16] *Darash* is the term used for "study." It properly means to examine, question, expound, or interpret. The word suggests that Ezra engaged in a careful investigation, a searching or probing, questioning back and forth, until the clarity of the truth emerged. The text hereby reminds us that the genius of study in the Jewish tradition, when applied to today, is mainly a "dialogical process," a timeless "conversation between faith communities of today and their ancestors in faith about their experiences of God."[17]

Ezra also set his heart to "do," "observe," or "practice" the Torah. The text uses the Hebrew infinitive, *la'asot*. One of the reasons the rabbis considered study to be one of the highest expressions of worship is because it led to *ma'asim tobim*, "good deeds." Note the direct connection between the verb *la'asot*, "to do," and the noun *ma'asim*, "deeds." Study affects character, actions, and how an individual lives. In short, "to know" is "to do." Ezra practiced the law and thus showed God's love of humanity through his willing obedience to God's revealed will in the Torah. In Judaism, study always leads to the pragmatic step of the outward; it is never stuck in the theoretical or contemplative world of the inward. A distinguishing mark of Judaism is "its focus on the social order as the medium for serving God, the community as the area of responsibility."[18] The same is true for Christian-

16. Charles F. Fensham, *The Books of Ezra and Nehemiah,* The New International Commentary on the Old Testament (Grand Rapids: Eerdmans, 1982), p. 101.

17. Philip A. Cunningham, *A Story of Shalom: The Calling of Christians and Jews by a Covenanting God* (Mahwah, NJ: Paulist Press, 2001), p. 66.

18. Bruce D. Chilton and Jacob Neusner, *Classical Christianity and Rabbinic Judaism* (Grand Rapids: Baker Academic, 2004), p. 262.

ity. Study entails more than the mere listening to Scripture. Hearing is not enough. "Do not merely listen to the word, and so deceive yourselves. Do what it says" (James 1:22).

The third verb in this series concerns teaching. The verb *lamad*, "to learn," appears in Ezra 7:10 in the *pi'el* or intensive stem (Hebrew infinitive, *lelammed*) meaning "to teach." From this root comes the form *limmud*, "learned," "practiced," "disciple." Learning and training come before teaching. Both learning and teaching imply discipline that is necessary for success. Only after one carefully examines and practices the truth of the text is one able to teach others. In the Hebrew Bible the Lord is frequently described as a teacher (see Job 21:22; Ps. 94:10); he communicates his commands and decrees to his people. The teacher within the community is but a representative of the divine, equipped and charged to impart to learners the divine word.

The teaching of Scripture involves making interpretive comments and explanations. In this, Ezra sets a biblical precedent. According to Nehemiah 8, at daybreak Ezra brought out the Book of the Law of Moses and gathered the people before the Water Gate in Jerusalem. Ezra, assisted by Levites, read aloud till noon as the people listened attentively to the Book of the Law (v. 3). According to verse 8, "They read from the Book of the Law of God, making it clear and giving the meaning so that the people could understand what was being read." The TANAKH translation of the Jewish Publication Society renders this verse, "They read from the scroll of the Teaching of God, translating it and giving the sense; so they understood the reading."

In this passage, Ezra instituted the important tradition of the public reading and explanation of the Torah. The return of the exiles from Babylon to Jerusalem required a linguistic adjustment that would bring a greater intelligibility of the biblical text. Ezra made the public reading understandable by translating the words of the Hebrew text into Aramaic, the lingua franca of the day. Thus, Ezra "made it clear" (Heb. *mephorash*) using the Aramaic language, a Semitic first-cousin language of Hebrew, and giving the meaning or explaining it.[19]

In the centuries after Ezra, the Targums ("translations"), written in Ar-

---

19. William L. Holladay gives two possible meanings for *mephorash* in Nehemiah 8:8: "expounded ex tempore," or "translated." William L. Holladay, ed., *A Concise Hebrew and Aramaic Lexicon of the Old Testament* (Grand Rapids: Eerdmans, 1971), p. 299. Also note the comment of *The Jewish Study Bible* on *mephorash*: "Unable to understand the Hebrew text, the returnees required both Aramaic translation and interpretation" (Megillah 3a; Nedarim 37b; Genesis Rabbah 36:8); *The Jewish Study Bible*, ed. Adele Berlin and Marc Zvi Brettler (New York: Oxford University Press, 2004), p. 1700.

amaic, became an important source for early Jewish studies. Some Targums were literal (e.g., Targum Onkelos), but most were free translations or paraphrases of books (or passages) of the Hebrew Bible, produced from about the third century B.C. to the third century A.D. The Targums are of particular interest to Christian scholars of early Jewish hermeneutics. For example, the Targums are useful in understanding the passages in the prophets and in the Psalms that were interpreted as referring to the Messiah.

Finally, the work of Ezra proved, in theory, if not in practice, to be a major step in furthering the "democratization" of the Word of God, of seeking to make it equally accessible to all the people. Pertinent are the words of Rabbi David E. Cahn-Lipman: "By making the text available to all people, Ezra further undermined the authority of the priesthood. Instead of being the sole caretakers of the Law, the priests were now viewed as a group answerable to the Law, which everyone could study and know."[20]

God proclaims to Israel, "You will be for me a kingdom of priests" (Exod. 19:6). Peter expands this concept of "royal priesthood" and applies it to the church, a "priesthood of all believers," those whose scriptural foundation and godly heritage derive from Israel (1 Pet. 2:9).

Guardians of the City

Jewish sages, scholars, and rabbis are always asking questions. This dialectical nature of Judaism is how Jews learn. Jesus fits this pattern. For example, as alluded to in a previous chapter, at age twelve, Jesus was found in the temple courts after a search of several days by his parents. They spotted Jesus "sitting among the teachers, listening to them and asking questions" (Luke 2:46). On seeing his parents, Jesus started to question them: "Why were you searching for me? Didn't you know I had to be in my Father's house?" (Luke 2:49). In the Jewish tradition, from youth Jews are taught to ask informative, and often probing, questions. So, our appropriate reply might be, "Why shouldn't they?"

One of the most powerful questions of rabbinic literature is found in the Jerusalem Talmud and also the Midrashim. The rabbis asked, "Who are the true guardians of the city?" (Jerusalem Talmud, Hagigah 1:7; Pesikta de-Rav Kahana 15:120b). In this modern world, especially after 9/11, our first

---

20. David E. Cahn-Lipman, *The Book of Jewish Knowledge* (Northvale, NJ: Jason Aronson, 1991), pp. 129-30.

reaction upon hearing this question might be to think of military might, physical force, or power. On "first response," we might think the expression "guardians of the city" mainly calls for people like local and state police, firefighters, National Guard, Homeland Security, or a branch of the military such as the Army or the Coast Guard. The "guardians" are mainly those governmental institutions empowered to patrol and to protect lives and property and to keep cities safe from invasion, harm, and destruction. As citizens, our typical first reaction on what must be done to guard and protect a city under siege or attack is to use physical force: we will meet the enemy head on with a display of physical strength and reliance on modern weaponry. Thus we will bring about the safety and protection of our citizens, their families, homes, schools, and public buildings.

The rabbis, however, suggested a more subtle, deep, and lasting defense to prevent destruction of a city. It would not be a show of military might but of moral power. As the above Talmudic text points out, to the rabbis, the true guardians of the city are "the teachers of Bible and Mishnah." By emphasizing *teachers* as the guardians, Dov Peretz Elkins points out, the rabbis expressed their belief that "the worst and most common kind of failure of a community comes from within. This kind of deterioration is one of inward moral rot."[21]

In short, for the rabbis, the antidote to moral decay and corruption is education in Scripture. It is the spiritual and ethical values of Hebraic heritage that have given inward strength to and sustained the people of God over centuries. Through study of the Scriptures, the Jewish people realized they must commit themselves to be empowered within. The rabbis believed that internal strength of character, developed through religious textual edification guided by dedicated teachers, brought about the best spiritual fortification to meet, resist, and survive any attack in life.

The rabbis directly linked their answer to the above question, "Who are the true guardians of the city?" to Psalm 127:1. The verse warns, "Unless the LORD watches over *(yishmor)* the city, the watchmen stand guard in vain." The verbal tense used in this verse for the Lord's "watching over" or "guarding" people implies an action not complete, but open-ended and ongoing. In a similar vein, teachers of Scripture (lay and professional) are the ever-vigilant moral and spiritual "watchmen on the walls," helping to guard the hearts of the students entrusted to them (see Isa. 62:6).

21. Dov Peretz Elkins, *The Wisdom of Judaism* (Woodstock, VT: Jewish Lights, 2007), p. 119.

Is this not the same timely divine admonition on the need to guard a city spiritually that Jeremiah gave to his fellow citizens of Judah shortly before idolatrous Jerusalem fell? "Let not the wise man boast of his wisdom or the strong man boast of his strength or the rich man boast of his riches, but let him who boasts boast about this: that he understands and knows me, that I am the LORD, who exercises kindness, justice and righteousness on earth, for in these I delight" (Jer. 9:23-24). The message of the teachers of Israel, like Jeremiah, is that one must not be deceived or seduced so as to trust in or rely solely on earthly power, or to seek to find ultimate security in the temporal. To do so is an illusion. Rather, a person must turn to the Lord and draw moral strength, spiritual encouragement, and ultimate deliverance through the Scriptures. Indeed, in the words of the psalmist, the Lord's pleasure is not in the "strength of the horse" or in the "legs of a man" but in those who "fear him" (see Ps. 147:10-11).

Many potential enemies seek daily to destroy a city from without and within. The often inconspicuous and unheralded guardians of any city, however, are the teachers of Scripture; their mission is to keep truth alive by "preserving the divine flame." The prophets of Israel teach that God's word is like a fire (Jer. 20:9; 23:29). As dedicated religious educators, teachers are called to guard the flame of Scripture and ignite a love for it in the hearts of their students; it cannot flicker or be extinguished.

In this tradition, the Gospels refer to Jesus as *didaskalos,* "teacher," forty-one times and as "rabbi" sixteen times. The early Christian centuries reveal that Jews brought with them to the diaspora their own spiritual teachings and religious traditions. Especially through their rabbis, scholar-teachers, and heads of families, they were committed to honoring and perpetuating this heritage and to safeguarding and transmitting it from generation to generation. "On the communal level, the synagogue was the main conduit for accomplishing these goals."[22]

In the big biblical picture, Paul, the rabbi from Tarsus, saw his mission to Gentile believers to be in a similar vein. That is, Paul deeply rooted his life in the Tanakh; it was the primary source for his theological and ethical teaching and preaching. In the corrupt and hedonistic society surrounding the young churches of the Mediterranean world, pastors of emerging flocks drew particular inspiration from the fresh apostolic teachings and also from the Old Testament Scriptures. In addition to reflecting upon the great reve-

---

22. Lee I. Levine, "The Synagogue," in *The Jewish Annotated New Testament,* ed. Amy-Jill Levine and Marc Zvi Brettler (New York: Oxford University Press, 2011), p. 520.

latory and redemptive events in Israel's history, these "pastor-teachers" (*tous de poimenas kai didaskalous;* see Eph. 4:11) drew heavily from the prophets and the Psalms out of which they established messianic connections, ethical imperatives, and encouragement for everyday spiritual living in the midst of persecution.

Rooted in the Bible of Jesus, the early church knew that God's truth "protects" (Ps. 40:11) and that understanding "guards" (Prov. 2:11). Thus, Paul urges fellow believers to defend themselves with moral and spiritual weaponry, by putting on the "full armor of God" (Eph. 6:11). Believers are commanded to "be strong" in God's mighty power (v. 10), taking in hand "the sword of the Spirit, which is the word of God" (v. 17). The good news is that the *shalom* of God will be present to protect believers inwardly with his tranquil, assuring presence whenever they need to face the moral and spiritual challenges of life. To be sure, the peace of God, says Paul, "will stand as a guard" *(phrouresei)* over the human heart (Phil. 4:7), a fortress divinely protected through faithful study and teaching of Scripture, the very heart of our Hebraic heritage (2 Tim. 2:2).

UNDERSTANDING CHAPTER FOURTEEN

1. In ancient Israel, who comprised the "educational backbone" of community life, and which locations served as "teaching hubs" within the tribal territories? Why did a major restructuring and reformulation of Judaism take place after A.D. 70? In what significant ways did the priesthood change? In the history of Christianity, can you think of any major readjustments or innovations brought about by political, social, or cultural changes of the times? Discuss the question of adaptability and change in religion. Are some things in religion temporal and others changeless? Explain.

2. In Jewish tradition, why was constant study of the commandments so significant? How was the practice seen as a spiritual duty, and why was no one exempt? Consider the fact that the task was passed from generation to generation (see Isa. 59:21); from a Christian perspective and from your experience, does Christianity carry a similar sense of intergenerational duty, or not?

3. What is the narrowest definition of Torah? To what is it often extended, however? Review Jacob Neusner's observations. How is studying Torah "Sinai revisited"? How is Torah study a type of communion with God?

4. In addition to studying Torah, what was viewed as God's "other book"? What role did this also play in communing with God? Review Psalm 19:1-4. How does creation join in praising God? What other biblical texts come to mind when you consider this "other book"?

5. While the memorization and repetition of Torah was never assumed to function as a guarantee, what power was it perceived to grant to its participants? Read Isaiah 55:11. Which passage does the author suggest as a New Testament equivalent? Does viewing the two passages together give you a heightened sense of the power and potential of God's Word? In what way?

6. What did Rabbi Johanan ben Zakkai found toward the end of the first century? Why did he advise against taking pride in accomplishing much study of Torah? How does *lishmah* translate, and how does it describe the way in which Torah study should be undertaken? In relation to this, what does biblical Christianity seek to balance? How does Jesus' parable of the talents demonstrate this?

7. Review the selections of commentary cited concerning the rabbis' debate about whether study or deeds is greater. What are some benefits of study? How are study and theology bound to action, and how do they combine to produce "action-faith"?

8. Are Byron Sherwin's words that "[t]he Jewish theologian is not only obliged to *do* what he or she believes, but to *believe* what he or she *does*" convicting to you? While Christianity is often perceived as more of a "creeds" than "deeds" religion, how does this undoubtedly ring true for Christians as well? In your opinion, does the church emphasize this enough?

9. Why is the study of Torah a continual calling rather than an activity that reaches an endpoint or can be finished? What does it mean to say that "the Torah has seventy faces" (see Numbers Rabbah 13:15)? How does the rabbinic perception of Jeremiah 23:29 illustrate this point?

10. Of what did the sage Ben Bag-Bag say there is "no better lot" (see Abot 5:22)? What did the sages teach about the wisdom of the world? How does H. G. M. Williamson describe the flexibility of Scripture?

11. What is "PaRDeS"? What four layers of meaning does the acronym represent, and which meaning did the rabbis say a text should be rooted in before other meanings were explored? How did the Christian Reformers insist on a similar prioritizing of interpretation? How is PaRDeS also a play on "paradise," both linguistically and conceptually?

In Genesis, what was the *etz ha-ḥayyim,* and how is this metaphorical of the Torah as a whole?

12. Why is Ezra a noteworthy example for all who would be "students of the Word"? How did Babylon develop into a center of copying and editing manuscripts, and what significant compilation of Jewish texts came out of Babylon? What do the Hebrew words *lebab, darash, la'asot,* and *lamad* mean (see Ezra 7:10)? How is study in the Jewish tradition a "dialogical process"?

13. What are *ma'asim tobim,* and how did the rabbis relate study to these? What does it mean to say that "to know is to do"? What distinguishing mark of Judaism reveals its pragmatic nature? Do you perceive the social order as a "medium" through which to serve God?

14. How is it that the verbs "to learn" and "to teach" come from the same verb in Hebrew? What close relationship exists between learning and teaching?

15. How did Ezra set a biblical precedent when he taught Scripture? What important tradition did he institute (see Nehemiah 8)? What translation did he provide in the public reading, and why was this necessary?

16. In the centuries following Ezra, which Aramaic texts became an important source for early Jewish studies? Why are they of particular interest to Christian scholars of early Jewish hermeneutics?

17. What does the author mean by saying that Ezra's work contributed to the "democratization" of the Word of God? According to David Cahn-Lipman, what effect did this have on the priesthood? How does the New Testament (see 1 Pet. 2:9) expand the Old Testament's original view of the priesthood (see Exod. 19:6)? Today, what do Protestant Christians mean in saying they uphold the "priesthood of all believers"? Are there any specific entitlements that accompany this expression?

18. Which dialectical tool does the author highlight as an instrument of Jewish learning? What question cited by the author is one of the most powerful questions of Jewish literature? What are some possible natural responses to this question according to the modern mind? Who were the guardians in the eyes of the rabbis, however, and in what way? To which text from the Psalms did the rabbis link their answer? How do Jeremiah's words in Jeremiah 9:23-24 convey a similar message?

19. How many times do the Gospels refer to Jesus as "teacher" and "rabbi"? How did the teachings of "scholar-teachers" of the day carry

on into the diaspora, and in the diaspora what was the main conduit for transmitting such teachings? How did Paul's work and teachings function similarly? What did "pastor-teachers" in the diaspora often draw on?

20. How did the early church view God's truth as protective? At the end of the day, who is the One standing guard over believers' hearts?

A Selective Bibliography

Ariel, David S. *What Do Jews Believe? The Spiritual Foundations of Judaism.* New York: Schocken, 1995.

Bader, Gershom. *The Encyclopedia of Talmudic Sages.* Northvale, NJ: Jason Aronson, 1993.

Baeck, Leo. *The Essence of Judaism.* New York: Schocken, 1948.

Bamberger, Bernard J. *The Search for Jewish Theology.* New York: Behrman House, 1978.

————. *The Story of Judaism.* 3rd ed. New York: Schocken, 1970.

Barth, Christoph. *God with Us.* Grand Rapids: Eerdmans, 1991.

Bavinck, Herman. *The Doctrine of God.* Grand Rapids: Eerdmans, 1951.

Berlin, Adele, and Marc Zvi Brettler, eds. *The Jewish Study Bible.* New York: Oxford University Press, 2004.

Berman, Louis A. *The Akedah: The Binding of Isaac.* Northvale, NJ: Jason Aronson, 1997.

Bivin, David. *New Light on the Difficult Words of Jesus: Insights from His Jewish Context.* Edited by Lois Tverberg and Bruce Ockema. Holland, MI: En-Gedi, 2005.

Bivin, David, and Roy B. Blizzard. *Understanding the Difficult Words of Jesus.* Austin, TX: Center for Judaic-Christian Studies, 1984.

Blanch, Stuart. *For All Mankind.* New York: Oxford University Press, 1978.

Blech, Benjamin. *The Secrets of Hebrew Words.* Northvale, NJ: Jason Aronson, 1991.

Blumenthal, David R. *God at the Center: Meditations on Jewish Spirituality.* Northvale, NJ: Jason Aronson, 1994.

Boman, Thorleif. *Hebrew Thought Compared with Greek.* New York: W. W. Norton, 1960.

Booker, Richard. *No Longer Strangers: Rediscovering the Jewish Roots of Christianity.* Woodlands, TX: Institute for Hebraic-Christian Studies, 2002.

Braaten, Carl E., and Robert W. Jenson, eds. *Jews and Christians: People of God.* Grand Rapids: Eerdmans, 2003.

Bright, John. *The Authority of the Old Testament.* Repr. Grand Rapids: Baker, 1975.

Browne, Lewis, ed. *The Wisdom of Israel.* New York: Random House, 1945.

Buber, Martin. *Hasidism and Modern Man.* Edited and translated by Maurice Friedman. New York: Harper & Row, 1958.

————. *I and Thou.* Translated by Walter Kaufman. New York: Scribner's, 1970.

Cahill, Thomas. *The Gifts of the Jews*. New York: Doubleday, 1998.

Cahn-Lipman, David E. *The Book of Jewish Knowledge*. Northvale, NJ: Jason Aronson, 1991.

Chilton, Bruce D., and Jacob Neusner. *Classical Christianity and Rabbinic Judaism*. Grand Rapids: Baker Academic, 2004.

Chumash, The. The Stone Edition, The Artscroll Series. Brooklyn, NY: Mesorah Publications, 1994.

Cohen, Arthur A., and Paul Mendes-Flohr, eds. *Contemporary Jewish Religious Thought*. New York: Free Press, 1987.

Cohen, Norman J. *The Way into Torah*. Woodstock, VT: Jewish Lights, 2000.

Cohn-Sherbok, Dan. *The Blackwell Dictionary of Judaica*. Oxford: Blackwell, 1992.

——. *The Jewish Heritage*. New York: Blackwell, 1988.

Cook, Michael J. *Modern Jews Engage the New Testament*. Woodstock, VT: Jewish Lights, 2008.

Cunningham, Philip A. *A Story of Shalom: The Calling of Christians and Jews by a Covenanting God*. Mahwah, NJ: Paulist Press, 2001.

Danby, Herbert, ed. *The Mishnah*. London: Oxford University Press, 1938.

Davies, J. G. *The Early Christian Church*. Grand Rapids: Baker, 1965.

Dickson, Athol. *The Gospel According to Moses*. Grand Rapids: Brazos, 2003.

Diprose, Ronald E. *Israel and the Church: The Origin and Effects of Replacement Theology*. Rome: Authentic Media, 2000.

Donin, Hayim Halevy. *To Pray as a Jew*. New York: Basic Books, 1980.

Dorff, Elliot N., and Louis E. Newman, eds. *Contemporary Jewish Theology: A Reader*. New York: Oxford University Press, 1999.

Doron, Pinchas. *Rashi's Torah Commentary*. Northvale, NJ: Jason Aronson, 2000.

Dosick, Wayne. *Living Judaism*. San Francisco: HarperCollins, 1995.

Doukhan, Jacques B. *Israel and the Church: Two Voices for the Same God*. Peabody, MA: Hendrickson, 2002.

Doukhan, Jacques B., ed. *Thinking in the Shadow of Hell*. Berrien Springs, MI: Andrews University Press, 2002.

Dumbrell, William J. *Covenant and Creation: A Theology of Old Testament Covenants*. Nashville: Thomas Nelson, 1984.

Dunn, James D. G. *Unity and Diversity in the New Testament*. 2nd ed. London: SCM Press, 1990.

Eckstein, Yechiel. *How Firm a Foundation*. Brewster, MA: Paraclete Press, 1997.

Edelman, Lily, ed. *Jewish Heritage Reader*. New York: Taplinger, 1965.

Elkins, Dov Peretz. *The Wisdom of Judaism*. Woodstock, VT: Jewish Lights, 2007.

Epstein, I., ed. *The Babylonian Talmud*. 35 vols. repr. in 18. London: Soncino, 1961.

Fieldsend, John, Clifford Hill, Walter Riggans, John C. P. Smith, and Fred Wright, eds. *Root and Branches: Explorations into the Jewish Context of the Christian Faith*. Bedford, UK: PWM Trust, 1998.

Fishbane, Michael A. *Judaism: Revelations and Traditions*. San Francisco: Harper & Row, 1987.

Fitzmyer, Joseph A. *Romans*. The Anchor Bible, vol. 33. New York: Doubleday, 1993.

Flusser, David. *Judaism and the Origins of Christianity.* Jerusalem: Magnes, 1988.

Flusser, David, and Steven Notley. *The Sage from Galilee: Rediscovering Jesus' Genius.* 4th ed. Grand Rapids: Eerdmans, 2007.

Frankel, Ellen, and Betsy Platkin Teutsch. *The Encyclopedia of Jewish Symbols.* Northvale, NJ: Jason Aronson, 1992.

Friedman, Maurice. *Abraham Joshua Heschel and Elie Wiesel: You Are My Witnesses.* New York: Farrar, Straus & Giroux, 1987.

Frieman, Shulamis. *Who's Who in the Talmud.* Northvale, NJ: Jason Aronson, 1995.

Frymer-Kensky, Tikva, David Novak, Peter Ochs, David Fox Sandmel, and Michael A. Signer, eds. *Christianity in Jewish Terms.* Boulder, CO: Westview, 2000.

Fuller, Daniel. *The Unity of the Bible.* Grand Rapids: Zondervan, 1992.

Gaer, Joseph, and Alfred Wolf. *Our Jewish Heritage.* North Hollywood, CA: Wilshire, 1957.

Garr, John D. *Family Worship.* Atlanta: Hebraic Christian Global Community, Golden Key Press, 2013.

———. *Living Emblems: Ancient Symbols of Faith.* Atlanta: Restoration Foundation, 2000.

———. *Restoring Our Lost Legacy: Christianity's Hebrew Heritage.* Atlanta: Restoration Foundation, 1989.

Glatzer, Nahum N. *Hammer on the Rock: A Midrash Reader.* New York: Schocken, 1962.

———. *A Jewish Reader: In Time and Eternity.* New York: Schocken, 1961.

Glustrom, Simon. *The Language of Judaism.* Northvale, NJ: Jason Aronson, 1988.

Goldin, Judah, ed. *The Living Talmud: The Wisdom of the Fathers.* New York: New American Library, 1957.

Goldscheider, Calvin, and Jacob Neusner, eds. *Social Foundations of Judaism.* Englewood Cliffs, NJ: Prentice Hall, 1990.

Gordon, Cyrus H. *The Common Background of Greek and Hebrew Civilizations.* 2nd ed. New York: W. W. Norton, 1965.

Gorg, Manfred. *In Abraham's Bosom: Christianity without the New Testament.* Translated by Linda M. Maloney. Collegeville, MN: Liturgical Press, 1999.

Green, Arthur. *These Are the Words: A Vocabulary of Jewish Spiritual Life.* Woodstock, VT: Jewish Lights, 1999.

Greenberg, Irving. *For the Sake of Heaven and Earth: The New Encounter between Judaism and Christianity.* Philadelphia: Jewish Publication Society, 2004.

———. *The Jewish Way.* New York: Simon & Schuster, 1988.

Greenberg, Irving, and Shalom Freedman. *Living in the Image of God.* Northvale, NJ: Jason Aronson, 1998.

Greenberg, Moshe. *Biblical Prose Prayer.* Berkeley: University of California Press, 1983.

Gulstrom, Simon. *The Language of Judaism.* Northvale, NJ: Jason Aronson, 1988.

Hagner, Donald A. *The Jewish Reclamation of Jesus.* Grand Rapids: Zondervan, 1984.

HaLevi, Baruch, and Ellen Frankel. *Revolution of Jewish Spirit.* Woodstock, VT: Jewish Lights, 2012.

Hammer, Reuven. *The Torah Revolution.* Woodstock, VT: Jewish Lights, 2011.

Harris, R. Laird, Gleason L. Archer Jr., and Bruce K. Waltke, eds. *Theological Wordbook of the Old Testament.* 2 vols. Chicago: Moody Press, 1980.

Hartman, David. *A Living Covenant: The Innovative Spirit in Traditional Judaism.* Woodstock, VT: Jewish Lights, 1997.

Heie, Harold, and Michael A. King, eds. *Mutual Treasure: Seeking Better Ways for Christians and Culture to Converse.* Telford, PA: Cascadia, 2009.

Heie, Harold, A. James Rudin, and Marvin R. Wilson, eds. *The Role of Religion in Politics and Society.* Wenham, MA: Gordon College and the American Jewish Committee, 1998.

Helyer, Larry R. *Exploring Jewish Literature of the Second Temple Period.* Downers Grove, IL: InterVarsity, 2002.

Hertz, Joseph H., ed. *Authorized Daily Prayer Book.* Rev. ed. New York: Block, 1948.

Hertz, Joseph H., ed. *The Pentateuch and Haftorahs.* 2nd ed. London: Soncino, 1975.

Heschel, Abraham J. *The Earth Is the Lord's.* New York: Farrar, Straus & Giroux, 1950.

———. *Essential Writings.* Edited by Susannah Heschel. Maryknoll, NY: Orbis Books, 2011.

———. *God in Search of Man.* New York: Farrar, Straus & Giroux, 1955.

———. *Heavenly Torah: As Refracted through the Generations.* Translated and edited by Gordon Tucker. New York: Continuum, 2006.

———. *The Insecurity of Freedom.* New York: Schocken, 1966.

———. *Israel: An Echo of Eternity.* New York: Farrar, Straus & Giroux, 1969.

———. *Man Is Not Alone.* New York: Harper & Row, 1951.

———. *Moral Grandeur and Spiritual Audacity.* Essays by Abraham Joshua Heschel. Edited by Susannah Heschel. New York: Farrar, Straus & Giroux, 1996.

———. *A Passion for Truth.* New York: Farrar, Straus & Giroux, 1973.

———. *The Prophets.* New York: Harper & Row, 1962.

———. *The Sabbath.* New York: Farrar, Straus & Giroux, 1975.

———. *Who Is Man?* Stanford, CA: Stanford University Press, 1965.

Heschel, Susannah. *Abraham Geiger and the Jewish Jesus.* Chicago: University of Chicago Press, 1998.

Hodes, Aubrey. *Martin Buber: An Intimate Portrait.* New York: Viking, 1971.

Holladay, William L., ed. *A Concise Hebrew and Aramaic Lexicon of the Old Testament.* Grand Rapids: Eerdmans, 1971.

Holwerda, David E. *Jesus and Israel: One Covenant or Two?* Grand Rapids: Eerdmans, 1995.

Hubbard, Robert, Robert Johnston, and Robert Meye, eds. *Studies in Old Testament Theology.* Dallas: Word, 1992.

Hunt, Steven A., ed. *Perspectives on Our Father Abraham.* Grand Rapids: Eerdmans, 2010.

Jacobs, Louis. *A Jewish Theology.* New York: Behrman House, 1973.

Jastrow, Marcus, ed. *A Dictionary of the Targumim, the Talmud Babli and Yerushalmi, and the Midrashic Literature.* London: Luzac & Co., 1886-1903. Repr. Peabody, MA: Hendrickson, 2005.

Johnson, Paul. *History of the Jews.* New York: Harper & Row, 1987.

Kadushin, Max. *Worship and Ethics: A Study in Rabbinic Judaism.* Evanston, IL: Northwestern University Press, 1964.

A Selective Bibliography

Kaplan, Edward K. *Spiritual Radical: Abraham Joshua Heschel in America, 1940-1972.* New Haven: Yale University Press, 2007.

Kessler, Edward. *Bound by the Bible: Jews, Christians and the Sacrifice of Isaac.* Cambridge: Cambridge University Press, 2004.

Kinzer, Mark S. *Post-Missionary Messianic Judaism: Redefining Christian Engagement with the Jewish People.* Grand Rapids: Brazos, 2005.

Kirzner, Yitzchok. *The Art of Jewish Prayer.* Northvale, NJ: Jason Aronson, 1991.

Klagsbrun, Francine. *Voices of Wisdom: Jewish Ideals and Ethics.* New York: Pantheon, 1980.

Klausner, Joseph. *The Messianic Idea in Israel.* Translated by W. F. Stinespring. New York: Macmillan, 1955.

Klenicki, Leon, and Richard John Neuhaus. *Believing Today: Jew and Christian in Conversation.* Grand Rapids: Eerdmans, 1989.

Knight, Douglas A., and Amy-Jill Levine. *The Meaning of the Bible: What the Jewish Scriptures and Christian Old Testament Can Teach Us.* New York: HarperCollins, 2011.

Küng, Hans. *Judaism: Between Yesterday and Tomorrow.* New York: Crossroad, 1992.

Kuschel, Karl-Josef. *Abraham: Sign of Hope for Jews, Christians and Muslims.* New York: Continuum, 1995.

Kushner, Lawrence. *Jewish Spirituality.* Woodstock, VT: Jewish Lights, 2001.

Kutsko, John F. *Between Heaven and Earth: Divine Presence and Absence in the Book of Ezekiel.* Winona Lake, IN: Eisenbrauns, 2000.

Lapide, Pinchas. *Hebrew in the Church: The Foundations of Jewish-Christian Dialogue.* Translated by Erroll F. Rhodes. Grand Rapids: Eerdmans, 1984.

Lapide, Pinchas, and Ulrich Luz. *Jesus in Two Perspectives: A Jewish-Christian Dialog.* Translated by Lawrence W. Denef. Minneapolis: Augsburg Publishing House, 1985.

Larsson, Goran. *Bound for Freedom: The Book of Exodus in Jewish and Christian Traditions.* Peabody, MA: Hendrickson, 1999.

Levenson, Jon D. *The Death and Resurrection of the Beloved Son.* New Haven: Yale University Press, 1993.

————. *Inheriting Abraham: The Legacy of the Patriarch in Judaism, Christianity and Islam.* Princeton: Princeton University Press, 2012.

Levine, Amy-Jill. *The Misunderstood Jew: The Church and the Scandal of the Jewish Jesus.* New York: HarperCollins, 2006.

Levine, Amy-Jill, and Marc Zvi Brettler, eds. *The Jewish Annotated New Testament.* New York: Oxford University Press, 2011.

Levine, Lee I. *Judaism and Hellenism in Antiquity: Conflict or Confluence?* Peabody, MA: Hendrickson, 1998.

Lohfink, Norbert. *The Covenant Never Revoked.* Mahwah, NJ: Paulist Press, 1991.

Lowin, Joseph. *Hebrewspeak.* Northvale, NJ: Jason Aronson, 1995.

Lutske, Harvey. *The Book of Jewish Customs.* Northvale, NJ: Jason Aronson, 1986.

Mansoor, Menahem. *Jewish History and Thought.* Hoboken, NJ: Ktav, 1991.

Martin-Achard, Robert. *An Approach to the Old Testament.* Translated by J. C. G. Greig. Edinburgh: Oliver & Boyd, 1965.

Matthews, Victor H., and Don C. Benjamin. *Social World of Ancient Israel*. Peabody, MA: Hendrickson, 1993.

Montefiore, Claude G., and H. Loewe. *A Rabbinic Anthology*. New York: Schocken, 1974.

Moore, George Foot. *Judaism*. Cambridge, MA: Harvard University Press, 1955.

Murphy, Frederick J. *Early Judaism*. Peabody, MA: Hendrickson, 2002.

Neuhaus, Richard John, ed. *Jews in Unsecular America*. Grand Rapids: Eerdmans, 1987.

Neusner, Jacob. *Judaism in the Beginning of Christianity*. Philadelphia: Fortress Press, 1984.

————. *Judaism in the Matrix of Christianity*. Philadelphia: Fortress Press, 1986.

————. *Questions and Answers: Intellectual Foundations of Judaism*. Peabody, MA: Hendrickson, 2005.

————. *A Rabbi Talks with Jesus*. Montreal: McGill-Queen's University Press, 2000.

————. *The Way of Torah*. 5th ed. Belmont, CA: Wadsworth, 1993.

Neusner, Jacob, ed. *Dictionary of Judaism in the Biblical Period: 450 B.C.E. to 600 C.E.* Peabody, MA: Hendrickson, 1996.

Neusner, Jacob, ed. *An Introduction to Judaism*. Louisville: Westminster/John Knox, 1991.

Neusner, Jacob, and Bruce Chilton. *Jewish-Christian Debates: God, Kingdom, Messiah*. Minneapolis: Augsburg Fortress, 1998.

Newman, Louis E. *An Introduction to Jewish Ethics*. Upper Saddle River, NJ: Pearson Prentice Hall, 2005.

————. *Repentance: The Meaning and Practice of Teshubah*. Woodstock, VT: Jewish Lights, 2010.

Novak, David. *Jewish-Christian Dialogue*. New York: Oxford University Press, 1989.

O'Hare, Padraic. *The Enduring Covenant*. Valley Forge, PA: Trinity Press International, 1997.

Patai, Raphael, and Emanuel S. Goldsmith, eds. *Thinkers and Teachers of Modern Judaism*. New York: Paragon House, 1994.

Pearl, Chaim. *Theology in Rabbinic Stories*. Peabody, MA: Hendrickson, 1997.

Petuchowski, Jakob J. *Understanding Jewish Prayer*. New York: Ktav, 1972.

Poling, Jason Alder. *Changing Jewish Perceptions of Evangelicals Through Interfaith Text Study*. Doctor of Ministry dissertation, Hatfield, PA: Biblical Theological Seminary, 2012.

Pryor, Dwight A. *Unveiling the Kingdom of Heaven*. Dayton, OH: Center for Judaic-Christian Studies, 2008.

Pryor, Keren H., ed. *A Continuing Quest*. Dayton, OH: Center for Judaic-Christian Studies, 2011.

Rabinowicz, Tzvi. *A Guide to Life*. Northvale, NJ: Jason Aronson, 1989.

Rahner, Karl, and Pinchas Lapide. *Encountering Jesus — Encountering Judaism: A Dialogue*. New York: Crossroad, 1987.

Richardson, Peter. *Israel in the Apostolic Church*. Cambridge: Cambridge University Press, 1969.

Rosenberg, Stuart E. *The Christian Problem: A Jewish View*. New York: Hippocrene Books, 1986.

Rosenthal, Gilbert S. *What Can a Modern Jew Believe?* Eugene, OR: Wipf & Stock, 2007.

Rottenberg, Isaac C. *Christian-Jewish Dialogue: Exploring Our Commonalities and Our Differences*. Atlanta: Hebraic Heritage Press, 2005.

———. *Judaism, Christianity, Paganism: A Judeo-Christian Worldview and Its Cultural Implications*. Atlanta: Hebraic Heritage Press, 2007.

Rubinstein, Aryeh, ed. *Hasidism*. New York: Leon Amiel, 1975.

Rudin, James. *Christians and Jews Faith to Faith*. Woodstock, VT: Jewish Lights, 2011.

Rudin, James, and Marvin R. Wilson, eds. *A Time to Speak: The Evangelical-Jewish Encounter*. Grand Rapids: Eerdmans, 1987.

Runes, Dagobert D., ed. *The Hebrew Impact on Western Civilization*. Secaucus, NJ: Citadel Press, 1976.

Safrai, S., and M. Stern, eds. *The Jewish People in the First Century*. Vol. 2. Philadelphia: Fortress Press, 1976.

Salkin, Jeffrey K. *Righteous Gentiles in the Hebrew Bible*. Woodstock, VT: Jewish Lights, 2008.

Samuel, Michael L. *Birth and Rebirth through Genesis: A Timeless Theological Conversation*. Coral Springs, FL: Aeon, 2010.

———. *The Lord Is My Shepherd: The Theology of a Caring God*. Northvale, NJ: Jason Aronson, 1996.

Sanders, E. P. *Paul and Palestinian Judaism*. Philadelphia: Fortress Press, 1977.

Sandgren, Leo Dupree. *Vines Intertwined: A History of Jews and Christians*. Peabody, MA: Hendrickson, 2010.

Sandmel, Samuel. *Judaism and Christian Beginnings*. New York: Oxford University Press, 1978.

Saperstein, Marc. *Moments of Crisis in Jewish-Christian Relations*. Philadelphia: Trinity Press International, 1989.

Sarna, Nahum M. *Genesis*. Jewish Publication Society Torah Commentary. Philadelphia: Jewish Publication Society, 1989.

Schafer, Peter. *Judeophobia: Attitudes toward the Jews in the Ancient World*. Cambridge, MA: Harvard University Press, 1997.

Schechter, Solomon. *Aspects of Rabbinic Theology*. New York: Schocken, 1961.

Schimmel, Solomon. *The Seven Deadly Sins: Jewish, Christian, and Classical Reflections on Human Nature*. New York: Free Press, 1992.

Schoeps, Hans-Joachim. *Jewish Christianity: Factional Disputes in the Early Church*. Translated by Douglas R. A. Hare. Philadelphia: Fortress Press, 1969.

Scott, J. Julius. *Customs and Controversies: Intertestamental Jewish Backgrounds of the New Testament*. Grand Rapids: Baker, 1995.

Sheriffs, Deryck. *The Friendship of the Lord: An Old Testament Spirituality*. Milton Keynes, UK: Paternoster, 1996.

Sherman, Franklin, ed. *Bridges: Documents of the Christian-Jewish Dialogue*. Vol. 1: *The Road to Reconciliation (1945-1985)*. Mahwah, NJ: Paulist Press, 2011.

Shermis, Michael, and Arthur E. Zannoni, eds. *Introduction to Jewish-Christian Relations*. Mahwah, NJ: Paulist Press, 1991.

Sigal, Phillip. *Judaism: The Evolution of a Faith*. Grand Rapids: Eerdmans, 1988.

Siker, Jeffrey S. *Disinheriting the Jews*. Louisville: Westminster/John Knox, 1991.

Silver, Abba Hillel. *Where Judaism Differed.* New York: Macmillan, 1956.

Small, Joseph D., and Gilbert S. Rosenthal, eds. *Let Us Reason Together: Christians and Jews in Conversation.* Louisville: Witherspoon, 2010.

Smith, Christian. *The Bible Made Impossible.* Grand Rapids: Brazos, 2011.

Snaith, Norman H. *The Distinctive Ideas of the Old Testament.* New York: Schocken, 1964.

Soloveitchik, Joseph B. *The Lonely Man of Faith.* New York: Doubleday, 1965.

Spangler, Ann, and Lois Tverberg. *Sitting at the Feet of Rabbi Jesus.* Grand Rapids: Zondervan, 2009.

Spong, John Shelby. *This Hebrew Lord.* New York: Seabury, 1974.

Steinsaltz, Adin. *Biblical Images.* Northvale, NJ: Jason Aronson, 1994.

———. *The Essential Talmud.* New York: Basic Books, 1976.

Stendahl, Krister. *Paul among Jews and Gentiles.* Philadelphia: Fortress Press, 1976.

Strack, Hermann L., and Paul Billerbeck. *Das Evangelium nach Matthaus.* Munich: C. H. Beck'sche, 1992.

———. *Kommentar zum Neuen Testament aus Talmud und Midrasch.* 4 vols. Munich: C. H. Beck'sche Verlagsbuchhandlung, Oscar Beck, 1928.

Tanenbaum, Marc H., Marvin R. Wilson, and A. James Rudin, eds. *Evangelicals and Jews in an Age of Pluralism.* Grand Rapids: Baker, 1984.

Tanenbaum, Marc H., Marvin R. Wilson, and A. James Rudin, eds. *Evangelicals and Jews in Conversation on Scripture, Theology and History.* Grand Rapids: Baker, 1978.

Telushkin, Joseph. *A Code of Jewish Ethics.* New York: Bell Tower, 2006.

———. *Jewish Literacy.* New York: William Morrow, 1991.

———. *Jewish Wisdom.* New York: William Morrow, 1994.

Toperoff, Shlomo P. *Avot: A Comprehensive Commentary on the Ethics of the Fathers.* Northvale, NJ: Jason Aronson, 1997.

Tverberg, Lois. *Walking in the Dust of Rabbi Jesus.* Grand Rapids: Zondervan, 2012.

van Wijk-Bos, Johanna W. H. *Making Wise the Simple: The Torah in Christian Faith and Practice.* Grand Rapids: Eerdmans, 2005.

Vermes, Geza. *Jesus and the World of Judaism.* Philadelphia: Fortress Press, 1983.

Visotzky, Burton L. *Reading the Book.* New York: Doubleday, 1991.

Volz, Carl A. *Faith and Practice in the Early Church.* Minneapolis: Augsburg, 1983.

Wenham, Gordon J. *Story as Torah: Reading Old Testament Narrative Ethically.* Grand Rapids: Baker Academic, 2000.

Wiesel, Elie. *Messengers of God: Biblical Portraits and Legends.* New York: Random House, 1976.

Wigoder, Geoffrey, ed. *Encyclopedia Judaica.* 16 vols. Jerusalem: Keter, 1971-72.

Wigoder, Geoffrey, ed. *Jewish Values.* Jerusalem: Keter, 1974.

Williamson, Clark M. *Has God Rejected His People?* Nashville: Abingdon, 1982.

Wilson, Marvin R. *Our Father Abraham: Jewish Roots of the Christian Faith.* Grand Rapids: Eerdmans, 1989.

Wilson, Marvin R., ed. *Study Guide* to the documentary, *Jews and Christians: A Journey of Faith.* Potomac, MD: Auteur Productions, Ltd., 2000.

Wilson, Marvin R., ed. *Study Guide* to the documentary, *Three Faiths, One God: Judaism, Christianity, Islam.* Potomac, MD: Auteur Productions, Ltd., 2005.

Wylen, Stephen M. *The Jews in the Time of Jesus*. New York: Paulist Press, 1995.

Wyschogrod, Michael. *Abraham's Promise: Judaism and Jewish-Christian Relations*. Edited and introduction by R. Kendall Soulen. Grand Rapids: Eerdmans, 2004.

Young, Brad H. *Jesus and His Jewish Parables*. Mahwah, NJ: Paulist Press, 1989.

————. *Jesus the Jewish Theologian*. Peabody, MA: Hendrickson, 1995.

————. *The Jewish Background to the Lord's Prayer*. Dayton, OH: Center for Judaic-Christian Studies, 1984.

————. *Meet the Rabbis: Rabbinic Thought and the Teachings of Jesus*. Peabody, MA: Hendrickson, 2007.

————. *Paul the Jewish Theologian*. Peabody, MA: Hendrickson, 1997.

Zucker, David J. *The Torah: An Introduction for Christians and Jews*. Mahwah, NJ: Paulist Press, 2005.

Zuidema, Willem. *God's Partner: An Encounter with Judaism*. London: SCM Press, 1977.

Index of Biblical Texts

Index of Rabbinic Literature

Index of Authors

Index of Authors

Index of Subjects

'abad (Heb. "to serve," "to worship"), 163

Abraham, 81-82, 183; "Abraham's bosom," 68, 89; in the ancestry of Jesus, 88; change of name (Abram to Abraham), 106, 120; as crucial to the beginning and the end of the New Testament story, 67-68; as a descendant of Noah's son Shem, 64; encounter with God in Ur, 43, 83; as an eschatological figure in the Gospels, 89-90; experience of God, 231; faith of, 32, 101-4; as father of both Jews and Christians, 65-67; God's call of, 96-98, 117, 118; God's covenant with, 98-100; Islam's view of, 81-82n3; Kabbalism on the gematria of Abraham's name, 87n21; mention of in the New Testament, 88; in the New Testament epistles, 101; "our/your father Abraham," 81, 83, 107-9; in the parable of the rich man and Lazarus, 89; as a prophet, 83, 106, 106n37; questioning of God, 234-35; as a "rock," 105-7; as a shepherd, 143. See also Abraham, significance of in Christian tradition; Abraham, significance of in Jewish tradition; Akedah

Abraham, significance of in Christian tradition, 88; Abraham's pilgrim-like lifestyle, 91-92; in Catholic Christianity, 92; Christians as disinherited children, 92-93; focus on the good and righteous qualities of Abraham, 90-91; in the New Testament epistles, 88-89; in the New Testament Gospels, 89-90

Abraham, significance of in Jewish tradition, 82-83; children of Abraham, 87-88; as a compassionate soul, 84; as the first "missionary," 85; as a man of justice, 84-85; as a person of character and faithful obedience, 83; and zekhut abot ("merit of the fathers"), 85-87

Adam and Eve, 156; encounter with God in the Garden of Eden, 31, 43. See also Fall, the

adon (Heb. "lord," "master"), 122-23; in proper names, 123

Adoption, as designation of the spiritual state of "sonship," 252

Afterlife: in Christian tradition, 223; in Jewish tradition, 223

Agnosticism, 116

Akedah, 87, 103-4, 209; in Christian tradition, 104n32; in Jewish tradition, 104; and the killing of one's own child in medieval times, 104

Akiba, Rabbi, 44, 157, 238, 261; martyrdom of, 238

Aleinu, 149-50

Amidah, 85-86

Amos, God's call of, 118

"Apocalypse of Isaiah," 90